An Extraordinary Woman

An Extraordinary Woman

SELECTED WRITINGS OF GERMAINE DE STAËL

Translated and with an Introduction by

Vivian Folkenflik

1987

Columbia University Press

New York

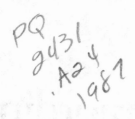

Columbia University Press
New York   Guilford, Surrey

Copyright © 1987 Columbia University Press

Library of Congress Cataloging-in-Publication Data

Staël, Madame de (Anne-Louise-Germaine), 1766–1817.
  An extraordinary woman: selected writings of Germaine de Staël

  Translated from the French.
  Bibliography: p.
  Includes index.
  1. Staël, Madame de (Anne-Louise-Germaine),
1766–1817—Translations, English.   I. Folkenflik,
Vivian.   II. Title.
PQ2431.A24   1987   848'.609   86-26871
ISBN 0-231-05586-2

Book design by J.S. Roberts

Contents

Acknowledgments

I am grateful to Paul de Man not only for helping to define this volume, but for his teaching and encouragement during a period of twenty-five years; his friends and students will understand why it is impossible to put that in the past tense. I would like to thank William Germano, then of Columbia University Press, for his original enthusiastic response as well as his subsequent unvarying patience; Joan McQuary and Karen Mitchell's able and sympathetic editing carried this project through. Susan Mango, at the National Endowment for the Humanities, offered useful suggestions. I am indebted to James Chiampi, James Mirollo, Luci Berkowitz, and Theodore Brunner for their efforts in tracking down some of Mme. de Staël's more obscure references. I would also like to thank Geoffrey Hartman and Christopher Lasch for their help at an early point in the work. I am deeply grateful to Patricia O'Brien and Nora Folkenflik for their perceptive and intelligent readings; and to Lore Iser, David Folkenflik, and Jacob Perlstein. Robert Folkenflik gave his wholehearted and energetic support to the project from start to finish; his own interest in this portrait of the artist as a woman is long-standing.

This book was completed with the assistance of a grant from the National Endowment for the Humanities.

Chronology

1766	Anne-Louise Germaine Necker is born in Paris.
1786	She marries Eric Staël von Holstein; writes fiction.
1788	She publishes *Letters on Rousseau*; meets Louis de Narbonne.
1789	The French Revolution begins, with Jacques Necker in office.
1790	She gives birth to Auguste. Necker is dismissed.
1792	She gives birth to Albert; saves Narbonne's life.
1793	The Reign of Terror. She publishes *Reflections on the Trial of the Queen*; lives in England; meets Adolphe Ribbing.
1794	She publishes *Zulma*. Mme. Necker dies.
1795	She publishes the *Essay on Fiction* and novellas; becomes involved with Benjamin Constant.
1796	She publishes *The Influence of the Passions*.
1797	She gives birth to Albertine; meets Napoleon.
1800	She publishes *On Literature*.
1802	She publishes *Delphine*; Eric de Staël dies.
1804	Napoleon is crowned. Necker dies while she is traveling in Germany; she begins her Italian travels.
1807	She publishes *Corinne*; travels to Vienna.
1810	Napoleon stops publication of *On Germany*.
1811	She writes *The Mannequin*.
1812	She gives birth to Louis; travels to Russia.
1813	She publishes *On Germany* and the *Reflections on Suicide*.
1814	Napoleon is defeated; the monarchy is restored.
1817	She dies, acknowledging marriage to John Rocca in her will.
1818	Publication of the *Considerations*.
1820	Publication of *Ten Years of Exile* and the *Complete Works*.

An Extraordinary Woman

Introduction

Reflection, for Germaine de Staël, is a response to a sudden awareness of feeling, whether enthusiasm or, more frequently, pain: it is
because she and her heroines love or suffer that they feel the need to observe and express themselves. In this system, the moment of self-
consciousness necessary to retrace the memory of one's own feelings permits us to constitute duration and establish the perspective necessary for
us to look at what we are experiencing. It is the essential moment for the
artistic and creative vision. It also provides the perspective implicit in her
political stance. As a woman, Germaine de Staël saw herself as speaking
for truths that challenged society in a dialectical confrontation: her sense
of the distance between consciousness and the outside world was essential to her. Her need to change the status quo is a feminist one: in part
because history had no place for her, she envisaged history as an ongoing
process of challenge. She overcame a sense of alienation from herself—
the physical self that was often a trial to her, the emotional self that was
an equal burden—by using it to define the critical distance as an essential
part of consciousness. At the same time, what could be seen as her need
for acceptance became, in her work, the impetus to establish a new af-
filiative connection as the source of her strength.

      Mme. de Staël has long been recognized as one of the first
women intellectuals to put her work at the center of her sense of self.
Ellen Moers calls her "the first woman of middle-class origins to impress
herself, through her own genius, on all the major public events of her
time—events political, literary, in every sense revolutionary."[1] Germaine
de Staël not only broke with conventional femininity herself, but created
popular heroines who did the same; she helped form the Romantic criti-

cal cogito; shaped French liberal political theory; served as a rallying
point for an entire continent's opposition to the tyrant of her day. This
phenomenon, influential as it was on generations of Europeans and
Americans including Byron, Goethe, Schiller, Stendhal, George Sand,
Elizabeth Barrett Browning, George Eliot, Harriet Beecher Stowe,
Margaret Fuller, Kate Chopin, and Henry James, has recently begun to
attract attention again. Modern readers may find that their own interdis-
ciplinary concerns are closer to Mme. de Staël's than the old arguments
about whether she was "really" a novelist, a historian, a literary critic, or a
social scientist suggest, and that their interests cut across these categories
of discourse in some of the same ways hers did.

    The wealth and position that Germaine de Staël found such
an advantage should not keep us from recognizing that she was an outsider in many respects. Because she was a woman, she was often treated
as an alien by the writers and thinkers she learned from, criticized, and
led, as well as by the aristocracy that held political power when she was
young and by those who took over during the Revolution and Empire.
Her response was dual: she simultaneously sought to obtain acceptance
and to define herself in opposition. In her critical and fictional writing,
this distance between the individual consciousness and its context is the
source of the tension from which language arises; in her political and
emotional life, that margin defines the arena of battle. The apparent dis-
ability one might expect to find in an ambivalent sense of self becomes,
then, a source of strength.

    Germaine Necker's sense of herself as a woman was a dif-
ficult one to achieve, both emotionally and intellectually. As a girl, she
was conscious that she could not make a place for herself by her looks,
according to the standards of the day. Later, she was often an object of
mockery as a full-bosomed middle-aged woman in the diaphanous,
almost transparent gowns of the Empire, not least because she openly
considered herself a sexual being throughout her life. She was attacked,
however, as unfeminine. The Prince de Ligne's portrait of her runs, "*He*
has a lot of intelligence, *she* has a very lively imagination. *He* is a thinker,
she is a poet. *He* is a libertine, *she* is almost chaste," and the recent
biographer who quotes this portrait himself describes her as "this man-
woman whose turban, black eyes and ardor made her look a little like a
Turkish janissary."[2] While some of the venomous attacks on her personal
appearance must be ascribed to hostility to her as a woman writer—the

Prince's portrait is such a mixture—it is also true that she felt that the main appeal of her physical presence lay in her conversation. She was, unusually for a woman of her time, a speaker. Her heroine Delphine faces some of the problems of a woman conscious of her talent and its attraction, interested in the intellectual content of the argument and uncomfortably aware that she is rejecting conventional femininity with every word she says.

The question of her femininity as a writer came up early and often. Her father's pet name for her when she was writing was *Monsieur de Sainte-Escritoire*—a fond nickname, "Lord Holy-Desk," but a masculine one, not entirely explained by the peculiarities of the French language. Republican pamphleteers, aristocratic enemies, Napoleon, and even some fairly sympathetic critics also saw her writing as unfeminine. The witty commentary on *Delphine* by her first lover, Talleyrand, was much appreciated: "Mme. de Staël has disguised both herself and me as women in her novel." She treats the problem of the woman writer's identity specifically in her second Preface to the *Letters on Rousseau,* her essay "On Women Writers," and her novel *Corinne,* but it is central to all her work. Her difficulties in defining herself as a woman writer made her a visible outsider in a world that had not noticed how much it had made outsiders of all its women. Her great strength was that she was able to use her critical consciousness of the distance at which she had been placed to help change the way the world saw women, as well as literature and history; the issues were inseparable in her mind.

Her birth had certainly put her at the center of everything she thought interesting and important. Germaine de Staël rejoiced all her life in her good fortune at being the daughter of Jacques Necker, Louis XVI's idolized minister of finances. Born in 1766, Germaine grew up in the years leading to the Revolution of 1789, when Paris was intoxicated by radical challenges and liberal attempts to accommodate them in a context still largely determined by an aristocratic sense of style. And if, as Talleyrand was to say, anyone who did not know France under the ancien régime did not know how sweet life could be, many of those who enjoyed the sweetness of that regime as well as those who wanted to change it looked to Germaine Necker's father as a savior.

The general French idolatry of Jacques Necker, the Swiss banker who bailed out the bankrupt royal treasury so that the starving could buy bread, can only be explained by the public's awareness that it needed a miracle worker. Necker was happy to fill the bill. He had arrived in Paris as a clerk and had managed to become a quick millionaire through shrewdness, luck, and the Catholic Church's ban on usury, which still prevented most Frenchmen from becoming bankers. His real, if limited interest in the welfare of the poor made him doubly valuable, and the troubled French monarchy became completely dependent on him to make its financial condition look stable to rich and poor alike. He succeeded as best he could, by presenting a balanced budget that some-how omitted the national debt; the very uncertainty of his achievement seems to have inspired a frenzied cult of himself as the only person who could make the system work. This lesson was not lost on the young Ger-maine, who would have been justified in feeling that the whole country was teaching her to idolize her father as the only man she could depend on.

At the outbreak of the Revolution, Necker was still revered as the savior of France, and it was partly because of his efforts that the commoners triumphed in 1789 when the Estates General insisted on voting as individual representatives instead of in three classes. King Louis XVI dismissed him as a traitor, and Mme. de Staël and her parents fled to Switzerland. En route, they heard that the mob had taken the Bastille in protest: Necker was recalled. Enthusiastic Frenchmen pulled Necker's carriage back toward Paris themselves. His daughter was never to forget the experience of their welcome, sharing in the nation's canonization of her father; it was the culmination of her own attitude toward him. In a little over a year, the events of the Revolution were to outdistance him, but this did not tarnish the memory for Mme. de Staël, who was to say later, as a woman of much experience, that nothing in her life had ever equalled the sensation.

But while this roar of welcome was the confirmation of the adoration Germaine had always thought due her father, it also became the model of what she was to want for herself, setting a standard that was difficult for a woman to achieve, and that she craved always: the approval of an entire world. If she was often viewed as "masculine," it may have been because the response she wanted was not defined as something a woman could have.

Mme de Staël's relationship to her father was, moreover, complicated by another factor. Necker was not only the model for what she would have liked to be, but also himself what she would have wanted to possess. In her early years she seems to have become a rival for her

father's affections in a peculiarly painful way, and she openly said in conversation and in her published essay *On the Character of M. Necker and
His Private Life* that she wished she had had him for a husband. As a
newly married woman, she wrote a drama about a young girl's serious,
and reciprocated, passion for her married guardian. Jacques and Suzanne
Necker's marriage functions as the "perfect union" Germaine de Staël
never managed to recreate in her own marriage, her love affairs, or her
fiction. Only in some of her essays do we see what such "love within
marriage" might mean, and there Mme. de Staël is writing as an
outsider.

  Her relationship with her mother was, understandably, a
troubled one: she seems to have craved an affection Suzanne Necker was
unable to return. An anxious, unhappy note she wrote at the age of
twelve about being separated from her mother got a reply criticizing the
intensity of the child's letter. Suzanne Necker had many virtues, but
warmth and spontaneity would not have been virtues to her; perhaps this
is why her daughter prized them so highly. Nevertheless, her influence
was crucial in introducing Germaine to the world, as to the family, in a
way that both placed her within it and made her aware of being an exception to it.

  The world to which Germaine Necker was introduced was
the best of Enlightenment Paris. In her husband's interests and her own,
Mme. Necker had used her intelligence and good looks to establish an
active and lively salon, and she enjoyed the results. If young Germaine
had few friends her own age, she knew the Encyclopedists Diderot,
d'Alembert, Helvetius, and Buffon, as well as the aristocrats and
diplomats with whom her father had dealings at court. Mlle. Necker was
brought up to be a prodigy whose opinion was gravely sought by these
luminaries, only half in jest. An early portrait by the Count de Guibert
calls her "Apollo's priestess," compares her to the muses of poetry and
history, and describes how everyone in the salon cries out when she appears. To other guests, though, such admiration was a mixed blessing,
even an invitation to ridicule. Their mixture of admiration and hostility,
the model of the public response Mme. de Staël encountered throughout her adult life, is partly the result of her mother's unusual ambitions
for her.

  Exactly what Mme. Necker was trying to accomplish is hard
to say; when in later years she was complimented on her daughter she
replied, "She is nothing, compared to what I wanted to make of her." A

rigid, doctrinaire woman, Mme. Necker seems to have thought she was educating her child according to Rousseau's principles of natural development, but she actually gave her large doses of Latin, English, dancing, classical French theater, sentimental fiction, and the joy of sitting on a little footstool in the salon, taking part in the world's cleverest conversation and observing the dangerous liaisons of ancien régime Paris. This experience was a formative one, not only because of what it taught Germaine about political, social, and literary matters, but also because of the importance it gave to the response of others. Moers identifies this as "performing heroinism": " 'The Spoiled Child' is not so far from 'Corinne au Capitole' as one might assume."[3] Other readers may see more of a distinction, but it is clear that the sense of self and other established in her mother's salon prepared Mme. de Staël to widen her horizons as soon as she became a married woman with an audience of her own.

Germaine Necker's marriage was certainly no perfect union. She was married at nineteen, in 1786, to a man she had no illusions about loving. The Neckers' choice had been limited: Protestant, presentable at court, willing to live in Paris. They settled for Eric Staël von Holstein, a thirty-six-year-old attaché to the Swedish ambassador, polite and pleasant but uninterested in his fiancée, whose father once broke in on their dancing to show how one "should" dance with such a young woman. M. de Staël had managed to acquire the title of baron, the friendship of Marie Antoinette, a number of mistresses, and more than the usual run of debts: he had been trying for Germaine Necker's enormous dowry since she was twelve. After negotiations involving the Swedish ambassadorship for M. de Staël, promises that his wife would never have to live in Sweden, and the island of Saint Barthélemy, the marriage contract was signed by the King and Queen.

Opinions differ as to what went wrong in the marriage, but little went right. M. de Staël was disappointed that his wife was not fonder of him; Mme. de Staël saw the marriage as giving her the relative independence of a married woman. They lived apart, and his death in 1802 was to affect her much less than her father's (1804). But the newly wed Mme. de Staël was presented to the King and Queen, though she tripped over her own dress; she established her own brilliant salon, though her husband did not like her friends; she gave birth to the only child she conceived within the marriage (1787), though baby Gustavine died before the age of two; she used her position as Swedish Ambassadress to make her own brilliant political entrée; she wrote stories and she published her *Letters on Rousseau* (1788). The remarkable thing, as eighteenth-century marriages went, was not that the marriage did not provide her with a center for her life, but that she made it give her a point of departure.

Indeed, after the birth of Gustavine Mme. de Staël soon began to extend her emotional and sexual experiences. *The Little Dictionary of Great Men of the Revolution* (1790) was dedicated to her by the royalist Antoine de Rivarol as a list of her burning admirers. Her first lover, Charles-Maurice de Talleyrand, then the powerful bishop of Autun, was to become the foremost diplomat of Europe under the monarchy, the Revolution, the Empire, and the Restoration. Her first great love, however, and the father of her sons Auguste and Albert, was the handsome Count Louis de Narbonne, an illegitimate offshoot of the French royal family; she worked to place him as Minister of War in 1791, a year after the birth of their first son, during the early constitutional phase of the Revolution. In 1792, after the failure of their plot to rescue the royal family, she saved his life and that of various friends, barely escaping Paris with her own; as soon as their second son was born she followed him to England, where the relationship began to disintegrate. Various aspects of it can be found in all her subsequent love affairs; physical attraction, disinterested enthusiasm, intellectual encouragement, devotion, political daring, suicide threats, and, often, financial generosity. Their affair is generally believed to be the source of *Zulma* (1794), though elements of that story can be seen in the fictions she wrote before meeting him. It also marked her first partial break from her parents, who were deeply shocked by her abandoning the month-old Albert at their chateau of Coppet in Switzerland.

Like Narbonne, Germaine de Staël's other lovers all found her too demanding sooner or later, and most ended the relationship with some relief. Her simultaneous demands for approval, passion, and respect would have been a difficult balancing act at the time even if her tactics had not included blackmail and her standard had not been the unquestioned devotion of her parents' marriage. As it was, all her friendships and sexual relationships demanded a very high level of intense involvement by all their participants, not lessened by frequent real or suspected infidelities. Yet a number of her ex-lovers and suitors remained her friends for many years, such as Mathieu de Montmorency, an aristocratic liberal who had led the nobility to divest itself of its privileges, and August Wilhelm Schlegel, a spokesman for German Romanticism who ended up spending most of his life at Coppet.

It is true that Mme. de Staël did not always observe the fidelity she tried to require of others; she was still involved with Narbonne in 1793 when she fell in love with Count Adolphe Ribbing, the regicide responsible for assassinating the King of Sweden the previous year at a masked ball. Nor was she faithful to the man with whom she was to have the most important remaining relationship of her life, whom she first met in 1794: Benjamin Constant, liberal politician and author of the novel *Adolphe* and a number of political, religious, and literary treatises. Although Mme. de Staël was much less attracted sexually to Constant than to Narbonne and Ribbing, he was her companion for many years, her partner in her dealings with Napoleon, and the father of her only surviving daughter, Albertine (1797). In the course of these years, Mme. de Staël was involved with other men, Constant treacherously married an old love (1809), and they both bickered endlessly about the dowry for Albertine's marriage to the liberal Duke de Broglie (1816). There remains much to admire: she and Constant supported each other in various ill-fated political enterprises during those Napoleonic years and incited each other simultaneously to write *Corinne* and *Adolphe*, painful as the discovery of the personal elements in these novels was to be. But Germaine de Staël was to find the total security she craved only in her late forties, in a secret marriage (1816) with a devoted young lieutenant named John Rocca, who was not in any sense her intellectual or social equal; she never acknowledged to anyone her love for him, or the retarded child, Louis, born of their premarital liaison.

In each of these passionate relationships, with the possible exception of the secret marriage, Germaine de Staël's incessant and limitless demands were the expression of an unfulfilled need for complete acceptance, while her own equally strong craving to be the person who structured that acceptance, determining its content and context, ensured that any such acceptance would be ultimately meaningless. Nevertheless, we should not trivialize the lifelong series of sexual relationships within the context of which her work was done, and out of which it grew, even though her role within these relationships was usually unhappy and more than occasionally undignified. The attitude epitomized by the title of J. Christopher Herold's best-selling biography,

Mistress to an Age, prevents us from seeing that if the acceptance she craved remained out of grasp, the resulting sense of an opposing self is not comic. Her fear of rejection, actual, imminent, or imaginary, gave Mme. de Staël an acute consciousness of the relationship of self and other, and the way the conscious self experienced its own emotions; her need to express these passions took precedence over the happy ending she claimed she craved for each of them.

If she sometimes blames her personal isolation on society's definition of her role as a woman rather than on the limitations of consciousness itself, if she saw separation from emotional ties as an evil to be remedied whenever possible instead of as a given that the mind must cope with, contemporary feminists may find this a revolutionary phenomenon rather than a self-seeking failure, as critics have done. As Lawrence Lipking says, Mme. de Staël, "the first major female critic, consciously built her own program from relations and affiliations that go beyond author and text."[4] Carol Gilligan suggests that for women, "connection, rather than seeming an illusion or taking on an explosive or transcendental cast, appears as a primary feature of both individual psychology and civilized life."[5] It is possible, then, to consider Mme. de Staël's complementary needs for connectedness and distance as a function of the identity as woman writer she was creating, rather than as a failure to achieve a relationship with the text structured by a masculine priority of independence. This new appeal, which is close to what Lipking calls the alternative canon of the "web of relationship," as well as her insistence on the interconnectedness of literature and society and her interpretation of history as the interplay between opposing cultures, can then be seen in terms of her feminist vision.

In her political life, the identity Germaine de Staël shaped was necessarily an identity as a woman. Her problem lay not in her Swiss-Swedish nationality or Protestant religion, but in her sex: nothing would have made it possible for her to hold office, and Necker's daughter knew very well that that was the way to hold power. Instead of being handicapped by this, however, she turned to writing political novels, essays, pamphlets, and treatises, becoming the first woman to make a theoretical and practical statement about the political problems of Europe, and one of the only French voices raised against the ruling power of her time.

We need not, then, belittle the limited sphere of Mme. de Staël's direct political activity, much of which consisted in negotiations undertaken on behalf of her friends and lovers, usually with unsatisfactory results. Narbonne lasted only three months as Louis XVI's Minister of War (1791); Talleyrand, recalled from exile in America thanks to her intercession with the Directory, snubbed her on his return to power (1795); her attempts to help Constant work with Napoleon (1799, 1802) were inevitably unsuccessful; a plan to replace Napoleon with her liberal friend Marshal Bernadotte ended when Talleyrand proclaimed the restoration of the French monarchy (1814). Through this activity, however, she gained energy from a sense of working toward the public good, even and especially in the face of opposition. Her notable bravery in rescuing both friends and enemies persecuted during the Revolution marks her as someone who enjoyed rising to a challenge, undeterred by great personal risk.

In time, through her work, she made her outsider's perch into a conscious stance. Though her various exiles during the Revolution and the Empire were involuntary, her enemies were right: she consistently made the statements that provoked them, and she gloried in using them. Her flight from Paris during the September Massacres was the basis for Delphine's; her exile to England during the Reign of Terror gave her a deeper understanding of the Northern culture she was to celebrate in *On Literature* (1800). Ordered out of Paris in 1803, she traveled to Germany, where her conversations with Goethe, Schiller, Schlegel, courtiers and commoners gave her the material for her work *On Germany* (1810); still unwelcome in France in 1805, she went to Italy, where she was publicly acclaimed like her half-Italian heroine Corinne, whose improvisations sing Italy's glories. Exiled to the chateau of Coppet, she made it the most interesting intellectual center of its day, and when she escaped from it in 1812 after Napoleon's suppression of *On Germany*, she wrote the account of her life there and of her flight to Russia, barely ahead of the Napoleonic invasion, in *Ten Years of Exile*. By the time she died in 1817, accepted by King Louis XVIII if not by all the aristocrats, her advantage no longer lay in having been born an insider. She had made her situation as opponent into the context for her vision of historical progress and perfectibility as a process of continuing challenge.

In the end, the distinction between practical and theoretical politics vanishes. By proclaiming her opinions, Mme. de Staël created and maintained the actual cause of liberal opposition to Napoleon. Her lasting political influence was great; her view of the French Revolution as an essential, though deeply disturbing, part of the struggle toward liberty became the foundation of French nineteenth-century liberal theory. In this respect too, it was Germaine de Staël's good fortune that she gained strength from overcoming the fact that she was excluded; that struggling for power as a woman became for her not a handicap but a source of vision. The distance at which Mme. de Staël had been placed became the distance within which she establishes the process of consciousness itself.

WORKS

Letters on Rousseau (1788)

If, as Mme. de Staël once said, the abduction of Richardson's Clarissa was one of the most important events of her girlhood, her reading of Jean-Jacques Rousseau was one of its formative experiences. Her first published words tell us of her need to recreate and interpret that reading: "There is still nothing in print to praise Rousseau: I felt a need to see my admiration expressed. I might certainly have wished for someone else to portray my feelings, but I have tasted a certain pleasure in retracing for myself the memory and sensation of my enthusiasm." She finds in Rousseau her concept of passion as inexorably linked to the origin of reflection, which brings unhappiness not because it fails but because, in Paul de Man's words, "it succeeds too well in understanding its object, the self, in the painful imprecision of its contingency."[6] The interest of the Letters lies partly in her recognition of Rousseau's influence, and also in her own statement of the nature of consciousness. Her insight that "the soul's elevation is born of self-consciousness" is seen by de Man as a landmark, while Georges Poulet suggests that "everything we could say . . . to be honest, about the entire European literary criticism that is just about to burst into bloom—is simply an explanation" of the first Preface.[7] The origin of the critical act, then, is not a classical evaluation, but the desire of consciousness to recreate the sensation of its own emotion. Here is the formation of the Romantic critical cogito: the critical act of admiration is an act of understanding that depends on reestablishing an emotion inspired by something outside the self.

The Preface of 1814 gives us the feminist perspective of the forty-eight-year-old woman looking back on her career as a writer, recommending "the process of developing and perfecting one's own mind" because for women, "everything goes downhill except for thought." The precarious and continually demanding nature of this "process of developing and perfecting" is what provides the challenge. A conventional upbringing without the exhilaration of intellectual experience creates nothing but "a doll who has learned her lesson well" (a theme explored in *The Mannequin*). This is a demand for the education of women in general, much stronger than what she had written in the original *Letters* at the age of twenty-two, though she goes on to be thankful for her own literary career.

Her discussion of Rousseau's *Letter on Spectacles* (1758) is a good example of her early limited feminism. Rousseau accused the theater of turning acts of vice into spectacles for our pleasure and corrupting us by staging them. Despite her love of the theater and amateur acting, Mme. de Staël defends not only his thesis but his incidental sexism, allowing him to reduce the role of women in theoretical republics if she can claim a better role for them in the existing monarchical society, where they do not feel debased like men because their "slavery" everywhere keeps them from noticing their exclusion. She settles for a vindication of women writers, a rhetorical tour de force in which her impassioned admiration of Rousseau disproves his poor opinion: women can obviously paint passion—Mme. de Staël has just done it. And there must be others who can: women, restricted to "a destiny whose only events are feelings," may be capable of a more touching language than the raptures of male poets. Because her vindication of the exceptional woman is based on her vision that all women are everywhere oppressed by lives whose "only events are feelings," it protests.the limitations society placed on all women's lives, even though the essay is supposedly defending Rousseau's opinion that these limitations should be stricter.

The chapter on Rousseau's widely read novel of love outside marriage, *The New Héloïse* (1761), begins by reestablishing the critical self: "I surrender myself to retracing the effect this book has had on me." She defines this process by reinforcing the distance between the "retracing" self and the self that experienced the original effect through the introduction of a temporal perspective: "I am therefore going to distance myself somewhat from my impressions as I receive them, and write about *The New Héloïse* as I think I would do if time had aged my heart." Here again, the sense of distance from her own feelings establishes the critical cogito.

The story is a dangerous one—Julie, like the medieval Héloïse for whom the novel is named, has sexual relations with her tutor Saint-Preux ("Saint-Gallant"), but marries the worthy Wolmar, though her first love remains pure and untouched. Assuming a moral aim on Rousseau's part, Mme. de Staël asserts the connection between abstract ideas and emotions, "since we must involve the soul through feelings to fix the mind on ideas—since we must mix passion with virtue to make anyone listen to both of them. . . . " As for the innocent girls who may be corrupted by such material, their innocence in our society is mere dependency on arranged marriages. What we want is the marriage for love Rousseau might have written an inferior novel about.

In talking about Rousseau's taste for music Mme. de Staël defines the act of listening as a temporary lessening of the critical distance so that we are "close" enough to ourselves, in reverie, to let involuntary memory establish a moment outside time's "regrets." The memories that come to us through music are not subject to the distance established by time: "for a moment music gives us back the pleasures it retraces, and we feel them again rather than recollect them." Music temporarily abolishes our sense of the gap; "while one listens, one's sensations are enough for both mind and heart, leaving no emptiness in either."

Rousseau's interest in botany also centers on memory. Mme. de Staël moves past her initial disagreement with him to focus on his now-famous periwinkle passage in the *Confessions*, abolishing time through a complex association of memories: "he found and felt every one of them again, and all at one time." In a characteristic critical trope, she has moved through judgment to participation.

If the act of critical appreciation is indeed an act of love, its course does not always run smooth. Mme. de Staël solves the dubious problem of Rousseau's character by concentrating on him as narrator of the *Confessions*: "I think he wrote his memoirs to shine as a historian rather than as the hero of the story. . . . He observed himself and painted himself as if he had been his own model." Here again she emphasizes the importance of the distance between the reflecting self and the self portrayed. Her analysis of the role of reflection in Rousseau's love affairs is significant in terms of her own emotional relationships: "his feelings increased through reflection ... concentrating on [a woman] in her absence. ... if you said one single word which could displease him he would remember it, examine it, exaggerate it, think about it for a week and end by breaking up with you, which made it almost impossible to set him straight."

But the essay then moves to relate to Rousseau in a way that reveals Germaine de Staël's early ambivalence toward herself as a woman writer. She begins by identifying with Rousseau as a man "all sensitive people ought to defend as their own cause"; his suicide, a hypothesis she was eager to embrace, is blamed on the world's insensitivity. Suddenly this identification with the artist changes, however, to an awareness of him as a man and herself as a woman: "Ah, Rousseau! How sweet it would have been to make you care about life again, to walk beside your footsteps in your solitary promenades, to follow your thoughts ...!" Here the very distortion of such a picture shows how difficult it is for the woman writer to see herself in the artist's role without ambivalence. She moves away to call for "an interpreter at last," invoking a "league of genius against envy! of superior men defending their predecessors, and giving a sublime example to their successors!" Here "superior men" is used to mean sexually undefined superior beings; but in her future writings Mme. de Staël will often be more aware of her ambivalence, or lay claim to a specific place for women. In these *Letters*, we find elements of conflict about her own femininity, together with great insight into the nature of consciousness and the workings of the mind.

Essay on Fictions (1795)

This ambitious theoretical work not only covers the whole of fiction, a daring act for a woman writer, but envisages a fiction beyond the range of any writers in the past. The tone of the *Essay* is that of someone who already has a public voice; Mme. de Staël had published her *Reflections on the Trial of the Queen* in 1793. Because the Reign of Terror has changed our world forever, fiction can no longer arouse "deep and terrible emotions" in us with elaborate devices, but may have to "follow a new path." Mme. de Staël therefore suggests that it extend beyond love stories to intrigues of power, ambition, and politics. Nineteenth-century readers such as Stendhal were to follow this advice, and Mme. de Staël follows it herself in *Delphine* and *Corinne*. Other ways in which literature develops historically through time will be suggested in *On Literature* and *On Germany*.

Through much of this essay, the "power of fiction" is seen as engaged in developing "among the people" a "mobility within the mind itself" that would prevent the "constant cruelty" of the "executioners of France." But a great writer, one who gives us "the only real happiness of which human nature is capable," does not work this way: his work "cannot be a genre, it cannot be a goal." In his work, the "eloquence of passion," suspending the action of our own passions "by substituting independent pleasures for them," provides the polarity within which Mme. de Staël moves between engagement and the independent workings of consciousness, the structure characteristic of her work throughout her life.

Novellas (1794–1795)

Mme. de Staël is thought to have written the first of three of these stories during the years of her engagement and marriage (1785–1786), and *Zulma* after her liaison with Narbonne. All four heroines of these stories achieve self-consciousness by recognizing the injustices imposed on them by society and the conventional men they love. The connection between the themes of femininity and slavery is a revolutionary one for the period.

Mirza is an African girl with a voice of her own. Not only does she make up her own songs about love of liberty and hatred of slavery, but she analyzes colonialism far more acutely than the anonymous French narrator: "'Europeans, . . . you condemn us to slavery so as to cultivate your land. Your self-interest is what makes you need our misfortune. . . . '" A similar self-interest permits Ximeo, an African prince, to accept Mirza's teaching and her love without realizing that he is being unfaithful to his fiancée, because he does not see Mirza as a woman in the same way.

The sexual role reversal in *Mirza* prefigures *Corinne* in its presentation of Mirza as artist. Ximeo says, "I no longer seemed to be listening to a woman, but to a poet." As Madelyn Gutwirth points out, "Mme. de Staël wants Mirza's gifts . . . to be construed by Ximeo as attractions, in the way a woman, within the conventions, would be expected to be drawn naturally to a bard, a warrior, a free spirit."[8] The ending, in which Mirza commits suicide after rescuing Ximeo from slavery, is often seen as self-justificatory, but within the story's framework the radical refusal to compromise is the only solution possible; if we object to this solution, such an ending implies, it is up to us to find a context in which another will be possible. The same problem will confront us in much of her other fiction.

The heroine of *Adelaide and Theodore* is a blonde orphan brought up with frivolous storybook ideas about love, married off and widowed young: she is popular, impulsive and, in Theodore's eyes, self-centered. Theodore is sensitive and dependent; he loves Adelaide, but threatens, in a conventionally feminine way, that he would die if she were ever to love him less. Adelaide marries him, but while "she could not have lived without Theodore, . . . she could amuse herself without him." Her independence is not altogether condemned, but she kills herself when she realizes how much she has hurt him. She dies on her own terms, however, not as a stereotypical female figure: after Theodore poisons himself she waits out her pregnancy and takes opium in the delivery room. Her life is not the "novel" she has thought it would be at the age of sixteen, but she does better, by taking control of her own story.

In *Pauline*, the link between conventional womanhood and slavery becomes stronger. "At the age of thirteen, ignorant of the importance of the engagement she was undertaking and without having ever reflected on either the present or the future," the heroine is chosen in marriage so that her husband can "buy a substantial number of Negroes . . . [with] Pauline's dowry." Seduced, passed from one man to another, abandoned, Pauline awakens from this unreflecting state to become, like Mirza, the singer of her own song, and to tell her self-righteous new love the truth before she dies. The victory lies in the consciousness achieved by a child who has been virtually sold in marriage and treated as an object by seducers, even though her moment of consciousness cannot sustain itself.

Zulma, published separately in 1794, was originally intended to be the chapter on love in The Influence of the Passions (1796). Thematically and structurally, it continues to develop along the lines laid out by the earlier stories, but by the time of this writing Mme. de Staël had become explicitly conscious of what constitutes a Staëlian heroine: an unhappy being "capable of observing its own self, and obliged to portray" its own feelings. The narrator, a prisoner of savages near the Orinoco river, hears Zulma tell her own story at her murder trial. The educated Fernand taught her everything she knows, giving her the "power of reflection" but "making no attempt to enlighten [her] as to the nature of the passions," which she has had to comprehend through her own suffering. Zulma is now capable of the Staëlian consciousness achieved through reflection on one's own passions, as Mme. de Staël says in the Foreword: "the soul recovers a sort of sang-froid that permits it to think coolly, while it is still suffering." Her refusal to feel guilt for Fernand's death establishes her right to self-definition: "I exist so strongly in myself that it is beyond my power to show myself as other." Her sense of her existence, constituted by a reflection on her own feelings and a refusal to accept herself as "other," takes priority over any judgment the outside world can make.

The Influence of the Passions
on the Happiness of Individuals and Nations (1796)

In this work Mme. de Staël poses the question of the relationship between personal revelation and theory in a way that was new at the time and is still being explored by feminists and other theorists today. What Mme. de Staël would have defined as the classical attitude has no room for personal problems in general theory. Here, "constantly slandered" and, as a woman, unable to defend herself directly, Mme. de Staël hopes that by writing about the happiness of individuals and nations she can make people understand her own life and character. In her next book,

On Literature, she will explicitly discuss the way society defines women's lives as private. In this work, she moves back and forth between personal revelation and her general theme.

The Introduction reasserts the Staëlian critical distance as the context of reflection. Because of the conflict between our desires for happiness and the "disastrous crisis" of the French Revolution, "we have been led to reflect more deeply than ever before on the nature of individual and political happiness" and also on the "rocks separating us from such a goal." But our reflections about the most intense of our experiences can begin only now; in 1793 we could not "separate ourselves for a moment from our impressions so as to analyze them." Even now, "the sensations created by [the Reign of Terror] absorb every other faculty"; she will keep her distance by talking about it indirectly.

Her definition of happiness as "the union of all contrary things" tries to acknowledge the gap established by the contradictions of the human mind. What individuals want is "hope without fear, activity without anxiety, glory without calumny . . . the good side of all conditions, talents, and pleasures, without their accompanying evils." The difficulty of achieving this on either the personal or national level is clear: "For nations, happiness would also be a reconciliation of republican liberty with monarchical calm," not easy to find.

As a theoretical statement, the chapter "On Vanity" contains a disturbing analysis of vanity in women. At first Mme. de Staël alternates betwen abstract statements that seem to limit women's ambitions ("In women everything is either love or vanity") and scathing accusations of the limits set by society ("The face of a woman is always a help or a hindrance in her life story, whatever the strength or range of her mind, however important the things which concern her"). In the end the ambivalence is resolved by a relentlessly practical description of the actual situation: "men see no kind of general utility in encouraging the successes of women in [public affairs], and praise which is not based on utility can never be deep, or lasting, or universal."

Nor can exceptional women escape, because they too need others to survive. The bind in which the author finds herself is painful: "Even glory does not give her enough support. . . . A woman who devoted herself to the solution of Euclid's problems would still want the happiness connected with the feelings we inspire or experience. Whenever women follow a career which puts them at a distance from these feelings, their painful regrets or ridiculous pretensions prove that nothing can compensate them for the destiny for which their souls were created." Not only do women need love more than men, but only women are prevented by this socially imposed "distance" from having both love and Euclid. The social structure will not finally accept a deserving few. From her analysis we might well wonder if vanity is the way society defines ambition in women, though Mme. de Staël herself does not draw this conclusion.

In "On Philosophy," as in the *Letters on Rousseau*, Mme. de Staël shocked public opinion by defending suicide, an issue that then aroused the bitterness of the current debates on abortion. Here she is supposedly recommending philosophy instead, but readers were not mistaken in focusing on the "horrifying . . . possibility of existing simply because we do not know how to die." She interprets the act of suicide as an act of consciousness and not of defeat: one must "embrace the tableau of one's misfortunes and the spectacle of one's end with the intensity of a single feeling and a single idea." For her heroine Zulma, whose story was intended to be part of this work, such an embrace permits victory. Mme. de Staël ends, however, by defining the difference between an act of suicide like Zulma's and her achievement by suggesting philosophy, the ability to "rise some distance above ourselves," as offering the ultimate happiness, "placing ourselves in relation to our own consciousness." The *Reflections on Suicide* (1813) will continue this argument.

The Conclusion is a lucid analysis of the Staëlian process of writing: "I have written to find myself, through so many sorrows, to free my faculties from the slavery of feelings, to elevate myself to a kind of abstraction that will let me observe the pain of my own soul. . . . " But "as reflection comes closer" to our own minds, we are lost: the human mind is not definable, but seems "only on the eve of its own creation, in the chaos of the day before." As de Man says, our limited understanding of the "painful imprecision of the contingency of the self" and our inability to mitigate the pain are both part of the structure of consciousness.[9] But the fact that Mme. de Staël considers human nature ultimately an "inexplicable phenomenon" does not prevent her from believing in the act of interpretation as the essential human endeavor.

On Literature Considered
in Its Relationship to Social Institutions (1800)

On Literature, a book that helped establish the Romantic canon, develops Mme. de Staël's critical insights and proposes a theory of the relationship of culture to society. In the Preliminary Discourse, she asserts the originality of her theory: a nation's literature arises from the context of its political structures, and these in turn depend on social structures and inherited patterns of consciousness interacting with the physical environment. Her application of this theory offers a new explanation of the problem of how the French Revolution went wrong. Instead of putting it down to the passion of vanity, as she had done in her last work, she is able to suggest a historical explanation: progress is slower than liberal thinkers had hoped because it takes time for society to react to new philosophical ideas. She uses Condorcet's concept of probability to analyze and predict past and future social, cultural, and historical events; the relationship of the historical moment to culture will permit her to claim Romantic literature as what we need to develop now.

Mme. de Staël's note to the Preface of the Second Edition parenthetically reminds us that the public responded to the first edition by criticizing not only her theory but also her writing anything at all. She pinpoints Molière's *School for Wives* (1662) as a *locus classicus,* but wonders how anyone can still believe that women should be uneducated nowadays. The form of this note may be evidence of some difficulty in dealing with the subject.

European civilization, as interpreted in the chapter "On Northern Literature," is the history of the relationship between North and South. This is an essential dialectic for Mme. de Staël: two tendencies of European culture, two possible directions for the human mind to take. Northern literature expresses the "sense of distance from life aroused by the harsh earth and mournful skies," leading to "philosophical ideas and reflection," whereas Southern literature involves a much more "immediate" connection between Nature and human feelings. The interplay between Northern literature and the classical frame of mind defines our current historical moment.

This dialectic also remains an important part of her own structure of consciousness, however. Both "North" and "South" are externalizations of processes of the mind; it is not a question of living *only* with distance or immediacy. Her own work is proof of her reliance on both elements of the polarity: she explains in *On Germany* what Northern literature can mean to the French, and develops the relationship between reflection and feeling in her half-English, half-Italian heroine Corinne.

Her outline of "the Present Condition of Intellectual Activity in France and its Future Progress" sketches out the dialectical theory of the Revolution found later in the *Considerations*. Out of conflict, "the introduction of a new class into the government of France," may ultimately come the enlightenment of "a greater mass of men" even though the immediate result has been cruelty and retrograde vulgarity. This opportunity for progress does not mandate it, however: what the polarity between the old world and the new offers us is an opportunity for our own theoretical and practical activity. Perfectibility, as the Second Preface to the *Letters on Rousseau* reminds us, is a process we can engage in, not a guarantee.

Mme. de Staël's chapter on German literature contains her remarkable analysis of Goethe's *Sorrows of Young Werther*, the most popular German novel of the day. Her vision of its suicidal hero, "the unfortunate man contemplating himself through his mind and succumbing to pain, directing his imagination toward himself, strong enough to watch himself suffer and incapable of giving his soul any kind of help," offers a revealing insight into her own work. What she admires is the ability "to portray self-reflecting passion, the passion that judges itself and understands itself without being able to conquer itself." In *Zulma*, *Delphine*, and *Corinne*, we see her own presentations of this self-consciousness. Her own position is clear: the simultaneous establishment of the critical distance and of what de Man calls the "inexorable link between reflection and passion" is at the heart of the discovery of the self.

In "On Taste and Civilized Manners and Their Literary and Political Influence," Mme. de Staël locates intellectual activity as arising from a specific cultural experiential context, as Montesquieu had done for politics. She analyzes the relationship of "the arbitrary demands of the old régime" to classical French literature in order to show "the horrible literary and political effects" of the Revolution, and accurately predicts the disappearance of the wit, "the tact and the instinct" peculiar to pre-revolutionary France: "When a particular way of life ceases to exist, we must give up everything that can only be learned in its context."

"On Women Writers" may be the most explicit call for sexual equality in Mme. de Staël's published work, based on the fact that women have now no way to define themselves at all: "at present, women belong neither to the natural nor to the social order." It describes the inferior status of women in society and the difficulties in trying to escape it through intellectual superiority, but beyond this it envisages radical change: "I believe a day will come when philosophical legislators will give serious attention to the education of women, to the laws protecting them, to the duties which should be imposed on them, to the happiness that can be guaranteed them." Under the ancien régime and the Revolution, "in both political structures, women are permitted to ignore household occupations only in favor of frivolous pursuits that keep them from making any real contribution to society." The solution to this inequality must go beyond politics, in "enlightening, teaching, and perfecting women together with men on the national and individual level." Until women are equally educated, the structural conflict created by inequality cannot be resolved: "this must be the secret for . . . the establishment of any permanent social or political relationship."

The woman intellectual is now, in contrast, very vulnerable: defined as private by a hostile public, "women have no way to show the truth, no way to throw light on their lives." Hostility comes not only from men, including the lover who is encouraged to abandon her, but from other women, who refuse to befriend or support "an extraordinary woman" in any way. "Like the pariahs of India, such a woman parades her peculiar existence among classes she cannot belong to, which consider her as destined to exist on her own, the object of curiosity and perhaps a little envy: what she deserves, in fact, is pity." This appeal poses a problem to some readers, who find it an embarrassing failure of energy on her part, or an inability to recognize such isolation as part of the structure of consciousness she herself describes elsewhere. But the unmediated call on our emotions is also a call for action: Mme. de Staël is reaching directly toward us to engage us in a social reformation that may help other women, and even the reader, in the future.

Delphine (1802)

This novel of revolutionary France, written when Mme. de Staël had been rejected by Ribbing, involved with Constant, and exiled by

Napoleon, further develops the theme of the individual self in conflict with society and becoming conscious of its own emotions. The power of the novel lies in Delphine's ability to reflect on her emotions; as Simone Balayé points out, "It is to show 'reflecting passion' that [Mme. de Staël] follows Goethe and Rousseau's example by giving her novel an epistolary form."[10]

In *Delphine*, Mme. de Staël follows her own advice in the *Essay on Fictions* and extends the novel to the world of recent politics. Delphine d'Albémar is a passionate defender of Rousseau and liberalism, while her equally aristocratic lover, a rigid monarchist, is shot by the Revolutionary Army. Napoleon and other readers objected to its views on the Revolution, emigration, and the disadvantages of Catholicism; moreover, the Revolution is shown in the early days when people were not being executed for what they said, a situation Mme. de Staël contrasts in her Preface with the "silent France" of 1802. But the book's popularity is suggested by a review in the *Journal de Paris*: the theaters and streets are empty because "everyone is home reading *Delphine*."

Like other Staëlian heroines, Delphine takes pleasure in her ability to express herself, though her freedom of speech both attracts the conventional Léonce and defines her to him as unfeminine. This, more than the official engagement, is what makes him marry her cousin Mathilde, whose dowry the generous Delphine has provided. Delphine's opinions on literary and political topics are the context for their love affair: "There was a kind of internal emotion within me, even when the discussion was purely literary. My mind kept its ease and fluency, but my soul felt disturbed. . . . That night I could not convince myself that something extraordinary had not happened." The impact of this first meeting is judged by others in terms of Delphine's conversation: "I would have thought I was listening to you for the first time today, madame." Within the story, society functions as Delphine's audience, the dialectic other to which she responds and, often, the subject of her speech. Politically and socially, this frightens Léonce, and Mathilde's mother Mme. de Vernon manages to keep them apart by playing on his weaknesses when she "happens to direct the conversation toward politics."

Understandable as it may be that everyone saw Talleyrand in the scheming Mme. de Vernon, the reasons behind her manipulative behavior are sympathetically presented within the specific feminine context of her education as a girl: "I soon realized that all the feelings that I expressed were being ridiculed, and that my mind was being forced into silence, as if it were an unsuitable thing for a woman to have." She is therefore well aware that Léonce will be disturbed not so much because Delphine has opinions "so repellent to people of your class" but because she voices them in public. Indeed, his embarrassment at her public presentation of self extends to her dancing—"I would have been happier watching her by myself"—and to her independence of action, both in helping her adulterous friend Thérèse d'Ervins and in rescuing an unchaste woman from public disgrace in the Queen's antechamber; he scans the crowd "to see the impression she has made." Such independence is sometimes involuntary on the part of Delphine, who would, in what Gutwirth calls a "pull towards immanence,"[11] often like nothing better than to be Léonce's ideal woman, but both independence and connectedness are essential to her being.

In her flight from Paris Delphine becomes completely isolated, trying to cut herself off even from her own reflections: "I drag through the days second after second, racking my brain to find the art to avoid the sensation of life and keep myself from reflecting on myself, as if I were guilty, and remorse were lying in wait for me within my heart." She tries to find refuge in a convent ruled by Léonce's possessive and frustrated aunt, Mme. de Ternan, but becomes even more of an outcast after her escape because she has taken the vows. In the end, society kills: Léonce is shot as a traitor by the Revolutionary Army, despite Delphine's impassioned speech to save him, while she takes poison at the scene. (In a second ending, added to avoid the controversial suicide, Delphine dies of grief and Léonce in the ranks of the counterrevolutionary forces.)

The novel is a feminist work in a number of ways. Delphine never renounces the married Léonce because her inability to find happiness with him is ultimately presented not as a function of the contingency of human nature but as part of society's hostile definition of femininity. Mme. de Ternan's account of the social death visited on even conventional middle-aged women underlines the difficulty of reaching any accommodation with society as it is constituted. The story's emphasis on politics serves to reinforce the power of a hostile external world, a problem none of these women can solve through individual acts, whether of conformity or of rebellion. The possibility remains that Delphine's gifts cannot offer her a solution because their audience is a private one. What happens to an unconventional woman whose talents offer her a wider audience is a problem Mme. de Staël explores in her next novel.

Corinne (1807)

At the end of *Corinne*, the artist heroine teaches a little girl to carry on for her after her death, and it sometimes seems as if every woman who read the book must have felt inspired to do the same. Corinne's popularity was immediate and astounding: the journalist and critic Sainte-Beuve called her "the ideal of all celebrated women" in the 1820s. Her fame spread across Europe and to England and America, influencing even fictional characters like George Eliot's Maggie Tulliver and and Charlotte Brontë's Angrian Zenobia, as well as their authors. Portraits of the heroine appeared on biscuit boxes, and Mme. de Staël herself was hailed as "Corinne" everywhere she went. The novel was admired by critics from Goethe on down, always with the exception of Napoleon, who had it condemned as anti-French. His objections were predictable: his Italian victories are ignored, though the date is 1794; the main characters are English and half-English; the Frenchman is a fop; English sailors are praised; Italian unification is encouraged. The rest of Europe and America, however, read it with passionate interest, and women everywhere adopted Corinne as a model.

    Corinne's subject is a revolutionary one: its heroine is a happy, independent, fulfilled, and recognized artist, We first meet her when she is being crowned as a poet on the Capitol in Rome, where Mme. de Staël herself had been honored by the Academy. Corinne's poetry consists of improvisations chanted to the accompaniment of her lyre, a recognized genre in the Italy of that time and a significant choice for this novel. Lipking suggests that Mme. de Staël was aiming at "nothing less than an alternative literary canon ... that would define civilization not in terms of power, refinement, or natural pride but as the communion of sensitive and enlightened beings." In such a view, texts would be "silent conversations or webs of relationship to which each reader might bring her own confidences."[12] Because Corinne is speaking in public, her text is in one sense a performance, but its improvisational quality, drawing its content as well as its energy from the audience, establishes her art as an affiliative relationship. Delphine's hostile audience has been replaced by a public willing not only to admire but to commune and to love.

In the beginning, then, far from being an uncertain outsider, Corinne not only has her public's approval but uses their admiration as the source of her own artistic expression. The narrative structure sets this up by introducing her through the sensitive but emotionally frozen Oswald, Lord Nelvil, who has traveled from Edinburgh to Italy to "protect himself" from his guilty grief at his father's death, always a sore point for Mme. de Staël. Simone Balayé documents the resemblances between Oswald and the self-protective Benjamin Constant;[13] if Corinne can make Oswald respond, she must be powerful indeed.

Oswald reponds: to the pleasures of the "brilliant Italian sun"; to a new Italian enthusiastic relationship to talent that, like all foreigners, he finds "contagious"; and to all Rome celebrating its "ecstasy" for a woman unlike any he has ever seen—Corinne, dressed in the robes and shawls of Domenichino's painting of the Cumaean Sibyl, riding in a chariot to be crowned on the Capitol. When she catches sight of Oswald there and begins to improvise with him in mind, his reserve is broken: "She was no longer a fearful woman, but an inspired priestess, joyously devoting herself to the cult of genius."

At this point Corinne proves herself an inspiring priestess in two ways. She has both constituted the Romans' historic and artistic past for them, as Prince Castel-Forte says in his tribute, and made Oswald capable of constituting his own. He seems almost to recognize her: "we often have a sort of innate image of the beloved in our heart that convinces us we are recognizing something we are actually seeing for the first time." What this connection makes him recognize is not some fleeting resemblance to her half-sister Lucile, but an acknowledgment of the change that has taken place in him, a recognition of the necessary other person who inspires emotion, and to whom the self must connect.

Corinne now takes center stage, with Oswald as the focus of her audience. But an improvisatory poet needs her public to inspire and define her, and whether we find this a narcissistic relationship or describe it in terms of Lipking's alternate canon, we can see the danger in her replacing that public with Oswald. His own relationship to the outside world is so problematic that it ultimately dictates his rejection of her as well as her isolation from the public he has replaced. But Corinne does not yet realize this: she wants both public acclaim for her genius and personal recognition from her beloved, and at first she does not see why she should not have it. Here is surely the source of the book's wide appeal: the "fantasy of the performing heroine," as Moers calls it, but also the much more powerful dream of having love and approval from the outside world simultaneously reciprocal with one's own love for it.

Corinne's independence, public persona, and disregard of social norms inspire growing hostility in Oswald—she has no known patronymic, she has had lovers, she does not observe the usual rules of dress or etiquette. Increasingly anxious, she arranges "one last brilliant day" on the Cape Miseno outside Naples for him to "hear her one more time, as he had heard her that day at the Capitol," before she feels ready to tell him her story.

It is not a story he finds reassuring. Corinne is, in fact, only half Italian, raised in Italy until her father, Lord Edgermond, brings her to England to live with his second wife and their little Lucile. There she suffers from the coldness of the climate and of the English attitude toward women. As her father explains, "Everything is different from Italy here. Women have no vocation among us, other than their domestic duties." Corinne will be expected not only to refrain from any "vocation," but to avoid expressing unconventional opinions or, for that matter, any opinions at all on a variety of subjects that might interest her.

The sixteen-year-old Corinne asks the essential Staëlian question: "What is happiness . . . if not the development of our abilities?" She fears for her talent; "Northern" creativity is not developed in women because society demands that they be cut off from their emotions. Miss Edgermond rescues herself by escaping to Italy, where, to her surprise, she finds that her talent has increased because of her contact with English culture: "I could therefore believe myself destined to unusual advantages, because of the special circumstances giving me a double education and two different nationalities. . . ." Her gift is now not the result of the superiority of either Northern or Southern cultures, but of her response to the interaction between them. With her father's legacy, she goes to Rome, where she knows no one, "and simply called myself Corinne, a name the story of the Greek Corinna, a poet and friend of Pindar, had made me love."

Oswald's sympathetic reaction to this story does not keep him from abandoning Corinne to marry her half-sister Lucile, thus repeating the experience of English rejection that enabled her to develop her talents; but she is now unable to use her gifts. The problem is her subject matter—she now thinks about her own pain instead of abstract ideas—and the nature of her altered relationship to her audience: concentrating on a man who has rejected her, she no longer gains from her public's response the energy to improvise. The connection has been broken. Nor does her insight help her bear his marriage; for Mme. de Staël, the ability to reflect on one's own grief does not necessarily lessen it. Corinne finds very little consolation in teaching Oswald and Lucile's little girl before she dies. Like most Staëlian fiction, the book ends with a radical refusal of the world society has structured. Mme. de Staël herself, exiled but acclaimed, went on to write *On Germany*.

On Germany (1813)

As Mme. de Staël relates in *Ten Years of Exile*, Napoleon stopped the printing of *On Germany* in the middle of the third volume, and it remained a controversial book well into the twentieth century. Her work to bring the new German philosophical ideas to France is, however, a development of her view of the progress of civilization as dialectic, which had been strengthened by her meetings in Germany with Goethe, Schiller, Wieland, Fichte, Humboldt, and Schlegel. As Gutwirth says, "what more precisely excited Mme. de Staël in Germany was not only the dialectic itself but also the dialectical mode of apprehension in which German culture was expressed."[14] Mme. de Staël envisaged her role in the historical process of civilization as challenging France with the stimulus of German culture. But while France may have exiled her, it remains her audience for this critique of the new German ideas; her enthusiasm is generated by the interplay between them.

Her first chapter, "On the Appearance of Germany," gives an example of this interplay as she presents the physical context for German culture. Her heart is gripped by the ruined castles, snow, and "something silent about both men and nature," but her reflecting mind keeps its distance: "once you have overcome these unreflecting sensations, the country and its inhabitants offer your observant mind something interesting and poetic." The chapter ends by describing German gardens containing Aeolian harps and grottoes that are "attempting to create an Italian nature; and there are some brilliant afternoons of the short summer when you manage to forget the difference." The active mind is what makes the connection.

The essay "On Women" defends the virtues developed by women whom society has made accustomed to suffering: in times when political circumstances do not let men "use their lives in a noble and worthy way," women can still find happiness because they live outside themselves, which, "whether through ideas, feelings, or virtues—makes the soul accustomed to a sense of elevation." German women accomplish this by making a religion of love, sometimes absurdly, sometimes sincerely, and have the "special charm" of appealing voices, blonde hair, and brilliant complexions. But Mme. de Staël's admiration for all this is qualified: "Nevertheless, German women rarely show the quick spirit that makes conversation live and ideas move." Once again, she opts for the quick-witted brunette Corinne over any quiet Northern Lucile. The play of language involved in French conversation "is an art for which imagination and soul are certainly very welcome, but which can also provide its own secret remedies to compensate you for the absence of either or both, if you so desire."

Goethe's presence in this book is the result of Mme. de Staël's interviews with him, at first rather strained. Unwilling to meet her, obliged to do so by pressure from the court, he wrote that an evil spirit made him "dialectically" contradict everything she said, but he enjoyed her responses.[15] Mme. de Staël, once she had "put Goethe at his ease," was struck by the play of his imagination: "It is a double existence, a double force, a double light which illuminates both sides of every question simultaneously." She enjoys this interplay in his writings as well, "thwarting the emotions he has aroused. . . . If he were not such a good man, we might be afraid of a superiority rising above everything to degrade and elevate, touch and tease, affirm and doubt successively and successfully." What she took from this dialectical structure illuminated her own mode of thinking.

Her famous division between "Classical and Romantic Poetry" is based on just such a dialectical structure: we have to divide the "realm of literature" into some opposition such as classical and Roman-

tic in order to think about either one at all. This temporal division, like
the geographic one between North and South, is partly a dichotomy that
structures the different aspects of the mind. In classical times, "reflecting
very little, man would relate the action of his soul to the outside
world. . . . The anxious reflection eating away at us like Prometheus' vulture would have looked insane among the clear, distinct relationships of
the civil and social state." But modern people are just the opposite, and
their "habit of turning continually inward upon themselves" demands a
new literature. Classical poetry is not inferior, but it has come to a dead
end for us: "Romantic literature is the only literature . . . that can still
grow and find new life." If we define ourselves as modern beings through
a process of reflection, the Romantic poetry that "evokes our life itself as
a phantom—the most powerful, terrifying phantom of all"—is the only
literature we can write, and a reading of German literature challenges us
to create it.

　　　　Mme. de Staël's presentation of Kant is a serious attempt to
offer French readers some notion of a philosophy "from which we can
get ingenious new insights nowadays, since the materialist perspective no
longer offers us anything interesting or original on any topic." She may
have underestimated the difficulty of trying to explain his work in so
short a space, but she is not talking down to her audience; she herself
sees no need for his "irritating" terminology ("There are already words
for everything") and "obscure metaphysics." Her hope is that French
philosophy will find a way to renew itself through studying him. She
identifies his relationship to his own predecessors in a characteristically
dialectical struggle: "Kant's doctrine feels the effects of the eighteenth-
century philosophy it is meant to refute, but that is because it is human
nature to come to terms with the spirit of one's times, even if one is fighting it." She was also interested in the relationship she sees in his work between abstract theory and "the simplest, strongest feelings," a connection
she saw as essential, and in its implications for morality and aesthetics,
which she treats elsewhere.

　　　　Her chapter on the romantic disposition in emotional life
moves through a discussion on the element of bad faith in "the whole
apparatus of sensibility" to a consideration of the distance imposed by
consciousness on feeling in all analysis, admitting that it may be impossible to write about sensibility "with perfect sincerity" because the very
process of speaking about it distorts experience one way or another:
"women try to present themselves like a novel, and men like a history

book." Her conclusion trusts that if someday someone discovers a way to "speak with absolute sincerity about all the things he has felt," we will find "that there is an unknown soul at the center of that soul about which all the stories are told." Until then, however, language remains at a distance from what it most wants to talk about: the soul's inmost experiences and feelings.

"Love Within Marriage" begins with an apparent contradiction: "In marriage, sensibility becomes an obligation." The previous chapter would suggest that this is a romantic disposition, but here Mme. de Staël takes the opposite view: men and women cannot find lasting happiness in this relationship because of the double standard with which society has structured it. She makes a sustained plea for the abolition of the "war between the sexes—a secret, constant, tricky, perfidious war that damages the morals of both." What she wants is a state of "harmony with the whole of human existence," and marriage fails to provide this because of the "inequality social opinion gives to the duties of the two spouses. . . . A number of prejudices from the days of women's slavery still exist." Given the double standard, educating women only makes things worse: "It would be better to lock women up like slaves, awakening neither their minds nor their imaginations, than to launch them in the middle of the social world and develop their faculties, only to refuse them the happiness these very faculties require." This slavery threatens consciousness itself: "if you still love the man who treats you as a slave, since he does not belong to you and has you in his power, despair takes hold of all your abilities and consciousness itself grows dim with misery." Critics have found this a conservative statement compared to the one in *On Literature*, but the comment on women's education should be read as highly ironic. Nor is Mme. de Staël begging the question of whether social reform can eliminate all unhappiness when she calls for an abolition of the sexual double standard as a practical means of eliminating the inequity that causes this particular form of suffering.

In "The Influence of Enthusiasm on the Enlightenment," Mme. de Staël reminds her French audience that "the terrible events we have witnessed have left us with souls blasé; everything related to thought pales beside the omnipotence of action." But if our reaction encourages a climate of enthusiasm, we may regain a sense of the interest and beauty of our own feelings and ideas, "the heart's reverie and the mind's whole range of thought." This optimistic ending poses the difficult question of why her stories and novels end so differently. Simone

Balayé believes that for Mme. de Staël, these two ways of expressing her-self are equally valid: "her truth is completely present in each."[16] The Staëlian structure of dialectic suggests that she may well have needed them both.

The Mannequin (1811)

This light-hearted comedy, intended for private performance at Coppet with young Albertine in the lead, recasts a classical plot in feminist terms. The heroine and her lover prove that her fiancé would just as soon marry someone else by substituting a two-dimensional mannequin for the "other woman," demonstrating not only how little importance women have as individuals for conventional men but that their ideal woman has no substance at all. Sophie is a lively talker, her lover a German artist, her fiancé a count who admires the shy femininity of Englishwomen who cannot speak French. Her trick is "to show you a woman who would not put forward her own opinion about anything, and broke none of the rules of etiquette: a real cardboard doll, just like all those living dolls."

The device may remind us of a theme Mme. de Staël was to take seriously in her Second Preface to the *Letters on Rousseau* (1814), where she warns us that a woman who cannot find intellectual freedom is "nothing but a doll." In order for the comedy to work at all, we must believe that some men really might prefer their women to be, literally, dummies; the mannequin onstage makes us realize the artificial nature of the everyday reality we accept. The comic ending offers us the possibility of reform with the Count's ambivalent "Let me hope, however, that somewhere in the world there are women less malicious than you, who are not, for all that, mannequins."

Reflections on Suicide (1813)

The problem of suicide raised by Goethe's *Werther* was, by 1813, well on its way to becoming a Romantic topos. For Mme. de Staël, it is a central moral issue, marking the boundary that keeps us from understanding other human beings. Suicide threats and attempts were common among her friends and heroines, and she was unhappy enough to consider it herself the year she wrote this work. Confined at Coppet by Napoleon, she had lost the company of her close friend Mme. Récamier, who had been ordered to keep away, and of Benjamin Constant, who had left with his wife after quarreling with John Rocca; she herself was inadmissibly and (at forty-five) uncomfortably pregnant, disguised as dropsical. She had just written a play in which the Greek poet Sappho, abandoned by her young man for a young girl, throws herself into the sea.

In *The Influence of the Passions* she had expressed her horror at continuing to exist "simply because we do not know how to die." Here she takes an opposite position: suicides are sick and weak. Nevertheless, "unhappy people are the ones to write for," because they are the ones who reflect on their feelings: "reflection is their safest refuge." Jean Starobinski sees in this work an "apologetic for a religion of unhappiness."[17] But the reflection prompted by unhappiness also suggests the possibility of consolation and the inevitability, if we survive, of change over time: "Look back after ten years on someone undergoing a great loss of any kind, and you will find that he is suffering and enjoying himself for very different reasons from the original loss that constituted his happiness ten years ago. This is not to say that happiness has come back to him."

If we are to go on living, then, in real life, Mme. de Staël recommends that we find consolation through hard work: "I do believe we can say with some confidence that hard, steady work has comforted most of those who have devoted themselves to it. There is a future in every form of occupation, and what man needs at every moment is a future." The retarded child Mme. de Staël carried within her physically that winter may have been short-lived, but the future she created with the intentionality of writing was not.

Considerations on the Main Events of the French Revolution (1818)

In the *Considerations*, Mme. de Staël develops her theory that the Revolution was not an aberration, but a necessary step forward in the development of human civilization. This now familiar theory, the foundation of French liberal thought, proposed a new approach to history: what seems like a break is actually a continuation of the process of struggle. Even the Reign of Terror is part of this process: "Where did the disorderly tendencies of the early years of the Revolution come from, after all, if not from a hundred years of superstition and arbitrary rule?" Our struggle toward perfectibility, often misrepresented as an automatic improvement, involves the effort of comprehension as well as of practical action.

"The Opening of the Estates General" shows us the moment of confrontation in the public astonishment at the emergence of a new force: procession of the three estates through Paris for the first time in centuries. The young Germaine de Staël reacts with "some very lively hopes," but the aristocrat nearby at the window, "a woman of no intellectual distinction whatsoever," is also right: "great disasters will come of this—disasters for France, disasters for ourselves." Mme. de Staël's position as a woman is necessarily that of an observer, but she moves from the personal to the historical level easily as the King and Queen enter the assembly room and her own father tries to keep his balance.

In her chapter "On Political Fanaticism" she tries to look at the "underlying principle": violence comes from "the will to dominate felt by those riding on top of the wheel of fortune," a will Mme. de Staël understood. Characteristically, she has faith both in representative government precisely because it is an "abstract power," and in the multiplication (though not the abolition) of personal and political connections between different classes of people. The Revolution occurred in France because there the lack of these connections was greatest and most resented; our next move to reestablish society must be to foster them.

As she did in *The Influence of the Passions*, she insists on the necessity of distancing herself from the undifferentiated destruction of the Reign of Terror: the threat of such a beginning, "staining one's imagination ineradicably in blood," now forces us into a stance of philosophical consideration. Her analysis of the institutionalization of fear during the Terror is complemented by her remarks on the way people were still reading sentimental fiction: in both cases the relationship of feeling to deliberate thought has been fragmented. But the great unhappiness of the French is at the source of this perversion: "if the Negroes of

Saint-Domingue have committed even greater atrocities, it is because they had been even more greatly oppressed."

Germaine de Staël's attitude toward Napoleon was not always so monolithic as she implies. There were moments when she and Constant tried to work with him, and she attempted to persuade him to pay back the money her father had lent Louis XVI's treasury. But her analysis of their relationship remains valid: she shows him persecuting her both as a woman and as someone who believes in the value of independent political thought.

In the essay "On Exile" his dislike of her as a woman intellectual is presented as a parvenu characteristic; the experiences of Delphine might suggest that such hostility was part of the aristocratic social structure, but Napoleon's went further. He pointedly told her at an early Talleyrand dinner that the most valuable woman is the woman who has the most children; and years later at a public reception he stared at her bosom and inquired, "You must have nursed your children yourself, I imagine?" Mme. de Staël cannot recount such stories in the *Considerations*, but her discussion of his "vulgarity" in this chapter goes beyond personalities to recognize that he cannot deal with independent women because they are outside the political power structure, a structure he is at pains to preserve.

Ten Years of Exile (1820)

Like many features of postrevolutionary France, internal exile was not really an "invention" of Napoleon's; Louis XIV used to send courtiers who had displeased him to their country estates. Mme. de Staël not only protests being exiled from Paris and from France, however, but does so in terms that show how much she was a child of the Revolution. In the chapter "Why Bonaparte Hated Me" she establishes herself as maintaining the revolutionary principle of liberty, untarnished by the Reign of Terror; she sees the political process as one that necessarily involves independent thought. "It's a question of what I think, not of what I want," is a statement that no one involved in politics would have dreamed of making in Louis XIV's time.

Mme. de Staël's analysis of "Bonaparte's System of Fusion" explains how Napoleon's use of politicians from opposing parties had created a "fusion" within which no real dialectical opposition was legitimate. The publication of her book On Literature thus became a hostile act. Here her trials as a woman writer are mentioned only as part of her dedication to liberty, by which she means her right to take a position opposing those in power. For Mme. de Staël they remained twin facets of her perception of herself.

The chapter "Suppression of On Germany; Exile from France" contains a spirited account of Mme. de Staël's life in exile and of the day she learned the news that publication of her book had been stopped. Mme. de Staël gives us enough in passing to let us know that she has made her life in exile a full one: the pleasure of knowing someone who will lend you his house when you are exiled from Paris, the delights of intimate conversation with long-term friends and complicated flirtatious games no one else can play; the enterprising determination of a woman in her midforties to investigate her property in America; the enjoyment of playing and hearing music, and the genuine curiosity about Indian rarities, encountered by chance. If she takes some satisfaction in this, we may be able to share it with her. Necessarily on the periphery, she had succeeded in making herself a life elsewhere. It was, and remains, no small achievement, even to readers whose own lives are very different. The reflective distance from feeling that Germaine de Staël established in her first theoretical work on Rousseau finds a parallel here in her geographical distance from the most stimulating experience she ever knew—the pleasure of talking in Paris. The connections she made across this distance, in both cases, are at the center of the reflections she offers us.

EDITOR'S NOTE

In this collection I have attempted to give a good sense of the impressive range of Germaine de Staël's writings, emphasizing the fiction and literary criticism but also suggesting the social, political, and historical interrelationships that were essential to her. The goal of the translation has been to convey the character of Mme. de Staël's intensely enthusiastic language, its drive, and also its hesitations in finding a voice in which to present the self-reflecting consciousness at the heart of her quest. I have introduced occasional additional paragraphing in places where entire pages without a break might be disconcerting to the modern reader; excerpts have been clearly marked. Her letters have not been included in this volume. The early short fiction has been placed according to its date of publication, except for *Zulma*, which introduces *Influences of the Passions*, of which it was intended to be a chapter. The standard edition of the complete works is the seventeen-volume edition (Paris, 1820–1821); I have also used the critical editions of *De la Littérature*, edited by Paul van Tieghem (Geneva: Droz, 1959), and of *De l'Allemagne*, edited by Mme. Jean de Pange and Simone Balayé (Paris: Hachette, 1958). The selected bibliography contains only works in English; a more extensive bibliography can be found in Madelyn Gutwirth's *Madame de Staël, Novelist: The Emergence of the Artist as Woman* (Urbana: University of Illinois Press, 1978).

1.

Letters on Rousseau

Preface to the Edition of 1788

There is still nothing in print to praise Rousseau; I felt a need to see my admiration expressed. I might certainly have wished for someone else to portray my feelings, but I have tasted a certain pleasure in retracing for myself the memory and sensation of my enthusiasm. Men of genius may be liable to the judgment of only a limited number of superior minds, but they have to accept tributes of gratitude from anyone and everyone. Books aiming at the happiness of the human race put their authors on the same level as men who have been immortalized by their actions: we who were not alive at the time may well feel some impatience to repay their ghosts, and place our homage on their graves even if we are aware of its inadequacy.

People kind enough to foresee some talent in me may blame me for rushing to deal with a subject far above any ability I could ever hope someday to have. But who can tell if time is going to give or to take? Who dares predict the progress of his own mind? How can we agree to wait, putting off the expression of urgent feelings to some uncertain future date? Time may be able to destroy our illusions, but it sometimes attacks the truth also: its destructive grasp is not always restricted to error. But in any case, don't we owe Rousseau the most gratitude while we are young? Here was a man who could use youth's good *and* bad qualities, transforming virtue into a passion, insisting on persuasion through enthusiasm, and making himself their master.

Preface to the Edition of 1814

These letters on Rousseau's writings and character were written the year I entered society and published without my consent, a stroke of chance that got me started on a literary career.[1] I cannot say I regret it: the study of literature has brought me more joy than sorrow. Anybody who is more hurt by criticism than pleased by praise must be violently affected by love of self. Moreover, the process of developing and perfecting one's own mind provides a continual activity—hope springing eternal—which the ordinary course of life simply cannot offer. In women's destiny everything goes downhill except for thought, whose immortal nature it is to keep constantly rising.

It is almost universally acknowledged that literary tastes and education are a great advantage to men, but there is no such agreement on the influence this same education might have on the destiny of women. There might be some point in fearing an increase in women's intelligence if there were any question of imposing domestic slavery on them, lest they be temped to revolt against such a fate. Christian society requires nothing but justice in family relationships, however; so the more enlightened reason becomes, the likelier it is to submit to the laws of morality. As we reflect on these laws, we see that in the long run they rule the world as infallibly as physical forces.

Feelings may carry us away in spite of enlightened education—but not because of it. Unusually bright women may often also be extremely passionate, but literary cultivation does not increase the risks of having a passionate character: it diminishes them. The mind's pleasures are made to calm the tempests of the heart.

Society is organized these days so that we are much more threatened by negative faults like coldness and selfishness than by any kind of exaltation. The common people may be capable of grand and beautiful virtues without cultivating their minds, but in the elegant leisure class our acquired habits dry our hearts out if we do not supplement them with revivifying study. When worldly habits are not combined with broad literary learning, all they teach us is how to say commonplace things in a facile way, expressing our opinions in formulas and our characters in curtsies. If you cannot find some compensation for all these sacrifices in a distinguished education—if you do not find a sense of the natural in spiritual exhilaration, and sincerity in a knowledge of the truth—if you do not finally breathe easy in some wider realm, you are nothing but a doll who has learned her lesson well, always singing the same note even if she changes the words.[2] Even if it were true (which it is not) that a woman under such discipline was more likely to submit to conjugal authority, what happens to communication between souls if there is no analogy between minds? What are we to think of a man whose pride is so modest that he prefers blind obedience in a wife to enlightened sympathy? The most touching examples of conjugal love are found in women worthy of understanding their husbands and sharing their fate. Marriage reaches its full beauty only when it can be founded on mutual admiration.

Nevertheless, many men prefer women to devote themselves to nothing but household cares—and to make sure of this, they would not mind if these women were incapable of understanding anything else. That is a question of taste. Distinguished women are few and far between, however, so men who do not want them will always have plenty of other choices available.

"We do not keep women from cultivating their minds in any way," some readers may object, "as long as those cultivated minds do not make them want to be authors, distracting them from their natural duties and making them the rivals of men, whom they were created solely to encourage and console." I must admit I would feel even greater respect for a woman of genius who had no ambition for the triumphs of self-love than for a woman of genius who was in hot pursuit of them; but we can only despise things that are within our power to achieve. There was once a Parisian who stooped every time he went under the Saint-Denis gateway, though it was a hundred feet high; it is the same for women who boast of being afraid of celebrity without having ever had the talent to achieve it. Talents may have their drawbacks, like all the other good things of this world, but I prefer such drawbacks to the boredom of a limited mind belittling things it cannot achieve or laying claim to things it cannot feel. Finally, if we consider only our relationship to ourselves, a greater intensity of life is always an increase of happiness. Unhappiness does penetrate deeper into more energetic minds; but take it all in all, there is no one who should not be thankful to God for giving him some talent extra.

ON THE *LETTER ON SPECTACLES*

[...] Rousseau's letter against the establishment of spectacles in Geneva is one of his works that have struck me the most.[3] It is an amazing combination of persuasive techniques, logic and eloquence, passion and reason. Rousseau never showed himself with greater dignity: love of country, enthusiasm for liberty, and an attachment to morality guide and enliven his thinking. The cause he supports, particularly as applied to Geneva, is perfectly just; all the brilliance he sometimes uses to sustain a paradox is devoted in this work to the support of truth. No effort is lost, no movement miscarries; he has all the ideas his subject can bring forth, all the elevation and warmth it should arouse.

It is in this work that he establishes his opinion on the advantages of men and women not seeing each other frequently in society. In a republic, such a custom is no doubt preferable: love of country is such a powerful motive that it makes men indifferent even to what we call glory; but in countries where only the power of opinion gives freedom from the master's power, applause and votes of confidence from women become an additional motive for emulation, the influence of which it is so important to preserve. In republics, men must keep even their faults: their harshness and roughness strengthen their passion for liberty. In a kingdom, however, these same faults would just make tyrants of everybody who might exert a little power. In a monarchy, too, women may preserve more feelings of pride and independence than men; the form of government does not touch them; their slavery, always domestic, is the same in every country. Women's nature is therefore not degraded even under despotism. But men feel debased when they no longer have the use of the liberty they were made for, and then they often fall beneath themselves.

Rousseau tried to prevent women from taking part in public affairs and playing a brilliant role, but how much pleasure he gave them when he talked about them! Ah! he may have tried to deprive them of some rights foreign to their destiny, but how he gave them back the ones that belong to them forever! If he tried to decrease women's influence on the way men make decisions, how much he consecrated the power they have over men's happiness! If he has made women come down from a

throne usurped, how he has replaced them on the throne nature destined for them! If he gets angry at them when they want to resemble men,
how he adores them when they present themselves to him with the
charms, weaknesses, virtues, and faults of their sex! Last of all, he believes
in love; he is forgiven; what does it matter to women that his mind
quarrels about power with them, when his heart submits to them? What
can it matter even to women naturally endowed with tender souls, if the
false honor of governing their beloved is snatched away from them? No,
it is sweeter for them to feel his superiority, to admire him, to believe
him a thousand times above them, to depend on him, because they
adore him; to submit voluntarily, to bring everything down to his feet
and to set the example themselves, asking no return except that of the
heart which they have deserved through love.

    I do reproach Rousseau on women's behalf with one wrong,
however: of claiming in a note to the *Letter on Spectacles* that women are
incapable of painting passion with warmth and truth. Let him deny
women, if he likes, the vain literary talents that make them struggle with
men instead of being loved by them; let him refuse women the intellectual power, the profound capacity for attention with which great
geniuses are endowed; women's feeble organs are opposed to this, and
their hearts too often preoccupied, monopolizing their minds, so that
they cannot concentrate on other meditations; but let Rousseau not accuse women of just being able to write coldly, and of being unable to
portray even love. The soul alone is what distinguishes women: the soul
gives women's minds some movement; the soul alone makes them find
any charm in a destiny whose only events are feelings, whose only interests are affections; the soul makes them identify with the fate of their
beloved, and arranges a happiness for them whose only source is the happiness of the things they love; finally, the soul takes the place of both
education and experience for them, making them worthy of feeling what
they are unable to judge. According to Rousseau, Sappho was the only
woman capable of making love speak.[4] Ah! women might blush to use
the burning language that is the sign of insane delirium rather than deep
passion, and still express what they feel: the sublime abandon, the
melancholy sorrow, the overpowering feelings that make them live and
die, would touch their readers' hearts more deeply than all the raptures
born of the exalted imagination of poets.

ON *THE NEW HÉLOÏSE*

The discourse I have been talking about so far are great and brilliant chiefly because of their depth and energy of style, but they also contain impulses of sensibility that foretell the author of *The New Héloïse*. It is with great pleasure that I surrender myself to retracing the effect this book has had on me, and I will try my best to forbid myself an enthusiasm that might be attributed to my own disposition instead of the author's talent. Real admiration inspires a wish to share one's feelings; one must restrain oneself to persuade, and slow down to be followed. I am therefore going to distance myself somewhat from my impressions as I received them, and write about *The New Héloïse* as I think I would do if time had aged my heart.

A novel may be a portrayal of manners and current absurdities; or a play of the imagination, gathering extraordinary events to capture the interest of curiosity; or a great moral idea set to action and dramatized. This last category is where we have to put *The New Héloïse*. The author's aim is apparently to use Julie's virtue as an example to encourage repentance in women guilty of her fault.

I will start by agreeing to every criticism anyone could make of this project. People will say that interesting anyone in Julie is dangerous, covering crime with charm, and that the damage this novel can do to girls who are still innocent is more certain than any use it can be to girls who are innocent no longer. This criticism is true. I wish Rousseau had portrayed Julie as guilty of nothing but the passion within her heart. I will go further—I think that morality should be written only for the pure of heart. In the first place, morality's real effect may be to perfect rather than to change, guide rather than to reform; in any case, a morality destined for honorable souls can still be useful to those who are honorable no longer. Portrayals of the misery and remorse caused by minor faults arouse such blushes of shame for serious ones! I think too that indulgence may be the only virtue it is dangerous to preach, though useful to practice. In the abstract, crime must arouse indignation. Pity is born only from the interest the guilty person inspires; the austerity should lie in the morality, the kindness in its application.

I admit, then, that I agree with Rousseau's censors: the subjects of *Clarissa* and *Grandison* are more moral.[5] But a novel's real usefulness lies in its effect rather than its plot, in the feelings it inspires rather than the events it narrates. Let us forgive Rousseau if we feel more quickened by love for virtue, care more about our duties, are more attracted by simple ways of life, kindness, retreat from society, after we have finished this reading. Let us stop condemning this novel, if this is the impression it leaves in our souls. Rousseau himself seems to have thought this a dangerous work; he believed that Julie's love was the only thing written in letters of fire, and that the image of virtue, her tranquil happiness as Mme. de Wolmar, would be colorless beside those searing tableaux. He was wrong; his talent for painting can be seen everywhere; and in his fictions as in reality, the storms of the passions and the peace of innocence rage and calm in turn.

What Rousseau meant to write was a work of morality: to do that he used the form of a novel, and he portrayed the dominating sentiment of the genre. But if it is true that men cannot be moved without the stimulus of passion—if few of them are set on fire by thought, or rise through enthusiasm for virtue by thought alone without any foreign sentiment giving charm and life to such an abstract love of perfection—if they are no longer affected by the language of angels, shouldn't even angels renounce such language? Why should we blame Rousseau for choosing love, if men have to be dragged into virtue, so to speak, if their imperfection means that we have to resort to the eloquence of passion to interest them? What other passion would have been closer to virtue? Ambition, perhaps? But ambition is always accompanied by hatred and envy. The desire for glory? But all men are not suited to this sentiment, and those who have never felt it do not even always understand it. What a stage—what talent that passion would demand! Whose task is it to inspire it, if not those whom nothing can keep from feeling it? What difference do books make to the tiny number of men who anticipate the progress of the human mind? No: only love could be of universal interest, filling every heart in proportion to its energy; and only love could become both a strong and a useful motive under Rousseau's direction.

In earliest times, men's only virtues may have been those that come from love. Love can sometimes provide all the virtues ordained by religion and morality. Such virtues have a less celestial origin, but it is easy to confuse them with the others: when the object of our adoration is virtuous, we soon become virtuous ourselves. One is enough to make two. We are virtuous when we love what we should love; we involuntarily do whatever duty commands. In the end our souls are made ready for virtue by that abandonment of self and contempt for everything vanity makes us seek; and when love has died, virtue will reign alone. Once we are accustomed to giving no value to ourselves except because of someone else, once we have completely detached ourselves from ourselves, there is no confusion, and love gives way to piety. That is the most probable history of the heart.

Kindness and humanity, gentleness and goodness seem part of love too. We get interested in unhappy people; the heart is always inclined to emotion, like stretched strings which resound at a breath. The beloved lover is a stranger to envy and also to men's injustice; their faults do not irritate him, because they cannot hurt him; he bears them because he does not feel them. His mind is on his mistress, his life is in his heart: he forgives any evil done to him elsewhere because he forgets about it. He is effortlessly generous. Far from me, however, to compare such momentary virtue with real virtue: and I am far from respecting it in the same way. But let me repeat: since we must involve the soul through feelings to fix the mind on ideas—since we must mix passion with virtue to make anyone lsiten to both of them—is Rousseau to blame? Did not human imperfection decree the wrongs he is accused of?

I know he is blamed for having portrayed a tutor seducing the pupil entrusted to him, but I must admit I hardly reflected on this at all when I was reading the book. First, it seems clear to me that this circumstance did not occur to Rousseau himself; he took it from the old story of Héloïse.[6] Then, too, the morality of his novel lies entirely in Julie's story; he thought of painting Saint-Preux only as the most passionate of men. His is a book for women: it was written for women; they are the people it can harm or help. Doesn't the fate of love depend entirely on them? This novel could indeed mislead a man in Saint-Preux's position; but a book is dangerous if it expresses feelings everyone may have, rather than when it narrates a combination of events that may never happen, and cannot authorize anyone. Saint-Preux has neither the language nor the principles of a seducer; Saint-Preux was filled with those notions of equality we still see in Switzerland; Saint-Preux was

Julie's age. They met in spite of themselves, and were carried away. Saint-Preux used no weapons but truth and love; he did not attack, he showed himself involuntarily. Saint-Preux had loved before wanting to be loved; he wanted to die rather than risk disturbing the life of his beloved. He fought his passion, which is the virtue of men; the virtue of women is to triumph over it. No; Saint-Preux's example is not immoral. But Julie's could have been. Julie's situation comes close to all situations that come from the heart, and the picture of her wrongdoing might be dangerous, if the effect of it was not canceled by her remorse and the rest of her life; if virtue were not painted in this novel in lineaments as ineradicable as love.

The picture of a violent passion is certainly dangerous, but other authors have dealt with principles in a light, indifferent way that not only presupposes much more corruption of manners, but also contributes more to that corruption. The guilty Julie is less of an insult to virtue than a woman who keeps her virtue without valuing it, hanging on to it through calculation and observing it without loving it. If indulgence were reserved for excessive passion, would there be much call for it? Would there be any need to despair of a heart that had felt such passion? No: its misguided soul could still recapture its energy. But nothing can be expected of a soul that has lost its taste for virtue through a slow process of corruption. Anything that happens gradually is always irrevocable.

Rousseau may have given in to the impulse of his soul and talent. He had something very violent to express: passion and virtue, in contrast and in combination. But look at his respect for conjugal love! He may have meant to use Julie's misfortunes and her father's inflexible pride as an example to attack social prejudices and institutions, following his usual line of thought. But he has such reverence for the tie to which nature has destined us! He tried so hard to prove that it is capable of making people happy, even people whose hearts have known other delights! Who would dare resist his morality? Is he a stranger to the passions? Does he fail to recognize their power? Hasn't he earned the right to speak to the tenderhearted, and teach them the sacrifices which lie within their power? Who would dare call such sacrifices impossible, when Rousseau teaches us that Julie, the most passionate of women, was capable of them, finding her happiness in the fulfillment of her duties without deviating from them again until the very last moment of her life?

We think ourselves excused from resembling perfect heroines; we would be ashamed not to have the virtues of a guilty woman.

Our customs keep young girls in convents. There is no fear of this novel's turning them away from marriages of convenience. Young girls never depend on themselves; everything around them is trying to protect their hearts from emotional impressions. Virtue watches over them, and often parental ambition too. Even men, bizarre as their principles may be, wait until girls are married before talking to them of love. At that point, everything around women changes: people stop trying to uplift their minds with romantic sentiments, and wither their hearts with chilly jokes about everything they have learned to respect. This is when women should read *The New Héloïse*. For one thing, in reading the letters of Saint-Preux they will feel how far the men around them are from even the crime of loving them; they will then see the sanctity of the marriage tie, and learn to recognize the importance of its obligations and the happiness such obligations can offer, even without the spell cast by sentiment. Who has ever felt this more strongly than Rousseau? What more striking proof could he have offered?

Suppose Rousseau had portrayed two lovers united by destiny, their whole lives made up of days any one of which would have beautified a good part of the year; lovers traveling the road of life together, indifferent to the countries through which they passed; lovers who adored a beloved image in their child, a being in which their souls were united, their lives merged together; lovers fulfilling all their duties as if they were giving in to impulses; lovers for whom the charm of virtue would be joined to the attraction of love, the sensual pleasures of the heart combined with the charms of innocence. Piety would also connect them to each other; they would thank the Supreme Being together. Can any happy person be an atheist? Some blessings are so great that they inspire a need for gratitude; it would be so cruel not to enjoy them forever that the heart seeks refuge in tangible hopes. These lovers would no longer be holding on to each other through some secret, unknown tie; before men and before God they would have formed the unbreakable bond. Their name, their children, their dwelling—everything would remind them of their happiness; everything would be saying it would last; every moment would give rise to some new pleasure. There are so many details of happiness in an intimate union! Oh! if Rousseau had shown us a union like that, his task would have been easy. But would what he had been preaching have been virtue? Would what he had given be a lesson? would it have been useful to mankind to make the unhappy envious, and tell the happy what they already know? No; the plan Rousseau followed was more moral than that.

Rousseau portrayed a woman married in spite of herself, tied to her husband by respect alone, carrying within her heart both the memory of another kind of happiness and something else to love; a woman who spent her entire life outside the whirlwind of society, which can make us forget both husband and lover, letting no thought or feeling predominate within us, extinguishing all passions and reestablishing calm through confusion and peace through upheaval. Instead, this woman spends her life in absolute retirement, alone with M. de Wolmar, in the country, close to nature and therefore disposed to all the heart's sentiments which nature inspires or retraces. This is the situation in which Rousseau portrays Julie, making her own felicity through virtue; happy through the happiness she gives her husband, the education she gives her children, the effect of her example on all around her, and the consolations she finds in her confidence in her God. There is certainly a happiness other than the one I have just portrayed, a more melancholy happiness one can taste despite an occasional tear. But here is a happiness more suited for beings passing through the earth they inhabit; a happiness one can enjoy without the regret of losing it; a happiness one can possess completely, from which reflection or fear takes nothing away; a happiness in which the pious find all the delights other people are promised by love. This is the pure feeling, so enchantingly portrayed, that makes this novel moral; this is the feeling that would have made it the most moral of all novels if Julie had always offered us the spectacle of virtue struggling not with misfortune, as the ancients say, but with passion, which is much more terrible—and if this pure and spotless virtue had not lost some of its charm by looking like repentance.[. . .]

There is one letter that is rarely praised, but I have never been able to read it without an inexpressible surge of tenderness: it is the one Julie writes to Saint-Preux at the moment when she is dying. Perhaps this letter is not so touching as I think; sometimes we fall under the illusion of a word which exactly answers our own heart, a situation which retraces chimeras or memories for us, and we think that the author is the cause of this effect of his work. But Julie telling Saint-Preux that she has never been able to stop loving him—Julie, whom I thought cured, showing me a heart wounded more deeply than ever; this sensation of happiness she gets from the end of a long struggle—this abandon authorized by death and soon to be ended by death—these somber, melancholy words, "adieu forever," mingled with the expressions of a sentiment meant for happiness in life—this certainty that she is dying, which gives all her words such a solemn, true character—this predominating idea, this thing that takes up her whole attention just at the moment when most men concentrate whatever is left of their thoughts upon themselves—this calm that unhappiness offers even more surely than courage at the moment of death; in short, every word of this letter filled my soul with the keenest emotion. Ah! it is so painful to see the end of a reading that has interested us as closely as something going on in our own lives, and that, without disturbing our hearts, has set all our thoughts and all our feelings in motion!

ON ROUSSEAU'S TASTE FOR MUSIC AND BOTANY

Rousseau wrote several works on music; he loved this art with passion all his life. *The Village Soothsayer* even shows some talent for composition. He tried to make melodramas adopted in France, using *Pygmalion* as an example, and perhaps this genre should not have been rejected.[7] When words and music follow each other, both effects are increased; sometimes they are improved by not being harnessed together. Music expresses situations; words develop them. Music can take on the portrayal of impulses beyond words; words can do feelings that are too nuanced for music. Pygmalion's monologue is so eloquent that it seems perfectly likely for the statue to come to life at the sound of his voice, and we are tempted to believe that the gods played no part in this miracle.

Rousseau composed simple, touching airs for a number of romances, the kind of melody that blends in with the situation of one's soul, the kind one can still sing when one is unhappy. A few of them seem national to me; as I heard them I felt myself transported to our

mountain peaks, when the sound of the shepherd's flute is slowly prolonged in the distance by a succession of repeated echoes. These airs remind me of the kind of music, calm rather than somber, that lends itself
to the listener's sentiments and becomes for him the expression of his
own feelings. Where is the sensitive man who has never been touched by
music? An unfortunate person who can listen to it is given the sweet
satisfaction of shedding tears, and his despair is replaced by melancholy;
while one listens, one's sensations are enough for both mind and heart,
leaving no emptiness in either. Some melodies put one in ecstasy for a
moment; a choir of angels always heralds rapture into heaven. How
powerfully memories are retraced by music! how inseparable it becomes
from them! What man in the midst of life's passions could be unmoved
by hearing the tune that enlivened the dances and games of his peaceful
childhood! What woman whose beauty has been withered by time could
keep from tears at the sound of the romance her lover once sang for her!
The tune of this romance, even more than its words, renews in her heart
the emotions of youth. No accessory circumstance such as the sight of
places or things that once surrounded us is connected to the events of
our lives the way music is. The memories which come to us through
music are not accompanied by any regrets; for a moment music gives us
back the pleasures it retraces, and we feel them again rather than
recollect them. Rousseau loved only melancholy airs; that is the kind of
music one wants in the country. All nature seems to accompany the
plaintive sounds of a touching voice. To feel such pleasures, one needs a
pure and gentle soul. A man disturbed by the remembrance of his errors
would not be able to bear the reverie into which we are thrown by
touching music. A man tormented by heartrending remorse would be afraid to get that close to himself, to make all his feelings alive again, to feel
them all slowly, one at a time. I am inclined to trust anyone who is enraptured by music, flowers, and the country. Ah! a penchant for vice must
surely be born within man's heart, because all the sensations he receives
from the objects surrounding him draw him away from it. I don't
know—but often at the end of a lovely day, in a country retreat, at the
sight of a starry sky, it has seemed to me that the spectacle of nature was
speaking to the soul of virtue, hope, and goodness.

    For a while Rousseau turned his attention to botany; this is
one way of taking a detailed interest in the countryside. He had adopted
a system which may show the extent of his belief that man's own memory

is what spoils the pleasure aroused by his contemplation of nature. Rousseau distinguished plants by their forms, rather than by their properties; he thought it degrading to relate them to the use man could make of them. I must admit I am not in favor of adopting this opinion; to consider the works of the Creator destined to a final cause is no desecration, and the world looks more imposing and majestic to someone who sees in it only a single thought. But Rousseau's poetic, savage imagination could not bear to link the image of a shrub or flower, ornaments of nature, to the memory of men's sicknesses and infirmities. In his *Confessions* he paints an enchanting picture of his rapture at seeing periwinkle again. The sight of it had the same effect on him as that tune it is forbidden to play to the Swiss army when they are out of their country, for fear they will desert. This periwinkle could inspire in Rousseau a passion to return to the Vaud country; this single circumstance made all his memories present to him. His mistress, his country, his youth, his loves—he found and felt every one of them again, and all at one time.

ON ROUSSEAU'S CHARACTER

I did not want to begin with a portrait of Rousseau's character. Rousseau wrote his *Confessions* only after finishing his other works, and did not solicit men's attention for himself until he had deserved their gratitude by giving them his genius for twenty years. I have followed the path he traced for me: it is by admiring his works, as anyone must, that I have prepared myself to judge his character, which has been often libeled and sometimes blamed, perhaps with some justice. I am trying not to find him a contrast to his works: I cannot combine contempt and admiration, and I really do not want to believe that the mind can imitate the stamp of truth in books, or that pure and sensitive hearts have no more accurate signs by which to recognize one another. In my attempt at portraying Rousseau, therefore, I will often believe what his *Confessions* have to say about him. The *Confessions* may not have the quality of elevation we could wish for in a man speaking about himself, a characteristic which excuses personality because we find it perfectly natural for anyone who possesses it to be important in his own eyes as well as in ours. All the same, his sincerity seems to me hard to doubt. Anyone would be much more likely to conceal the things admitted in the *Confessions* than to invent them. The events related in them seem true in every detail. Some are circumstances which could not possibly be created by the imagination. And Rousseau has a feeling of pride which answers for the veracity of his memoirs. He believed himself to be the best of men; he would have blushed to think that he needed to dissimulate a single fault to show himself to them. Finally, I think he wrote his memoirs to shine as a historian rather than as the hero of the story. He cared about the portrait rather than the face. He observed himself and painted himself as if he had been his own model: I am convinced that his primary wish was to make himself a good likeness. I believe, then, that one can portray Rousseau according to his *Confessions* exactly as if one had spent a long time living with him; studying what he says does not mean one cannot disagree with it. The way a man judges his own character permits us to understand him even if we do not adopt his opinion.

Rousseau must have had a face that would be unremarkable if one passed him in the street, but unforgettable once one had watched him speak. His eyes were small, and had no particular character of their own, but took on the various emotions of his soul. He had rather prominent eyebrows, as if they were intended to promote his wildness by preserving him from the sight of other men. He generally went around hanging his head, but not from servility or fear; meditation and melancholy had made it lean over like a flower bowed down by its own weight or by the storm. When he was quiet, his face was quite expressionless. His thoughts and affections were portrayed on his face only when he was mingling with the conversation, and took refuge in the depths of his soul if he kept silent. His features were ordinary, but they sparkled when he spoke. He was like those gods Ovid sometimes depicts leaving their earthly disguises by degrees, and finally making themselves known by the brilliant rays of lights darting from their glances.[8]

Rousseau had a slow wit and an eager soul; he grew passionate through thinking. Apparently, at least, he had no sudden impulses; his feelings increased through reflection. He might fall in love with a woman little by little, concentrating on her in her absence. She would leave him quite cool, and come back to find him blazing with passion. On the other hand, he would sometimes leave you still in love with you, but if you had said one single word that could displease him he would remember it, examine it, exaggerate it, think about it for a week and end by breaking up with you, which made it almost impossible to set him straight. No flash of illumination could ever destroy errors so slowly and deeply engraved in his heart. It was also very hard to stay close friends with him for long: a word or gesture would become the subject of his deepest meditations. He linked the most trivial coincidences together as if they were geometrical propositions, finally arriving at what he called a demonstration. I believe that imagination was his primary faculty, and it may even have absorbed all the others. He dreamed rather than lived, and the events of his life went on in his head rather than outside of himself. This way of life might seem to preclude mistrust, as it does not allow for observation, but it did not keep Rousseau from looking: all it meant was that he did not see very well. He had a tender soul; how can anyone who has read his work doubt that? But his imagination sometimes came between his affections and his reason, destroying their power. If he seemed insensitive sometimes, it is because he did not notice the way things were, and his heart would have been more deeply touched than ours if he had had the same eyes as we do. The most serious charge of which his memory can be accused of is that of having abandoned his children. Well, this same man would have been capable of the greatest examples of paternal love, of risking his life for them twenty times over, if he had not believed that someone wanted to make modern Seides out of them.[9] The worthless woman who spent her life with him had learned enough about him to be able to make him unhappy; and the story I have been told of the ruses she used to increase his fears and confirm his doubts, reinforcing his faults, is almost incredible.*

Rousseau was not mad, though he had a demented imagination. He had a powerful rational hold on abstract material, on things whose only reality is within the mind, and he was extravagantly silly about everything related to a knowledge of the world. He went too far in everything; he came close to madness because of his superiority. He was

---

*A man from Geneva who lived with Rousseau for the last twenty years of his life has often given me a picture of his wife's abominable character and the atrocious way she urged him to put his children in the orphanage, constantly repeating that all his supposed friends would attempt to make them feel a mortal hatred of him, and trying to fill him with pain and distrust through her lies and her own feigned terrors. It is certainly mad to listen to such a woman, or to love her. Once we assume such madness, however, all the other crazy things seem true to life.[10]

a man made to live in retirement among a small number of people of limited intelligence, so that nothing would add to his inner turmoil, and he would be surrounded by peace and quiet. He was good; the lower classes, who are usually the ones to enjoy this quality, adored him. But Paris had upset him. He was born for natural rather than institutional society. All his work expressed the loathing he felt for the latter; he could neither understand nor suffer it. He was a savage from the shores of the Orinoco, who would have been happy to spend his life watching the water flow by.[11] He was born contemplative, and found his greatest happiness in reverie; his mind and his heart took hold of him in turn. He lived in his imagination: the world went smoothly along under his eyes, and he would concern himself with religion, mankind, love, or politics. After walking alone all day long, he would come back calm and tranquil. Do the wicked profit from being alone with themselves this way?

All the same, we cannot call Rousseau virtuous, because such praise requires action, and consistency in action. He was a man who should have been left alone to think, without any other demands upon him—led like a child, and listened to like an oracle. His heart felt everything deeply; he should have been treated, not with ordinary precautions, but with the precautions such a character required. His own innocence should never have been trusted. Rousseau had less than anyone else the divine power of reading in others' hearts; people should have shown themselves to him for what they were, and displayed their feelings for him openly. I know it will be said that this is not the highest form of love, but I find that in affairs of the heart the only rule is to make the object of our affections happy. All the rest of the rules are invented not by delicacy, but by vanity.[. . .]

Whether we read Rousseau's works or listen to people who loved him talk about him, we find impulses and feelings in his life and writing that belong only to the pure and good. When we see him in contact with men, we are less fond of him; but as soon as we find him back with nature again, all his impulses find echoes in our hearts, and his eloquence develops the feelings in our souls. He paints a really delightful picture of his stay at Charmettes. How happy he was in the quiet of the countryside! Young people usually like activity, and call their need of it vivacity. Really passionate souls dread it, however, foreseeing what it will cost them to leave their peace and quiet, and feeling that any fire that can be lit can burn. Rousseau, at peace in his retreat, had no desire to exer-

cise his genius; dreaming was enough for his faculties. Loving—no matter what the object of his affections, he staked all his fantasies on that object. What he was dreaming about was love, not Mme. de Warens. Her
own feelings did not torture him; he did not study in his mistress's eyes
the degree of passion he was inspiring in her. What he needed was someone to love. Mme. de Warens made his happiness without getting involved herself. Perhaps the truth is that no great man dominated by the
genius of thought has ever experienced a passion that came from the
heart alone, and this is especially true of Rousseau. Such a passion would
have distracted him, and would have been no use to his imagination.
The faculties of his mind had to play some part in his feelings, he had to
feel the need to endow his mistress. A perfect woman would have been
his best friend, but not the object of his love. I am sure Rousseau never
made any but peculiar choices; I am also sure that the person he was
most in love with in the whole world was Julie. Rousseau was a man who
could become passionate only about illusions—and he was lucky if they
did not trouble his heart more violently than reality itself. He was born
good, sensitive and trusting, but once in the grip of the cruel folly of
men's injustice and ingratitude, he became the most miserable of
creatures. These sweet moments of his youth which he portrayed so
charmingly were never renewed. His reveries were hopes, and became
regrets. Once in Turin a sign from his young mistress enraptured his
heart; now the bow of an old wounded veteran who seems not to hate
him is the only boon he craves.* But remember how much respect he
had for people in his youth! If he has changed more than the average
man, it is because he was less ready for the sad enlightenment he was
forced to acquire. But who feels no sorrow at losing the blind goodness
of his youth? the laughing hopes and sweet confidence of that first stage
of life? Rousseau was unable to bear this trial—but where is the man of
feeling whose heart *does* shrink painlessly, and whose imagination fades
without regret?[. . .]

      People blame Rousseau—yes, there are plenty to accuse this
man all sensitive people ought to defend as their own cause. The ac-
cusers blame Rousseau for wanting to be unusual: "Should a man who
was happy to obtain the palm of glory have been making himself con-

---

*One recalls the charming tableau Rousseau makes in his *Confessions* of Mme. Basile, the Turin
shopkeeper, who gestured in the mirror to him with her finger, telling him to get down on his knees
before her; in his insane *Dialogue of Jean-Jacques with Rousseau* he paints his thrill when an old pen-
sioner salutes him, "not yet having joined in the universal conspiracy against me," as he says.[12]

spicuous with such eccentricities? And when the superiority of his genius made him so extraordinary, why on earth did he try to make himself be extraordinary through such puerile originality?" They say he wanted to make himself remarkable in every possible way; and this was a man who loved solitude more than any other man ever has! Look how happy he was during the whole time he spent on the isle of Saint-Pierre! What an enchanting stay! a delightful refuge! That is where Rousseau's soul still wanders; in those places that aroused his thoughts we must go to pay homage to his memory. Sensitive people will easily understand the happiness experienced in this retreat. Rousseau gave himself up to his profound meditations there; but others might have abandoned themselves to sweeter thoughts. While he was reflecting on time, the world, and life, an unhappy woman would have felt the calmness of nature gently penetrating her heart.[...]

Ah! You who were accusing him of playing a role, of feigning unhappiness, what did you say when you found out that he had killed himself?* It is at this price that people who are slow to feel sorry for others must believe in misfortune. But who or what could have inspired Rousseau with this fatal plan? I am told that it was the woman who had become the only person he trusted, and had become necessary to him by detaching him from all his ties to anyone else. Perhaps too, those long reveries ended by plunging him into despair. The first few days are bewitching: one discovers oneself, one enjoys one's own sentiments and feelings; but can anyone fix his gaze for long on the human destiny without falling into melancholy? Most of all, are there any minds strong enough to endure an inactive life and habitual contemplation? By reflection, Rousseau intensified all the ideas that afflicted him. In no time a glance, a gesture from someone he met, a child who ran away from him looked like fresh proofs of the universal hatred he thought directed at

---

*The reader will perhaps be surprised that I accept Rousseau's suicide as certain. But the Genevan I mentioned above had recently received a letter from him that seemed to suggest such a plan. Afterward, inquiring with great care as to his last moments, this man found out that the morning of the day Rousseau died, he got up in perfect health, but said that he was going to look at the sun for the last time, and drank some coffee he had made himself before leaving the house. He returned a few hours afterward, and steadfastly forbade anyone to call for help although he was in horrible pain. Not long before this sad day, he had noticed his wife's vile inclinations for a man of low estate; he seemed struck by this discovery, and stayed at the edge of the lake for eight hours in profound meditation. I think that if one combines these details with his habitual sadness and the unusual intensification of his fear and distrust, it is impossible to doubt that this great, unhappy man ended his life voluntarily.[13]

him; but, despite this cruel mistrust, he always remained the best of men. He believed everything around him was conspiring to hurt him, and the thought of revenge or prevention never entered his mind. He believed himself destined to suffer, and did not act against his fate. [...]

How harsh I find those who say it takes a lot of pride to believe oneself the object of the whole world's attention! It must have been a very sad pride that made him think there was no one on earth who did not hate him! Why didn't he meet some tender soul who might have given herself to reassuring him, to restoring his downcast courage, someone who would have loved him profoundly? He would have trusted this person in the end: feeling uncontaminated by self-love and self-interest is so pure, so tender, so true that every word proves it, every glance makes doubt impossible. Ah, Rousseau! How sweet it would have been to make you care about life again, to walk beside your footsteps in your solitary promenades, to follow your thoughts, and to bring them slowly back to pleasanter hopes! [...]

Rousseau may have allowed himself to commit suicide without remorse because he found himself too much alone in the immense universe. We feel we will leave so small an empty space if we have no place in a heart that will live on after us, that we may count our life as nothing. What! the author of Julie is dead because he was not loved! One day, in those dark forests, he said to himself: "I am alone on the earth, I suffer, I am unhappy, and my existence is useful to no one; I can die." You who accused him of pride: did he lack success? Could he not have had more and more successes every day? But whom would he have shared them with? Who would have rejoiced in them so that he might enjoy them? He had admirers, but he had no friends. Ah! Now in vain a tender feeling mingles with the enthusiasm he inspires! His works, so full of virtue and love of the human race, make him beloved now that he is no more. While he was alive, calumny kept people away from him, triumphing until his death: that is all she asks.

Day by day the tears of unhappy people are wearing away the simple inscriptions carved by friendship on Rousseau's tomb. I demand that the gratitude of all those he enlightened, people whose happiness concerned him all his life, should find an interpreter at last. Let eloquence take up arms for him, let it be her turn to serve him. What great man could despise the task of ensuring this great man's glory? How beautiful it would be to see in every age this league of genius against envy! of superior men defendng their predecessors, and giving a sublime example to their successors! One day the monument they built would be the pedestal for the statue of themselves. If calumny dared attack them too, they would already have made her look untrustworthy, blunting her arrows; and the justice posterity rendered them would repay the gratitude of the abandoned shade whose glory they had protected.

2.

Essay on Fictions

Introduction

Man's most valuable faculty is his imagination. Human life seems so little designed for happiness that we need the help of a few creations, a few images, a lucky choice of memories to muster some sparse pleasure on this earth and struggle against the pain of all our destinies—not by philosophical force, but by the more efficient force of distraction. The dangers of imagination have been discussed a good deal, but there is no point in looking up what impotent mediocrity and strict reason have said on this topic over and over again. The human race is not about to give up being stimulated, and anyone who has the gift of appealing to people's emotions is even less likely to give up the success promised by such talent. The number of necessary and evident truths is limited; it will never be enough for the human mind or heart. The highest honor may well go to those who discover such truths, but the authors of books producing sweet emotions or illusions have also done useful work for humanity. Metaphysical precision cannot be applied to man's affections and remain compatible with his nature. Beginnings are all we have on this earth—there is no limit. Virtue is actual and real, but happiness floats in space; anyone who tries to examine happiness inappropriately will destroy it, as we dissolve the brilliant images of the mist if we walk straight through them. And yet the advantage of fictions is not the pleasure they bring. If fictions please nothing but the eye, they do nothing but amuse; but if they touch our hearts, they can have a great influence on all our moral ideas. This talent may be the most powerful way there is of controlling behavior and enlightening the mind. Man has only two distinct faculties: reason and imagination. All the others, even feeling, are simply results or combinations of these two. The realm of fiction, like that of imagination, is therefore vast. Fictions do not find obstacles in passions: they make use of them. Philosophy may be the invisible power in control of fictions, but if she is the first to show herself, she will destroy all their magic.

When I talk about fictions, I will therefore be considering them from two perspectives of content and charm: this kind of writing may contain pleasure without useful purpose, but never vice versa. Fictions are meant to attract us; the more moral or philosophical the result one is trying to achieve, the more they have to be decked out with things to move us, leading us to the goal without advance warning. In mythological fictions I will consider only the poet's talent; these fictions could well be examined in the light of their religious influence, but such a point of view is absolutely foreign to my subject. I will be discussing the writings of the ancients according to the impression they create in our times, so my concern must be with their literary talent rather than their religious beliefs.

Fictions can be divided into three groups: (1) marvelous and allegorical fictions, (2) historical fictions, (3) fictions in which everything is both invented and imitated, where nothing is true and everything is likely.

This topic should really be discussed in an extensive treatise including most existing literary works and involving thoughts on almost every topic, since the complete exposition of any one idea is connected to the whole chain of ideas. But I am only trying to prove that the most useful kind of fiction will be novels taking life as it is, with delicacy, eloquence, depth, and morality, and I have excluded everything irrelevant to that goal from this essay.*

---

*I have read several chapters of a book called *The Spirit of Religions*, by M. Benjamin Constant, which offers some extremely ingenious insights into this whole question. The world of letters and philosophers ought to insist that the author of so great a work finish it and publish it.[1]

I

The fiction of the marvelous gives us a pleasure that wears thin almost immediately. Adults have to make themselves into children to like these supernatural tableaux, and be touched by feelings of terror and curiosity which do not originate in truth. Philosophers have to turn themselves into common people if they want to grasp useful ideas through the veil of allegory. Classical mythology sometimes contains the sort of simple fables transmitted to idolatrous religions by credulity, time, and priests, but mythology may generally be considered as a series of allegories: personifications of passions, talents, and virtues. There is certainly an initial felicity in the choice of these fictions, a burst of imagination that must guarantee their inventors real glory for devising a style and a language which constantly reminds us of ideas exclusively devoted to poetry, thus saving itself from the vulgarity involved in the continual use of worn, habitual expressions; but new works adding to these accepted fictions would be completely pointless. It takes more talent to get great effects from unassisted nature; there are natural phenomena, metamorphoses, and miracles in human passions, and this mythology is inexhaustible, opening heaven and hell for anyone capable of bringing it to life.

The fiction of the marvelous, on the other hand, casts a pall on every feeling associated with it. There are a thousand different ways to give pleasure if the only goal is a pretty picture. The eyes are always children, the saying goes; this really applies to the imagination. The imagination needs nothing but amusement; its end is contained in its means. Imagination serves to cheat life, steal time, give night's dreams to the daylight. Its lighthearted activity takes the place of repose, suspending at one blow everything that could move or concern us. When we are trying to make the pleasures of this same imagination serve some moral and coherent end, however, we need a simpler, more logical plan.

Even our impression of Virgil's and Homer's poetry is damaged by this alliance of heroes and gods, men's passions and destiny's decrees. The inventor is scarcely able to obtain our indulgence for a genre whose chief merit is its inventiveness. When Dido loves Aeneas only because she has held Love in her arms, disguised by Venus as Ascanius, we miss the talent that could have explained the birth of this passion by a simple portrayal of the workings of the heart. When the gods command anger, pain, and Achilles' victories, our admiration is focused on neither Jupiter nor the hero; the first is an abstract being, the second destiny's slave. The absolute power of the character escapes through the marvels surrounding him.[2]

Moreover, there is something about this element of the marvelous—predictable one moment and unpredictable the next—that takes away all the pleasures associated with terror or anticipation according to one's own feelings. When Priam is about to ask Achilles for Hector's body, I would like to be afraid of the dangers he braves for love of his son—to tremble as I see him enter the tent of dread Achilles—to hang on every word of this unfortunate father—and to feel at the same time, through his eloquence, the sensation of the emotion that eloquence expresses and a portent of the events it will determine.[3] But I know perfectly well that Mercury is leading Priam across the Greek camp; that Thetis, at Jupiter's command, has ordered his son to return Hector's corpse. I have no doubts as to the outcome of Priam's enterprise, and my mind has stopped paying attention. Without the name of divine Homer I would not read even one speech that followed the event instead of leading up to it.

I said above that there was something unpredictable about marvelous fiction which, by a contrary effect, takes away the pleasure of anticipation. This happens when the gods undo the best-laid plans, giving their favorites invincible support against the most powerful forces and refusing to let events bear any relation to what we can expect of human beings. The gods are only playing the part of fate, of course: this is chance personified. In fiction, however, it is better to avoid the influence of chance. Everything that is invented should be likely. The reader has to be able to explain every shock by a sequence of moral causes. Not only will the work make a more philosophical effect, but it will provide more of a challenge to talent. Situations which can only be resolved through a stroke of fate are always badly planned, whether they are real or imaginary.

In short, I think that it is better to derive the greatest possible effects from man's character when dealing with mankind. Here is the inexhaustible source from which talent should draw deep and terrible emotions. The bloody crimes we have just witnessed make Dante's underworld take second place.[4] The epic poems most remarkable for the marvelous quality in their fictions are really sublime because of a beauty quite independent of it. What we admire in Milton's Satan is a man; what stays with us about Achilles is his character; what we want to forget in the passion of Rinaldo for Armida is the magic mixed with the attractions inspiring it; what strikes us in the *Aeneid* is a range of emotions belonging to all hearts down through the ages.[5] When our tragic poets have taken topics from ancient authors, they have detached them almost completely from the magical machinery we associate with the beauties of the ancient world.

Chivalric romances make us even more sharply aware of the disadvantages of the marvelous, affecting the characters' development and feelings as well as our interest in the events. Heroes are larger than life, passions far beyond truth. This imaginary moral nature has greater disadvantages than the prodigies of mythology and fairyland. Falsehood is more closely intertwined with truth, and the imagination has less to do. It is no longer a question of inventing, but of exaggerating and caricaturing what is beautiful in real life in a way that would make valor and virtue ridiculous if truth could not be set back in its rightful place by historians and moralists.

In judging human things we should avoid absolute statements, and I do admire the creative genius of these poetic fictions which nourished the human spirit for so long, giving us so many successful and brilliant comparisons.[6] Nevertheless, we may well want the talent of the future to follow a different path. I would like to restrain—or rather to raise to a simple imitation of truth—the kind of strong imagination that is as likely to be inspired by phantoms as by scenes from life.

In works whose primary characteristic is gaiety, we might miss Ariosto's delightful use of his ingenious fictions. But there are no rules or goals in the good fortune that creates this kind of amusement. The impression it makes cannot be analyzed; reflection gets us nowhere. There is so little cause for gaiety in the true-to-life that works trying to inspire gaiety do sometimes need the marvelous. Nature and thought are inexhaustible sources of sentiment and meditation, but pleasantry is a kind of good luck in expression or insight whose twisting path is impossible to predict. Every idea that makes people laugh may well turn out to be the last anyone will ever find: there is no highway leading to this genre, no fountainhead from which to draw success. We know the result exists, because it happens again and again, but we know neither cause nor means: the gift of pleasantry is much closer to inspiration than even the loftiest enthusiasm. This kind of literary gaiety, which does not arise from a sensation of happiness, and is enjoyed by the reader much more than the writer, is a talent won and lost all at once, and all at a stroke. It can be controlled, but never replaced by any other faculty of even the greatest mind. If I have recognized an analogy between the marvelous and the lighthearted, it is because neither of them can really portray nature. Passion, destiny, truth, have no gaiety about them at all—and yet amusing contrasts only emerge from passing nuances of these positive ideas.

The comic talent is a far superior genre, though it too creates funny situations. The comic genre draws its strength from characters and passions in nature; like all serious works, it would be adulterated and weakened by a use of the marvelous. If the characters in *Gil Blas*, *Tartuffe*, or *The Misanthrope* were miraculous in any way, these masterpieces would be much less able to attract and impress our minds.[7]

Imitation of the truth always makes more of an effect than supernatural means. Higher metaphysics may let us assume the existence of thoughts, truths, and beings superior to human knowledge in things beyond the reach of our intelligence; but as we have no conception of these abstract realms, our use of the marvelous does not come anywhere near them, and remains beneath even our known reality. Our power of understanding is limited to the nature of things and men; what we call our creation is only an incoherent assemblage of the ideas we draw from the same natural world we are trying to escape. The stamp of divinity is on the truth. People associate the word "invention" with genius, but the only way for genius to merit the glory of being called creative is by retracing, reuniting, discovering what actually exists.

Allegories are a form of fiction whose effect seems to me inferior even to the effect of the marvelous. I think allegories weaken the idea, just as the marvelous spoils the tableau of passion. In the form of the apologue, allegories can sometimes popularize useful truths, but the very example shows that in giving this form to thought we think we are bringing it down to the level of the common people. The need of images to understand ideas is an intellectual weakness in the reader: any thought which can be perfectly apprehended this way necessarily lacks some degree of abstraction or subtlety. Abstract thought is superior to images, having a kind of geometric precision that lets us express it only in its own positive terms. The absolute delicacy of the mind escapes allegories. Nuances in tableaux are never so delicate as metaphysical insights; things that can be shown in relief are never the most ingenious, subtle part of what one is thinking.

Quite aside from the damage to the ideas it is trying to express, however, allegory is a genre that almost never gives anybody any kind of pleasure. Its aim is both to make some moral truth stand out and to attract us by the fable emblematic of it. Each usually fails because of the attempt to achieve the other: the abstract idea is represented vaguely and the tableau has no dramatic effect. Allegory is a fiction within a fiction. The events in an allegory can interest no one, since they exist only as the incarnation of philosophical conclusions, and understanding them is much more tiring than their pure metaphysical expression. We have to separate abstract from image, discover the ideas represented by the names of characters, and begin by guessing the riddle before we understand the thought. If we try to explain the cause of the monotony in the charming poem *Telemachus*, we realize that it is the character Mentor.[8] Being both marvelous and allegorical, Mentor has the disadvantages of two genres at once. Marvelous, Mentor keeps us from feeling any suspense as to Telemachus' fate as we grow certain of his triumph over any possible danger with the help of the goddess; allegorical, Mentor completely spoils the effect of the passions, which comes from their internal struggles. In Fénelon's poem, the two powers distinguished by moralists in the human heart exist as two characters: Mentor has no passion, Telemachus no control over himself. Man falls in between; our interest in unable to focus. Pointed allegories in which Willpower goes out to seek Happiness (as in *Thélème and Macare*),[9] or interminable allegories in which every stanza narrates the struggle between a chevalier who represents some virtue and his adversary vice (as in Spenser's *Faerie Queene*), these are boring no matter what sort of talent is decorating them.[10] We finish the poem so tired of the tale told by the allegory that we no longer have the strength to understand its philosophical meaning.

Fables with talking animals were first used as apologues whose meaning would be easier for the common people to grasp. Afterward they became a literary genre, practiced by many writers. One—La Fontaine—must have been unique in this line of work, as his completely natural manner kept him from ever repeating or imitating himself; he is able to make his animals speak as if they were some sort of thinking creatures who exist before the reign of prejudice and affectation. His talent keeps one from thinking of allegory in connection with his work, because the character of each species is personified according to what is right and fitting for it. The comedy in his fables comes from the actual portrayal of the manners of the animals onstage, not from allusions. This success was necessarily a limited one, and the other fables people have written in various languages all fall back into the nuisances of allegory.[11]

The Orientals made much use of allegories, no doubt primarily because of the despotism of their governments. They had to tell the truth under a veil, so that subjects could understand things escaping their master; even when they dared to wish that this truth might reach the throne, they thought that linking it to emblems drawn from the laws of physical nature could separate it from human influence and opinion, always dependent on the sultan's wishes. When this truth was presented as a story, the moral was never drawn by the author, who could therefore flatter himself that the sultan would be merciful to this conclusion, should he notice it, as if to a discovery of his own intelligence. But the devices to which we are condemned by despotism should be banished along with its power; they lose all their interest as soon as they are seen to be unnecessary.

Works of allusion are another kind of fiction that appeals only to contemporaries. Posterity judges such writings without reference to the application they might have had at some other time, or to an awareness of the difficulties their authors had to overcome. Whenever talent operates relatively, it loses its brilliance when it loses the circumstances that originally set if off. For example, people may call *Hudibras* a witty poem, but we have to hunt for the author's meaning through what he is saying, with innumerable notes to understand his jokes, and preliminary instruction on how to find it funny or interesting. The merit of this poem is therefore no longer generally appreciated.[12] A philosophical work may require research, but fiction can only produce a convincing effect when it contains within itself whatever the readers need for a complete impression of it at every moment. Actions are useful, and therefore immortal in glory, insofar as they are adapted to immediate circumstances; the written word, however, achieves greatness only by detaching itself from current events and rising to the unchanging nature of things. As Massillon says, whatever writers do for today is time wasted for eternity.[13]

Comparisons are a derivation of allegory, but they distract our attention less because they are shorter, and almost always a further development of the thought that precedes them. All the same, a feeling or an idea is rarely at full strength if it can be expressed by an image. The line "That he die!" in *Horace* would have been impossible to do as an image.[14] When we read the chapter where Montesquieu tries to give us some idea of despotism by comparing it to the acts of Louisiana savages, we might well prefer to this image a reflection of Tacitus—or of Montesquieu himself, who has so often outdone the best writers of antiquity.[15] We would be too severe if we rejected all such decorations: the mind often needs them as a relief from inventing new ideas, or to vary familiar ones. Images and tableaux constitute the charm of poetry and whatever resembles it. But everything relating to reflection gains greater power and more concentrated intensity when the expression of thought draws its power from itself alone.

We must now discuss allegories whose only aim is a combination of humor and philosophical ideas, such as Swift's *Tale of the Tub, Gulliver, Micromégas,* etc.[16] I could repeat what I said about marvelous fictions: if they make people laugh, the goal is achieved. But this sort of work has a higher goal—to set off some philosophical object—which it never really accomplishes. When an allegory is amusing in its own right, most people remember the fable rather than its result, more likely to be fond of Gulliver's story than taught anything by its moral. Allegory invariably falls between two stools. If the point is too clear, it bores us; if it is hidden, we forget it; and if an attempt is made to divide our attention, it no longer arouses any interest at all.

II

In this second part, as I said, I am going to talk about historical fictions: inventions with a basis of truth. Tragedies and poetry drawn from history cannot manage without fiction. History cannot provide an adequate model when all the emotions have to be evoked and concentrated in the course of twenty-four hours and five acts, or when a hero has to be kept up to the level of epic poetry. But the invention essential to historical fiction bears no resemblance to the marvelous. It does not involve another nature, but a choice in the framework of existing nature: the work of Apelles, who composed beauty by gathering together individual delightful details.[17] Granting that the language of poetry has its own distinguishing characteristics, all our emotions are involved when we judge beautiful situations and great epic or dramatic characters. These characters and situations are borrowed from history—not to disfigure them, but to detach them from mortality and consecrate their apotheosis. Nothing in such fiction goes beyond nature: the same pace is observed, the same proportions. If a man born for glory heard a masterpiece such as the *Henriad*, *Gengis Khan*, *Mithridate*, or *Tancred*, he would probably admire it unsurprised, enjoying it without ever thinking about the author, or suspecting that anything in these scenes of heroism had been created by talent.[18]

But I wish another kind of historical fiction were absolutely banned. This consists of novels grafted onto history, such as *Anecdotes of the Court of Philippe-Auguste*.[19] Such stories might be pretty enough, if we could detach them from proper names, but they put themselves between you and history, presenting you with details whose invention imitates the ordinary course of daily life and thus blends with the truth so closely that it becomes very difficult to separate the two.

This kind of historical fiction destroys the morality of history by loading the action with a lot of motives that never existed. Such fiction can never achieve the morality of the novel, either, because it has to fit onto a real canvas, so that the plan cannot be devised with the liberty and coherence which a work of pure invention can afford. The interest added to novels by famous names from history is offered by the advantages of allusion; as I have tried to show, fiction that depends on souvenirs instead of internal developments is never perfect in itself. Then too, it is dangerous to make such changes in truth. Such a novel never shows anything but love affairs, because every other event taking place at the time has already been related by historians. The author then tries to explain these other events by the influence of love, so as to make the subject of his novel look more important, and ends by giving us the falsest possible view of human life. These fictions weaken the effect that should be produced by history itself—that same history from which the original idea was borrowed—just as a bad copy of a painting can damage our impression of the original, which it brings to mind lamely, with a few random strokes.

III

The third and last part of this essay must deal with the usefulness of natural fictions, as I call them, where everything is both invented and im-itated, so that nothing is true but everything looks true to life. Tragedies with completely imaginary subjects will not be included here; they por-tray a more lofty nature, an extraordinary situation at an extraordinary level. The verisimilitude of such plays depends on events that are ex-tremely rare, and morally applicable to very few people. Comedies and other dramas are in the theater what novels are to other fiction: their plots are taken from private life and natural circumstances. However, the conventions of the theater deprive us of the commentary which gives ex-amples of reflections their individuality. Dramas are allowed to choose their characters among people other than kings and heroes, but they can show only broadly defined situations, because there is no time for nuance. And life is not concentrated like that—does not happen in contrasts—is not really theatrical in the way plays have to be written. Dramatic art has different effects, advantages, and means which might well be discussed separately, but I think only the modern novel is capable of achieving the constant, accurate usefulness we can get from the pic-ture of our ordinary, habitual feelings. People usually make a separate case of what they call philosophical novels; all novels should be philosophical, as they should all have a moral goal. Perhaps, however, we are not guided so inevitably toward this moral goal when all the episodes narrated are focused on one principal idea, exempting the author from all probability in the way one situation follows another. Each chapter then becomes a kind of allegory—its events are only there to illustrate the maxim at the end. The novels *Candide, Zadig,* and *Memnon,* while delightful in other respects, would be much more useful if they were not marvelous, if they offered an example instead of an emblem and if, as I say, the whole story did not have to relate to the same goal.[20] Such novels are at the same disadvantage as teachers: children never believe them, because they make everything that happens relate to the lesson at hand. Children unconsciously know already that there is less regularity than that in real life. Events are also invented in novels like Richardson's and Fielding's, where the author is trying to keep close to life by following with great accuracy the stages, developments, and inconsistencies of human history, and the way the results of experience always come down to the morality of actions and the advantages of virtue, nonetheless. In these novels, however, the feelings are so natural that the reader often believes he is being spoken to directly, with no artifice but the tactfulness of changing the names.

The art of novel-writing does not have the reputation it deserves because of a throng of bad writers overwhelming us with their colorless productions; in this genre, perfection may require the greatest genius, but mediocrity is well within everyone's grasp. This infinite number of colorless novels has almost used up the passion portrayed in them; one is terrified of finding the slightest resemblance in one's own life to the situations they describe. It has taken the very greatest masters to bring this genre back again, despite the writers who have degraded it. And others have dragged it even lower by including disgusting scenes of vice. Despite the fact that fiction's main advantage is to gather around man everything in nature that might be useful to him as a lesson or model, some writers supposed we might have some kind of use for these detestable paintings of evil habits. As if such fictions could ever leave a heart that rejected them in the same state of purity as a heart that had never known them! The novel as we conceive of it, however—as we have a few examples of it—is one of the most beautiful creations of the human mind, and one of the most influential on individual morality, which is what ultimately determines the morality of the public.

There is a very good reason why public opinion does not have enough respect for the writing of good novels, however. This is because novels are considered to be exclusively devoted to the portrayal of love—the most violent, universal, and true passion of them all, but also the passion which inspires no interest at any other time of life than youth, since youth is all it influences. We may well believe that all deep and tender feelings belong to the nature of love, and that hearts which have neither known nor pardoned love cannot feel enthusiasm in friendship, devotion in misery, worship of one's parents, passion for one's children. One can feel respect for one's duties, but no delight or self-surrender in their accomplishment, if one has not loved with all the strength of one's soul, ceasing to be one's self to live entirely in another. The destiny of women and the happiness of men who are not called upon to govern empires often depend for the rest of their lives on the role they gave to the influence of love in their youth. Nevertheless, when people reach a certain age, they completely forget the impression love made on them. Their character changes; they devote themselves to other goals, other passions; and these new interests are what we should extend the subjects of novels to include. A new career would then be open to authors who have the talent to paint all the emotions of the human heart, and are able to use their intimate knowledge of it to involve us. Ambition, pride, greed, vanity could be the primary topic of novels which would have situations as varied as those arising from love, and fresher plots. Will people object that such a tableau of men's passions exists in history, and that we should look for it there? History does not reach the lives of private men, feelings and characters that do not result in public events. History does not act on you with sustained moral interest. Reality often fails to make an effect; and the commentary needed to make a lasting impression would stop the essential quick narrative pace, and give dramatic form to a work that should have a very different sort of merit. And the moral of history can never be completely clear. This may be because one cannot always show with any degree of certainty the inner feelings that punish the wicked in their prosperity and reward the virtuous in their misery, or perhaps because man's destiny is not completed in this life. Practical morality is founded on the advantages of virtue, but the reading of history does not always put it in the limelight.

Great historians (especially Tacitus) do try to attach some moral to every event they relate, making us envy the dying Germanicus, and hate Tiberius at the pinnacle of his grandeur.[21] But they can still portray only those feelings certified by facts. What stays with us from a reading of history is more likely to be the influence of talent, the brilliance of glory, the advantages of power, than the quiet, subtle, gentle morality which is the basis of individual happiness and the relationship between individuals. Everyone would think me ridiculous if I said I set no value on history, and that I preferred fictions—as if fictions did not arise from experience, and as if the delicate nuances shown in novels did not come from the philosophical results and mother-ideas presented by the great panorama of public events! However, the morality of history only exists in bulk. History gives constant results by means of the recurrence of a certain number of chances: its lessons apply to nations, not individuals. Its examples always fit nations, because if one considers them in a general way they are invariable; but it never explains the exceptions. These exceptions can seduce each man as an individual; the exceptional circumstances consecrated by history leave vast empty spaces into which the miseries and wrongs that make up most private destinies could easily fall. On the other hand, novels can paint characters and feeling with such force and detail that they make more of an impression of hatred for vice and love for virtue than any other kind of reading. The morality of novels belongs more to the development of the internal emotions of the soul than to the events they relate. We do not draw a useful lesson from whatever arbitrary circumstance the author invents as punishment for the crime; what leaves its indelible mark on us comes from the truthful rendition of the scenes, the gradual process or sequence of wrongdoing, the enthusiasm for sacrifices, the sympathy for misfortune. Everything is so true to life in such novels that we have no trouble persuading ourselves that everything could happen just this way—not past history, but often, it seems, the history of the future.

Novels give a false idea of mankind, it has been said. This is true of bad novels, as it is true of paintings which imitate nature badly. When novels are good, however, nothing gives such an intimate knowledge of the human heart as these portrayals of the various circumstances of private life and the impressions they inspire. Nothing gives so much play to reflection, which finds much more to discover in details than in generalities. Memoirs would be able to do this if their only subjects were not, as in history, famous men and public events. If most men had the wit and good faith to give a truthful, clear account of what they had experienced in the course of their lives, novels would be useless—but even these sincere narratives would not have all the advantages of novels. We would still have to add a kind of dramatic effect to the truth; not deforming it, but condensing it to set it off. This is the art of the painter: far from distorting objects, it represents them in a way that makes them more immediately apprehended. Nature sometimes shows us things all on the same level, eliminating any contrasts; if we copy her too slavishly we become incapable of portraying her. The most truthful account is always an imitative truth: as a tableau, it demands a harmony of its own. However remarkable a true story may be for its nuances, feelings, and characters, it cannot interest us without the talent necessary for the composition of fiction. But despite our admiration for the genius that lets us penetrate the recesses of the human heart, it is impossible to bear all those minute details with which even the most famous novels are burdened. The author thinks they add to the picture's verisimilitude, blind to the fact that anything that slows down the interest destroys the only truth fiction has: the impression it produces. To put everything that happens in a room onstage is to destroy theatrical illusion completely. Novels have dramatic conventions also: the only thing necessary in an invention is what adds to the effect one is creating. If a glance, a movement, or an unnoticed circumstance helps paint a character or develop our understanding of a feeling, the simpler the means, the greater the merit in catching it—but a scrupulously detailed account of an ordinary event diminishes verisimilitude instead of increasing it. Thrown back on a positive notion of what is true by the kind of details that belong only to truth, you soon break out of the illusion, weary of being unable to find either the instruction of history or the interest of a novel.

The greatest power of fiction is its talent to touch us; almost all moral truths can be made tangible if they are shown in action. Virtue has so much influence on human happiness or misery that one can make most of life's situations depend on it. Some severe philosophers condemn all emotions, wanting moral authority to rule by a simple statement of moral duty. Nothing is less suited to human nature. Virtue must be brought to life if she is to fight the passions with any chance of winning; a sort of exaltation must be aroused for us to find any charm in sacrifice; misfortune must be embellished for us to prefer it to the great charm of guilty enticement; and the touching fictions which incite the soul to generous feelings make it unconsciously engage itself in a promise that it would be ashamed to retract in similar circumstances. But the more real power there is in fiction's talent for touching us, the more important it becomes to widen its influence to the passions of all ages, and the duties of all situations. The primary subject of novels is love, and characters who have nothing to do with it are present only as accessories. It would be possible to find a host of new subjects if one followed a different plan. *Tom Jones* has the most general moral of any novel: love appears in it as only one of many means of showing the philosophical result. The real aim of *Tom Jones* is to show the uncertainty of judgments founded on appearances, proving the superiority of natural and what we may call involuntary virtues over reputations based on mere respect for external etiquette. And this is one of the most useful, most deservedly famous of all novels. *Caleb Williams*, by Mr. Godwin, is a recent novel which, despite some tedious passages and oversights, seems to give a good idea of this inexhaustible genre.[22] Love plays no part in this fiction; the only motives for the action are the hero's unbridled passion for the world's respect and Caleb's overpowering curiosity, leading him to discover whether or not Falkland deserves the esteem he enjoys. We read this story with all the absorption inspired by romantic interest and the reflection commanded by the most philosophical tableau.

Some successful fictions do give pictures of life unrelated to love: several *Moral Tales* of Marmontel, a few chapters of *Sentimental Journey*, various anecdotes from the *Spectator* and other books on morality, some pieces taken from German literature, whose superiority is growing every day.[23] There is still, however, no new Richardson devoting himself to paint men's other passions in a novel completely exploring the progress and consequences of these passions. The success of such a work would come from the truth of its characters, the force of its contrasts and the energy of its situations, rather than from that feeling which is so easy to paint, so quick to arouse interest, pleasing women by what it makes them remember even if it cannot attrack them by the greatness or novelty of the scenes it presents. What beautiful things we would find in the Lovelace of ambition![24] What philosophical developments, if we were eager to explain and analyze all the passions, as novels have already done for love! Let no one object that books on morality are enough to teach us a knowledge of our duties; such books cannot possibly go into all the nuances of delicacy, or detail the myriad resources of the passions. We can glean a morality purer and higher from novels than from any didactic work on virtue; didactic works are so dry that they have to be too indulgent. Maxims have to be generally applicable, so they never achieve that heroic delicacy we may offer as a model but cannot reasonably impose as a duty. Where is the moralist who could say: "If your whole family wants you to marry a detestable man, and you are prompted by their persecution to give a few signs of the most innocent interest to the man you find attractive, you are going to bring death and dishonor upon yourself"? This, however, is the plot of *Clarissa*; this is what we read with admiration, without a word of protest to the author who touches us and holds us captive. What moralist would claim that it is better to abandon oneself to deep despair, the sort of despair that threatens life and disturbs the mind, rather than marry the most virtuous man in the world if his religion is different from your own? Well, we need

not approve of the superstitious opinions of *Clementina*, but love struggling against a scruple of conscience and duty winning out over passion
are a sight that moves and touches even loose-principled people who
would have rejected such a conclusion disdainfully if it had been a
maxim preceding the tableau instead of an effect that followed it.[25] In
novels of a less sublime genre, there are so many subtle rules for women's
conduct! We could support this opinion by quoting from masterpieces
like *The Princess of Clèves, The Count of Comminge, Paul and Virginia,
Cecilia,* most of the writings of Madame Riccoboni, *Caroline,* whose
charm is felt by everyone, the touching episode of Caliste, the letters of
Camilla, in which the mistakes of a woman and their miserable consequences give a more moral and severe picture than the spectacle of virtue itself, and many other French, English, and German works.[26] Novels
have the right to offer the severest morality without revolting our hearts;
they have captured feeling, the only thing that can successfully plead for
indulgence. Pity for misfortune or interest in passion often win the
struggle against books of morality, but good novels have the art of putting this emotion itself on their side and using it for their own ends.

There is still one serious objection to love stories: that they
paint love in such a way as to arouse it, and that there are moments in life
when this danger wins out over every kind of advantage. This drawback
could not exist in novels about any other human passion, however. By
recognizing the most fleeting symptoms of a dangerous inclination from
the very beginning, one could turn oneself as well as others away from it.
Ambition, pride, and avarice often exist without the least consciousness
on the part of those they rule. Love feeds on the portrait of its own
feelings, but the best way to fight the other passions is to make them be
recognized. If the features, tricks, means, and results of these passions
were as fully shown and popularized by novels as the history of love,
society would have more trustworthy rules and more scrupulous principles about all the transactions of life. Even if purely philosophical
writings could predict and detail all the nuances of actions, as do novels,
dramatic morality would still have the great advantage of arousing indignant impulses, an exaltation of soul, a sweet melancholy—the various effects of fictional situations, and a sort of supplement to existence. This
impression resembles the one we have of real facts we might have witnessed, but it is less distracting for the mind than the incoherent panorama of events around us, because it is always directed toward a single

goal. Finally, there are men over whom duty has no influence, and who could still be preserved from crime by developing within them the ability to be moved. Characters capable of adopting humanity only with the help of such a faculty of emotion, the physical pleasure of the soul, would naturally not deserve much respect; nevertheless, if the effect of these touching fictions became widespread enough among the people, it might give us some assurance that we would no longer have in our country those beings whose character poses the most incomprehensible moral problem that has ever existed. The gradual steps from the known to the unknown stop well before we reach any understanding of the emotions which rules the executioners of France. Neither events nor books can have developed in them the least trace of humanity, the memory of a single sensation of pity, any mobility within the mind itself for them to remain capable of that constant cruelty, so foreign to all the impulses of nature—a cruelty which has given mankind its first limitless concept, the complete idea of crime.

There are writings whose principal merit is the eloquence of passion, such as the "Epistle of Abelard" by Pope, *Werther*, the *Portuguese Letters*, and especially *The New Héloïse*.[27] The aim of such works is often moral, but what remains with us more than anything else is the absolute power of the heart. We cannot classify such novels. Every century has one soul and one genius capable of achieving this—it cannot be a genre, it cannot be a goal. Who would want to proscribe these miracles of the word, these deep impressions which satisfy all the emotions of the passionate? Readers enthusiastic about such talent are very few in number; these works always do their admirers good. Let ardent, sensitive souls admire them; they cannot make their language understood by anyone else. The feelings that disturb such beings are rarely understood; constantly condemned, they would believe themselves alone in the world, they would soon hate their own nature for isolating them, if a few passionate, melancholy works did not make them hear a voice in the desert of life, letting them find in solitude a few rays of the happiness that escapes them in the middle of society. The pleasure of retreat is refreshing after the vain attempts of disappointed hope; far from this unfortunate creature, the entire universe may be in motion, but such eloquent, tender writing stays near him as his most faithful friend, the one who understands him best. Yes, a book must be right if it offers even one day's distraction from pain; it helps the best of men. Of course there are also sorrows that come from one's own character flaws, but so many of them come from superiority of mind or sensitivity of heart! and there are so many that would be easier to bear if one had fewer good qualities! I respect the suffering heart, even when it is unknown to me; I take pleasure in fictions whose only effect might be to comfort this heart by capturing its interest. In this life, which we pass through rather than feel, the distributor of the only real happiness of which human nature is capable would be someone who distracts man from himself and others, suspending the action of the passions by substituting independent pleasures for them—if the influence of his talent could only last.

3.

Novellas

Preface

No one will have any difficulty in understanding that the *Essay on Fictions* was written after these stories, which do not deserve to be called novels. The situations in them are sketched out rather than fully explored, and their only virtue is in the portrayal of a few of the heart's sentiments. I was still not twenty when I wrote them, and the French Revolution had not yet taken place. Since then, I hope, my mind has grown strong enough to devote itself to more useful work. Everyone says that unhappiness accelerates the development of moral faculties, but sometimes I am afraid it produces the opposite effect, plunging us into a depression which detaches us from ourselves and other people. The magnitude of the events around us makes us so acutely aware of the nothingness of general ideas and the impotence of individual feelings that, lost in life, we no longer know the path hope should follow, the motives which should arouse our efforts, or the principle that will guide public opinion through the errors of party spirit, showing once again, in every walk of life, the dazzling goal of glory.

MIRZA,
OR, LETTER FROM A TRAVELER

Let me tell you a story of my travels, madame; it may have some claim to interest you. A month ago, at Gorea, I heard that the

Governor had induced a Negro family to come and live a few leagues
away, so as to establish a plantation like the ones in Saint-Domingue.[1] He
may have flattered himself that such an example would arouse Africans
to grow sugar, so that the Europeans who gained control of the free sugar
trade would stop kidnapping them from their homeland and making
them suffer the hideous yoke of slavery. The most eloquent writers have
tried in vain to get this revolution from men's virtue. An enlightened ad-
ministrator, hopeless of triumphing over personal self-interest, might try
to enlist self-interest on humanity's side, by preventing it from finding
any further advantage in opposition. The Negroes, however, lacking
foresight for their own futures, are even less capable of bringing their
minds to bear on future generations: they refuse present hardship for
themselves without comparing it with the fate such hardship might en-
able them to avoid. An African whom the Governor rescued from
slavery was the only one who had lent himself to his plans. A prince in his
own country, this man had been followed by a few subordinates, who
cultivated his plantation under his direction.

  I asked to be taken to this plantation. After walking for part
of the day, I reached in the evening a house I was told Frenchmen had
helped build; it had something savage about it, nevertheless. When I approached, the Negroes were enjoying their recreation period; they were
amusing themselves by shooting with bows and arrows, nostalgic perhaps
for the time when such pleasure was their only occupation.

  Ourika, the wife of Ximeo (the name of the Negro head of
the plantation), was sitting some distance away from the games, absently
watching her two-year-old daughter play at her feet. My guide advanced
toward her and told her that I asked for shelter on behalf of the
Governor.

  "The Governor sends him!" she cried. "Oh, let him come in
and be welcome—everything we have belongs to him." She ran up to
me. Her beauty fascinated me. She had the true charm of her sex, everything that delineates grace and weakness.

  "Where is Ximeo?" asked my guide.

  "Not back yet," she answered. "He is on his evening walk.
He will return when the sun is no longer on the horizon and even dusk
no longer reminds us of daylight, and then it will no longer be night for
me." As she finished speaking, she sighed and retreated; when she re-
joined us, I noticed traces of tears on her face.

  We entered the cabin, and were served a collation of local

fruits. I tasted them with delight, eager for new sensations. A knock at the door: Ourika trembles, springs to her feet, opens the door and throws herself into the arms of Ximeo, who kisses her without seeming to realize what he is seeing or doing.

I approached Ximeo. You cannot imagine a more attractive face. His features had none of the faults of men of his color. His look affected me in a way I have never felt before: it had one's soul at its command, and the melancholy it expressed went straight into the heart of anyone it touched. His figure was as perfect as that of the Apollo Belvedere—too slender for a man, perhaps, but the depressing misery revealed by his gestures and portrayed on his face was more consistent with delicacy than strength.[2]

He seemed impervious to any emotion other than his obsession, and showed no surprise at seeing us. We told him who had sent us, and the object of our voyage.

"The Governor has the right to my gratitude," he said. "Even in my condition, if you can believe it, I have a benefactor." He spoke to us for a while about his motives for deciding to cultivate a plantation. I was astounded by his intelligence and his fluency, as he noticed. "You are amazed," he said to me, "when we are not on the level of the animals whose destiny you impose on us."

"No," I answered, "but even a Frenchman could not speak his own language better than you do."

"Ah! you are right," he replied. "When one has lived near an angel for a while, one keeps a few rays of light afterward." And his beautiful eyes looked down, so as to see nothing of the outside world. Ourika was crying; in a little while he noticed this. "Forgive me," he cried, taking her hand. "Forgive me. You have the present; bear with these memories." He turned back toward me. "Tomorrow," he said, "tomorrow we will go over my plantation together. You will see if I can flatter myself that it lives up to the Governor's wishes. The best bed will be prepared for you. Sleep well; I would like you to feel comfortable here. Men who are unfortunate in love," he went on in a low voice, "do not fear the sight of other people's happiness—they even wish for it."

I went to bed, but without closing my eyes. I was filled with sorrow. Everything I had seen carried the mark of unhappiness. I did not know its cause, but I felt moved, as if contemplating a picture representing melancholy.

I arose at daybreak to find Ximeo even more depressed than

he had been the night before; I asked him why. "My unhappiness is fixed in my heart," he said, "neither increasing nor decreasing. The uniformity of daily life makes it pass more quickly, however. New events, whatever they are, inspire new reflections, and those are always new sources of tears."

Ximeo showed me his whole plantation with great care. I was surprised by the methodical order to be seen everywhere. The plantation yielded at least as much as a comparable amount of land cultivated in Saint-Domingue by the same number of men, and the fortunate Negroes here were not overwhelmed with work. I saw with delight that cruelty was, in addition to everything else, useless. I asked Ximeo who had advised him about the cultivation of the land and the organization of the working day.

"I have had very little advice," he answered. "Reason can reach what reason has found. Since death was forbidden me, I have had to consecrate my life to other people. What could I have done with it on my own behalf? I hated slavery—I could not comprehend that barbarous scheme of men of your color. Sometimes I thought that their God—an enemy of ours—had commanded them to make us suffer. When I heard that it was a crop produced in our own country, neglected by us, that was giving the unhappy Africans all this trouble, I accepted the offer to show them how to cultivate it. Let free trade be established between the two halves of the world! Let my unfortunate countrymen give up their primitive life, devote themselves to work to satisfy your greed, and help save a few of themselves from the most horrible fate! Let even the Africans who delude themselves into thinking they may escape such a fate be equally eager to guarantee their fellow countrymen freedom from the most dreadful fate imaginable!"

As he was talking, we approached a gate that led to a thick wood bordering one side of the plantation. I thought Ximeo was going to open the gate, but he swerved to avoid it.

"Why don't you show me—" I began.

"Stop!" cried he. "You look like a man of feeling. Can you listen to long tales of sorrow? For two years I have not spoken—what I have been saying to you is not speaking. You can see I need to get it off my chest. You should not be flattered by my confidence, but it is your goodness that encourages me and makes me count on your pity." "Ah! have no fear," I replied. "You are not deceived."

"I was born in the kingdom of Cayor.[3] My father was of

royal blood, the chief of several tribes that had been entrusted to him by
the King. They trained me from an early age in the art of defending my
country, and I was familiar with the use of the bow and javelin in my
childhood. That was also when they decided that Ourika, my father's sister's daughter, should be my wife. I loved Ourika as soon as I could love
at all: the faculty of loving developed in me for her and through her. Her
perfect beauty struck me all the more when I had compared it with other
women's, and I came back voluntarily to my first inclination.

"We were often at war with our neighbors the Jaloffes. We
both had the atrocious custom of selling our prisoners of war to the Europeans, so a deep hatred never permitted the slightest communication
between us, even in peacetime. One day, hunting in our hills and drawn
farther than I intended, I suddenly heard a woman's voice, remarkable in
its beauty. I listened to what it was singing, and I could not recognize any
of the words young girls enjoy singing over and over again. Love of
liberty and hatred of slavery—these were the subjects of the noble songs
that struck me with admiration.

"I drew closer. A young woman arose. Struck by the contrast between her age and the subject of her meditations, I looked into
her face for something supernatural, some sign of the inspiration that
might take the place of maturity's long reflections. She was not beautiful,
but her noble, regular form, enchanting eyes, and lively features made it
impossible for even love to wish her face had been different. She came
toward me and spoke to me for a long time without my being able to
reply. At last I managed to portray my astonishment, which grew even
greater when I found that she had written the words I had just
heard.

" 'Do not be surprised,' she said. 'A Frenchman living in
Senegal has come to live among us, discontented with his fate and unhappy in his country. This old man has had the kindness to take great
pains with my young years, and has given me something we may well
envy the Europeans: the knowledge they abuse and the philosophy
whose lessons they fail to follow. I have learned French and read a few of
their books, and I enjoy coming out on the mountains alone to think.' At
each word she spoke, my interest and curiosity doubled. I no longer
seemed to be listening to a woman, but to a poet; the men of our tribe
who had devoted themselves to the gods had never seemed filled with
such noble enthusiasm.

"When I left her, I obtained permission to come back and

see her again. Her memory followed me everywhere. I was filled with admiration rather than love, and counted on this difference for some time, so that I saw Mirza—the name of the young Jaloffe girl—without thinking I might be offending Ourika.

"At last one day I asked Mirza if she had ever been in love. I trembled as I asked this question, but Mirza's quick wit and openhearted character allowed her to answer without embarrassment.

" 'No,' she said. 'People have sometimes loved me, and I may have wished they had moved me—I wanted to know this feeling that takes hold of one's whole life and determines the fate of every minute of one's day all by itself. I think I must have done too much serious thinking to experience that illusion, however. I feel all the impulses of my heart, and see other people's, but so far I have never been able to fool myself, or be fooled.'

"This grieved me. 'Mirza,' I said to her, 'how I pity you! The pleasures of reflection are not enough to occupy one completely; only the pleasures of the heart can satisfy all the faculties of the soul.'

"Meanwhile, with inexhaustible kindness, Mirza went on teaching me. I soon learned everything she knew. When I interrupted her with my praises, she would not listen; as soon as I stopped, she went on, and I could see by what she said that she had been thinking only of me while I was praising her.

"Finally, intoxicated by her grace, her wit, her glances, I felt I loved Mirza and dared to tell her so. What expressions I used to convey to her heart the exaltation I had found in her mind! I was dying of fear and passion at her feet. 'Mirza,' I repeated, 'tell me you love me and put me on top of the world. Open heaven to me so that I can enter it with you.'

"As she listened to me she became upset, and tears filled the lovely eyes which had heretofore shown me only the expression of genius. 'Ximeo,' she said, 'I will answer you tomorrow. Do not expect the artfulness of your countrywomen from me. Tomorrow you will read into my heart. Think about your own.'

"With these words she left me. It was long before sunset, the usual signal for her to retire, but I did not try to keep her. Mirza's influential character made me submit to her wishes. Ever since I had known her, I had been seeing less of Ourika, whom I deceived, pleading the excuse of traveling, putting off the date of our wedding, pushing the future away from myself instead of coming to any decision about it.

"At last, the next day—it seemed centuries away from the night before—I arrive. Mirza takes the first steps toward me. She had spent the day in tears, out of foreboding or tenderness.

"'Ximeo,' she said softly but firmly, 'are you quite sure that you love me? Is it true that no one in all your vast country has ever been the object of your love?'

"Solemn oaths were my reply.

"'Well . . . I believe you. The only witness to your promises is nature, all around us. I know nothing about you except what I have learned from your own mouth. My only security lies in my isolation and my lack of reserve. What mistrust—what obstacle have I ever opposed to your wishes? You would be deceiving nothing in me except my esteem for Ximeo; you would be taking your revenge on nothing but my love. As for my family, friends, fellow citizens—I have taken my distance from everything in order to depend on you alone. I should be as sacred to you as weakness, childhood, misery—no! I can fear nothing! no!'

"I interrupted her. I was at her feet, I thought I was being sincere. The force of the present had made me forget both past and future. I deceived and persuaded, and she believed me. Gods! she found such passionate terms to express herself! She was so happy in loving!

"Two months slipped by this way, during which her heart had everything love and happiness could offer. I took pleasure in that, but I grew calmer. Human nature is so bizarre! I was so struck by the delight she took in seeing me, that I began to come for her sake rather than my own: I was so sure of her welcome that I no longer trembled as I approached her. Mirza did not notice this. She would speak, answer, weep, console herself; her active soul acted and reacted on itself. Ashamed of myself, I needed to get away from her.

"War broke out at the other end of the kingdom of Cayor, and I made up my mind to rush over there. I had to annouce this news to Mirza. Ah! at that moment I still felt how dear she was to me. Her sweet, trusting sense of security deprived me of the strength to tell her of my plan. She seemed to live through my presence to such an extent that my tongue froze when I tried to speak about my departure.

"I decided to write to her. This art that she had taught me was to be her misfortune. I left her twenty times, twenty times I came back again. The unfortunate girl was delighted by this, mistaking my pity for love. Finally I went off, writing her a letter to the effect that my duty forced me to leave her, but that I would come back and kneel at her feet more tenderly than ever. What an answer I got back from her! Love's language, so enchanting when the mind makes it shine! She was so desperate at my going away! so passionately eager to see me again!

"At that point I trembled at the thought of the excessive love of which Mirza's heart was capable; but my father would never have called a Jaloffe woman his daughter. All the obstacles came to my mind once the veil hiding them from me had fallen. I saw Ourika again. Her beauty, her tears, the authority of one's first attachment, the urging of the whole family—I don't know!—everything that seems overwhelming when one's strength no longer comes from the heart made me unfaithful, and my bonds with Ourika were formed in the presence of the gods.

"Meanwhile, the time I had set with Mirza for my return was drawing near. I wanted to see her again. I hoped I could soften the blow I was going to deal her. I believed this possible: when one is no longer in love one can no longer guess at love's effects. One cannot even make use of one's memories. How I felt traveling through the same places that had witnessed my vows and my happiness! Nothing had changed except my heart, and yet I could hardly recognize them.

"As for Mirza, I think that she felt during the moment she first saw me all the happiness people scarcely taste throughout life. That must be how the gods settled their debt toward her.

"How can I tell you the dreadful steps by which I made the unfortunate Mirza understand the state of my heart? My trembling lips pronounced the word 'friendship.'

"'Friendship!' she cried. 'Your friendship, barbarian! Does my soul deserve an offer like that? Go ahead and give me death. Go on—that is all you can do for me now.' Her excessive pain seemed to be leading her to that result: she fell motionless at my feet. What a monster I was! That was when I should have deceived her—that is when I was sincere. 'Unfeeling man, leave me,' she said. 'The old man who took care of me in my childhood, who was a father to me, may still have some years to live. I must live for him. I am already dead here,' she added, putting her hand on her heart, 'but he will need my care; leave me alone.'

"'I couldn't do that,' I cried. 'I couldn't bear your hatred.'

"'My hatred!' she answered. 'Have no fear of that, Ximeo. Some hearts only know how to love; their violent passions turn only on themselves. Goodbye, Ximeo. Another woman will—'

"'No, never!' cried I. 'Never!'

"'I do not believe you anymore,' Mirza went on. 'Yesterday your words would have made me doubt the sun that shines on us. Hold me to your heart, Ximeo, call me your beloved mistress in your voice of yesterday! Let me hear it again—not to enjoy it, but to remember it—but it is impossible. Goodbye; I will find it again myself. My heart will always hear it; it is the cause of death I carry and keep within my breast. Ximeo, goodbye.'

"The touching note of that last word and the effort she made as she moved away are still in my mind; she is before my eyes. Gods! make the illusion stronger! Let me see her for one moment, the better to feel what I have lost, if that is possible. I stayed immobilized for some time in the place she had left, lost and disturbed like someone who has just committed a great crime. Nightfall took me by surprise before I thought of going home. Remorse, remembrance, and the sensation of Mirza's unhappiness clung to my soul; her ghost haunted me as if the end of her happiness had been the end of her life.

"War broke out against the Jaloffes, and I had to fight against Mirza's countrymen. I wanted to win glory in her eyes, justify her choice and still deserve the happiness I had renounced. I did not much fear death; I had made such sad use of my life that I may have taken some secret pleasure in risking it.

"I was dangerously wounded; while recovering I learned that a woman was coming to the threshold of my doorway every day. She would stand there motionless, trembling at the slightest noise. Once I was worse, and she lost consciousness; when people rushed to her side, she came back to life and said: 'Let him remain ignorant of the condition in which you have seen me. I am much less than a stranger to him, and my interest could only give him pain.'

"Then came a day, a dreadful day! I was still weak; my family and Ourika were with me. I was calm when I could gain some distance from the memory of the woman I had driven to despair—or at least I thought I was calm. Fate had led me, I had acted as if fate had ruled me, and I dreaded the moment of repentance so much that I was using all my strength to restrain my mind, ever ready to fix itself on the past. Suddenly our enemies, the Jaloffes, pounced on the city where I was staying. We were defenseless. We withstood a fairly lengthy attack, but they finally carried the day and took a number of prisoners: I was among them. What a moment for me when I saw myself in chains! The cruel Hottentots just

destine the vanquished to death, but we—more cowardly in our bar-
barity! we serve our common enemies, and justify our crimes by becoming their accomplices.[4]

"A company of Jaloffes made us march through the night.
By the time daybreak came to enlighten us, we found ourselves on the
shore of the Senegal River. Boats had been prepared. I saw white men; I
was certain of my fate. Our leaders soon began to discuss the vile conditions of their infamous bargain. The Europeans examined our age and
strength curiously, to find some reason for hoping we might be capable
of bearing the evils they planned for us. My mind was already made up: I
hoped that as I was passing onto the fatal boat, my chains would loosen
enough so that I could leap into the river, and that they would be heavy
enough to drag me down to the bottom of the abyss in spite of the
prompt rescue of my greedy owners. My eyes fixed on the ground, my
mind riveted to the terrible hope I was embracing, I was as if separated
from the things around me.

"Suddenly a voice I had learned to know through happiness
and pain made my heart tremble and tore my from my paralyzed meditation. I looked up and saw Mirza, beautiful like an angel—not a mortal,
for her soul was depicted on her face. I heard her asking the Europeans if
they would hear her speak. Her voice was moved, but what had changed
it was not fear or tenderness. A supernatural burst of emotion had given
her whole person new character.

"'Europeans,' said Mirza, 'you condemn us to slavery so as
to cultivate your land. Your self-interest is what makes you need our misfortune; you are not like the god of evil, and our suffering is not the aim
of the pain you have in mind for us. Look at this young man, weakened
by his wounds. He will be able to bear neither the long journey nor the
work you require of him. Let me be a slave in Ximeo's place. I will live—
since that is the price at which you will have granted me Ximeo's liberty.
I will no longer think slavery debasing—I will respect the power of my
masters: they will hold that power from me, and their good deeds will
have consecrated it. Ximeo must cherish life—Ximeo is beloved! For
myself, I hold fast to no one on this earth; I can disappear off the face of it
without leaving any empty heart to feel that I no longer exist. I was going
to end my days, but a new happiness makes me outlive my heart. Oh! let
yourselves be moved! and when your pity is no longer at war with your
self-interest, do not resist pity's voice.' As she finished these words, the

proud Mirza, whom the fear of death would not have made fall to the feet of the kings of the earth, humbly bowed her knee. She still kept all her dignity in this position, however; shame and admiration were the share of those to whom she begged.

"There was a moment when she could believe I was accepting her generosity. I had lost the power of speech, and I was in torment at my inability to regain it. The barbarous Europeans were crying out as one man: 'We accept the exchange! She is young, she is brave—we want the Negress! and we will leave her friend.'

"I regained my strength; they were about to approach Mirza. 'Savages,' I cried, 'this is up to me—never, never—respect her sex and weakness. Jaloffes, how can you let one of your countrywomen be a slave in the place of your own worst enemy?'

"'Stop being noble and generous,' Mirza said to me. 'This virtuous act is for yourself alone. If my happiness had been dear to you, you would not have left me. I prefer you guilty, when I know you are indifferent. Leave me the right to feel sorry for myself, since you cannot take away my sorrow. Do not tear from me my only remaining happiness, the sweet thought of holding on to you by the good I have done you, at least. I have followed your fortunes, and I die if my life is not useful to you. This is the only way you have to save my life. Persist in your refusal if you dare!'

"Since then, I have remembered all her words; I don't think I heard them at the time. I was shuddering at Mirza's plan, trembling lest these vile Europeans should second it. I did not dare proclaim that nothing should separate me from her. Those greedy merchants would have dragged us both off. Their hearts, incapable of sensibility, were perhaps already counting on the results of ours, promising themselves to choose in the future captives whom love or duty could oblige others to buy back or follow, studying our virtues to make them serve their vices.

"But the Governor comes forward like an angel of light, informed of our struggles, Mirza's devotion, my despair. Who would have believed he was not bringing us happiness? 'Be free, both of you,' he told us. 'I give you back to your country and your love. Such greatness of soul would make any European blush to call you his slaves.'

"They took off my chains. I kissed his knees and blessed his goodness in my heart as if he had been sacrificing legitimate rights. Look

how usurpers, by renouncing their injustices, attain the rank of benefactors! I stood up. I had thought that Mirza was with me at the Governor's
feet; I saw her at a distance, leaning against a tree and deep in
thought.

"I ran toward her, feeling and expressing love, admiration, gratitude.

"'Ximeo,' said Mirza, 'the time for that is past. My unhappiness has cut too deep for even your hand to reach it. I can no longer hear
your voice without trembling in pain, and your presence freezes the
blood that once ran hot in my veins for you. Passionate souls know
nothing but extremes, and they leap the interval between these extremes
without stopping. When you told me my fate, I doubted it for some time.
You might have come back then—I would have thought I had dreamed
your inconstancy. But to destroy that memory now, you would have to
pierce my heart, from which nothing can efface it.' As she spoke those
words, the fatal arrow was in her breast.

"Ye gods who held my life in suspense at that moment, did
you give it back to me to avenge Mirza through the long torture of my
misery? For a whole month the chain of my memories and thoughts was
interrupted. Sometimes I seem to be in another world, whose hell is the
memory of the first. Ourika has made me promise not to attempt suicide;
the Governor has convinced me that I should live to be useful to my unfortunate countrymen, respecting Mirza's last wish; he says that as she lay
dying she begged him to watch over me and console me in her name. I
obeyed. I have locked away in a tomb the sad remains of the woman I
love now that she lives no longer, the woman I failed to appreciate when
she was alive. There, alone at sunset, when all nature seems to clothe itself with my mourning, when universal silence permits me to hear nothing but my own thoughts, lying on her tombstone, I experience the
pleasure of unhappiness, the total feeling of her sorrows. My excited imagination sometimes creates phantoms—I think I see her—but she never
shows herself as an angry lover. I hear her console me and concern herself with my sorrow. I am uncertain of the fate that awaits us after life; I
respect the memory of Mirza in my heart, and I am afraid that if I killed
myself I might destroy everything that remains of her. In these two years,
you are the only person to whom I have confided my sorrow. I expect no
pity. Can a savage who has caused the death of the woman he mourns
expect to interest anyone on his own behalf? I wanted to talk about her,

though. Promise me not to forget the name of Mirza; you will tell it to your children, and after my death you will keep the memory of that angel of love and this victim of unhappiness."

Ximeo's face was the picture of somber reverie as he finished his story. Bathed in tears, I tried to speak to him. "Do you think you should try to console me?" he asked. "Do you think anyone can have a thought about my misery that my heart has not already discovered? I wanted to tell you about it because I was convinced you would *not* soften it. I would die if you took it away from me. Remorse would take its place—take over my whole heart; and the pains of remorse are dry and burning. Farewell. Thank you for listening."

His somber calm and tearless despair easily persuaded me that my efforts would be in vain. I could no longer try to speak to him. Sorrow inspires respect; I left him, my heart filled with bitterness. I am telling his story to keep my promise and consecrate, if I can, the sad name of his Mirza.

ADELAIDE AND THEODORE

The fortune and education of Adelaide, an orphan at a very early age, had been entrusted to her uncle the Baron d'Orville, who found the obligation of bringing her up so wearisome that he seized the first opportunity of getting rid of her. The Baron was a likeable man, easy to live with, but so flighty that it would have been impossible to get his attention for a quarter of an hour even if half his fortune had been at stake. This had made him quite an entertaining person. In his youth his insouciance was thoughtlessness, in his old age they called it philosophy— the results were the same, only the name had changed. He never did anything difficult, whether for good or evil; he simply let himself drift one way or the other through weakness. He was not a man of systematic morality or immorality; he generally thwarted anything that was logical or profound, anything that required taking trouble or making an effort. His feeling that he was not cut out to raise a young girl was so strong that he left Adelaide in the country until she was fourteen, at the home of one of his relatives named Mme. d'Orfeuil.

Mme. d'Orfeuil was a woman of thirty who believed herself madly in love with a husband who had abandoned her. Or, at least, devout as an angel, she had never allowed herself to let go of that sentiment, for fear of feeling a need for someone else. Born with a good deal of natural wit, she had cultivated it poorly, thinking of nothing but love and reading about nothing but religion. She did not know the world, because she had lived in a land of fairy tales. The result of this contrast between her romantic ideas and her religious practice was a character more agreeable to her friends than useful to her pupil. Adelaide loved her passionately. Together they read novels; together they prayed to God. They waxed enthusiastic together; they were tender together. Adelaide's young soul was in constant turmoil.

It was in this frame of mind, and at the age of fourteen, that Adelaide arrived at the home of the Baron d'Orville. He had let her come alone, without even a waiting-woman to attend her, but every conceivable invention of luxury awaited her there. His women friends gathered around young Adelaide, and each of them took it on herself to direct some aspect of her toilette, as a proof of friendship. She was given neither good advice nor bad; these ladies left her behavior to chance and concentrated on her pride, because they put some value on her triumphs. When middle-aged women are not jealous of a young girl, they make her the object of their vanity. A success has to belong to them one way or another for them to take any pleasure in it.

Adelaide was stunned by everything she saw. She would try to talk about love; these ladies replied that the best way to inspire it was to avoid wearing bright colors if you were a brunette, or pale ones if you were blonde. She wanted to be devout; the Baron d'Orville loaded her down with jokes. She meant to read, but the ladies gave her no time. Without being evil or indecent, in short, they were so frivolous that they had the knack of making the day disappear without one's being made aware of it by either pain or happiness.

Meanwhile, the Baron was getting bored by all the things he had to take into consideration for a young girl, and worried about fulfilling this responsibility. Then one morning M. de Linières, a decent enough man but as foolish as could be found in France, came to say that he was sixty years old, had twenty-four thousand livres a year, loved the

Baron's niece very much, and would marry her, if that were acceptable, in a week. The Baron saw no objection to this suitable proposition, so he gave his word.

At the same time, the matter was discussed with Adelaide, who was in despair. Her novel of happiness was destroyed. She struggled for longer than one might expect from a girl of fifteen, but they finally gained her consent at a ball. The morning after the fateful day, she wrote a melancholy letter to her aunt. "There is no more hope for me," she wrote. "They have finished my future. The happiness of love is forbidden me forever. I will die without having felt what it is to live—nothing interesting can happen to me—it is all the same to me." And a few days later she wrote, "One has to stun oneself, to let the whirlwind carry one along. I feel neither sadness nor happiness; I cannot dream with any pleasure; I give in to the flood. I enjoy anything that wastes my time."

In fact Adelaide very soon gave herself completely to the pleasures of her age. She was young, clever, and agreeable; her vanity was flattered. People made her love her triumphs. She was often unhappy about the way she used her time during the day, but the fear of finding herself alone with her husband made her leave the house, and the chain-linked schedule of social pleasures did not allow for going back home. In endless protest against the life she led, she would always find the next day the same as the one that had gone before.

Two years went by like this. No feeling occupied Adelaide's soul, but she learned to live in a vacuum, content with the pleasures of vanity. Her mind and heart were superior to her fate, but her character needed solitude: the world could intoxicate it, and its instability made the choice of the things around it important. The sight of a beautiful countryside made her dream, the sound of a violin brought her back to town. Rousseau's sensitive morality was made for a young, flexible soul like hers.

This lightness went only as far as secondary characteristics, however. A little vanity and some taste for amusements were faults cured by the countryside and instantly restored by the city. But her sensibility, her goodness, and her honesty were inalterable, and she readily avowed her faults, which gave the envious some consolation and her friends a topic for fresh, welcome merriment. Her sweet, delicate face, her blonde hair, her dazzling pale complexion and—more than anything else—her romantic and tender expression were contradicted by her great liveliness, but they suffused her whole person with an air of modesty and sensibility that interested people in her. Even in her delight at parties and triumphs, she was good to her husband. She could not stand it when people ridiculed him in any way; even foolish people have their pride. He was content when Adelaide gave him a few kind words and asked him to go places with her, a favor which his own lack of anything to do always made him happy to grant.

After two years M. de Linières fell sick, and Adelaide nursed him zealously. He died. A feeling of horror seized her; her imagination was struck by the gloomy spectacle she had witnessed. It was the first time she had thought about death. The loss of those we love makes us so unhappy that it makes terror disappear. With people we do not care about, however, we are looking at the end of life, an idea which abandons us to sad and philosophical thoughts, easily frightening the heart of a woman.

The Baron d'Orville and his set understood Adelaide so little that she felt she needed to escape from them. She decided to spend her year of mourning at the home of her beloved aunt, Mme. d'Orfeuil. Her aunt had never stopped missing her, even though she found fault with the life her niece had been living.

It was April when Adelaide arrived at Mme. d'Orfeuil's. She had not seen nature for two years, and it thrilled her heart. Her childhood impressions retraced themselves with all their charms, and she was happy to find Mme. d'Orfeuil once more. No pleasure had ever delighted her heart so much as the sweet melancholy these delightful places made her feel. The daily occupations—the schedule of the hours of each day—everything was quickly decided. Adelaide found that life passed more quickly and sweetly this way: one felt it more strongly, and it was less of a burden. In the end, her imagination, completely devoted to the charms of the countryside, portrayed the city to her as altogether loathsome.

She had been living in the country for scarecly two weeks when Mme. d'Orfeuil suggested that they go to visit the Princess de Rostain, whose château was two leagues away. The Princess was a very proud woman, but famous for her wit, her character, and her passion for her son, Count Theodore de Rostain, whom she had finally cured of the failings of his youth, running up debts and loving women. These two faults, which ordinary people treat as such crimes, and which one's competitors use so nicely to lead one astray from the path to good fortune, really do oneself much more harm than they do other people. Moreover, interesting qualities can sometimes be their cause and their excuse.

Mme. de Linières had heard people speak of the Count de Rostain. No one had a greater reputation for wit and amiability. She knew that he had retreated from society four months ago, because of his pain at the infidelity of his mistress, Mme. d'Etampes, a woman of light conduct whom he thought he had steadied, whom he had sincerely loved, and from whom he had parted with equal self-respect and sensibility. She also knew that he had taken up residence in Paris; that he lived in bad company there because he visited only people he liked; and that he was a ne'er-do-well because he gave all his money to his friends. Since one's opinion about men who have no reason to appear in public life is easily formed, Mme. de Linières believed Count Theodore was just like the portrait people had painted of him. However, her curiosity for the charms of such a famous wit got the better of every other consideration.

Adelaide was talking about the Count de Rostain along these lines when Mme. d'Orfeuil answered her by saying, "People have given you a false impression of the Count. They have not exaggerated the charm of his conversation, serious and lively by turns, but he has an extremely sensitive soul and the proudest character imaginable. He is so right about everything that he must have left the path of reason because he was carried away by his heart. He has a lively mind and a melancholy heart. I know what I am talking about. His mind is not romantic—he exaggerates nothing and expresses himself very little—but he feels love a thousand times better than we think."

At this point in their conversation, the two women arrived at their destination. Adelaide was eager to see a man whom the court called delightful and her aunt called sensitive; both advantages were perhaps necessary to her mind and heart. She had never, therefore, concentrated so hard on pleasing.

They entered a château that was furnished simply, but nobly. As they approached the drawing room, they heard some friends of the Princess burst into laughter. Upon opening the door, they saw her son talking to two old ladies. Adelaide could not bring herself to speak to them, but she felt it was good that someone was taking care of them, and she respected Count Theodore for doing it. He came up to her; his face was noble and interesting, and his manners showed grace and dignity, inviting one to be at one's ease while forbidding familiarity. Most of all, his gaze had something sensitive and dreamy about it as soon as he had said or done anything to express gaiety, and seemed to show that gaiety was not the natural condition of his soul.

Mme. de Linières went to some trouble to please him. He replied without any eagerness to show himself off, but with a readiness to make the most of her: instead of worrying about his own answer, he set up Adelaide's. If she had had less wit herself, she might have thought the credit more hers than his.

The visit came to an end. The Count asked permission to see them home; he came back the following day and every day thereafter. No business affairs kept him from coming; he devoted his whole life to it. He was always at Adelaide's command, anticipating her schedule, forestalling her wishes, silent about his own feelings, which he expressed by his devotion or by the religion he made of Adelaide's charms. Should we call the fascination he expressed while she was speaking to him flattery? That is a different art from the art of praise; it is the gift of love. Theodore had this charm in an irresistible way: he seemed to live in what he loved, serve pride by abandoning himself to his heart's impulses, act involuntarily just as reason might have advised him. Like Emile carrying his mistress to the goal, he called victory for her sake.[5] In short, he added such beauty to his beloved's existence—pleasure, glory, happiness, everything was so much his own work—that when he left, one lost both him and one's own self all at once. One could no longer find either his graces, nor the graces he inspired. Nothingness followed life; pleasures apparently quite independent of him all vanished in his absence.

Theodore was becoming less amiable, however, and more lost in reverie. Irresistibly attracted to him, feeling that she had been on the verge of betraying her feelings time and again, Mme. de Linières could not understand his silence. He was free, she was free, no obstacles separated them. His actions, his words, even his involuntary glances proclaimed the deepest love. What could be the cause of his silence? Adelaide wanted to confide her feelings to her aunt, but Mme. d'Orfeuil was careful to avoid this conversation.

At last one evening the two women were out for a walk, waiting for Rostain at the edge of a stream on a dark path, near the pavilion separating the garden from the forest. "Well! Don't you ever want to talk to me about the Count de Rostain?" asked Adelaide.

"We have been talking about him for the last hour," replied Mme. d'Orfeuil.

"Could you explain his incomprehensible behavior to me?"

"First I must understand what mystery I am supposed to unravel."

"Ah! my friend," cried Adelaide, bursting into tears, "if you cannot guess that I love him, you do not love me anymore."

Mme. d'Orfeuil was touched by her sincerity. "Come," she said, "I would not be opposed to his passion for you if I thought your heart was worthy of his."

"Opposed to my happiness?" Adelaide asked. "You?"

"If you understood the soul that is devoted to you! Such sensitivity! Such delicacy! He is putting his life in your hands."

"My tenderness makes me worthy of it—that and the principles my aunt has engraved on my heart."

"I have the greatest respect for you. I am even sure that your ardent soul is capable of a most tender love—but your mind is so mobile and your head so light that your lover or husband could easily be uncertain of your heart. I know Rostain. He has the best character in the world for other people, and the most unfortunate for himself. The world that makes hearts wither has only made his heart more liable to distrust; experience has not detached him from the happiness of love, but it has taught him all too well how rare it is to get it."

"Aunt," Adelaide answered, "do not judge me by the two years I spent in society. Then I was not in love. Today I feel I must possess Rostain's heart or die . . . but is it true that he loves me?"

As she was finishing these words, Rostain approached.

"Well," Mme. d'Orfeuil said, "I am beaten. I think Adelaide is in love with you, and I no longer oppose the confession you want so much to make."

"Oh Adelaide! Listen to me," cried Rostain. "This is not the first time I am speaking to you about my love. You guessed it a long time ago. Let me lay my soul bare before you, however. I no longer have any chance not to love you, but there is still time for me not to give in to the hope of inspiring some return. Let your heart reflect for a moment: I am putting my life in your hands. I am certainly willing to lose it for the sake

of enjoying one day of such sweet illusion, but the instant that would enlighten me—the instant before my death—would be so cruel that I do
not feel the strength to risk the danger. I have sought happiness
everywhere. A woman of light virtue held me in thrall for four years; I
thought she was in love with me. When she was unfaithful, I abandoned
the world; I would have abandoned life, if one could be wholeheartedly
in love with something one does not respect. Simple tastes filled my
time; the days went past without any regrets or anticipation on my part;
the action of my soul was suspended. Then I saw you. I had a notion of
some kind of happiness beyond anything I could imagine; it seemed to
me that I could find in you all the charms of love and virtue; that I could
see you freely; that marriage would sanctify love's bond.

"The shudder that went through me at this hope would be
incomprehensible to anyone who did not love Adelaide, or feel passion
with his heart, as I do. For the two months I have known you, this fear
has held me back. My own character has created it. Adelaide has a pure,
tender soul; she will give her lover, her husband, cause for nothing but
respect. This is not enough for me. My heart has banished suspicion, but
it is constantly pervaded by anxiety; I am not only jealous, but extremely
susceptible to jealousy. Happiness does not exist for me if it is darkened
by the least little cloud; my imagination is so somber that any pretext
throws me into despair. Most men are concerned with fame or fortune,
but only one thing can make me unhappy. My strength is completely
concentrated on my heart—that is where I live or die. If one day you
were to love me less—and forgive me for thinking that I am loved by you
now—I would not complain. Reproaches never bring love back, and my
soul is too proud and scrupulous to give in to them. But I would die of it.
This much-abused expression would tell my story, and the sight would
tear Adelaide's heart to pieces. It is for her that I fear it—for her sake that
I question her heart."

This speech was pronounced with a solemn sensibility
that Adelaide found deeply moving. She abandoned herself to her
feelings, crying, "Theodore! My tenderness is worthy of yours."

"Lord! this is the most holy of vows," he answered. "My
happiness is overflowing—I can feel it—I can doubt it no longer." And
floods of tears streamed from his eyes.

Adelaide was overjoyed. Mme. d'Orfeuil pressed their
clasped hands. They felt all the bliss the human soul is capable of enjoy-

ing; then, growing calmer so as to experience their happiness in detail, they talked about how they could go about ensuring it.

Adelaide, naturally a scatterbrain, had been concentrating on Count Theodore rather than his mother. This proud woman had taken a dislike to Adelaide, entirely unsuspected by the two lovers. Full of confidence, Theodore resolved to ask her consent the very next day, though Adelaide's mourning did not allow her to remarry yet.

The Princess de Rostain told her son that she would never consent to this marriage. He had spend on his friends the fortune he had inherited from his father; he needed his mother to make up his losses.

Theodore felt deeply indignant at such a refusal. A respectful son, he broke out for the first time in his life in bitter reproaches and, leaving his mother impetuously, arrived at Mme. de Linières' at the limits of anger and despair.

As soon as she understood the reason for this, Adelaide asked him if at the age of thirty he could not control his own fate.

"Yes," he replied, "but my fortune—"

"Do I not have enough for both of us?"

"You are right," he answered. "I will not thank you for this sentiment, which fits into my heart so well that it is no surprise to me in yours."

Perhaps it would have been better for Adelaide to advise her lover not to disobey his mother, but at that time neither of them had any virtues but those of love. Adelaide stopped visiting Mme. de Rostain, but the Count spent half the day with his mistress, and the inexpressible joy of being together lent a charm to the most ordinary occupations.

At last the time they had set for their wedding approached. Mme. d'Orfeuil, their only confidante, had obtained the necessary papers. The marriage was to be secret: this was a necessary precaution because of Adelaide's mourning, Mme. de Rostain's refusal, and the Baron d'Orville's indiscretion. Theodore, so quick to anxiety, felt none. He was confident of the heart of his delightful friend, he found some new reason to love and respect her every day, and every instant of his life seemed an age of happiness. Adelaide was intoxicated. Her heart seemed even more moved than Theodore's; she showed all her feelings, she hid nothing.

The morning of the happy day, Theodore led Adelaide into the pavilion which had witnessed their first vows. "Tonight they will ask you to love me in the name of religion and the name of law," he said. "Let another ceremony, equally solemn but more tender, give you to me forever. Swear to God—our hearts must believe in His existence, since happiness like ours must come from Him—swear to your devoted lover that you find it sweet to give him your life. As for myself, I swear at your feet that I will die if your love or happiness changes. My Adelaide, you must believe there never has been a truer vow." Passion had never spoken more strongly.

Mme. d'Orfeuil came to interrupt them. "The priest is waiting for you," she said.

"Why do we need a priest?" cried Theodore. "I have received her vows."

A wave of fear took possession of Adelaide. Her knees trembled and her eyes filled with tears; her happiness was beyond her strength. Neither of them could speak, but their whole beings expressed the fatal, beloved, "yes." Slowly they regained the château, leaning on each other, plunged in the melancholy of happiness, so sure of understanding each other that they felt no need to speak. Mme. d'Orfeuil looked at them with a sweet, sad feeling, as this spectacle reminded her of her own sorrows. They noticed it, and the thought made them break a silence they could have kept for some time; they took care to console her, because they did not want there to be any unhappiness in the world. That day Mme. d'Orfeuil was just another person to them; they loved the whole world equally.

They spend a month in a state of calm, passionate happiness, perhaps unique. During that time, the Baron d'Orville kept writing to his niece to make her promise to return to Paris. Theodore had to divide his time between his mother and his wife; and winter was coming on.

One day Adelaide suggested to her husband that they spend three months in Paris. Theodore turned pale and kept silent for a moment. After a little while, he told her that she was right. His mother had been proposing such a trip for a month; he had refused until now, but he was going to agree.

"Would this plan distress you?" asked Adelaide.

"No," Theodore answered; "it pleases you."

Adelaide did not notice the cloud covering Theodore's face; she was more aware of her own emotions than other people's. She was thoroughly sorry that she would miss her aunt, but she left—eighteen years old, passionately in love with her husband, but enchanted at seeing Paris again.

Theodore was acquainted with the Baron d'Orville, and the day of Adelaide's arrival he came to supper at his house. When Adelaide made her entrance, the salon resounded with the applause her beauty deserved. The countryside had made her more beautiful. Her husband's wit and grace outshone whatever Paris had to offer, and he soon gave his attention to setting Adelaide off to advantage. The two of them were attractive together, and each through the other.

Theodore came to see Adelaide the next day. "No one has ever shown so much charm and gaiety as you do," she told him. "You must love society—no one seems better suited to it."

"My dear Adelaide," he said, "these social triumphs have become a matter of indifference to me. I will seek them because they give you pleasure, but they have not flattered me for some time."

Taken for a widow, rich and beautiful, Adelaide attracted everyone's homage. She did not love Theodore any the less, but she felt a taste for society as well. Love still exerted its control over her, but it no longer occupied her completely. She would never have gone to a fete to which Theodore had not been invited, but she sometimes preferred to go to a ball rather than stay alone with him. While she dedicated her triumphs to him, she did want to have triumphs. If he spoke to her in the middle of a crowd, she stopped everything to answer him; if he left her to dance or sparkle in conversation, however, she devoted her whole evening to that. She could not have lived without Theodore, but she could amuse herself without him.

If Adelaide had ever noticed this change in herself, she would have put a stop to it. She found it easy to love society, though, and to take pleasure and succeed in it. Assuming that her husband shared this sentiment, she had not the slightest doubt that he felt it.

The first cloud of sadness that Adelaide noticed on Theodore's face hurt her so much, and she immediately offered him with such good faith to sacrifice absolutely all the pleasures of society, that he was unwilling to accept the offer. They reassured each other completely; Adelaide began to indulge her tastes once more, and Theodore, who had begged her to do so, did not dare admit that he would prefer not to have his wishes granted quite so completely. The day we make it a rule to hide any of our feelings from the object of our affections, the impression that feeling makes on our inmost selves becomes incalculable. Explanations, complaints, reproaches may leave no trace, but silence devours the heart that commands itself to be silent.

Proud and sensitive, Theodore let his sorrows accumulate in his soul, and his temper felt the results. Adelaide tried to distract him. Taking embarrassment for effort, he rejected her interest rather coldly. Adelaide was offended by the fact that her attentions were useless, repelled by Theodore's unfairness, and even repelled by her own feeling of tenderness for him. With a tacit agreement of tact or vulnerability, they avoided occasions when they might be together. Adelaide was so convinced she loved nobody but Theodore, and Theodore so convinced that he had done nothing wrong, that neither of them wanted to justify himself to the other.

Time and love would have led to a reconciliation if an unfortunate coincidence had not allowed jealousy to take hold of Theodore's heart, which unhappiness and constraint had made ready for it. Adelaide had thoughtlessly attracted a friendship with a woman who confided in her: this friend was passionately in love with the Count d'Elmont, and begged Adelaide to invite him often, as this was the only way she could see him. Adelaide, always deeply interested in love, agreed. Theodore kept finding the Count d'Elmont at his wife's house, and when he spoke to her about it she was disturbed by her promise not to reveal her secret.

The kind of acrimony that makes trust impossible soon set in. Adelaide found Theodore demanding. Theodore thought her insensitive; he made up his mind to leave her forever.

It was at about this time that Adelaide realized she was pregnant. "Ah! I will get him back," she cried. "I will atone for my errors—I will leave Paris—our happy days will be born again."

Theodore enters the house. Adelaide goes toward him, but she stops short at his icy manner. One of her friends, deceived by appearances, had just thrust a dagger in Theodore's heart by saying that he thought Mme. de Linières was in love with the Count d'Elmont.

Theodore did not suspect his wife's virtue. He had seen her insist on receiving the Count d'Elmont only when her friend was present. He persuaded himself that she mistrusted her own heart; combining that bitter thought with the pain he felt at Mme. de Linières' fickle vanity, he was convinced he was beloved no longer. His decision was prompt and irrevocable. "I have received an order to rejoin my regiment," he told Adelaide. "I am leaving immediately. I have come to say goodbye."

A thunderbolt could not have struck Mme. de Linières with such force. "You are leaving?" she asked.

"Yes. I must go."

"You say so with such indifference!"

"I will see you again in a little while," he replied. And quickly assuming an air of detachment, he began speaking of things that were indifferent to them.

Adelaide had been about to tell him about the new bond uniting them, but she kept a profound silence, cut to the quick by his coldness. Then she arose. They moved toward each other, their secret almost escaping them. I do not know what craving for misery made Theodore keep silent, but suddenly he turned away, with a cry of pain.

"Adelaide!" he cried. "Adelaide, adieu!"

At first Adelaide stood still, frozen. Then she darted after him to call him back; she saw his carriage moving quickly away, and her voice could not be heard. She hurried to his house, but he had not gone back; she sent to the country, but they had no news of him there.

Mad with despair and anxiety, she went to her uncle, confessed her marriage, and begged him to go and ask the Princess de Rostain what had become of her son.

The Baron d'Orville understood nothing of his niece's despair. "He has gone on a trip," he said. "Well, what harm will that do him?" He went in the end, nevertheless, to satisfy his niece.

Adelaide's uncle came back after an hour that felt like a century to her. "Your mother-in-law is the most abominable woman in the world," he said. "I could get nothing out of her except insults about you, tears for her son, and this letter." Adelaide seized the letter with rapture. It said: "Dear Mother, I will be away for two months. Forgive me for not telling you where I am going; I do not want anyone to know. I swear I will see you again. I will come back in two months to your estate, near Mme. d'Orfeuil's, to live or die at your feet." Upon reading this letter,

Adelaide fainted. Her uncle brought her back to life and tried to console her, but she pushed him away.

Unable to bear that world any longer, the cause of all her wrongdoings and misfortunes, Adelaide left to go back to Mme. d'Orfeuil. She made so many painful reflections on the road! felt such remorse! reproached Theodore so many times!

At last she came to the château that had witnessed her happiness. Her messenger had preceded her, but no one came to meet her. This show of indifference on Mme. d'Orfeuil's part filled her with sadness. She entered the salon; Mme. d'Orfeuil arose, bowing coldly.

"Good God!" cried Adelaide, "you were saving this last misfortune for me!"

She spoke with such despair that Mme. d'Orfeuil was touched, and felt impelled to reproach her. "Heartless creature!" she said. "What did Theodore ever do to you, that you should unite his destiny to yours, making his tender heart the victim of your unbelievable flightiness? Read this," she cried. "Read your sentence in this unhappy letter. It has torn me apart—I am rightfully sorry for him and fatally fond of you."

Adelaide read the letter without answering. "Everything is at an end for me, my friend. One moment of happiness—too much, perhaps, for mortal man—has deprived me of the strength to bear unhappiness. I am not writing to the woman who caused it. Complaints and reproaches would escape me; she would want to justify herself, I would cling to my chimera once again, I would be condemning myself to live. As you realize, Adelaide knows me as well as you do. In my view, any shadow of change in my beloved's heart is just as great a misfortune as the complete loss of her affection. I have seen such a change. I do not impugn Adelaide's virtue—her soul is pure. My sorrow is painful, but not bitter. I can still adore the beloved object I have lost. But her heart is no longer the same. Someone else may have been able to please her. At the very least, the world has distracted her from her husband: she is no longer the Adelaide who lived for us alone. Ah! Madame, I am no longer necessary to her happiness. Why should I go on living?

"However, I am going alone up to the mountain peak, to reflect in the presence of heaven and earth on my fate and men's right to put an end to their existence. If I can go on living without happiness, I will leave everything that was dear to me, consecrating my time and en-

ergy to some useful work and dedicating my life to other people as my
brothers, but no longer as my friends. If I do not have enough courage to
make this effort, I will come back to die near you and my mother—and
perhaps, perhaps I may need to catch sight of her once again before closing my eyes forever. Goodbye, my friend. Goodbye."

It is impossible to portray Adelaide's state of mind. Why
was Theodore not there to see it? Mme. d'Orfeuil could not resist it, and
very soon concerned herself with consoling her. But Adelaide's anxious
pain could not be soothed in any way. She wanted to leave, she wanted
to stay; she dared not hope, she was horrified of fear. No plan was adopted, none was rejected. Her misery showed itself in all sorts of ways and
exhausted every kind of courage. Her eagerness to justify herself made it
easy to see that remorse was tearing her apart. Mme. d'Orfeuil did not
dare flatter her with any promise of seeing Theodore again. She was too
cognizant of the depth of his feelings. He had promised, however, to
come back in two months. What days those were for Adelaide! Her misery made her truly worthy of her husband. It is so easy for such deep,
painful feelings to erase the faint traces of dissipation and vanity!

Adelaide still felt a need to hope. There are some misfortunes we cannot understand ahead of time. One of these is death:
nothing can give any idea of that.

One day while she and Mme. d'Orfeuil were walking along
the road leading to the château of Rostain, they saw some peasants coming sadly back the other way. Mme. d'Orfeuil questioned them.

"Oh, if you knew how our young master has changed!"

"Your young master?"

"Yes—Count Theodore."

At these words, Adelaide lost consciousness. They carried
her back to the château; she had hardly regained her senses when she
threw herself to Mme. d'Orfeuil's knees. "Go and find him!" she said.
"Justify me to him. Take these letters—they will prove that it was my
friend who was in love with the Count d'Elmont, and that my only
wrong was in having such a secret. Paint him a picture of the despair you
have witnessed for the last two months. Tell him everything, except that I
have a child within me. If he rejects the mother, both must perish. Justify
me—obtain my pardon. Ah! Go and return; think about the state I shall
be in."

"I will obey you," Mme. d'Orfeuil answered. "It will be easy to obtain your pardon: he will take my word about your heart. Now, alas, it is all too worthy of him. But they did tell you that he was greatly altered?"

"Those are peasants; his careless dress might—oh, my friend, fly to his side."

Mme. d'Orfeuil left immediately. During the three hours she was gone, Adelaide could hardly breathe. Her beating heart heaved, lifting her gown; every minute, every noise, intensified an emotion which seemed beyond human strength. At last Mme. d'Orfeuil returned. Adelaide did not dare go meet her; she entered with an effort of constrained gaiety that was more frightening to Adelaide than the darkest gloom. The need to listen, however, kept her alive.

"He forgives you," said Mme. d'Orfeuil. "He loves you—but he is very ill."

"Ah well," answered Adelaide. "I thank heaven. Now I can die. When will I see him?"

"He begs you to wait a few more days."

"What condition is he in?" She asked this so mournfully that Mme. d'Orfeuil felt obliged to reassure her.

Adelaide did not answer, lost in deep reverie. At two o'clock in the morning she asked her aunt to go to bed, saying that she herself wanted to sleep. At daybreak, however, she had herself driven to the Rostain estate, bribed a gardener, and hid in the shrubbery where Rostain's mother came to have breakfast every morning. She did not ask the gardener any questions. She opened her mouth to ask him the latest news about his master twenty times; twenty times the words died on her lips. Hidden in the shrubbery, she could see without being seen.

By ten o'clock the weather was perfectly beautiful; she saw Mme. de Rostain arrive, sad and tearful. A quarter of an hour later, a shadowy figure drew slowly near, leaning on two men whose feelings seemed to make their steps falter. Adelaide did not recognize him at first—or rather remained uncertain for a moment, trying to deceive herself as one would avoid the thrust of a dagger. Very soon, however, the sound of that dear voice struck her ear; crying out, she fainted. The noise attracted the attention of Rostain's supporters, who rushed into the woods and brought his unconscious Adelaide to his feet. What a spectacle for him—and for his mother!

As Adelaide was opening her eyes, Mme. de Rostain cried

with rage, "Take that woman who killed my son out of my sight. Take
away that barbarous creature he calls his wife."

At these words Rostain recovered his strength, crying, "Do
not insult her, Mother. My life depends on it. My respect for you
depends on it—I would no longer know myself."

"Go on, die at her feet," his mother said. "That is all she
wants. Farewell."

Adelaide heard none of this. Fixing her eyes on Rostain, she
was trying to decipher a few signs of life in his disfigured features.

Left alone together, Adelaide and Theodore kept silent at
first. All of a sudden Adelaide broke the silece, talking rapidly and
passionately. She justified herself, kissed his knees, spoke about nothing
but her love, trying to persuade herself that her own fate depended on
convincing her husband of her love for him.

"Alas, Adelaide," answered Theodore, "I believe my heart
to be unjust, and yours pure. I accuse no one of our unhappiness but
myself."

"Our unhappiness!" she cried. "Cannot the future put
things right? This dear bond uniting us, this child I am carrying . . . "

"Good Lord! This child! You may be a mother?"

"I am one."

"Oh my God, what have I done that you connect me to life
once again?" As he finished these words, Theodore fell into a state of
such violent, painful grief that his strength abandoned him.

Adelaide screamed; people rushed up to her. She had such
a cruel spectacle before her eyes—such dreadful symptoms of decline
and death!

Mme. de Rostain, brought back by Adelaide's scream,
pushed her away with abhorrence.

"Alas, madame, you will regret your injustice," Adelaide
told her. "You will see whether or not I love him."

Rostain, regaining consciousness, saw the picture of horror
painted on every face. "Let Adelaide stay near me, Mother," he said. "I
cannot be separated from her anymore. And let me speak to my
doctor alone."

They brought Rostain back to the château; Adelaide
followed without a word. Only her trembling betrayed her condition;
her face was stony. The doctor went in and out, and she did not move

from the door against which she was leaning. He stopped in front of her, gently taking her hand.

"Leave me alone," she said, "leave me alone. Do you know who killed him? It is I. Go away."

Rostain asked to see his mother, who walked past Adelaide in fury and left shortly afterward in tears. "Go on in," she said to Adelaide. "Go on, he wants to see you. Look at your handiwork."

"Madame," said Adelaide, "I need to live for one more hour. Let me have it." Then she went into Rostain's bedroom without raising her eyes to him, and sat down at his side.

"Adelaide," he said, "you have a brave, sensitive soul; I am asking you to listen to me carefully. I have done you great wrong. My disastrous imagination convinced me I was no longer loved, when your heart was still willing to respond to my love for you. Pain—and more violent measures—guaranteed me that my life was at an end, that in coming here I could be sure of carrying death with me. I will not deny that your presence and tenderness, this pledge of our love, have made cruel regret and remorse spring up in my heart. But the thread of life cannot knot itself again! and I wanted to tell you so myself, because I think I am the only person who can teach you to bear losing me."

"Do you think that your murderer—the woman who thrust the dagger in your heart—will survive you? Shall I not avenge you?"

"No, Adelaide. You will respect the child whose mother you will be. You will want to keep this image of a husband you loved. You will give my mother this child. You will not want me to die completely, so that my memory would not remain in your heart and my features in your child! You will not commit this crime—you will not cause me this grief."

Upon hearing these words, Adelaide fell into a deep reverie. "True," she said to herself, "his child must be sacred to me. Perhaps we can hold on to his life, delay his death—well!" she cried aloud, getting up. "Well, Theodore, before God I answer for the life of your child."

"Oh, Adelaide, I can die in peace. You swear that he will see the light of day—that you will care for him and raise him."

"No," Adelaide said in the firm, grave voice that comes from unshakable resolution. "No. I have promised only to give him life. That is all he will get from me."

"Adelaide, what do you mean? Do you want me to carry these heartrending fears to the grave?"

"You savage," she cried. "When you left me forever, when you made the poison that is killing us run in your veins, did you take pity on me? You are tearing the thing I love from me, you are making me a murderer—and you speak to me of surviving? Forgive me," she said, throwing herself to his knees. "Forgive me. All right. You will hear no more of these painful complaints. I submit to my destiny. But ask your heart. Let it teach you what I suffer, let it forbid you to order me to live."

As Adelaide was finishing these words, Mme. de Rostain entered the room. Theodore charged her in the strongest terms to look after both his wife and his child. Cast down with grief, the unhappy mother could not utter a word. Her violence, tenderness, faults, good qualities—all were gone.

Adelaide's eyes were fixed on Theodore; when he began to breathe with difficulty she lost her breath. She seemed to be dying with him. All of a sudden she saw him grow pale. "Theodore," she cried.

"Adelaide, come and put your hand on a heart which lived for you alone," he cried. "Believe that you are not guilty. Believe I am leaving you both my son and my mother. Do not forget me." He leaned his head on Adelaide's breast, and there he died.

His mother's cries called for help. Everyone wanted to come near him; Adelaide waved them away. They made another attempt to tear her away from that spectacle. "No," she said. "Leave him to me. You see he wanted to rest on my heart." She remained in that position for twenty-four hours, occasionally asking for nourishment in a careful way that contrasted oddly with her grief.

Mme. d'Orfeuil came to beg her to leave the lifeless body. "Soon you will no longer be able to recognize him," she said.

"Very true," replied Adelaide. "Let us not expose his disfigured face to people's stares. What are his last wishes?"

"He wants his tomb to be in the little wood where you saw each other again. That is where he said he would have wanted to live; that is where his ashes should repose."

"He is right," Adelaide answered. "I will conduct the ceremony."

"You?"

"Yes."

"Why should you want to tear your own heart in pieces?"

"No, my friend. With these thoughts I can fill the time I still have to spend. Let me do as I wish. I want to live—this child I am carry-ing must see the light of day. Let me direct my heart myself; it is so nearly gone from me. Go and ask Mme. de Rostain if my presence will be other than hateful to her."

Mme. d'Orfeuil came back to say that Theodore's mother would receive her without trouble.

For the first time, Adelaide entered her own house without fear. She found Mme. de Rostain in convulsions of despair, and having difficulty hiding her horror at the sight of Adelaide.

"Do not restrain yourself, madame," said Adelaide. "You can add nothing to my situation. Your hatred will not last. Let me love your son's child, since I am his mother—that is all I dare hope for."

At first Mme. de Rostain had been angry at Adelaide's calm, but as she watched her, something so solemn and grave spread over Adelaide's whole being that she could not prevent herself from being touched. Her eyes and voice softened. Adelaide did not notice, how-ever, and went out into the garden.

As she came near the shrubbery, she trembled; but she soon found her courage again, and called for the man responsible for the mon-ument. "Make it very simple," she told him, "that will fulfill his inten-tion. Two urns will be placed on this tomb."

"Two?"

"Yes, two. He would have permitted it; he has forgiven me."

The fatal day of the ceremony, Adelaide led the funeral pro-cession with indescribable courage. When it stopped, she could be seen to tremble, and throwing herself to her knees she prayed for some time. Then she got up and said to Mme. d'Orfeuil, "Take me back. It is too much."

As she returned home, she was seized by a burning fever. "Take good care of me," she told Mme. d'Orfeuil. "In my condition, you might think that death would come as a favor from heaven. But you do not realize that I have to live to keep my promise. I have to."

Adelaide's life was saved by Mme. d'Orfeuil's care and her own reason. Mme. de Rostain paid a good deal of attention to her. Adelaide was touched by this, but without expressing it very keenly; she was lost in a deep reverie which she interrupted only to make well-disposed but cold signs of gratitude.

For the four remaining months of her pregnancy she could often be seen alone, writing a great deal, walking endlessly near her husband's tomb, speaking little, and trying to keep away from cares and even feelings. She was silently attentive to Mme. de Rostain, but anyone could see that she did not want to be loved by her, and that she only wished to see Mme. de Rostain happier and in a better state of health.

At last one evening she felt the onset of birth pangs. She was with Mme. d'Orfeuil, and for the first time an involuntary word escaped her. "Oh God!," she cried. "Here is an end to it!" Mme. d'Orfeuil did not understand her.

During the hours of her labor, Adelaide gave no sign of suffering. Her thoughts were so deeply absorbed that her soul had already separated itself from her. Everyone around her was amazed by the contrast between her convulsed muscles and her tranquil gaze. Immediately after the delivery, she asked for her child, and raised him to heaven with a faltering hand. "Theodore!" she cried. "Dear Theodore! I have kept my promise." Then, so quickly that no one could see what she was doing, she took some grains of opium that she had hidden under her headboard and, coming out of the stupor in which she had been plunged for so long, begged Mme. de Rostain and Mme. d'Orfeuil to come to her.

"For four months I have been holding in a grief which would have been enough to end my days, but the process has been hastened by a quicker relief," she said. "I must tell you so." She was interrupted by their cries. "Do not grieve for me," she went on. "For some time I have not really been living. No feeling penetrated my heart, I no longer loved anything. I had grown wild. If you keep some memory of the Adelaide who lived before the loss of Theodore, if you have forgiven me the unhappiness my guilty flightiness caused you, Mother, take care of your child. The experience of wrongs and unhappiness have made my mind and soul go more quickly. The woman who planned this death four months ago judged life without any prettifying illusions. Make my child read what I have written for him. Speak to him often of his father; let him listen to me and imitate him. If my wrongdoing angers him against me, let my unhappiness and death efface its horror."

She spoke for some time more, without weakness or emotion. Her deepest thoughts were about God, death, and the future. Nothing tender escaped her, however, until the moment when her ideas grew confused; then the names of Theodore, his mother, her child, and her friend wandered ceaselessly on her lips. A few hours later she died, like someone whom death had rescued.

Adelaide was buried next to her husband, as she had wished

and deserved. Mmes. de Rostain and d'Orfeuil, united by one wish and one regret, did not separate; they raised Adelaide's attractive son together, and the firmness of one woman, tempered by the other's sweetness, made an accomplished being of the unfortunate fruit of love and unhappiness.

PAULINE

In one of those torrid climates where most men think about nothing but a savage trade and profit, apparently lacking any ideas or feelings to make such things repugnant to them, a thirteen-year-old girl named Pauline de Gercourt was married to a businessman who was very rich and eager to be richer.[6] This man's whole life was taken up by his plantations, commerce, and travel. In order to buy a substantial number of Negroes he had suddenly needed a great deal of money, which was provided by Pauline's dowry, and this was why he had married. Pauline was an orphan who had been badly brought up by her tutor, a friend of her husband's and very much like him. She married M. de Valville at the age of thirteen, ignorant of the importance of the engagement she was undertaking and without having ever reflected either on the present or on the future.

Pauline had a sensitive and pleasing nature, but at that time of life what good is such a gift if it is not developed by education? One can find it again later on, when the time comes to develop oneself by using one's own experience; but even the best of natural dispositions succumbs to its first impressions of the world if there are no good principles to protect it. Pauline was as beautiful as the dawn, the incarnation of everything novels tell us about regular features and charming expressions. Her youth still had something childlike about it, but her face often had a characteristically melancholy look.

Unfortunately for Pauline, her husband had a frequent visitor named M. de Meltin. This was a man of thirty-six, likeable and clever but so depraved that nothing, not even delicacy, filled the gap left by the complete absence of moral principles in his soul. Pauline was left alone all day by her husband and had no notion of what to do with her time or high spirits; M. de Meltin amused her. He tried to attract her as well, but he very soon realized that he would be unsuccessful in this, and therefore decided on the horrible approach of corrupting her first and taking his turn with her afterward. Pauline's age is no obstacle: he consecrates her to misery. It is true that he attached no importance whatever to feminine virtue, so he was merely acting in accordance with his ideas.

Meltin introduces one of his cousins to her, a young, apparently sensitive man named Theodore; this apparent sensitivity of his gives him an extra way to deceive others. Theodore pays attention to Pauline. He has read a few novels; he speaks their language. He touches her, he attracts her—or rather her young soul, believing it feels love because it needs to love, fixes on its first impression.

Theodore was certainly more sensitive than his cousin, and quite incapable of plotting an immoral project in advance, but easily led by Meltin's plans. He would have felt ashamed to show Meltin that he had any scruples at all, and he behaved lightly toward the women he loved, as he had no respect for them. He sang and danced to perfection, talents shared by Pauline—it was the only part of her education anyone had seen to. These common tastes and occupations drew them closer together, and M. de Meltin's continual efforts to unite them made them closer still. Real feelings do arise spontaneously, but a third person can arouse a young mind even more than the object of its affections. The fact that this third person seems to be disinterested makes him better at persuading. We assume that he has no illusions, and believe him rather than our own eyes.

One day M. de Meltin gave a large ball, attended by the whole town of Cap.[7] Pauline's beauty and Theodore's grace enchanted everyone; people said they ought to be in love, and Pauline and Theodore believed it. In accordance with his infamous plans, Meltin encouraged Theodore, who had grown timid since falling sincerely in love. The great heat forced Pauline out into the garden; Theodore followed her.

The night, the silence, the intoxication of pleasure and triumph were Pauline's downfall. They then separated, Pauline in a state of confusion and despair beyond the strength of her age or its ability to reflect, Theodore upset rather than happy; he did not love Pauline enough to take charge of her life, but neither was he insensitive enough to look with indifference at the fate menacing the child. In this condi-tion, he went to find his cousin.

Far from calming him down, Meltin did his best to disturb Theodore still further. Theodore loved to be independent; his cousin painted him an exaggerated picture of the slavery to which he would be doomed, spoke enthusiastically about the advantages of a post Theodore was being offered in France, and urged him to set out on his journey right away. Theodore was shaken by this advice: he was ambitious, and still dominated by his own interests.

However, he went to see Pauline. He could hardly recognize her. The child had turned into a passionate lover; her young language was as eloquent as could be. An observer might have noticed that she was waxing enthusiastic about her feelings so as to mitigate her wrong-doing in her own eyes, but in any case she held forth to Theodore on every lofty and romantic notion love can devise.

This picture frightened Theodore much more than it at-tracted him. Pauline was struck by his coolness, and abandoned herself to the bitterest pain, swearing she would stop living if he did not feel exactly the way she did. Theodore was still dumbfounded by her violent speech. Despite the folly of his age and situation, he could feel a few noble, pure impulses in his soul that gave him some regret. Nevertheless, Pauline's misery, far from bringing him back to her, was just one more nuisance from which to escape.

Theodore struggled against this longing for another two weeks. Pauline could see his withdrawal all too clearly, but as she had not been taught how to captivate a man so fond of his independence that he was afraid of being loved, she kept on writing him long letters in which her young and tender soul portrayed itself in a strange, incorrect style combining childlike characteristics and adult sentiments.

Meltin tried to console her, but he failed. She was possessed by the wildest plans; her body, too frail for such thoughts, was on the verge of breaking down. Frightened by her condition, Theodore decided to abandon her. He was too tenderhearted to bear the sight of her pain, and found it easier to exacerbate it by going away. He therefore left for France, sending Pauline a letter in which he said that he was going to a nearby island for two months, and expressly forbidding his cousin to reveal his secret.

At this news, Pauline felt such violent despair that Meltin feared for her life. He took great care of her, frightened himself by the web into which his dreadful plots had led her. No one had less respect for women than Meltin; he had never been willing to believe that a first seducer should feel any guilt, and from this first to a second he thought that the only difference was random chance. His opinion on this subject had relaxed his moral principles in other ways too: morality is a whole that cannot exist without all its parts. He was generally considered an honorable man, however, as he had been cruel and treacherous toward no one but women.

Away from her husband, without a family to take care of her, and with no intimate companion but Meltin, the unhappy Pauline spent day after day talking to herself about her misery. Her reputation had already alienated a number of women. Some who wanted people to forget their own youthful errors began by forgetting them themselves, and showed an unconquerable aversion for a young girl making such an unpromising debut. Others, closer to her age, were trying to use their choice of companions to gain a respect they could not have earned on personal merit alone. Some, simply envious of her beauty, seized the pretext not to be seen with her; while those who were trying to attract a reputation for kindliness said with heartwarming sorrow in their voices, "What a pity that Pauline is a light woman! I thought she was so appealing—I must admit nothing has ever hurt me so much as the dreadful acts people are accusing her of committing." This tender interest destroyed Pauline more completely than any overt criticism. She knew what everyone was saying about her, and did not dare show herself in society.

Uneducated and unaccustomed to occupying herself, Pauline could not bear to be alone; solitude nourished her despair. Meltin tried to persuade her that the only way she could get out of her misery was by giving in to some other affection. When she talked to him about repentance, he would tell her that such repentance would only stop if she adopted principles lifting her above childhood prejudices. In short, he pictured the rest of her life as either a series of hardships, endless days all devoted to one idea, or a varied train of triumphs and delights.

In her heart, Pauline was not entirely convinced, but her mind, wild with despair, sometimes persuaded her that she should try anything to get away from the pain. She was too young to bear unhappiness, and too weak to overcome it.

After two months of misery, she finally receives a letter with a French stamp, addressed in Theodore's handwriting. She faints at the sight of it. Regaining consciousness, this child—or woman—waited two hours before opening the letter: her destiny was in it. She may have been terrified not only by love, but also by fear of the fate awaiting her and the abyss into which Meltin would drag her. At last she read the fatal lines announcing that Theodore, now in France, was abandoning his country forever, and begged her to forget even the memory of the man she had deigned to prefer to all others.

Such coolness and comtempt annoy her; she hates Theodore. No sweet, tender thoughts or consoling memories soften the bitterness in her soul. All week she wanders in the gardens as if wild; when Meltin tries to speak to her, she rejects him. Her disturbed soul seems to be in a state of madness.

One day she approaches Meltin with a more sinister look on her face than her young features would seem able to express. "Listen," she says. "I am still not fourteen years old. You have been leading me around for a year now. I am a child—but I am dying of unhappiness. Take me out of the abyss into which you have led me. What should I do so as not to die?"

"Love the man who adores you."

"Love you!" she exclaimed. "Impossible. I am unfair—even ungrateful—but I do feel an aversion from you."

"Be mine, and you will no longer be unhappy. What will become of you otherwise, without friends or relatives? I am the only person who can guide you with care and advice, and help you regain the respect you have lost in society. I know how to love and understand you—to judge your fault and forgive it. If I leave, you will succumb to your regrets and misfortunes. I am the only person capable of making them disappear, guiding you, and taking the place of father, husband, and lover." Meltin was trying to seduce a soul that vice revolted instinctively rather than intellectually.

"What!" said Pauline to herself. "That I—I myself—should no longer be capable of enough self-respect to feel pity for myself! Will I dare think of Theodore once I break the ties that bind me to him? Light, unfaithful women do not feel pain like mine. Meltin assures me that they are happy. But to think of their disgrace—and to think what my own fate will be!"

Such were the thoughts of the unhappy Pauline. She was alone and desperate under the hot equatorial sky, her mind almost unhinged. Afraid of losing his conquest, Meltin threatened to leave her, frightening her about the future. With the skill gained from a study of women in general and Pauline in particular, he was able to throw her into such panic and uncertainty that he could see she was on the verge of losing her mind and life together. In that instant, her defeat was easy. It might seem as if any man would have respected this child, whom despair had put in his power; but not Meltin.

"So I am now a lost woman!" Pauline said to him, shuddering. "Those vile creatures everyone despises are like me! There is no going back to virtue—I know that virtue so little, though I hold its name so dear. Well, then! take charge of my destiny. You have sworn to keep me from despair, and that is all I ask. I am no longer capable of doing anything for myself; you are responsible to me for that." As soon as she had finished speaking, she left him. He remained almost disturbed by his victory, and did not dare reflect on it; he had no wish to reproach himself.

A week passed, during which the terrified Pauline repelled her lover. She did not do this out of remorse: her soul was not developed enough for her to feel remorse, at least not consciously. Nor was her involuntary withdrawal caused by resentment of Meltin's behavior. Pauline had thrown herself into the abyss, or at least so she thought. The art that had driven her was invisible to her eyes. But she felt an invincible loathing and horror of a choice dictated by despair, combined with the obligation of loving—and loving someone who had a right to despise his mistress, without love as an excuse. All this brought an unattractive wretchedness and regret to her heart, without giving her any sweet memories; she remained ignorant of such memories' power to disturb, as well as of their emptiness.

In this perplexity, unable to formulate any wishes or imagine any hopes, Pauline learned that her husband had been shipwrecked on his way back from Jamaica. His will gave her control of a considerable fortune. Pauline shed no tears for a man she scarcely knew: no artificial sentiments entered her soul, none of those feelings one arouses in oneself so that one can exhibit them in good conscience to other people. But she trembled at her youth, her mistakes, and her independence.

As for Meltin, turning his plan of seduction into a plan for making his fortune, he congratulated himself on an event which would permit him to find the best of matches in the prettiest of mistresses. It was so easy to bring Pauline's soul back to decent feelings that he must have felt sure he could convince her to marry him, and even persuade her that her very faults had made it her duty. And Pauline, disturbed and anxious as she was, would certainly have accepted his hand; but an unforeseen event saved her from this ultimate misfortune.

Theodore had fallen acutely ill upon arriving in Le Havre.[8] All sorts of care had been lavished on him by an American woman living nearby, a relative of Pauline's, but nothing could avert the mortal blow. His conviction that he was dying changed his soul—or perhaps at the edge of the grave where all illusions vanish he saw life as the wise man must. Pauline's plight touched him; he spoke of her frequently to the respectable woman kept at his side out of pity. By portraying her cousin's plans and habits and showing her Pauline's letters, he aroused this lady's lively interest.

Mme. de Verseuil was a woman of great character and superior intelligence who had once been in love with Pauline's father. Her parents had been opposed to their union. Her subsequent marriage had made her unhappy, but she had fulfilled all her obligations virtuously. Now a widow for four years, childless, wealthy, and independent, she had come to live in the country at the seaside. She sometimes went into Le Havre to perform some service for her compatriots, and always inquired after Pauline, keeping up her interest in the daughter of the man she had loved and deeply regretted, whose memory was enough for all her reveries.

Theodore portrayed Pauline as in such danger that Mme. de Verseuil was moved to an ecstasy of feeling. She was a person who considered evil the only impossibility: she made a plan to go find Pauline, and save her through good advice. Theodore died asking her to think of his young, unhappy friend, and Mme. de Verseuil set sail after hearing him sigh his last.

Upon arriving in Saint-Domingue, Mme. de Verseuil inquires after Pauline. She learns that Pauline is a widow, and flatters herself that she can simply take her away. Her name is familiar to Pauline; the reputation she had left behind on the island and the services she had done various colonists in Europe made it impossible not to know of her virtues and intelligence. She arrives at Pauline's house, choosing a moment when she knows Meltin has gone to town.

Moved and disturbed by the visit, Pauline believes at first sight that Mme. de Verseuil must know everything: she must be her conscience. Mme. de Verseuil starts by telling her of Theodore's death. Pauline's dreadful shock and flowing tears show her emotion, a mixture of remorse and regret. She is given a letter Theodore wrote as he lay dying, in which he exhorts her to follow the advice of this respectable woman who is interested in her fate, and begs her to give up his cousin Meltin's society forever. The letter finished with a few feeling words and more reflections dictated by repentance and morality.

Mme. de Verseuil spoke to Pauline for some time. Pauline's impression as she listened was indescribable. Her soul was growing; feelings until now uncertain and confused were becoming clear and distinct; she heard a language she had been unconsciously craving; she could see the path she had sought opening up before her. She found in Mme. de Verseuil a character she had thought mythical, and had imagined without ever having seen.

She was just abandoning herself to her first sensation of pure happiness when all of a sudden she reflected on the second fault she had committed. She drew violently away from Mme. de Verseuil.

"No, madame," she said, "no. I am not worthy of your interest. I am an unfortunate being whom Meltin has ruined all over again. Nothing can lift me out of such degradation. Marrying Meltin is the only way I can expiate my shame."

"What a mistake!" cried Mme. de Verseuil. "You are not yet fifteen years old, and you want to devote yourself to the torture of marrying someone you cannot respect?"

"But I deserve everyone's contempt. He is the only person who has no right to reject a misfortune he has caused himself."

"You are still very young, and not really in your soul an accomplice of the errors you have been made to commit! Do you really believe that these errors cannot be put right?"

"Never—never. The disgrace cannot be erased."

"Not true, Pauline," said Mme. de Verseuil. "In my eyes, this disgrace no longer exists. In the name of your father, whose virtues would have saved your young self from these traps, in the name of the tender feeling that his memory and your presence have aroused in my heart, come and follow me to another country. Put the wide seas and a virtuous education between your childhood and your youth, and I will be responsible for making you forget the first."

Pauline was thunderstruck. In the end she gave in, falling to her knees and swearing to follow Mme. de Verseuil.

"Listen. We have to hide this secret from Meltin," said Mme. de Verseuil. "Behave generously toward him. He has taken it on himself to manage your affairs; let him keep doing so. Write to him without any fuss, but in such a way that he has no hope of ever seeing you again. Tomorrow, while he is away, come to my house. He does not know that I am in Saint-Domingue; in two days we will have left it. Two days from now, you will be cut off from pain and disgrace forever."

Pauline agreed to everything, and spent the whole day in some sort of joy. She had not yet reflected enough to have any notion of the unhappiness brought by the memory of the faults she had committed. It seemed as if everything had been fixed. She shuddered when she saw Meltin, and avoided the necessity of lying by claiming that she had a headache; she knew nothing of lying, a guilty art to which we are condemned by illegitimate love in what may be its most criminal act.

At the appointed time the next day, Pauline went to see her benefactress. As she entered the room, Mme. de Verseuil cried aloud, "Thank you, God. She belongs to you." They set sail the following day.

A fortunate sea journey allowed them to reach Mme. de Verseuil's charming house, a league from Le Havre, in very little time. With the sea on one side and a thick wood on the other, the situation of the house was somber and melancholy. There Pauline found her father's portrait; there, little by little, Mme. de Verseuil enlightened her mind. Mme. de Verseuil's speeches to lift her soul were not all inspired by austere morality; she was tactful, so as not to torment Pauline's heart with remorse. Moreover, she had been in love herself, and she was sensitive; her memory and that characteristic gave her virtue a sympathetic, tender quality which kept it from looking too formidable. "Unhappiness" and "love" were two words whose meaning she had always understood. She never rejected anyone in tears, anyone capable of love, even if the person was not worthy of her.

Pauline's gaiety did not increase. Far from that: it was decreasing daily. As she adopted the perfect morality preached so delightfully by Mme. de Verseuil, she grew horrified at her past life; her kindhearted teacher kept having to extenuate her faults to her. When she and Mme. de Verseuil read works containing strict, pure precepts, Pauline often had to run away abruptly deep into the forest; Mme. de Verseuil would find her there, the ground wet with tears. Even when she allowed herself to read novels, she would often say to Mme. de Verseuil: "Those people followed the rules of delicacy, at least; *they* had love for an excuse."

Mme. de Verseuil could not buoy up this soul weighted down by remorse. Pauline was at once the most virtuous of women and the most guilty; the past pursued her constantly, inseparable from the present. When she was alone, she invariably kept busy; how could she have enjoyed her reveries? She seemed happy when she was doing something for Mme. de Verseuil or performing charitable tasks, increasing them through her own good deeds; but at the least little word reminding her of America, she fell back into despair.

One day Mme. de Verseuil tried to talk to Pauline about her youth, the happiness of love, and the need to be loved. Pauline rejected this idea with horror. "Then I would have to reveal my disgrace to the man I chose—that or hide it from him!" said she. "I would rather die." She spoke these words with such energy and seemed disturbed for so long afterward that Mme. de Verseuil sought to distract her from these dark thoughts rather than to fight them.

Mme. de Verseuil was very far from judging her friend so strictly; she was thinking about arranging a marriage for her, burying the last year of Pauline's childhood in oblivion forever. The fact that Pauline was living in a new world favored such a plan. Mme. de Verseuil had been guided by a strong mind and pure morals all her life, but the extreme delicacy of a young, timorous soul looked more like madness than virtue to her. But her influence on Pauline did not go that far; she had been able to bring Pauline back to the path of honor, which she herself had never left, but Pauline's excessive remorse and regrets were beyond her.

Four years went by like this. Nothing could make Pauline agree to accompany Mme. de Verseuil on her trips into Le Havre. The sight of men horrified her; the only things she liked were solitary reading and Mme. de Verseuil's company. She acquired all sorts of knowledge, and developed her mind in many different ways. Her beauty grew in the quiet of solitude; there was no one more accomplished than Pauline at the age of nineteen. Something dreamy and wild gave her face a romantic quality, and the shock of admiration was a tribute no one who met her could deny her.

She had refused, as usual, to accompany Mme. de Verseuil on a trip to Le Havre, when she received a letter saying that her friend was sick with fever. Anxiety obliged Pauline to leave. She arrived in town to find Mme. de Verseuil recovered; she wanted to go home immediately, but her friend kept her in spite of herself. As soon as company arrived, however, Pauline locked herself away in her own apartments.

In the evening, Mme. de Verseuil reproached her, and said that her conduct had aroused the interest and curiosity of Count Edouard de Cerney, colonel of a regiment of dragoons garrisoned at Le Havre. She spoke of this young man with great enthusiasm.

Pauline paid very little attention, but the next morning she gave in to her friend's wishes and went with her to a fete given by the Count de Cerney. Many women went straight to the promenade; they all liked the Count de Cerney, but he had no preference among them. At the age of twenty-five, he lived alone most of the time; his first love was study, and the expressivity of his face convinced one of his sensitivity much more than his conduct could do. Friendship and love did not fill his life in any way; the only links anybody could have with him seemed to be benevolence and kindness.

This was how Mme. de Verseuil portrayed him to Pauline, as they were walking on the esplanade together. She did not notice that Pauline was being followed by all the young men of the town, exclaiming, "How beautiful she is!" and surrounding her with an eagerness which was beginning to be a nuisance.

"Why have you brought me here?" asked Pauline, very much disturbed. "That is what everyone kept saying in Saint-Domingue—that is what I cannot hear without horror."

The crowd was increasing, and Pauline's fear and distress were making her almost unable to stand, when Count Edouard broke his way through and came up to her. Seeing her agitation, he gave her his hand to lead her to the house nearby, saying, "This is the first time such tributes have ever inspired simple terror in anyone, madame. Since you wish to be protected from admiration, let me place you on one of these amphitheater steps and surround you with a few soldiers, so that the crowd will not be able to come near you." Pauline curtsied in reply; still trembling at the sight of society after four years of complete solitude, she followed Mme. de Verseuil, and placed herself on the raised amphitheater with her.

Somewhat reassured, she could not keep herself from admiring Count Edouard. His charming face portrayed both daring and sensitivity; a slight pallor aroused one's interest, and his glances were animated by courage and pride. Strong features marked his face, but his blond hair, his coloring, and his long eyelashes mingled sweetness and even shyness with a soldier's intrepidity.

For almost an hour the Count gracefully commanded his dragoons in their maneuvers. Every time he passed in front of Pauline, he bowed to her with an expression of respect remindful of the days of chivalry. During the last maneuver, he was about to end these military games when he heard the cries of a dragoon who was being trampled by a portion of his regiment. Moved by these cries, the young Count forgot his own danger. Twisting around on his horse, he was himself thrown in the cavalry charge, and disappeared under the horses' hooves.

Mme. de Verseuil rushed forward, terrified. Pauline was even more frightened, but she did not trust herself; her heart had flown ahead of her friend, but her footsteps followed more slowly. All the dragoons had gotten down from their horses in consternation. The man for whom Edouard had risked his life, who was only wounded, wanted to kill himself in despair.

Edouard had actually lost consciousness, and his breathing was impeded by a severe blow to the chest. He was carried back to Mme. de Verseuil's house, a portion of which contained his own living quarters. The surgeons arrived; they examined Edouard's wounds and then went directly outside to reassure his regiment, which was laying siege to the door.

Pauline drew near them to ask questions, but she could not pronounce a word; her face expressed her meaning so clearly, however, that they answered without waiting for her to speak. "His wounds are alarming," they said, "but with good care we can hope to save him." This answer threw her into such a deep reverie that for a moment she did not notice that she was alone in the midst of twenty officers. Suddenly realizing this, she hurried upstairs.

Back in her apartment, she was concerned by the agitation

in her own soul and frightenend by the concern she was feeling. The memory of her early faults had left her perpetually distrustful of herself, and much more apprehensive than a woman of unstained virtue. She therefore forbade herself to send for news of Count Edouard, an exaggerated scruple which made her spend five hours in useless agony.

Mme. de Verseuil had not left Count Edouard; she sent for Pauline, who went downstairs. Mme. de Verseuil then reproached her for her absence, saying that the Count had complained of it as soon as he regained his senses. "You must come and see him with me," she went on. "All the ladies are there, and your absence would be censured."[9] Pauline did not answer, and followed tremulously.

Count Edouard was greatly changed. It was impossible to see him without feeling touched—all the women showed it, and even exaggerated it as a point of honor in their own eyes and to impress Edouard. This last goal, however, they failed to achieve; Edouard answered their excessive sensibility with simple politeness.

When Pauline entered, however, he was deeply moved. She made such a brilliant appearance! All the other women were nothing in comparison. Edouard spoke to her more warmly and courteously; Pauline answered with such great reserve that he did not dare continue. She was obliged to stay as long as Mme. de Verseuil did, but as she scarcely spoke, the other women easily convinced themselves that this beautiful creature lacked even common sense, an opinion they expressed as soon as she had left the room. Edouard opposed this hotly, making them a speech on the principles of feminine virtue which they considered less than gallant on his part.

Despite Pauline's resistance, Mme. de Verseuil forced her to spend two hours of every day in Edouard's bedroom. He was spitting blood, and they feared for his lungs. How natural it is to love someone we are afraid of losing! It is also only natural for such a situation to make us aware of our interest more quickly. How closely the care we take of someone we favor connects us to him—and how necessary he becomes when he needs us!

The only way anyone could have noticed Pauline's feelings was by her altered countenance; no word or gesture betrayed her, and her willpower dominated everything she could control. But she was quietly observing Edouard, and everything she saw made her respect and admire him.

Edouard had an energetic soul. His only touch of youth was his exaggerated goodness; his mind was clear, though his heart might feel things too keenly. He had one fault—or perhaps virtue: this was the great austerity of his habits. He had been raised by a scrupulously virtuous father, now dead for two years. Filled with respect for his father's ideas and maxims, Edouard merely grew more convinced of them, perhaps exaggeratedly, whenever he met with opposition in society. He held to these notions partly out of love for his father, but also because of his own natural firmness. There was nothing severe in what he said or pedantic in what he did, nothing to alienate others; but he had such a keen, steady sense of perfection that he drew away from one friend after another because none of them could understand him. Whenever there was any question of helping them, he still thought he loved them, but these feelings did not contribute to his own happiness in any way. He had turned down the most advantageous matches, because no woman resembled the model of charm and virtue that his imagination and soul were hoping to find. His mind was already amazingly powerful, and capable of developing further; and his heated language did not impair the soundness of his reasoning.

Pauline was struck by all this. She often had to leave the room to hide her tears when Edouard, who secretly admired her modesty and reserve, took pleasure in speaking in front of her about some woman's virtue and sense of decency; or tried to make her understand that he could never love any woman less perfect than himself; or happily repeated that a woman's heart was not worthy of the same homage—worship—once it had known love. Far from loving Edouard less because of this, though, she approved of feelings which were in harmony with her soul, while they might censure her conduct.

Every day she found new reasons both to cherish Edouard and to leave him. She had never experienced such feelings. There is no comparison between this pure, tender love, mingling your life with someone else's, and the madness of a wild imagination, leaping ahead of happiness, taking the first thing that offers itself to view, and trying vainly to prolong its own illusion as soon as it is undeceived.

Pauline could read her own heart, and judge the force of the passion she was feeling, but she was so set on dominating it that Mme. de Verseuil could not guess at it. Trembling and diffident, Edouard did not dare address a single word of love to his beloved object. She would chat freely to him about indifferent things. Carried away by his own wit and Pauline's, he found great charm in these conversations. A lively interest seemed to animate whatever they said; they spoke of nothing together as they would have spoken to other people. But as soon as the Count tried to approach the subject he wanted so much to discuss, Pauline's cold, serious air forced him to stop immediately.

Meanwhile Edouard's health was no better, and it had been two months. Country air was prescribed, and Mme. de Verseuil offered him an apartment in her country house. Her dearest wish was to unite Edouard and Pauline, and she was partial to his sentiments. Pauline showed her great annoyance at this invitation, reproaching her friend keenly. This was so unlike her that it drove Mme. de Verseuil to complain of her ingratitude toward someone who wanted nothing but her happiness, and thought she could guarantee it by marrying her to Count Edouard.

Deeply moved, Pauline was sorry to have displeased her friend, and knelt before her in tears. "Have you forgotten who I am?" she cried. "What daydream are you chasing for me? What vile gift are you trying to give a man you love?"

"You are being cruel," Mme. de Verseuil answered. "Don't I have a right to judge you? Didn't I form your soul? Don't I know how well it deserves Edouard?"

"Then erase these degrading memories from my heart. If you make me capable of tolerating myself, maybe I will believe I can deserve other people's good opinion. Why should I hide it from you? Edouard is the most perfect object I could imagine; there is no doubt about that. But I have too much respect for myself to think I deserve him; it would cost me too much to entrust my shame to his virtue. I am condemned to the eternal torture of feeling an attachment I do not deserve to inspire. Nothing can save me from the spell the past has cast on my life. My new feelings have inspired my heart with keener regrets, but no new hope."

Edouard came in just as Mme. de Verseuil was about to reply. He saw that Pauline had been weeping; he rushed up to her. She covered her face, but he grasped her hand, pronouncing her name twice with great emotion.

"Never," she said, answering his thought, "never." She ran off instantly. Edouard remained motionless. Mme. de Verseuil tried to reassure him, blaming her niece's timidity and fear of forming new ties for the extraordinary emotions he had witnessed. She put new life into his hopes, and all three of them left for the country together.

Seeing and speaking to each other continually, Edouard and Pauline felt their passion grow every day, but Pauline's resistance seemed to increase in direct proportion to her admiration. This incomprehensible mystery drove her lover to despair; he begged Mme. de Verseuil to explain it, and her vague replies were not satisfactory.

One day while out for a walk and listening to Edouard praise the purity of Pauline's heart, Mme. de Verseuil asked him if he did not believe it possible to love and respect a woman who had recovered from the early wildness of her young days and had expiated it through her repentance.

"I believe her misdeeds are all obliterated before God and men," he answered. "There is only one person in whose eyes she cannot make amends, and that is her lover or husband. I am not considering this question as a moralist—it should generally be resolved by indulgence. But as a sensitive man capable of a love verging on idolatry, I do not hesitate to say that there can be no happiness with a woman whose memories are not pure. A woman like that is always anxious about the opinion her lover has of her; he himself is afraid of pronouncing a single word that might humiliate her, and this mutual distrust makes them feel that they are two separate beings. A woman's heart reaches its full perfection only when it is not conscious of itself. Impressions a woman recognizes, emotions she retraces never have the same strength. If this is the first time she is in love, despite her past errors, her heart has been withered before being touched; if she has already known love, she is always comparing her past experiences with what she is feeling now. Memories cast a spell over feelings; they are always more moving in the distant past. Then too, any woman who makes a second choice knows by experience that one may stop loving—and as soon as one conceives that idea, true love becomes impossible."

"How harsh! How unfair!" cried Mme. de Verseuil. "Do you really think a heart cannot be purified through repentance? Can't you see? A woman who has been unhappy in the wildness of her youth will attach herself all the more fervently to the man who forgives her for it! Don't you realize that she adds the bonds of gratitude to her passion, believing she owes her whole existence to this man? Some acts of wrongdoing are so foreign to the soul, so thoroughly excused by extenuating circumstances, that they are more like misfortune than faults."

"Possibly," replied Edouard, "but I want to marry someone I admire, not someone I forgive. I feel this so strongly that if I were in love with a woman who had all Pauline's charms without having always had her virtues, I would die of sorrow, but I would leave her. Not for my sake, but for hers. Not even because of her wrongdoing, perhaps, but because I would be aware of her wrongdoing, and because she would be unhappy and almost humiliated by the generosity I was practicing on her behalf."

These last words attracted Mme. de Verseuil's particular attention, because they seemed to confirm that she should follow her plan. She had an honorable soul, but she wanted to marry Pauline off at any price, and this fervent wish led her astray.

Edouard was showing himself to be so tender, speaking about his love with such energy and about his unhappiness with such dark despair, that Pauline had softened and was about to reveal her secret to him. In spite of everything, he did not guess it. Pauline would sometimes say to him, "An invincible obstacle is separating us: I am not worthy of you." But nothing could arouse suspicion in Edouard's heart; his enthusiasm for her was so great, and Pauline's character so perfect, her conduct so pure. Sometimes he would praise her with an enthusiasm which struck her to the quick, and pushed aside the unhappy admission that she was about to make.

At last one day Pauline went to see Mme. de Verseuil and portrayed her love for Edouard. "I have to choose between admitting my shame and sacrificing my love completely," she said. "I cannot go on seeing Edouard; I cannot nourish a feeling that will make him unhappy. I have to separate myself from this beloved object, or give him the strength to do it himself, by showing myself to him—not as I am, but as I have deserved to be judged."

The terrified Mme. de Verseuil then repeated part of her conversation with Edouard, with some alterations. She managed to capture Pauline's confidence, using her influence over her and, perhaps, the value Pauline placed on Edouard's love, which she was afraid of losing along with his respect. She drew a forceful picture of Edouard's austerity and swore to Pauline that he was wise enough to want to remain in ignorance of the faults of the woman he loved; strengthening the feelings of shame and modesty which had held Pauline back so many times, she obtained Pauline's promise to keep her fatal secret.

But nothing could keep Pauline from telling the Count to go away and renounce her forever, not even the pleas of her real mother, to whom she owed much more than life. She went to find Edouard. Speaking unceremoniously and very quickly, as she did not have the strength to maintain her self-control much longer, she asked Edouard to go away from her, and never to see her again.

On hearing these words, Edouard fell unconscious at her feet. Pauline nearly died at the sight; she called for help, and lavished all the tenderest names on him. Her broken, disconnected words at the moving spectacle of her beloved lover dying at her feet showed a passionate, despairing delirium. Mme. de Verseuil ran up; Edouard was brought back to life. Reassured, Pauline retired.

For two days, Mme. de Verseuil, acting as an interpreter between the lovers, tried in vain to shake her resolution. At last Edouard sent word to Pauline that he was leaving the following day. Pauline asked Mme. de Verseuil how he had spoken these terrible words. "Sadly and firmly," she replied. "That's all I noticed. You are ensuring his unhappiness and mine, Pauline, and that is not virtue." She left after making this reproach, leaving Pauline to her reflections.

It was a most beautiful evening, after a beautiful day. Pauline took up the harp she had played so many times for her lover. Flattering herself perhaps that chance might lead him under her window, she sang this romance; she had never dared let him hear it before, because it would have been enough to enlighten him:

> Edouard, do not follow me
> I do not deserve your trust
> I cannot live to make you happy
> But I can die for you, and must.
> From now on that's the only glory
> That can make my heart rejoice
> My memory's an open story
> While my life is your disgrace.
>
> Your heart so pure, which I admire,
> Lays down its law that we must part

I have profaned what it inspires,
The past has fastened on my heart.
Drunk with love, in vain I try
To look at future time-to-be
My soul is all too soon picked dry
By souvenir's dread agony.

I cherish yet the hopeful sense
That you might still feel love for me
But ah! despite this confidence
I must hasten now to die.
My secret could your trust destroy
And in the depths of pain I fear
I might, for one brief day of joy,
Deprive my tombstone of your tears.

After finishing her song, Pauline listened for a while. She could hear nothing. Situations conducive to some sort of explanation between her and her lover seemed to be slipping by her, and she lacked enough courage to make them happen. She had not gone outside because she was afraid of meeting Edouard, who was going to leave that very night. She would never see him again. He might think she was ungrateful, insensitive. She was gripped by remorse, blaming herself for a guilty personality, which had prevented her from making her lover think less of the value of what he was losing. All these reflections were aroused and reinforced by her need to hear the voice of the man she loved so madly.

At first she went down into the garden, hoping chance would be on her side. She walks out to the seaside, deep in reverie, dreaming of the unchanging tableau of the past and the frightening appearance of the future. Her soul rises from its melancholy depths toward heaven: nothing but the indulgence of heaven can blot out memories. Hidden by a grove of trees, she hears a noise and looks out toward the rock that protrudes into the sea. There she sees her lover on his knees, his hair disheveled, in an attitude of despair. She instantly guesses his plan—she is sure of it—and she is frightened by how long it will take her to reach him.

"Edouard!" she cries. "Edouard! Stop!"

He hears her voice, gets up, and sees her ready to rush toward him.

"Don't come near me! I would throw myself to the bottom of the sea to get away from your influence."

Pauline, afraid, does not dare approach. She falls on her knees, begging, "In the name of my love for you, Edouard!"

"Love! Cruel woman! You should say hate."

"Come down. Come here to me."

"No, no," he answers in fury. "You are going to enjoy this!" He makes a terrifying gesture.

"I am yours!" she cries out. "I am your wife." She could say no more; but he heard.

"Listen. Do not trick me. Swear that you love me before God—before this sea in which I would have found shelter—swear that your fate will be united to mine forever."

"I swear it." Pauline fainted as she spoke. Terror had captured her soul for a moment on the edge of flight; now that she felt reassured, she no longer had the strength to go on living.

Intoxicated by his own happiness, and perhaps also touched by having looked upon death at such close quarters, Edouard brought Pauline back to the château like a man deranged. He did not notice the danger of her condition: he believed she was listening to him and answering him. Mme. de Verseuil drew him out of this frightening self-absorption by taking care of Pauline. He was overjoyed, and as soon as Pauline had recovered consciousness he rushed into Le Havre to prepare the ceremony for the following day.

Mme. de Verseuil remained alone with Pauline. She pointed out forcefully that anyone who presented an obstacle to their union would be killing Edouard all over again. Pauline was not herself, shaken by the dreadful spectacle she had witnessed and the image of her lover ready to throw himself into the sea. The combination of the great happiness awaiting her and her awareness of her own imminent wrongdoing drove her into a sort of wild aberration; it was impossible to tell what the effects of it would be.

Edouard came back; Pauline would not utter a single word. He was anxious about his happiness, and well aware that he had stolen it. As he did not want to admit this to himself, he spoke only a few disconnected phrases, often contradicting himself, about Pauline's condition. Mme. de Verseuil did not leave them alone, and restrained her pupil by the influence of her presence. Anyone would have said that Edouard was

in league with Mme. de Verseuil to confirm what she had told Pauline;
he said again and again, as if still fearful, that his life depended on
Pauline's not changing anything; that he felt he could not possibly lose
any of his happiness without dying of the loss; that he had never experienced what he was feeling now; and that he had realized for the first
time that there are moments in life when one has no power over oneself
at all. He interrupted her whenever she tried to speak, afraid of hearing a
single word that might disturb the sensation of happiness he had so
recently begun to enjoy.

Pauline and Edouard had not been alone together for one
moment when the priest arrived that evening, though he had supposedly
been asked to come the following day. Pauline pronounced the vows so
dear to her heart as if she were consecrating herself a victim. Despite her
unhappiness, she had reassured her husband of her passion again and
again—if she had not done so, her obvious distress would have kept him
from accepting her hand. Certain of being loved, however, Edouard attributed her dreadful condition to modesty and eccentricity. Mme. de
Verseuil reinforced him in this notion, and his own happiness did the
rest.

As soon as the ceremony was over, Mme. de Verseuil took
Pauline aside, saying, "I am sure I do not need to tell you that you would
now be the world's guiltiest human being if you told your husband your
secret. You would wreck his happiness forever, and he would be absolutely right to blame you for a secret which you had kept and broken
just to make him miserable."

"No doubt!" said Pauline. "No doubt a first fault leads to
the second—but you are the person who had led me to it. You alone
have made your guilty Pauline criminal and desperate."

"Cruel," sobbed Mme. de Verseuil. "Am I so guilty for
burying a secret from which time and the sea will separate us forever? A
secret which you alone could tell your husband—and which he would
hate to know? Is this how you reward my affection?"

"My mother! my friend! Forgive me," cried Pauline. "Forgive me. The die is cast. Let him be happy. May you never be sorry for
what you have done for me!"

Edouard entered the room with a letter he had just
received, obliging him to go to Paris in a few days to look after his affairs.
He asked Pauline to go with him, but she begged him to let her live in

this solitude forever, and by dint of reminding him of her tastes and promises she finally obtained his permission.

The first days of Pauline and Edouard's marriage bore no resemblance to the start of what can be the happiest tie on earth, when it has been formed by love. Pauline was feeling unhappy and ashamed; she had a simultaneous desire and fear of speaking which must have looked extraordinary to her husband. Edouard attributed this trouble to timidity—though it bore no resemblance to timidity. All his fears were calmed by Pauline's distress at his departure and her passion for the solitude which would reunite them without any outside distraction.

At last he took his leave, a sad moment marked by Pauline's tears. He was away for two months, during which Mme. de Verseuil tore up several letters in which Pauline recited her faults. Pauline's uncertainty came to an end, however, when she realized she was pregnant; her mind was made up. She felt a need to bind the father to the mother through the child, and to the child through the mother, and she was less tormented by her secret.

Edouard came back, already intoxicated by the joy of being a father. When Providence combines this cherished bond with all the glamour of love, when the child one would love as one's own is also the image of the beloved object, when one finds the soul it is so sweet to know in the soul it is so sweet to develop—what greater happiness can there be than this intimate blend of sentiments so perfectly suited to the human heart? Cursed is the woman who has not known the joy of being a mother! A thousand times more cursed is the unfortunate woman who has known this joy and lost it, seeing in every passing year a year that should have increased her child's charms or virtues! And cursed is the woman who has received this boon without enjoying it, and whose heart fails to recognize this ineradicable, involuntary attraction!

Pauline and Edouard were able to enjoy this happiness. All their duties, quickened by the liveliest passion, occupied their minds. From the day on which Pauline gave birth to a son, she was truly happy. She pushed painful regrets away from her so as to busy herself with her husband, her son, and Mme. de Verseuil. She avoided conversations that might lead to the time of her first marriage. If these memories still cost her a few tears, she convinced herself that such pain was the way she was paying the tribute unhappiness exacts of human nature.

Alas! what a mistake! There is a sad law of fate that makes all destinies equal—though this is no consolation to the kindhearted, who would be better able to bear their own misfortune if they could contemplate other people who were happier.

Edouard had gone into Le Havre one day for dinner, and came back later than he had planned. When Pauline went to meet him, she saw an indescribable change on his face. He tried to deny it, but she was only the more convinced. Her emotion instantly grew so intense that Edouard was no longer master of the situation. He had not kept even a passing impulse secret from her for the last year; in such a union there are no secrets.

"Well, if that's what you want," said Edouard. "It may be annoying for you to see me angry when I should have been simply contemptuous, but my excuse must be my passion for you and your reputation. I was invited to dinner today by a businessman of our acquaintance. One of the guests was a stranger, newly arrived from Saint-Domingue; I did not know his name. The conversation fell upon the beauty of women, and a young officer said that the most beautiful woman he had ever seen was Mme. de Verseuil's pupil.

"'Who?' cried the stranger. 'Pauline de Gercourt, the widow of M. de Valville?'

"'Yes,' replied the officer.

"'Ah! I knew her very well,' continued the stranger. 'What you say is perfectly true, though if her character is as well developed as her features, she must be rather a lively one by now. When she left Saint-Domingue at the age of fourteen, she had given in to inclination only twice. I can well believe that you must all have managed to conquer such strict principles since that time.'

"I was beside myself with fury. At first people tried to warn him about our marriage, but I insisted on silence. The stranger kept up his horrible slander; by the time he finally realized his imprudence I had covered him with insults which made him unable to take it all back. His name is Meltin."

As Edouard was finishing his story, Pauline's face grew deathly pale; her whole body was trembling, and her violent agitation prevented her from uttering a single word. Edouard looked at her with an indescribable mixture of astonishment and terror. Pauline's tongue had frozen; was this from indignation, or some other sentiment? Could this possibly offer some interpretation of the inexplicable mystery which had delayed her marriage to him for so long—and those repeated speeches of hers, which never seemed to make any sense? A terrible light began to spread over the past, bleaching the future of color.

The two of them remained in this horrible situation for some time. Suddenly Edouard was afraid that Pauline suspected him of not having rejected this mortal injury courageously enough, and she kept silent because she felt unable to say so. "I am to meet him tomorrow," he said. "Filthy liar that he is."

Pauline understood these words only too well; they gave her the strength to speak. "No, you will not see him again," she cried. "The man is not a liar. He spoke the truth. He himself was one of the choices disgracing me; the other man died here, in this very place. I hid my disgrace from you to keep your respect. Losing it is only fair; dying of it bliss; but if my passion for you has earned me your pity, give up this horrible duel—I am not worth it. Spare me that torture. Kill me—but not by a torture worse than any crime! I beg it of you. I expect no less of your pity."

Edouard could no longer hear her. He felt annihilated; the destruction of the world would have surprised him less. Everything seemed as if it were crumbling away before his eyes. For a moment he thought Pauline had been driven wild by fear for the danger he would be running. He seized on this gleam of hope.

"Calm down," he cried. "Some kind of crazy madness must be driving you wild." As he spoke these words, he tried to hold her to his heart.

"Do not come near me," said Pauline with somber dignity. "I am not worthy of you. You will find me again in the arms of death; I will speak to you again then, and only then. Leave me now." Edouard, on the ground before her, felt both fear and respect.

During this dreadful moment, Mme. de Verseuil entered the room. Pauline shuddered at the sight of her. "Madame," said she, "I have followed your advice. Behold the result." Then, in a stifled voice, she explained what had just happened to her husband. "You can imagine whether or not I can go on living now," she went on. "But help me make Edouard give up this dreadful duel; it is torturing me. It is my last wish."

What a dreadful moment for Mme. de Verseuil! She was sorry for her disastrous advice, but as she was still eager to make excuses

for Pauline she told Edouard the whole story of the extenuating circumstances of his wife's first wrongdoing, and the force she herself had
exerted to prevent her from revealing it.

Edouard seemed to be listening most closely to this last part
of Pauline's justification. When Mme. de Verseuil had finished speaking,
he turned back toward Pauline. Her disfigured face struck terror into his
soul, and he threw himself at her feet.

"Pauline," he said to her, "Pauline—do you think I no
longer love you?"

"You love me!" she cried. "You love me—oh thank God.
My last moments will not be so dreadful, and my child will sometimes be
able to speak his mother's name." This tender impulse was quickly
followed by another emotion, however, and she knelt before Edouard,
begging him not to go back to Le Havre.

Edouard soon made Pauline aware that what she was asking
for was his dishonor. She said a prayer for a few minutes, convinced of
this horrible truth. Then, as she rose, she turned toward Edouard, who
had seen day break and was already counting the minutes until his
departure.

"This sunrise may be the last for the two of us," she said to
him. "I can no longer live for my husband; but I still have the right to die
for him. Bless your child," she went on, leading Edouard to the cradle. "I
can bless him too, because I know my remorse has led me to God's
mercy. As for you," she added, "you whom I still adore, let me tell you
something while you are kneeling in prayer. You are about to risk your
life for me. My wrongdoing and my disastrous dissimulation are leading
you into this terrible danger—but you are kind and generous; you still
feel pity for me, because you know in your heart that I am suffering."

Edouard tried to speak to her. "Do not say anything at all,"
she answered. "Everything has been said already." The hour was ap-
proaching; Edouard leaves. With the courage born of despair, Pauline
sees him to the door and says goodbye.

Uneasy at this apparent tranquillity, Mme. de Verseuil anx-
iously followed everything Pauline did. She was terrified to see her walking at the edge of the sea. "Be calm," Pauline told her. "Do I need to kill
myself? Is there any doubt that unhappiness will do it for me?"

Two mortal hours went by this way, more dreadful for
Pauline perhaps than for someone still hoping for happiness. A messenger arrives, carrying a letter for her from Edouard.

I have had the misfortune to kill my adversary. Whatever his guilt, his death makes me tremble. This cruel business will keep me here a few hours longer. I beg Pauline, whom I will always hold dear, to keep calm as she waits.

"See for yourself," said Pauline to Mme. de Verseuil. "A man's death falls on me—I am the one who has made Meltin die. I am surrounded by so many horrible things! So many crimes! You are my mother—save me." Mme. de Verseuil, desperate herself, tried to calm this mortally wounded creature, but in vain.

The two women saw Edouard return. Pauline did not dare to go meet him. He came toward her, but it was easy to see that he was already afraid of not showing her enough attention. He pretended to be at a distance from the painful subjects that were tearing away at him. Pauline, observing this effort, knew that he was thinking about them much more than if he had spoken about them.

Edouard could see that Pauline was changing day by day. "Have I not stayed the same for you?" he asked.

"You have grown better," she said, "but you are not the same. Do you see that shadow following me, that man whose death I caused? Do you see a future for our troubled happiness and your lost faith in me? Let me die, Edouard."

Edouard was the unhappiest of men. His character made it impossible for him to forget a wrong that had touched him so deeply, and his love for Pauline made him afraid to show his pain. Anxious and disturbed when he was near her, he would often walk out alone. Pauline did not dare go look for him, staying near her child's cradle. He would find her there bathed in tears, and try to speak to her, but she always interrupted him. Uncertain himself about what he meant to say, he would talk about something else. Mme. de Verseuil kept blaming herself for the advice she had given Pauline, because what was driving Edouard to despair was the fact that Pauline had made her faults a mystery to him.

Time might have made this retreat happy once again, but one morning one of Pauline's maids came to tell Edouard that her mistress had been disturbed by a burning fever all night long. Edouard sends for a doctor instantly, and runs to Pauline's room to find her delirious, repeating his name over and over with these words: "He does not love me anymore!" What a spectacle! What remorse he felt! He banished every other notion from his heart. This was his Pauline, just as he had loved her, just as she had once been in his eyes; this was the woman he loved.

Mme. de Verseuil, seated next to Pauline's bed, was even more frightened. She knew the heart she had shaped; she had judged the depth of its despair. The doctor arrived, and seemed anxious. Edouard encouraged the doctor to deceive him, rejecting a terror that might tear away at him too sharply.

Three days went by like this, and Pauline did not recover her reason. The things she said were all the more touching. Her delirium made her repeat the beloved name whenever it entered her mind; she kept expressing the idea ruling her mind in the same words, as it invariably made her unhappy each time in exactly the same way, which gave her husband fresh pain at every moment.

Three days later she finally became rational again; Edouard believed her life was saved. Pauline noticed this error, which was not shared by the unhappy Mme. de Verseuil. "My dear," she said to him, "let this illusion go; it could make the moment of our separation very bitter. We must say goodbye forever."

"Cruel!" Edouard cried. "You are the one who wants to leave me—it is you who despise me enough to be suspicious about my affection! Very well: I forswear everything I believed before knowing you—I swear at your feet that you are as perfect, as sublime, in my heart as in the happy days we had together. Time and love have purified your soul. Live to raise your child; live to be adored by an unfortunate man who believes that he alone is guilty."

"Do not believe that my death is the result of a fanatical imagination, exaggerating in my eyes faults erased before God by my remorse," replied Pauline. "I believe God has forgiven me, and I die unafraid. But happiness in love depends on more subtle feelings. The errors of my youth—and the greater wrong of hiding them from you—have faded that happiness forever; its very perfection made it incapable of change. By dying I feel worthy of you. It proves the excess of my passion for you; it is the last memory I leave you, the only one that comes to mind when the beloved object exists no longer. Look, Edouard, how happy I am to annihilate the barriers separating your soul from mine. We will be together again in heaven, and until that moment my image will remain in your heart exactly as it used to be. And you, my mother," she went on, turning to Mme. de Verseuil, "you to whom I own the feelings and perhaps the virtues which honor and console me! Console Edouard, and watch over our child with him."

      Pauline's child was brought to her bed. Her husband's cries, her child's caresses, and Mme. de Verseuil's tears exhausted her strength; little by little she grew weaker and died. I will not portray the despair of her husband and Mme. de Verseuil. After Pauline, how could anybody else possibly be of interest? I will simply say that Mme. de Verseuil's days were shortened by sorrow and the remorse she felt for the advice she had given Pauline. As for Edouard, devoured by regret and tormented by the well-deserved apprehension that he had been unable to conquer his character while there was still time, he locked himself away in absolute solitude, where he lived only to raise the child so precious to him because of his love for Pauline.

ZULMA, A FRAGMENT

Foreword

This episode was originally intended to take the place of the chapter on love in the work *On the Influence of the Passions*, the first chapter of which I have just published. As I then decided to keep that whole book analytical, I am printing this piece separately. I tried, in portraying love, to present the most terrifying picture possible, the most passionate in character. It seemed to me that this emotion could possess the maximum energy imaginable only in the combination of a savage soul and a cultivated mind, because the faculty of judging increases unhappiness greatly, when it has not reduced one's ability to feel. Finally, I tried to find a situation of despair and calm all at once, in which the unhappy being was capable of observing its own self, and was obliged to portray what it was feeling. Such a being is not, therefore, in the more appealing but less bitter state of disturbance in which one loses the ability to express oneself. When misfortune is irrevocable, the soul recovers a sort of sangfroid that permits it to think coolly, while it is still suffering. In such a condition passion must be at its most eloquent: that is where I tried to put Zulma. My excuse for these observations is the interest I take in this piece of writing, which belongs to my soul more than anything else I have done.

I was a prisoner of the savages who live on the shores of the Orinoco. My ransom had been requested, however, so I enjoyed some liberty among them. A long stay in their country had given me the opportunity to learn their language, and an old man I had once known on one of his journeys to Lima was particularly friendly.[10] His age entitled him to take part in their government; as these savages have no notion of property, the primary base of all social relationships, the leaders chosen by their nomadic tribes were men whom long experience had given a sense of conservation, which is the guardian angel of human destiny.

The sound of military instruments awoke me one morning; at first I thought the war had broken out again. My aged protector came and said to me, "This is the cruelest day of my life. I am to give my fellow citizens a painful proof of devotion: chance and my age make them call on me to judge a guilty person. Seven of us are condemned to this unhappy duty. They say the crime we are to hear about is unpardonable—but when I hear my voice pronounce the death sentence, how can I be sure in my tortured heart that I am not abusing the rights one man can have on another? How can I be sure I am not preempting divine vengeance? I will not see you for a week after pronouncing sentence. That is our custom: judges who have pronounced the death sentence are locked up alone for a week, reassembling again afterward to confirm or vacate their judgment. In your country, the decisions of the first tribunal are reviewed by a second. Here, we appeal from social man to solitary man, from a momentary impression to eternal conscience. We bless this procedure, which often makes us revoke our severe judgments.

"Follow me, my friend, to the enclosure where the case is being tried; it will be done in public. You will see the family of the accused—even more anxious than he is, because our laws banish the parents of a guilty child, and they often die of misery and isolation in the desert. This fatal responsibility is a prejudice we share with you. Compound errors are frequently accepted before the most natural truths! But as our nomadic habits do not let our government supervise us in a complete and constant way, we may have needed to seek every possible means of tightening family ties. This retroactive punishment has had that good result, whatever you may think of it otherwise. Come and listen

carefully, then, to the various motives they will explain to us. If you excuse a crime I might be ready to condemn, be quick to tell me so. Save
your friend from the irrevocable pain of murdering an innocent man."

I therefore followed the good old man toward the great
plain where everyone had gathered. I was amazed to get so close without
any noise warning me of the many men gathered there.

"They are collecting their thoughts in the contemplation of
unhappiness and death," said the old man. "They are brave warriors and
they weep for dangers they do not share."

I took my place behind the tribunal, among the crowd. In
the distance was a latania palm surrounded by cypress. That was the tree
criminals had to face when they were condemned to die; the executioner's bow hung from one of its branches. In front of the judges was
the amphitheater destined for the accuser, the accused, and his family.

As I approached the amphitheater, I saw a young man
pierced by a deadly arrow lying on a bed of grass. His blood had stopped
flowing and his limbs were stiff, but I had never seen such beauty in all
my life. I felt a simultaneous pain and admiration, and wept for this
young man as if I had known him when he was alive.

"That is the man who has just been murdered," I was told.
Filled with horror, I condemned the murderer in my heart. The young
man's mother was at his feet; she lifted her veil to speak, but her misery
kept her from expressing herself. The name of her son Fernand escaped
her lips several times, and through her sobs she seemed to be accusing a
young girl named Zulma of his murder. Seeing my wonder, the people
around me explained the words of this unfortunate mother.

At that moment, Zulma appeared. I was seized by an impression of misery as I looked at her face. She approached me slowly, which
gave me time to notice the charm of her features, but soon my soul was
gripped by their expression, and stirred by each of the various emotions
portrayed in succession on her face. She passed in front of the fatal tree
destined for her execution, and paused a few instants to look at it. I
could see nothing but great attentiveness on her face: not the slightest
sign of emotion. She bowed to the judges with respect and dignity. Then,
as she turned to go toward the amphitheater, she caught sight of Fernand's body. Her limbs trembled at the sight. She leaned on her bow at
first; then she tried to move closer to the dreadful object. When she
recognized the desolate mother shuddering at her approach, however,

she stopped and sighed deeply. Making a great effort, she collected her wits and began to speak.

"Honorable woman," she said to Fernand's mother, "forgive me for not speaking to you alone. I cannot look for long on what you are holding in your arms. There is still some question of my living, so this is not the moment for me to look at it. I have to justify myself to save my parents the shame of my execution—I have to do that, and I can do it, to the judges and the people. But you! Unfortunate mother, you loved him. You need nothing but my death. I do not think that your grief can be intensified by what I am about to say in my own defense; woe on me if I cannot sense what might afflict and wound your heart! What would be the use of all this suffering, if I had not learned how to spare pain?"

Zulma stopped at that point; shortly afterward, however, she got up in front of the tribunal which was to decide her fate, apparently trying to stifle in herself all the emotions which demand pity. "Judges of my fate," she told them, "I shot that bloody arrow into Fernand's heart. I alone have done it; and your laws condemn me to death. Before God, though, I do not believe myself to be guilty. You are a proud people: you will absolve me. Old men, hear the language of the passions. Call your memories back to your hearts, and let the long history of my feelings be their own interpreter of their amazing catastrophe.

"You are all weeping for Fernand: you remember his charm, his talent, his bravery. And you are right: not even a man of delirious vanity could have thought himself his equal. As a child Fernand was the prisoner of a Spanish general, so he had learned the terrible, seductive arts which capture and captivate others in civilized countries. But his proud soul could not suffer the yoke of European laws. He came back among us so as to find himself in the presence of nature once again, instead of being separated from it by the very institutions which seem as if they should perfect it. You remember that day when he won the prize for hunting, thanks to the new arts he had wrested from our enemies? He was indignant at a success that he did not owe to his own strength. He was too proud to use the skills he had gained in the various tasks to which your trust had called him—he was so independent of them that we even doubted their usefulness! In this land where the law establishes no distinction, Fernand seemed to create for himself the majesty of genius. He did not wish for it; the people themselves did not realize they were paying him homage; but the ranks opened to let him pass, in the hope of seeing him better. He was followed—not through servility, but because people wanted to stay close to him. His invincible charm acted on all of you—you who are listening to me—and on your old men, your children, even people who might have been envious of him. Every one of them was his friend before there was time to think of becoming his rival. Ah! Go on weeping for him, because his life was your glory, and his death bereaves the world.

"But the world must die, when passion so commands. The storm born secretly in the depths of the heart overturns all nature. Everything seems peaceful around me; only I know that the earth has trembled, and is about to gape open under my feet.

"While you were all admiring Fernand, a more tender feeling had begun to grow in my heart. I sought out the crowd to hear his name pronounced. Your voices would cry, 'Long live Fernand!' and I would lower my veil to repeat those words. I was following everyone's example, but trembling lest I attract attention. I had no hope of controlling myself enough to pass for merely enthusiastic. I was crying 'Long live Fernand!' and it is through me that he is dead. Love alone could have sacrificed him; what man's hatred could have invented this horror?

"Fernand singled out my face—unrecognizable today, marked by the stamp of his death. Fernand spoke to me! That day is so present to me now that its memory still brings with it a sensation of joy. My embarrassment intrigued him; he pretended he could not guess the reason for it, and insisted on trying to please me exactly as if he had not been sure of being loved. He concerned himself with teaching me what he had learned in his travels, he managed to make me understand the books of the Europeans—and it is to that very study that I owe the talent with which I can portray the frightful image of my misery to you.

"I grasped at Fernand's lessons eagerly; my memory did not lose the least little trace of them. Could I forget any word his voice had spoken? The care he was taking to shape my mind and soul seemed to me an absolute guarantee of his fidelity. He was trying to identify me with his own ideas, to direct my thoughts and feelings according to his opinions, his character. He knew perfectly well that to learn to live without him I would have had to be born again! He knew Zulma no longer had a single independent faculty with which to detach herself from Fernand! Everything that constitutes man's control over himself—the power of reflection, the gift of ideas—in me all that was Fernand's work, and could not rebel against its author. For me, the connection between ideas and the interrelationship of objects was all Fernand. Once cut off from the man who had constituted it, my soul could do nothing but despair.

"In the beginning, I realized the danger I was in. I could feel my passion growing every day, and judging that I had almost no time left to control it I decided to talk to Fernand about the anxieties he was caus-ing me. I asked him to follow me to the pine forest on the Orinoco shore, choosing a wild shelter where no trace of mankind could break the spell of our solitude. That was where I questioned my lover, in the presence of the pure sky and the rushing river—pure and turbulent as my soul.

"'I know nothing of human destiny,' said I. 'I have just em-erged from childhood through the violent passion of youth, and I can glimpse a happiness which belies everything people say about the imper-fection of man's condition. Why is everyone so afraid of love, if the heart can gain such sweet delights? Why isn't love the religion of old age and youth alike, the first hope, the only regret, the only motive with which anyone would try to govern the universe?'

"Fernand made no attempt to enlighten me as to the nature of the passions. He accused the insensitivity of men, and swore he would love me always.

"'Listen,' I said. 'Listen. If you do not need me for your hap-piness, if your heart is not sure it needs mine to exist, leave me. I love you—but that feeling began to rule my heart only a little while ago. It has still not transformed me completely. Every path still does not retrace your footsteps for me; every day is not yet marked once and for all as the anniversary of what you said or how you looked. In life, in space, in my mind, I still have sanctuaries in which to run away from you. Habit and passion—such contradictory powers!—have not forces to enslave me yet. But if you once let my heart say "Fernand will never leave me!" I am done for. And you will be the one responsible for my existence.

"'But the heart of man is independent of his will: so I will ask nothing of you except a vow which will always be in your power to keep. If you ever feel that your soul is ready to break itself off from mine, swear that you will kill me before I could find out. You tremble at the word; your fear is misplaced. Oh, Fernand! you should have been trem-bling for me when I was talking about your infidelity. What false pity could make you fear the end of my life more than an eternity of my des-pair! Is it possible that we do not understand each other?'

"Fernand reassured me with tender expressions inspired by his love and interpreted by mine. Everything else faded from my sight—parents, friends, country. This universe is said to be the work of a single idea; for me it became the image of a unique, all-powerful feeling. Multiplied by its own passion, my soul gave Fernand everything it could think of to make him happy—the most tedious errands, the most ingenious, painstaking attentions. I could tell you the countless things I did that cry out for gratitude, things that would form a sacred bond between two friends or comrades in arms. But when all the powers of the heart are concentrated on one object alone, what difference does it make which particular combination of random events gives that devotion a more or less favorable chance to prove itself? Passion paints its own self-portrait, all by itself. Nothing that derives from it is its equal; the heat of its rays can be felt only at its own sublime hearth.

"I will sketch my story for you quickly, though. There was a day when Fernand's mother was carried away by the current of the great river which makes our country fertile and keeps it from harm. She would have died in the waves, if I had not thrown myself in after her and found enough strength to carry her back to shore. At that instant Fernand ran toward us. 'Here is your mother,' cried I. 'I have lived long enough.' As I spoke those words I lost consciousness, but when I regained it Fernand was at my feet, thanking me for his mother's life. The pleasure of owing her life to me was already mixed with the joy of having her back. His love was painted in every tone of his voice, and reigned supreme in his soul. Ah! his gratitude was so charming that if his voice could still be heard, he would have the right to ask me if *he* was not *my* benefactor, at least for that moment. Cruel! Should you have let anyone you were going to abandon taste such intoxicating rapture? Was that any way to prepare me for losing you? Was my soul, plunged deep in the ecstasy of love, learning to save some strength for the onslaught of misery?

"A day came when slander led you to misjudge Fernand. You accused him of being in league with your enemies, of plotting to deliver you to their power. His sentence of death had been pronounced. You shudder, but you were the ones who decided on his death—the greatest crime in the world for anyone but Zulma. The ingenuity of my love managed to hide him from your sentries—but please do not think I am reminding you of that time in order to accuse Fernand of ingratitude. Far be it from me to call anything prompted by an irresistible impulse of my soul a good deed! But I look at myself with amazement when I see the very object I saved from unthinkable dangers for so many days murdered by my own hand. I believe I am my own enemy, I no longer know where I live. The only way I can recognize myself through the horror and the contrast between my feelings and my misfortunes is by putting my hand on my heart, and feeling it still consumed by the same passion.

"For one year I followed Fernand into the deserts where your cruel verdict forced him to hide out. In those barren places, he often came close to lacking the necessities of life. A spring or palm tree would mark an epoch in our lives. I would sometimes unpin my long locks of hair and hold them up in my hands as he slept to shield his head from the burning rays of the sun. I do not know whether or not I suffered during that dreadful time. I was so completely devoted to the hope of softening some of his pains that I can remember nothing about that year except the memory and impression of a single feeling. My last memories of happiness are associated with fearful rocks and burning sands. When his country had rejected Fernand and nature itself abandoned him, refusing him the food of life, a woman surrounded him with tenderness and love. Still sovereign in the desert, he could see life and happiness depend on one of his glances. My self-abandon and enthusiasm reminded him of power and glory. My love was always there to interpose itself between his reflections and men's injustice. He judged himself in my heart; he loved me, he lived—oh, God!"

Zulma's voice was stifled by sobs at this point. As she was painting this picture of her happiness, I had watched her strength gradually abandoning her. I looked at the old men, still motionless and stern as if they considered Zulma's condemnation inevitable. More easily touched, the crowd was murmuring the world "mercy."

This noise brought Zulma to herself, and she immediately went on speaking. "People," she cried, "you are too quick to forgive the greatest of crimes. I am outraged for Fernand's sake at such quick mercy. Listen to me. In the end, Fernand's fellow citizens saw the light about his virtues and talents. You came in search of him, offering your admiration and esteem. Trusting his noble soul, with good reason, you brought him back from exile to be the commander in chief of your armies. He accepted the command, despite my prayers. My ardent pleas could not dissuade him. I was horrified at his danger, and I had no more need of his glory. In the early days of my passion, I had loved anything that could justify its excesses. Sometimes I had even been proud of Fernand's triumphs, daring to think he was secretly proud of dedicating them to me. At this point, though, what external event could decrease or increase our love? My soul had passed into his, so that what he needed before me was not actions but feelings, exactly as if before the tribunal of his own conscience.

"He left, all the same. Three times he came back victorious: the rumors of his triumphs told me I was happy. Every time he left me, dreadful forebodings filled me with terror. I realize that the feelings people call supernatural are caused by wild unhappiness; the soul's own ruling passions act on it as if with some outside inspiration, making it believe its own impressions are oracles. But isn't that what anyone would want—for the soul to be warned of the onset of great misery, as the earth trembles before the abyss gapes open, and the sky is covered with clouds before the lightning strikes?

"One day there was a rumor that Fernand had died in battle. I wandered through the horrors of the battlefield, but the spectacle made no impression on me, despite the fact that I was seeing it for the first time. Through all the blood and dead bodies, what I was looking for was Fernand. That dreadful sight was simply an obstacle I had to overcome. Hours later, exhausted, I collapsed at the foot of a tree. There, in the violence of such deep unhappiness that I felt myself exist only through my pain, I tried to calm myself by remembering my early decision not to outlive Fernand. 'What is there about his death that I cannot escape by dying myself?'

"But what frightened me more than eternity was the instant I would have to live through in order to hear that Fernand was no longer alive. My mind could not find peace, even in the grave into which his death was about to dash me. My mind had never been able to imagine absolute nothingness, and I could see myself pursued by the attack of pain like this in whatever form I existed. Absorbed in paralyzed despair, examining myself with ferocious attention, I saw Fernand appear. Good God! What I had regained was not life, but heaven. I had all kinds of contradictory feelings—it was he! My soul grew weak with the weight of its own joy. Anyone who lives through a day like that uses up the existence of many years; for me there is no more time. Even now, my God, down in the pit of human miseries, I thank you for having existed. You collected for me in one day all the various good things of life. That day, my passionate soul was able to touch the limits separating human nature from your divine essence.

"Fernand was wounded lightly; but we soon learned that our savage enemies had dipped their arrows in deadly poison, and that the only way for him to be saved was for someone who was not afraid of the danger to suck his wound. I felt as if destiny was taking such good care of my happiness! I was going to make the poison threatening Fernand's life pass into my veins. Ah! in all the melancholy fantasies capable of pleasing tender souls, what more enjoyable situation could ever happen! I overcame his resistance, I deceived him as to the dangers I would be running; my successful efforts plucked death from his breast. Then it was my turn for a long struggle against death; the strength of my youth won out. People say that the destructive powers of that cruel poison disturbed my mind; this is not my excuse, or Fernand's either. My other ideas may have been thrown into confusion, but as long as I was alive my love had not changed in any way. Zulma was the same for Fernand: he had no right not to recognize her. Oh! there is no explanation for my crime, except my heart. What impulses of madness could be as strong as the madness of the very passion they were being used to justify?[11]

"Fernand asked if he could leave me for a few days. Feeling bitterly sorry for myself, I fought against this decision. What made me think I had some rights over Fernand was not my good deeds, but memory, the impression of my old feelings: that was what made me believe in my power over him. It seemed to me as if I had within my soul a power of love that should have dominated him, that a man so passionately beloved could not think that he was free. Suspicion could not come near me; that uncertain feeling was not suited to my soul. In the end I agreed to Fernand's wishes, and he left.

"At the time set for his return, I was waiting for him. On a day like any other, lit by the same rays of the sun, I was walking by myself, weak, lost in those very places which were still so full of the past. I was going into the heart of the forest, when I caught sight of Fernand at the feet of the young Mirza. That is the last thing my eyes ever saw. That dreadful tableau is all before me now, keeping me from seeing the preparations for my execution. The sight of them would be sweeter to me. I had no time to reflect, I acted without thinking, my hand seized the bow on which it was resting and the fatal arrow was launched; Fernand fell. At first I could think of only one thing: he had stopped loving Mirza. But when his blood began to flow, and the pallor of death . . . I don't know what was going on within my being. I lost my identity afterward, the memory of my existence. The only thing that could bring me to myself was the despair of my family; they came to tell me that my conviction would necessarily result in theirs, so that I had to justify myself to save them. They still want to live. I have had to obey them.

"You have heard my story. None of you has felt the slightest doubt as to its truth; not one tone of my voice can have sounded like an imitation. You are unjust if you condemn me now. Which of you can think himself more suited to avenge Fernand's death than I am? Which of you has saved his life a thousand times? which of you still loves him now? I had the right to pronounce his fate: if my heart judged him guilty, which of you dares to pardon him? Should his glory have been tainted and his name be borne by someone who was no longer Fernand? I have rescued my lover: he has remained immortal, his shade applauds my courage. I am sure no hatred touched his heart as he lay dying. No—no tribunal, no nation, not even heaven can judge between Fernand and me. The love which united me to him cannot make anyone mad or criminal. It is above men's laws and opinions. It is truth, the flame, the pure element, the first idea of the moral world. The feelings which give all of you life are only a faded imprint of it. Death, which man considers the most terrible and absolute thought, vanished completely in the presence of the thought occupying my mind. What is Fernand's life, or mine, compared to that love which is enough for eternity?

"Let men abstain from judging things that are not within their province. Let my heart pronounce its own verdict. Can you invent any form of torture which would not be a relief to me? You will punish only my family, which is innocent, ignorant of emotions which nothing can inspire or restrain. Save them the shame of my conviction. Listen to me when I tell you that such a verdict would be unjust. Do you think me blind about myself? Do you think me deceived by self-interest? Ah! Zulma is the most impartial of all her judges. Even my parents' safety could not make me resort to deception—and how could I? I exist so strongly in myself that it is beyond my power to show myself as other. Fernand's ghost, listening to me, fills me with more respect than you do. People, I have spoken. Old men, judge me."

With these words, Zulma stopped speaking. The emotion she had inspired kept the crowd silent for one more moment, but as soon as her voice could no longer be heard dark, tumultuous cries arose in her favor. Either the judges shared the crowd's emotions, or they thought it impossible to resist; Zulma's pardon was granted. Her family surrounded her; the people, always extreme, tried to crown her, as if on a day of victory.

"Stop," she cried. "Is my family absolved?"

"Yes," they shouted.

"Their daughter's name will never be cast up to them?"

"Never."

"Then the long task is over." And with an unforeseen motion, she took one of the arrows hanging at her side and buried it in her breast. A wave of terror and astonishment seized those around her.

"Did you think I would let Fernand's murderer live?" she asked, with a last effort. "If I had been able to exist without him, his unfaithfulness would have been justified." She turned toward Fernand's body and his unhappy mother. "Sacred objects," she cried. "I can look at you now, Fernand. And you, his mother; let me draw near him. Does not my trail of blood give me the right to come toward you? I am going to rejoin Fernand in that land where he can love only me, where man is free from everything except love and virtue. We will both wait for you there. I am dying . . . "

The unfortunate Zulma fell lifeless at the feet of her lover's mother. At that moment the unhappy woman seemed to mingle these two objects, the one sacrificed by the other, in her tenderness and pity. But she very soon succumbed under the weight of maternal sorrow, seeming to lose consciousness of an existence which old age gave at least some promise of bringing to an end.

4.

The Influence of the Passions
on the Happiness
of Individuals and Nations

Quaesivit caelo lucem, ingemuitque reperta.[1]

Foreword

The author may be thought overeager for publishing part I of her book before part II is written. In the first place, each of these parts can be considered as a separate work, despite their interconnections; but it may also be true that, since I am condemned to celebrity without being understood, I feel a need to make myself be judged through my writings. Constantly slandered, and finding myself so unimportant that I cannot resolve to talk about myself, I have given in to the hope that by publishing the fruit of my meditations I could offer some true notion of the habits of my life and the nature of my character.

Lausanne, July 1, 1796

Introduction

What a time I have picked to write a treatise on the happiness of individuals and nations! Have I really done this right in my middle of a disastrous crisis touching everyone's destiny, when lightning is striking the valleys and high places alike? at a time when being alive is enough to drag one into universal commotion? a time when peace is disturbed even in the grave's embrace, when the dead are judged anew, and the urns dedicated to them by the people are being thrown out of the temple in which political factions had thought to immortalize them?[2]

Yes: I have done this now, when the human race has risen up out of hope or the need for happiness—in this century when we have been led to reflect more deeply than ever before on the nature of individual and political happiness, on the way to achieve it, on its limitations, on the rocks separating us from such a goal. I would have been ashamed if I had been capable of writing this work during the two terrible years of the Reign of Terror in France; if I had been able to imagine any plan, or foresee any result to that horrible mélange of human atrocities! Perhaps the next generation will examine the cause and effect of those two years; but we, the contemporaries and compatriots of the victims sacrificed in those days of blood, how could we have been able to generalize ideas, meditate on abstractions, separate ourselves for a moment from our impressions so as to analyze them then? No—even today, the rational mind cannot come anywhere near that incommensurable time. To judge those events—whatever words one uses to designate them—is to make them reenter the order of existing ideas, ideas for which there already were words or expressions. At that horrible image, all the impulses of your soul are born anew: you shudder, you are on fire, you want to fight, you wish you were dead; but your thinking mind still cannot grasp any of these memories, because the sensations created by them absorb every other faculty. I will therefore try to assemble some impartial observations about government without referring to this monstrous time, using some of the other main events of the French Revolution and the history of all nations. If these reflections lead me to agree with the first principles of France's republican constitution, I ask that even now—even amid the furors of partisan spirit tearing apart France, and through France the rest of the world—the reader should be able to imagine that enthusiasm for certain ideas is not mutually exclusive with contempt for certain men, and that hope for the future may be reconcilable with hatred for the past. Then, even though the heart is forever torn by its wounds, the mind can still, after a while, rise to general meditations.*

---

*It seems to me that the true partisans of republican liberty are those who feel the deepest hatred for the wrongs committed in its name. Their adversaries may certainly feel the just horror of the crime, but as these very crimes are useful arguments for their theories, they cannot make these adversaries feel all the varieties of pain at once, as the friends of liberty do.

We must now consider the nature of the great questions determining man's destiny, not merely their relation to the misfortunes which have accompanied them. Or at least we must find out if these misfortunes are essential to the institutions people are trying to establish in France, or if the effects of the revolution are really different from the effects of the constitution. Finally, we must have enough confidence in the elevation of our own souls to have no fear of being suspected of indifference about crime because we are examining ideas. It is with the same independence of mind that I have tried to paint the effects of the passions of man on his personal happiness in part I of this work. I do not know why it should be more difficult to be impartial about politics than about morality; the passions certainly have as much influence on life's outcome as politics, but nevertheless in the quiet of retreat people talk reasonably about the feelings they have experienced. I would think it should be no more painful to talk philosophically about the advantages and disadvantages of republics and monarchies than to analyze precisely ambition, love, or any other passion which has determined your existence. In both parts of this work, I have tried to use only my mind, and to disengage it from every momentary impression: we will see if I have succeeded.

The real obstacle to individual and political happiness is the impulsive force of the passions, sweeping man away quite independently of his own will. Without the passions, government would be as simple a machine as any lever the force of which is proportional to the weight it has to lift, and man's destiny would be evenly balanced between his desires and the possibility of satisfying them. I will therefore only consider morality and politics from the point of view of the difficulties posed to them by the passions. Dispassionate characters spontaneously place themselves in the most suitable position, which is almost always the one chance has pointed out to them—or if they alter it in any way, they do so only with whatever offers itself. Let us leave them, then, in their happy calm; they do not need us; their happiness seems as varied as the different fates destiny has allotted them, but the base of this happiness is always the assurance of never being disturbed or dominated by any force stronger than the self. The existence of these impassible beings is no doubt subject to material accidents which overturn fortunes, destroy health, etc., like that of all men; but such sorrows are delayed or prevented by positive calculations rather than by emotional or moral thoughts. The happiness of passionate characters, however, is completely dependent on what is going on within them; they are therefore the only ones to whom the reflections one can awaken in their souls can offer any solace. Their natural tendency to be carried away makes them vulnerable to the cruelest misfortunes, so they are more in need of a system whose only aim is the avoidance of pain. And passionate characters are the only ones who, through various points of resemblance, can all be the object of the same general consideration. Other people live one by one, without analogy and without variety; their existence is monotonous, though each of them may have a different goal; there are as many tints as individuals, without a single real color in sight. [. . .]

Before going any further, we may need a definition of happiness. Happiness, as people wish for it, is the union of all contrary things. For individuals it is hope without fear, activity without anxiety, glory without calumny, love without inconstancy, imagination to embellish our possessions in our own eyes and fade the memory of what we have lost; the intoxication of moral nature, the good side of all conditions, talents, and pleasures, without their accompanying evils. For nations happiness would also be a reconciliation of republican liberty with monarchical calm, the emulation of talents with the silence of factions, a military spirit abroad and respect for laws at home. Happiness, as man imagines it, is the impossible in every genre. Happiness as one can get it, the happiness on which man's reflection and will can act, is obtained only through a study of the best ways to avoid the greatest sorrows. This book is intended to seek that goal. [. . .]

I believe it would be a good thing to discuss on a purely abstract level some issues which have been caught up by contrary passions. By looking at the truth away from individual men and these times, we come to a demonstration more readily applicable to current circumstances. No matter how general the point of view from which one has discussed these great questions, however, it seems impossible not to end by specifying their relationship to France and the rest of Europe. Everything invites France to remain a republic; everything commands Europe not to follow her example. One of the most intelligent books of our time, by Benjamin Constant, has discussed the question of the current situation in France.[3] Two sentimental motives strike me with particular force: would anyone want to suffer a new revolution to overthrow the one which established the republic? and should the courage of so many armies and the blood of so many heroes have been wasted in the name of a chimera, whose only memorial would be the crimes it has cost?

France must persist in her great experiment: its danger is past, its hope is still to come. But can we inspire enough horror of revolution in the rest of Europe? Foreign philosophers will never be persuaded by the vehement declarations of the intolerant fanatics who detest the principles of the French constitution, show themselves the enemies of any liberal idea, and make it a crime to love even the idea of a republic—as if the scoundrels who polluted France could dishonor the cult of a Cato, a Brutus, a Sidney.[4] But let Europe listen to the friends of liberty, the friends of the French Republic who hastened to adopt it as soon as they could do so without crime, as soon as it did not have to be paid for in blood. There now exists no monarchical government so abusive that a single day of revolution would not wring out more tears than all the evils the revolution was trying to correct. To want a revolution is to abandon both innocent and guilty to death; to condemn our dearest beloved, perhaps! and it is impossible to get oneself whatever one wanted at such a horrible price. In this dreadful movement, no man finishes what he began; no one can flatter himself that he directs an impulse which has been taken over by the nature of things. The Englishman who wanted to go down the waterfall of the Rhine at Schaffouse in a rowboat was not so crazy as the ambitious man who thinks he can steer his way through a whole revolution. Let us in France fight, win, suffer, die, in our affections, in our dearest inclinations—and be born again, perhaps, for the surprise and admiration of the world. But let a century pass on our destinies. Then you will know if we have acquired the true science of human happiness; if the old man was right all along, or if the young man did better with his property, the future. Alas! aren't you glad that a whole nation has put itself in the avant-garde of the human race to confront prejudices and try out principles? You, the contemporary generation, wait—keep away from hatred and death sentences for a while. No duty can require such sacrifices; on the contrary, every duty makes it a law to avoid them.

I hope I will be forgiven for having been carried away beyond my subject—but who can be alive at this time, who can write, without feeling and thinking about the French Revolution? [...]

Whatever people think of my plan for this book, my only goal is plainly to struggle against unhappiness in all its forms, to study the thoughts, feelings, and institutions which make men unhappy and to try to discover the reflection, the impulse, the combination, which could diminish something of the intensity of the soul's torments. The image of misfortune in any shape pursues and overwhelms me. Alas! I have so often experienced suffering that an inexpressible wave of tenderness and painful anxiety comes over me when I think about the unhappiness of everyone and anyone; about the inevitable afflictions and torments of the imagination; the downfall of the honest, and even the remorse of the guilty; the heart's wounds, the most touching of all, and the regrets one blushes for without feeling them any the less; about everything that makes tears flow, those tears the ancients collected in a sacred urn because of their great respect for human unhappiness. Oh! It is not enough to swear that within the limits of one's existence, no matter how one has been wronged, one will never voluntarily be the cause of pain or give up the chance of soothing it. Beyond that, one has to try and see if some shadow of talent, some ability to meditate could find the voice with which melancholy gently moves the heart, or help discover a philosophical height beyond the reach of wounding blows. Finally, if time and study could teach us how to give political principles enough evidence so that they would stop being the object of two religions and a most bloodthirsty frenzy, it seems as if we would have offered a thorough examination of the way man's destiny is abandoned to the power of unhappiness.

ON THE LOVE OF GLORY (1.1)

Love of glory is the most commanding of all the passions to which the human heart is susceptible. Traces of its impulses can be found in the primitive nature of man, but this is a feeling that reaches its real strength only in the midst of society. An emotion must absorb all the soul's affections to deserve the name of passion; the soul's pains and pleasures must be all related to the full development of its powers.

Next to the sublime kind of virtue that makes us look in our own consciences to find motives and aims for our conduct, love of glory is the most beautiful of the principles capable of moving our souls. I am giving the world "glory" its rightful greatness by not separating it from the real value of the actions it designates. In fact, genuine glory can never be acquired through relative celebrity. We always appeal to the universe and posterity to confirm the award of so august a crown; nothing but genius or virtue can keep it for long. When I think about ambition I will discuss the ephemeral success which imitates or reminds us of glory, but now I want to think about glory itself, which is truly great and just; and in order to judge the influence it has on happiness I will not shrink from showing it in all its alluring brilliance.

An honest, worthy lover of glory proposes a remarkable bargain to the human race. He says: "I will devote my talents to serving you; my ruling passion will keep arousing me to make an ever-increasing number of men enjoy the fruits of my labors. Nations and peoples I have never heard of will be entitled to the rewards of my insomnia; every thinking creature will be my kin. Free from the confines of individual feelings, I will measure my happiness only by the extent of my good deeds. All I ask of you in return for such devotion is this: that you celebrate it. Make fame acquit your gratitude. Virtue is capable of taking pleasure in herself—I admit that—but I am in need of you to give me the reward I need to fuse the glory of my name with the merit of my actions." This contract is so frank! So simple! How can it be that no nation has ever happened to live up to it, and that only genius ever fulfills its side of the bargain?

It is certainly an intoxicating pleasure to fill the universe with your name, existing so far above yourself that you can fool yourself about the extent and length of your life, and believe you possess some few of the metaphysical attributes of infinity. Your soul fills with pride and gratification as it grows accustomed to feeling that all the thoughts of a large number of men are concentrated on you—that you exist in the presence of their hope—that any meditation of your mind may influence the fate of many—that great events are happening within you, demanding, in the name of the populace counting on your brilliance, the keenest possible attention to your own ideas. The crowd's applause arouses the soul by inspiring reflections as well as arousing commotion; youth is swept away with hope and set afire with emulation by all the lively forms glory takes. The paths leading to this great end are filled with delights; the occupations imposed by the desire to succeed are pleasurable in themselves; and the happiest part of the career of success is often the sequence of interests which precede it, taking an active hold on life.

Literary glory is subject to very different conditions from the glory of action. Literary glory may borrow something from solitary pleasures and participate in their rewards, but it cannot embody all the signs of the great passion glory; it is not the same as the dominating genius that sows, reaps, and crowns itself in a single instant, instantly determining through its sweeping eloquence or victorious courage the fate of centuries and empires. Nor is literary glory the omnipotent emotion that commands others by inspiring identical wishes in them, taking for the present all the pleasures of the future. Active genius is excused from waiting for the belated justice time drags in its wake; it makes its glory march ahead like the pillar of fire that lighted the way for the Israelites.[5] The celebrity gained from writing rarely comes in one's own lifetime—and even when one is fortunate enough to obtain that advantage, a literary career does not have the same instantaneous effects and blazing brilliance; it cannot give the same total feeling of physical and moral strength, guarantee the exercise of all one's abilities. or intoxicate one with the certainty of one's own strength. We have to concentrate on the highest peak of happiness attained by love of glory if we are to be accurate judges of the obstacles and misfortunes it brings with it. [. . .]

ON VANITY (1.3)

You may well ask if vanity is a passion; the inadequacy of its object would make anyone have his doubts. If you observe the violence of the impulses vanity inspires, however, you will see the characteristic signs of the passions, and you will recognize their concomitant miseries in the servile way this feeling makes you dependent on the circle of those around you. Love of glory is based on the noblest elements in man's nature; ambition comes from the most positive side of human relations; but vanity fastens onto things which have no real value to oneself or other people, to specious advantage and passing effects. It lives on the leftovers of the other two passions. Sometimes it reinforces their power; man can reach his utmost limits through its strength and its weakness. More usually, however, those who experience it find that it overwhelms everything else within them. The agonies of this passion are very little known, because those who feel them keep it a secret. As this is a sentiment everyone has agreed to despise, no one ever admits to the memories or fears it involves.

[...]

This passion, great only in the pain it causes, and worthy of being treated on a par with the others only for that reason, reaches its full development in the emotional fluctuation of women. In women everything is either love or vanity. Whenever women want to have wider or more brilliant relationships than the relationships arising from the gentle affections they may inspire in those around them, they are laying claim to the triumphs of vanity. The same efforts which can earn glory and power for men almost never get anything for women except ephemeral applause and a reputation for intrigue—a kind of triumph which springs from vanity, a sentiment in proportion to their strengths and their destiny. It is in women, then, that we should examine vanity.

Some women put their vanity into advantages that have nothing to do with them personally, such as birth, rank, and fortune. It would be hard to show less feeling for the dignity of one's sex. The origin of all women is divine, because they owe their power to the gifts of nature: by concentrating on pride and ambition, they make everything magical about their charms disappear. As the credit women gain by this is invariably limited and fleeting, it earns them none of the respect that comes with great power. The successes women do win are characteristic of the triumphs of vanity, presupposing neither esteem nor respect for whoever is granted them. Women thus arouse antagonistic feelings in people who only meant to love them. There is a genuine absurdity clinging to women's efforts, the kind of absurdity that comes from a contrast with the essence of things. Whenever women oppose the plans and ambitions of men, they excite the acute resentment inspired by unforeseen obstacles. If they meddle in political affairs while they are young, modesty must be the loser; if they are old, the revulsion they inspire as women harms their claims as humans. The face of a woman is always a help or a hindrance in her life story, whatever the strength or range of her mind, however important the things which concern her. Men have wanted it to be this way. And the more determined men are to judge a woman according to the advantages or faults of her sex, the more they hate seeing her embrace a destiny contrary to her nature.

These reflections are in no way intended to turn women away from any kind of serious occupation, obviously, but rather to lead them away from the misfortune of taking themselves as the object of their own efforts. If the role they play in public affairs comes from their attachment for the man in control—if sentiment alone dictates their opinions and prompts their actions—they are not leaving the path nature has laid out for them. They love, they are women. When they abandon themselves to an active personality, however, when they try to make everything that happens revolve around themselves, thinking about events in relation to their own influence and individual interests, they are hardly worth even the ephemeral applause which constitutes vanity's triumphs. Women are almost never honored by any sort of pretentions. Even intellectual distinctions, which might seem to offer them a wider career, often just earn them an existence on the level of vanity. The reason for this ruling, fair or unfair, is that men see no kind of general utility in encouraging the successes of women in this career, and praise that is not based on utility can never be deep, or lasting, or universal. Chance provides a few exceptions; if there are a few souls carried away by their talent or their character, they may escape the common law—a few laurels may someday crown them. Even so, these women cannot escape the inevitable unhappiness which invariably clings to their destiny.

   With every kind of personal ambition, women's happiness is the loser. When women are trying to please simply in order to be loved, when this sweet hope is the only motive for their actions, they are concerned with perfecting themselves rather than showing themselves, with molding their minds for one man's happiness rather than for universal admiration. Once they aspire to celebrity, though, their attempts and successes both alienate the sentiment that necessarily determines their life's fate under one name or another. A woman cannot exist by herself alone. Even glory does not give her enough support. The insurmountable weakness of her nature and her situation in the social order have placed her in a daily dependency from which even immortal genius would not be enough to rescue her. In any case, nothing eradicates the distinguishing characteristics of women's nature. A woman who devoted herself to the solution of Euclid's problems would still want the happiness connected with the feelings we inspire and experience. Whenever women follow a career which puts them at a distance from these feelings, their painful regrets or ridiculous pretentions prove that nothing can compensate them for the destiny for which their souls were created. A famous woman's brilliant triumphs might seem to offer her lover some pleasurable sensations of pride, but such enthusiasm will probably not outlast an attraction based on the most trivial advantages. The criticism that always follows praise destroys the illusion through which all women need to be seen. Imagination can create or beautify an unknown object with its fantasies, but it has no more to offer anyone who has been judged by the whole of society. Real worth still remains, but love is much more taken by what is gives than by what it receives. Man delights in the superiority of his own nature; like Pygmalion, he bows down only to his own work.

In the end, if the brilliance of a woman's reputation attracts any homage in her wake, it is thanks to a feeling quite foreign to love—a feeling that looks like love, but which is a kind of means of access to the rising power one wants to flatter. People approach a woman of distinction like a man in a position of power: the language is different, but the motive is the same. Her admirers may mutually excite each other, intoxicated by the coincidence of tributes surrounding the woman they are concentrating on; but they are dependent on one another for this emotion. The first to leave could detach the ones who are still there, and the woman who is apparently the object of all their thoughts soon realizes that she is only keeping each of these men by the example of them all.

What feelings of jealousy and hatred are focused on a woman's great success! Envy's innumerable ways of persecuting her cause so much grief! Most women are against her, whether out of competitiveness, stupidity, or principle. Whatever a woman's talents may be, they always arouse anxiety in other women. Women deprived of intellectual distinctions can find a thousand ways to attack them when it is a woman who possesses them. A pretty creature who manages to thwart such distinction flatters herself that she is setting off her own advantages. A woman who considers herself remarkable because of the prudence and moderation of her mind, and who wants to look as if she has rejected things she never understood in the first place, never having had two ideas in her head in her life, can step out of her usual sterility to point out a thousand absurdities in a woman whose mind is giving the conversation life and variety. Mothers of families, who believe with some justice that the triumphs of even genuine wit are not in accordance with women's destiny, take pleasure in watching attacks on those women who have obtained any such success.

As for a woman who has achieved real superiority, and

might therefore think herself beyond the reach of hatred, capable of using her mind to raise herself to the destiny of the most famous men: she could never achieve their characteristic calm and determination. Imagination would always be her most important faculty: her talent might gain from this, but her soul would be too deeply disturbed. Fantasies would upset her feelings, illusions mislead her actions. Her mind may deserve some glory for giving her writings the accuracy of reason; but the combination of great talents and passionate imagination deceives us about personal relationships, however enlightening about general conclusions it may be. Sensitive, mutable women are the perfect example of that bizarre union of truth and error which distributes oracles to the universe and neglects the simplest advice for oneself. If we examine the small number of women with any real claim to glory, we see that their nature has always made this effort at the expense of their happiness. After singing the sweetest teachings of morality and philosophy, Sappho flung herself from the rock of Leucadia; after conquering the enemies of England, Elizabeth died a victim to her passion for the Earl of Essex.[6] Before women begin a glorious career, whether aimed at Caesar's throne or the crown of literary genius, they must realize that to gain this glory they have to renounce the happiness and peace of the destiny of their sex—and that in this career there are very few fates which are worth the most obscure life of a beloved wife and happy mother.

So far I have been evaluating the brilliance of great fame; what shall I say of all those pretensions to petty literary triumphs for which so many women's feelings and duties are neglected? Absorbed in this interest, these women renounce the distinguishing characteristic of their sex even more thoroughly than the female warriors of the age of chivalry: it is far better to share the dangers of those we love in combat than to drag ourselves through the battles of self-love, forcing sentiment to do homage to vanity and drawing from the eternal well to satisfy fleeting impulses and limited desires.

A more natural pretension, closer to the hope of being loved, is the disturbance that makes women experience a need to please through the charm of their faces; this offers a striking picture of the torments of vanity.

Look at a woman in the middle of a ballroom, wanting to be thought the prettiest and terrified of failure. The pleasure which is the nominal occasion for the gathering simply does not exist for her. There is no moment when she can enjoy this pleasure, for there is no moment free from her obsession and the efforts she makes to hide it. She watches the glances, the slightest signs of other people's opinion, with the attention of a moralist and the anxiety of a social climber. She may be trying to hide the torment of her mind from everyone's eyes, but her travail is apparent in her affected gaiety at her rival's triumph, the turbulence of the conversation she insists on having while her rival is being applauded—in short, the superfluity of her efforts. Grace, the ultimate charm of beauty, develops only in the serenity of natural self-confidence; anxiety and constraint deprive us of whatever advantages we may have. One's face changes with the contractions of self-love. People are not slow to notice it, and the pain of this discovery only increases the evil one is trying to remedy. Pain multiplies pain, and one's goal recedes through the action of desire itself. This picture may look like a child's story, but presents an adult's sorrows, the impulses which lead to despair and make us hate life; it is so true that our interests increase according to the intensity of the attention we pay them! and the sensations we experience come from the character receiving the sensation rather than from the object transmitting it!

Well, after this ballroom tableau illuminating vanity with some very frivolous pretensions, we will observe the full development of vanity in the greatest event to disturb the human race: the French Revolution. This emotion, so petty in its goal and motives that we might well have hesitated to place it as a passion, was one of the causes of the greatest shock ever to shake the universe. I can scarcely call vanity an impulse which carried twenty-four million men to reject the privileges of two hundred thousand: that is the revolt of reason—that is nature seeking its own level. I will not even say that the resistance of the nobility to the revolution was caused by vanity: the Reign of Terror brought down on this class persecutions and misfortunes which no longer permit us to recall the past. But within the internal process of the Revolution, we can indeed observe the rule of vanity in the craving for ephemeral applause—*the need to create an effect*—that native French passion, understood only very vaguely by foreigners. Many opinions were dictated by a craving to surpass the orator who had just spoken, and to ensure that one was applauded after him. The mere introduction of spectators to the room where debates were going on was enough to change the direction of public affairs in France. In the beginning, people conceded nothing to applause except a sentence here and there. Before long, however, they were giving up principles, proposing decrees, even approving of crimes, to get that applause. In a reciprocal and disastrous reaction, everything done to please the crowd made its judgments even wilder, and this wilder judgment then demanded new sacrifices. The primary reason for the consecration of barbaric decrees was not to satisfy feelings of hatred and fury, but to make the tribunes clap their hands. This noise intoxicated the orators and threw them into the same condition as savages are thrown by alcohol. The spectators themselves, who were applauding, were eager to create an effect on their neighbors by such signs of approval, and delighted in influencing their representatives. There is no doubt that the rule of fear followed the emulation of vanity, but it is vanity that created this power which destroyed all the spontaneous impulses of men for some time. Very soon after the Reign of Terror ended, it was clear that vanity was born anew. The most unimportant people were boasting of having been listed among the banished. Most of the Frenchmen one meets nowadays either claim to have played a leading role or assure one that nothing would have happened in France at all if people had believed the advice they gave somewhere, sometime, somehow. We are now surrounded by men who all call themselves the center of that immense whirlwind—men who would each have saved France single-handed from its misfortunes if they had been named to the highest government positions, but who all, by the same token, refuse to have any trust in superiority or recognize the influence of genius or virtue.

Does vanity help or hinder the maintenance of liberty in a great nation? This important question should be asked of those who think about philosophy and public affairs. In the beginning it certainly presents a real obstacle to the establishment of any new government; it is enough for a constitution to have been made by certain men for other men to refuse to adopt it. As happened after the session of the Constitutive Assembly, the innovators have to be banished for the institutions to be adopted; all the same, institutions die if they are not defended by their authors. Envy, glorified by the name of mistrust, destroys emulation, banishes brilliance, detests the combination of power and virtue, tries to divide them to oppose them to each other, and creates the power of crime, as the only power which degrades its possessor.

However, it may be possible for vanity to be useful in the maintenance of free institutions if it is the general temper of a nation at a time when lengthy misfortunes have beaten the passions down, when we need laws so much that we think of people only as they relate to the legal power entrusted to them. Vanity makes the rule of any one man hated, so it supports the constitutional laws which make the most powerful men soon return to private life. It generally supports what the laws want, because law is an abstract authority shared by everyone and giving glory to no one. Vanity is the enemy of ambition; it enjoys overthrowing what it cannot get for itself. Vanity gives rise to disseminated pretensions in all classes and in all individuals. This puts an end to the power of glory, as bits of straw keep back the sea from the coasts of Holland. In the end, the vanity of all throws such obstacles and annoyances into the public career of each that a time will come when there will no longer exist in France the main disadvantage of republics—the need they create to play a role. Hatred, envy, suspicion, every child of vanity will make people permanently sick of ambition for public office and public affairs. No one will go near them except through love of country and devotion to humanity, generous and philosophical feelings which make men as imperturbable as the laws they are charged to carry out. This hope may be only a chimera, but I truly believe that vanity is willing to submit to laws as a way of avoiding the personal brilliance of proper names, and that it may be able to preserve a free and populous nation with an established constitution from the danger of having any one man as its usurper.

ON PHILOSOPHY

I believe that philosophy, most exalted in its nature, could be a useful and possible source of help for passionate souls. We must place ourselves above ourselves in order to control ourselves, and above others in order to expect nothing of them. Weary of trying in vain to secure happiness, the last illusion, we must resolve ourselves to abandon it; it will take all the others with it when it goes. We must learn to conceive of life passively, to suffer its uniform flow, to make up for everything by thinking, to find in our thoughts the only events which depend on neither fate nor men. As soon as we have told ourselves that happiness is unobtainable, we are a good deal closer to reaching something like it, just as men whose fortunes have toppled are comfortable only after they have admitted to themselves that they are ruined. Once we have sacrificed our hopes, everything coming in on their account is an unexpected asset, possessed without forebodings of anxiety.

There are a thousand fragmentary delights in existence, none coming from a single source but all offering different pleasures to anyone with a soul at peace and ready to savor them; while a grand passion absorbs them all, refusing even to let us be aware of their existence.

The lover can see nothing but "her" footsteps; there no longer are flowers in any garden through which she has strolled. At the sight of villages surrounded by every gift of nature, the ambitious man wants to know if the governor of this district has a good reputation, or if the peasants living in it can elect a deputy. External objects represent only one idea in the eyes of the passionate man, because they are judged by only one feeling. The philosopher has, by a great act of courage, freed his thoughts from the yoke of passion: he now no longer focuses them on a single object, and enjoys the pleasant impressions each of his ideas can provide for him in turn and individually.

What would really lead us to think of life as a voyage is that there never seems to be any preordained place to rest. Just try to fix your life to the absolute power of one idea or one feeling—it all turns into obstacles or misfortunes at every step. But if you let your life drift at the will of the wind which sends it wandering through a variety of situations, trying to find pleasure in each day without making it contribute to the whole happiness of all destiny—then it all comes easily. When the events of our lives are not heralded by burning desires or followed by bitter regrets, we are able to find enough happiness in the isolated pleasures aimlessly distributed by chance.

Youth could perhaps be devoted to the long odds of the passions if it were the only stage of man's existence, but the moment when age demands a new way of life is a transition which can be suffered painlessly only by the philosopher. We could enjoy some happiness at any age if our faculties and the desires to which they give birth were always in tune with our fate; but our faculties and our desires do not die simultaneously. Time often degrades our destiny without weakening our faculties, or weakens our faculties without deadening our desire. The soul's activity outlives the means of exercising it; desires last longer than the goods they make us crave. The pain of destruction is experienced with all the force of existence—it is like being present at one's own funeral, violently attached to this sad and lengthy spectacle, renewing the torture of Mezentius, linking life and death together.[7]

On seizing control over the soul, philosophy certainly makes it place much less value on everything it possesses and hopes for. The passions inflate all the values to a much higher level; once this moderate price scale has been fixed, however, it lasts throughout the ages of life. Each moment is sufficient unto itself; one stage does not anticipate the next; the storms of passion do not confuse or hurry them. The years and everything they bring with them follow along peacefully according to the intention of nature, and man takes part in the calm of the order of the universe.

As I have said, anyone can enter the career of the passions if he is willing to put suicide on his list of resolutions; he can devote his life to this career, if he feels capable of ending that life as soon as a bolt of lightning overthrows the object of his prayers and efforts. But we have a sort of instinct of preservation, closer to physical nature than moral sentiment, even when every instant of life brings new pain with it. Can we run the almost certain risk of a misery which will make us hate living, and a spiritual disposition which will make us afraid to end it? Not that there is any charm left to life in such a situation—but one has to assemble all one's motives for misery together at one time to conquer the indivisible idea of death. Unhappiness is spread over the length and breadth of one's days, whereas the terror inspired by suicide concentrates itself entirely in a single instant; and in order to kill oneself one would have to embrace the tableau of one's misfortunes and the spectacle of one's end with the intensity of a single feeling and a single idea.

But nothing is so horrifying as the possibility of existing simply because we do not know how to die. Such is the fate that may be lying in wait for all grand passions, however—and this nightmare is quite enough to make us love the power of philosophy for maintaining man on the level of life, without making him any too attached to it but also without making him hate it.

Philosophy is not insensitivity. The kind of philosophy offering the help I recommend here may decrease the effect of acute pain, but it also demands great strength of soul and mind. Insensitivity is not the result of a victory, but an ingrained habit. Philosophy is affected by its origin: invariably born of profound reflection and frequently inspired by a need to resist the passions, it requires superior qualities and provides an enjoyment of one's own faculties unknown to the insensitive man. Such a man is more suited to the world than the philosopher; he has no fear of society's turmoil disturbing the peace he enjoys. The secluded philosopher, owing this peace to the work of his own mind, enjoys his own pleasure in himself.

The self-possession acquired through meditation offers a satisfaction which is completely different from the pleasures of the man interested in his own personal self. The selfish man needs other people; he is demanding; he suffers every wound impatiently; he is dominated by his egoism, and if that feeling were capable of energy it would bear all the characteristic marks of a great passion; but the happiness a philosopher finds in self-possession is the feeling that gives real independence.

In a kind of pleasurable abstraction, we rise some distance above ourselves, watching ourselves think and live. We have no desire to control any event, so we think of all events as modifications of our being, exercising its faculties and hastening the process of its perfectibility in one way or another. We are now placing ourselves in relation to our own consciousness, instead of to fate. Renouncing any influence over men and destiny, we take more pleasure in the action of the power we have kept for ourselves, in our self-control; and every day we make some discovery or change in this, the only property over which we believe we have any rights or influence.

For this kind of occupation one needs solitude—and if it is true that the philosopher finds a means of enjoyment in solitude, he must be the happy man. Not only is living alone the best of conditions, because the most independent, but it also provides a satisfaction which is the touchstone of happiness: its source is so intimate and so deep-seated that even when one really possesses it, reflection always brings one closer to the certainty of experiencing it.

Solitude is an extremely dangerous situation for people whose souls are disturbed by great passions. Nature invites us to this repose; it seems man's immediate destiny; its enjoyment would seem to come before the need of society, especially after we have been living in society for any length of time; but this repose is a torture for the man dominated by a great passion. The calm all around him contrasts with his inner agitation, and only increases the pain of it. The way to try to weaken a great passion is through distraction. There is no point in starting a war with man-to-man combat; one must already have acted upon oneself before taking the risk of living alone.

Passionate characters are not at all afraid of solitude—far from that, they crave it, which is the very proof that it nourishes their passion instead of destroying it. Troubled by depressing feelings, the soul is convinced that it can soothe its pain by paying more attention to it. The first instants when the heart is abandoned to reverie are delightful; but this pleasure consumes it very quickly. One may have put some distance between one's imagination and the source of the blaze, but the imagination has remained the same, and it pushes every opportunity for anxiety to the limit. In its isolation the imagination surrounds itself with chimeras; in silence and retreat, never touched by the real world, it gives an equal importance to everything it invents. It wants to escape the present, and gives itself to the future, which is much better suited to it and much more likely to disturb it. Its ruling idea has been left behind by events, and diversifies in a thousand different ways through the workings of the mind; one's brain is on fire and one's reason becomes weaker than ever. In the end solitude frightens the unhappy man, who believes his pain to be eternal. The peace all around him becomes an insult to the turmoil in his soul; the sameness of the days does not even offer him any change of misery. The violence of such misfortune in the heart of retreat is one more proof of the disastrous influence of the passions, which put a distance between us and everything simple and easy. Their origin may be in man's nature, but they constantly struggle against his real goal.

Solitude is the most important asset of the philosopher, however. His reflections and resolutions may abandon him in the middle of society, and his most deeply held general principles yield to particular impressions. This is when self-government demands the surest hand. In retirement, the philosopher relates only to the pastoral setting around him; his soul is in harmony with the peaceful sensations inspired by this setting, and uses them to think and live. People hardly ever come to philosophy without having first made some attempt at obtaining goods closer to youth's fantasies, and in renouncing them the soul creates its happiness out of a sort of unexpectedly pleasant melancholy, toward which everything seems to tend sooner or later. There is such an analogy between this moral disposition and the sights and happenings of the countryside that it is tempting to think Providence intended everyone to achieve it, and everything to coincide in inspiring it in us as soon as we reach the time of life when the soul is weary of working on behalf of its own fate, tired even of hope, with no ambition but the absence of pain. All nature seems to lend itself to the feelings men experience then. The sound of the wind, the burst of thunderstorms, a summer evening, winter's hoar-frost—these contradictory motions and tableaux produce similar impressions, and give rise to the soul's sweet melancholy, man's true feeling, the result of his destiny, and the only disposition of his heart which allows meditation its full action and all its power.

Conclusion

[. . .] In writing this work, where I pursue the passions as destructive to happiness and hope to provide resources for keeping life going without their help, it is myself too that I have been trying to persuade. I have written to find myself, through so many sorrows, to free my faculties from the slavery of feelings, to elevate myself to a kind of abstraction that will let me observe the pain of my own soul, to examine in my own impressions the movements of moral nature, and to generalize the experience provided by thought. Since complete abstraction is impossible, I tried to see if meditating on the very things that concern us would not lead to the same result—if the phantom did not vanish faster when we approach it than when we distance ourselves from it. I tried to discover whether the painful sharpness of personal experience was not blunted a little if we placed ourselves in the vast tableau of destinies, where everyone is lost in his century, the century lost in time, and time lost in the incomprehensible. I tried it, and I am not sure I succeeded in this first attempt to try my doctrine out on myself. Am I the best person, then, to affirm its power? Alas! as reflection comes closer to everything that makes up the human character, we lose ourselves in vacant melancholy. Political institutions and social relationships offer almost certain ways to happiness or sadness, but the depths of the soul are so hard to sound! Sometimes supersition keeps us from thinking and feeling, upsets our ideas, moves all our impulses contrary to their natural direction, and somehow bonds us to our unhappiness itself, if it is caused by a sacrifice, or can become the object of one. At other times, blazing, frenzied passion cannot bear any obstacle or accept the most minor deprivation, but disdains the future, pursuing each instant as the only instant, and awakens only at the end or in the abyss. What an inexplicable phenomenon is man's spiritual existence! If we compare it to matter, all the attributes of which are complete and in accord, it still seems only on the eve of its own creation, in the chaos of the day before. [...]

5.

On Literature Considered in Its Relationship to Social Institutions

Note from the Preface to the Second Edition

Even after refuting the various objections people have made to my work, I realize perfectly well that there is another kind of attack, capable of endless repetition: this consists of the many insinuations aimed at blaming me, as a woman, for writing and thinking. I offer in advance a translation of all these criticisms in the following verses of Molière:

> I'll have nothing to do with an uplifted wit
> For a woman who writes is more knowing than fit.
> My own wife's understanding will not be sublime—
> She should never have even *heard* of a rhyme—
> And all my wife needs to be able to do
> Is to pray God, to love me, to spin flax, and sew.
> —Arnolphe, in *The School for Wives*.[1]

I can see how such jokes may please people, even though they are rather worn out, but I cannot understand how my character or writings can possibly inspire bitter feelings. People may talk that way for all kinds of motives, but to tell the truth I am incapable of believing anybody really feels that way.

Preliminary Discourse

I have decided to examine the influence of religion, customs, and laws on literature, and the influence of literature on religion, customs, and laws. There are treatises in French on the art of writing and the principles of taste which leave nothing to be desired; but I think no one has adequately analyzed the moral and political causes that modify the spirit of literature, or considered the way in which human abilities have gradually developed through famous works in every genre, from Homer's time to our own.*

I have tried to give an account of the slow but steady march of the human mind in philosophy, and its quick but intermittent triumphs in the arts. Ancient and modern works on morality, politics, and science give evidence of the successive progress of the mind from the beginning of its history. The same is not true of the poetic beauties which belong exclusively to the imagination. As I observed the characteristic differences between the writings of Italians, Englishmen, Germans, and Frenchmen, it seemed to me I might be able to prove that the greatest factors in these constant variations were political and religious institutions. Then too, as I contemplated the hopes and ruins jumbled together by the French Revolution, I thought how important it was to understand the power that this revolution had over enlightened minds, and the things one could hope to do as a result some day if liberty, morality, and republican independence were combined in a wise and politic way.

Before giving a more detailed overview of this work, I must retrace the importance of literature considered in its widest sense, including philosophical writings and imaginative works, in fact everything involving the exercise of the mind in writing except for the physical sciences.

I will start by examining the relationship of literature in general to virtue, glory, liberty, and happiness; even if it is impossible not to see the power of literature over these great feelings, the primary motives of mankind, perhaps that will just make people more interested in joining with me to follow and observe the progress and ruling characteristics of the writers of different times and countries.

*The works of Voltaire, Marmontel, and La Harpe.[2]

Why can't I bring every enlightened mind back to an enjoyment of philosophical meditations? A revolution's contemporaries often lose all interest in the quest for truth. So many events determined by force, so many crimes absolved by success, so many virtues withered by blame, so many misfortunes insulted by power, so many generous sentiments the object of mockery, so many vile calculations glossed with such hypocrisy—everything makes even men who are devoted to the cult of reason get tired of hoping. But they should take heart from this observation: in the history of the human mind there has never been a useful thought or a profound truth that has not found its century and admirers. The effort to carry forth our interest and expectations toward our descendants—strangers very far from us, unknown to us, men whose image and memory cannot be drawn in our minds—may well be a sad one. But alas! After ten years of revolution, most of the people you recall (except for a few constant friends) sadden your heart, stifle your impulses, and even inhibit your talent, not by their superiority but by the kind of ill will that saddens the gentlest and hurts those who do not deserve to suffer.

So let us rise up under the weight of existence. Let us not give our unjust enemies and ungrateful friends the triumph of having beaten down our intellectual faculties. They reduce people who would have been satisfied with affection to seeking glory; well then, we have to achieve glory. These ambitious attempts may not remedy the sorrows of the soul, but they will bring honor to life. To devote life to a constantly disappointed hope of happiness is to make it even sadder. It is better to direct one's efforts to going down the road from youth to death with some degree of nobility, and with reputation.

ON NORTHERN LITERATURE (1.11)

There are two completely different kinds of literature, it seems to me, Southern and Northern: the literature that comes from Homer and the literature that starts with Ossian.* What I am going to call Southern

---

*To repeat what I have already said in the preface to this second edition: the chants of Ossian, a fourth-century bard, were known by the Scots and by English men of letters before being collected by Macpherson. By calling Ossian the start of Northern literature, I am merely pointing him out as

literature includes the Greeks, the Romans, the Italians, the Spanish, and the French of Louis XIV's time. English works, German works, and a few writings of the Danes and Swedes must be classified as Northern, along with the literature which began with the Scottish bards, Icelandic fables, and Scandinavian poetry. I think I will have to consider the main differences between these two literary hemispheres in general before describing individual English and German writers.

English and German writers have certainly often imitated the Greeks and Romans. They have drawn useful lessons from this fruitful study; but their original creations, those stamped by Northern mythology, have a sort of likeness among themselves, a poetic greatness of which the primary example is Ossian. English poets are considered remarkable for the philosophical turn of mind displayed in all their writings, some people may object, but Ossian has hardly any reflective ideas at all: he narrates a series of events and impressions. I would answer this objection by saying that the most characteristic images and ideas in Ossian are those recalling the brevity of life, respect for the dead, celebration of their memory, and worship of those who are gone by those who remain. The poet may not have added moral maxims or philosophical reflections to these feelings, but that is because the human mind of his time was not yet capable of the abstraction necessary to draw much in the way of conclusions. But the shock the imagination receives through Ossian's chants does predispose the mind to deep meditation.

The kind of poetry most in harmony with philosophy is melancholy poetry. Sadness lets us understand much more about the human heart and destiny than any other emotion. The English poets who followed the Scottish bards have added the appropriate reflections and ideas to their tableaux, aroused by the tableaux themselves; but they have preserved the Northern imagination, which gives pleasure at the seashore, amid the howl of winds, on the wild heath, carrying the soul

---

the earliest poet in whom we find the distinctive character of Northern poetry. Ninth-century Icelandic and Scandinavian poetry, the foundation of both English and German literature, greatly resemble the characteristic traits of Gaelic poetry and the poem of Fingal. A lot of scholars have written about runic literature, Northern poetry, and the ancient art of the North. All their scholarship has been summarized by M. Mallet, however, and a reading of the various ninth-century odes included and translated by him ("King Regner-Lodbrog," "Harold the Valiant," etc.) will be enough to convince us that these Scandinavian poets sang the same religious ideas, used the same warlike images, and worshiped women in the same way as the bard Ossian who lived almost five centuries before them.[3]

weary of its destiny toward the future and another world. The imagination of Northerners shoots beyond the limits of the world they live in, flying through the clouds edging their horizon which seem to represent the dark passage between life and eternity.

To make a general choice between the two kinds of poetry exemplified by Homer and Ossian is impossible. All my impressions and ideas make me tend toward Northern literature—but the point here is to examine its distinguishing characteristics.

Climate is certainly one of the main causes of differences between the images that delight us in Northern countries and those we enjoy recalling in the South.[4] Strange things may come out of the reveries of poets, but habitual impressions always turn up in anything one creates. To avoid the memory of these impressions would be to lose the greatest of all possible advantages: that of painting from one's own experience. Southern poets mix images of coolness, woody glades, clear streams, with all the emotions of life. They cannot portray the heart's delights without bringing in the kindly shade protecting them from the sun's burning rays. This vivid nature surrounding them arouses emotional impulses in them rather than abstract ideas. I think it is wrong to call Southern passions more violent than Northern. We see more varied interests there, but less intensity in any single thought: and fixity is what creates miracles of passion and willpower.

Northern people are more concerned with pain than pleasure, so they have more fertile imaginations. The sight of nature acts on them strongly, and as it shows itself to be in those climates: dark and uncertain. This tendency toward melancholy may vary according to the circumstances of individual lives, but it and it alone bears the stamp of the national spirit. In nations, as in individuals, we must look for the characteristic feature. Other traits are the result of a thousand different chances: only that characteristic feature constitutes its being.

The spirit of a free people is much better suited to Northern poetry than Southern. The Athenians, who were the first known founders of Southern literature, were a nation very jealous of its national independence; but the Greeks were more easily enslaved than Northerners, all the same. A love of the arts, the beautiful climate, all those enjoyments lavished on the Athenians gave them some sort of compensation. The first and only happiness of Northerners was independence. Servitude must have been unbearable to them because of the spiritual pride and sense of distance from life aroused by the harsh earth and mournful skies. Long before anybody in England knew about constitutional theory and the advantages of representative government, the warlike spirit so enthusiastically celebrated in Erse and Scandinavian poetry gave man a stupendous idea of his individual strength and willpower. Independence existed for individual men before liberty was constituted for all men.

During the Renaissance, philosophy began in Northern nations, where it was much easier to fight religious prejudice. The ancient poetry of the North presupposes much less superstition than Greek mythology. The *Edda* may contain some dogmatic beliefs and absurd fables, but almost all Northern ideas fit in with high reason.[5] The shadows bending down from the clouds are simply memories, brought to life by tangible images.*

The emotions aroused by Ossian's poetry can be found in all nations, because their ways of moving us are all taken from nature; but it takes prodigious talent to make Greek mythology fit into French poetry naturally. Religious beliefs transplanted to a country where they are just ingenious metaphors are lifeless and affected. Northern poetry is hardly ever allegorical; its effects can strike the imagination without the help of superstition. Reflective enthusiasm and pure imagination are equally suited to all peoples: that is the real poetic imagination, felt by everyone, though expressed only by genius. Poetic inspiration maintains a heavenly reverie making one love solitude and the countryside; it inclines the heart toward religious things and arouses in privileged beings a sense of virtue and the inspiration of uplifting ideas.

Man owes his greatest achievements to his aching sensation of unfulfilled destiny. Mediocre minds are usually more or less content with common life; the illusions of vanity permit them to round out their existence and compensate for any gaps. But the sublime element in mind, feeling, and action comes from a need to escape the boundaries

---

*People say there are no religious ideas in Ossian. There may be no mythology, but there is throughout an elevation of soul, respect for the dead, confidence in a life to come—feelings much more analogous to Christianity than Southern paganism is. The monotony of *Fingal* has nothing to do with the absence of mythology, as I have explained. Modern writers would be condemned to monotony too, if the only way to vary imaginative works was by using Greek fables; the more admirable these fables are in ancient poetry, the harder it is for our poets to use them. An imagination working on a topic about which nobody is allowed to invent anything at all soon gets terribly boring.[6]

limiting the imagination. People who feel a need for the preternatural pleasures of moral heroism, enthusiastic eloquence, and ambition for glory are exalted, melancholy souls weary of the measurable and temporary—weary of any limit, no matter how far away. This temperament is the source of all generous passions as well as all philosophical ideas, and Northern poetry is particularly able to inspire it.

I am far from comparing Homer's genius with Ossian's. What we know of Ossian cannot be considered his complete work—it is a collection of popular songs handed down in the Scottish mountains. Ancient traditions must have existed in Greece well before Homer wrote his poem. Ossian's poetry is no more advanced artistically than those pre-Homeric Greek chants must have been.* There is no parity, then, between the *Iliad* and *Fingal.* We can nonetheless still judge whether the images of nature presented in the South arouse as noble and pure emotions as those in the North; if the images of the South, more brilliant in some respects, give rise to as many thoughts and have as immediate a relation to the soul's feelings. Philosophical ideas go with dark images, as if spontaneously. Voluptuous Southern poetry is very far from harmonizing with meditation and inspiring the things reflection should prove; it almost entirely excludes ideas above a certain level.

Ossian has been called monotonous, but this fault is less common in the English and German poetry that is derived from his work. Culture, industry, and commerce have varied the landscape in several ways. The Northern imagination always keeps more or less the same characteristics, though, so we still find something in common among Young, Thompson, Klopstock, etc.[8] Melancholy poetry is not capable of infinite variety. The shudder we feel at certain natural beauties is always the same feeling; the emotion that the poetry retracing this feeling inspires in us is very close to the effect of the harmonica. The soul, gently shaken, takes pleasure in prolonging this condition as long as it can bear it. What makes us feel tired after a while is not the poetry's fault, but the weakness of our own organs; what we feel is not bored, but exhausted, as if by aerial music which we have been enjoying a little too long.

---

*Some people have said I compared Homer with Ossian; I have not changed a word of the above passage for this second edition. People nowadays feel free to say the exact opposite of the truth, which is useful for those who do not read. Non-readers never believe that one's critics, however partial, are saying things in complete contradiction to the facts.[7]

The great dramatic effects of the English and their German followers never come from Greek subjects or Greek mythological dogma. The English and Germans arouse terror by other superstitions closer to our own times. They have been able to do this especially well by portraying the unhappiness they have felt with such pain in their profound, energetic souls. The effect the idea of death has on human beings depends to a great extent on religious opinion. The religion of the Scottish bards was always more somber and spiritualized than that of the South. Apart from some sacerdotal fabrications, the Christian religion comes very close to pure Deism, annihilating the imaginary cortege surrounding man at the gateway to the tomb.[9] For the ancients, nature was peopled with protective beings inhabiting the forests and rivers and ruling over night and day; but nature has gone back to her solitude, and man's fears have grown all the greater. Christianity, the most philosophical religion of all, is also the one that leaves man most to his own devices. The natural effects created by a picture of the soul's emotions has not always been enough for the tragic poets of the North, and they have used apparitions, ghosts, and superstitions analogous to their dark imagination; but however deep the terror produced this way may be, it is a fault rather than a beauty.

The talent of the dramatic poet increases when he lives among a nation which is not too easily credulous. He then has to look for the sources of emotion within the human heart, and invoke the fearful phantoms which will strike the imagination with an eloquent phrase, a heartfelt emotion, a pang of remorse. The supernatural is always amazing, but however it is managed it never equals the impression of a natural event when that event involves all the things by which the soul is stirred. The Eumenides in pursuit of Orestes are less terrifying than the sleep of Lady Macbeth.[10]

Northern people have always respected women in a way unknown in Southern countries, if we judge by the traditions handed down to us and by Germanic customs. Women enjoyed independence in the North; elsewhere they were condemned to slavery. This is another of the principal causes of the sensibility characteristic of Northern literature.

The history of love can be considered from a philosophical point of view in every country. The way this sentiment is portrayed seems to depend only on the feelings of the individual writer expressing it. But the influence of the environment on writers is so great that they submit the very language of their most intimate feelings to its customs. In his own life, Petrarch may have been more in love than the author of *Werther* or English poets like Pope, Thompson, and Otway.[11] But wouldn't anyone think, reading Northerners, that they belong to another nature, other relationships, another world? The perfection of some of this poetry may certainly prove the genius of their authors, but it is no less certain that the same men would not have written these same poems in Italy, even if they had felt the same passion. It is so true that literary works aim at success that they usually give us less evidence of the writer's personal character than of the general spirit of his nation and his time.

The last thing that gives modern Northern nations a more philosophical turn of mind is the Protestant religion adopted by most of them. The Reformation is the historical period which has been of most real use to the perfectibility of the human race. Protestant religion has no living seed of superstition within its breast, and still gives virtue the support provided by sensitive opinions. The Protestant religion is not a hindrance to philosophical inquiry in countries where it is professed, and it is a very effective way of maintaining pure moral standards. To go into this question at length would be a digression, but let me ask enlightened thinkers for a way to link morality to the idea of a God without letting it become an instrument of power in the hands of men. Would such a religion not be the greatest good one could ensure for human nature—for a humanity becoming more dried out and pitiable every day, and breaking every day a few more links of delicacy, affection, and kindness?

ON GERMAN LITERATURE (1.17)

German literature* dates only from this century. Until then the Germans had concentrated on science and metaphysics—with a

---

*I must remind readers of the aim of this work. I am not claiming to analyze every one of the distinguished works which make up any literature; I am trying to characterize the general spirit of each literature as it relates to religion, mores, and government. I have certainly quoted a lot of books and writers in the course of this discussion, but I have been using them as examples to support my argument, not judging or debating their individual merits for a complete literary encyclopedia. This observation is particulary relevant to the following chapter. There are a lot of good books in German I have left out, because the ones I have quoted are enough to prove what I am saying about the general character of German literature.

good deal of success, but in Latin rather than in their natural tongue; there was nothing characteristically original about the work of their minds. In some ways, the causes of this delay in the progress of German literature are still keeping it from perfecting itself. A literature that develops later than those of the nations around it is under a real disadvantage: the imagination of such prior literatures often takes the place of its own national genius. Let us examine the major causes shaping the spirit of literature in Germany, the character of the truly beautiful works it has produced, and the drawbacks it must guard against.

The formation of taste was a more difficult process in Germany than in France because of the division into states, which meant that there was no single capital city to concentrate national resources and provide a meeting place for men of distinction. A great number of petty circles may multiply the effects of emulation, but no one judges or criticizes severely when each town wants to have superior men in its own lap. It is also hard for the language to take definitive shape when there are several universities and academies of equal authority on literary questions. Many writers then think they have a right to keep on inventing new words; this looks like abundance, but it only leads to confusion.

I think everyone realizes that federation is a political system favorable to happiness and liberty; but it is almost always unfavorable to the fullest possible development of arts and talents, which requires the perfecting of taste. When men of distinction are in the habit of communicating in a common central place, a sort of literary legislation is established, directing everyone's mind in the right direction.

The feudal regime governing Germany does not permit it to enjoy all the political advantages associated with federation. All the same, German literature is stamped with the characteristic of a free people. It is easy to see why. German men of letters live among themselves as in a republic; the more revolting the abuses of aristocratic despotism, the more enlightened men isolate themselves from society and public affairs. They consider every idea in its natural relationships; the institutions existing around them are too contrary to the simplest philosophical notions to have any influence on their reasoning at all.

The English are less independent in their general way of considering anything related to religious and political ideas. They find repose and freedom in the order of things they have adopted, and are willing to modify some philosophical principles; they respect their own happiness; they treat certain prejudices with care, like a man who has married for love and is therefore inclined to support the indissolubility of the marriage. Philosophers in Germany are surrounded by vicious institutions; they have neither excuses nor advantages, and have therefore devoted themselves entirely to the rigorous examination of natural truths.

Division into a number of governments may not assure political liberty, but it almost inevitably establishes liberty of the press. In a country so divided, there is no controlling religion or opinion; the establishment is maintained by the protection of higher powers, but the rule of each government over its subjects is extremely limited by public opinion. Anything can be talked about, because nothing can be acted upon.

Society offers even fewer delights in Germany than in England, so most German philosophers live solitary lives. The powerful English interest in public affairs is almost nonexistent there. German princes treat men of letters with distinction, often awarding them honors. But the people generally called upon to take part in German politics are the ancient nobility; and the only way to give all classes a direct interest in public affairs is through representative government. In this situation, the minds of men of letters inevitably turn toward self-examination and the contemplation of nature.

German writers are very good at portraying painful feelings and melancholy images. In this respect, they are close to all Northern and Ossianic literature. However, their meditative lives also inspire them with a sort of enthusiasm for the beautiful and an indignation against the abuses of the social system, saving them from the boredom to which the English are so liable in the vicissitudes of their careers. Enlightened Germans live only to study, and their minds keep going of their own accord, through a livelier, steadier kind of inner activity than the English mind.

In Germany, ideas still interest people more than anything else in the world. Nothing in any German government is great or free enough to make philosophers prefer the pleasures of power to those of thought, so their souls are not dried up by continual contacts with other men.

The work of German writers is less useful in a practical sense than that of English writers. As it has absolutely no influence whatsoever on their national institutions, the Germans are more likely to surrender to systematic theories and aimlessly abandon themselves to the random action of their thoughts. They adopt every mystical religious sect, one after the other; they find a thousand ways to waste time and their lives, because they have nothing to fill their lives except meditation. There is, however, no country in which writers have done more to explore the feelings of passionate man, the soul's suffering, and the philosophical resources which can help us bear them. The general characteristics of literature are the same in all Northern countries, but the distinguishing traits of German literature are related to the German political and religious situation.

The most remarkable book the Germans have is *Werther*; this is the one they can hold up to compete with the masterpieces of other literatures. Many people do not realize that *Werther* is a serious work, as it is called a novel. But I know of no book containing a more striking and truthful portrayal of the aberrations of enthusiasm—or a more piercing glimpse into unhappiness, that abyss of nature in which all truths are uncovered to the eye capable of seeking them.

The character of Werther is necessarily different from that of most men. It is an undiluted presentation of the harm a bad social system can do to an energetic mind. Such characters are found more often in Germany than anywhere else. People have tried to blame the author of *Werther* for making the hero of his novel suffer from something besides love, letting his soul show the raw pain of humiliation and a deep resentment against the aristocratic pride that caused it. As far as I am concerned, this is one of the book's strokes of genius. Goethe wanted to portray a human being suffering through all the feelings of a proud, sensitive soul. He wanted to portray the motley assortment of evils which lead a man to the ultimate stage of despair. The trials of nature may still leave us some recourse; for reason to become completely contaminated and death a necessity, society has to add its poisons to the wound.

What a sublime combination of thoughts and feelings, enthusiasm and philosophy we find in *Werther*! No one but Rousseau and Goethe has ever been able to portray self-reflecting passion, the passion that judges itself and understands itself without being able to conquer itself. This examination of one's own feelings by the very being they consume would stop our interest cold if it were attempted by anyone but a genius. Yet nothing is more touching than this mélange of pain and meditations, observations and delirium, showing the unfortunate man contemplating himself through his mind and succumbing to pain, directing his imagination toward himself, strong enough to watch himself suffer and incapable of giving his soul any kind of help.

Werther has also been called a dangerous book, glorifying feelings instead of controlling them; this assertion is supported by various examples of the fanatic response it has aroused. The particular enthusiasm *Werther* has aroused in Germany comes from the fact that this work is in complete agreement with the national character. Goethe did not create it; he portrayed it. In Germany everyone's mind is predisposed to enthusiasm, as I have said; and *Werther* does such a character good.

The example of suicide can never be contagious. Moreover, we are most deeply impressed by the feelings the novel develops, not the plot it invents. The spiritual illness which begins with high-mindedness and ends by making life hateful—that sickness is perfectly described in *Werther*. All sensitive, noble people have felt themselves on the verge of succumbing to it from time to time; indeed, excellent creatures hounded by ingratitude and slander may very well wonder if any virtuous man can stand life as it is, and if the whole organization of society does not weigh down on sincere, tender souls, making their existence unbearable.

Reading *Werther* teaches us to understand how glorifying integrity can lead to madness. It shows the degree of sensitivity at which we become too disturbed to stand even the most natural events. Every reflection, every occasion, every moral treatise may warn us about guilty inclinations, but when we feel we have a noble-hearted, sensitive nature we trust it, and can easily get to the ultimate stages of misery with no sign of the sequence of errors by which we were led to it. The example of Werther's fate is useful for such characters; it is a book that reminds virtue of the necessity for reason.

PART II
ON THE PRESENT CONDITION
OF INTELLECTUAL ACTIVITY IN FRANCE
AND ITS FUTURE PROGRESS

General Idea of Part II

I have traced the history of the human mind from Homer until 1789. In my national pride, I regarded the French Revolution as a new era for the intellectual world. Perhaps it was simply a terrible event! perhaps the strength of former habits will not let this event lead to productive political institutions or philosophical results for some time to come. However that may be, there are a number of general ideas on the progress of the human mind in this portion of my work, and these ideas may be usefully developed even if they can only be applied to some other time or country.

The literature that should characterize a great people is always interesting to examine, I believe: the literature of an enlightened people, who have established liberty, political equality, and manners in harmony with such institutions. Right now the Americans are the only nation in the universe to which these reflections are applicable. Americans may still have no developed literature, but when their men in public office are called upon to address public opinion they obviously possess the gift of touching all the soul's affections with simple truths and pure feelings. Anyone who can do that already knows the most useful secrets of style. Let us grant, then, that although the following considerations were written for France in particular, they will often have a more general application.

Every time I talk about the changes and improvements we can hope for in French literature, I presuppose the existence and duration of liberty and political equality. Does that mean I believe in the possibility of this liberty and equality? I am not going to try to resolve such a problem. I am even less willing to give up such a hope. My aim is to try to understand what would be the influence on intellectual activity and literature of the institutions required by these principles and the social mores they would bring with them.

When thinking about France, it is impossible to separate such observations from the results already produced by the French Revolution—results which we must admit have been damaging to manners, letters, and philosophy alike. In the course of this work I have shown how the mixture of Northern and Southern people resulted in a period of barbarism, though it was followed by great progress for enlightenment and civilization. The introduction of a new class into the government of France had, inevitably, a similar effect. In the long run this revolution may enlighten a greater mass of men; but the vulgarity of language, manners, and opinion will make taste and reason lose ground in many ways for some years.

No one denies that literature has lost a great deal since the Reign of Terror in France reaped its harvest of men, characters, sentiments, and ideas. Without analyzing the results of this horrible time (which we must consider as completely outside the circle of life's events, as a monstrous phenomenon nothing ordinary can explain or produce), we can say that it is in the nature of revolution itself to stop the progress of enlightenment for a few years, and then to give it a new push forward. We therefore need to look at the two principal obstacles to intellectual development: the loss of urbanity in manners and the loss of the emulation which could be aroused by the rewards of public opinion. I will then consider how literature and philosophy may be perfectible, if we can correct our revolutionary errors without forswearing along with them the truths which interest the whole of thinking Europe in the foundation of a free and just republic.

My conjectures as to the future will be the result of my observations on the past. I have tried to show how Greek democracy, Roman aristocracy, and the paganism of both nations gave a different character to the fine arts and philosophy; how the combination of Northern ferocity and Southern degradation and the modification of both by Christianity were the principal causes of the medieval state of mind. I have tried to explain the bizarre contrasts of Italian literature by remembrances of liberty and habits of superstition. The monarchy with the most aristocratic habits and the royal constitution with the most republican habits seemed to me the primary origin of the most striking differences between English and French literature. I must now examine the changes which the new French institutions may bring to the character of writing in terms of the influence that laws, religions, and customs exert on literature. If certain political institutions have led to certain literary results, one ought to be able to predict, by analogy, how similarities or differences in the causes would modify the effects.

The new literary and philosophical progress I am proposing to outline will continue the development of the system of perfectibility I have traced since Greek times. It is easy to show how the steps we could take in this direction would be faster if all the prejudices around which the road of truth must be laid were flattened out, and if the only thing left to do in philosophy was go straight ahead from demonstration to demonstration. This is the procedure adopted in the positive sciences, which make a new discovery every day and never go backward at all.

Yes—even if this future I enjoy sketching were still far away, it would still be useful to discover what might come to pass. We must conquer the discouragement the public feels in times when things are only judged according to fears or by calculations completely foreign to the immutable nature of philosophical ideas. The reason we study how the opinion of the moment is moving is to gain credit from the forces in power; but anyone who wants to think and write must consult only the solitary belief of a meditative mind.

We must clear our minds of the ideas circulating around us, which are only a metaphysical representation of various personal interests. At times you may be ahead of the wave of the people, at times behind it; it goes beyond you, meets you, abandons you; but eternal truth stays with you.

The mind's belief cannot be as firm a support as the conscience of the soul. Morality's command is never doubtful in action; but we often hesitate and retract our own opinions when hateful men take them over for their own misdeeds; and the flickering light of reason still does not offer enough assurance in the torments of life.

All the same, either the mind is a useless faculty or men must tend toward new progress to bring forward the age in which they live. We cannot condemn thought to go back in its own footsteps, hopeless and regretful; deprived of hope, the human mind would fall into wretched degradation. Let us look for this future, then, in literary productions and philosophical ideas. Perhaps some day these ideas will be applied to more mature institutions; meanwhile, the faculties of the mind will still have some useful direction, serving the national glory.

If you bring superior talents to the midst of human passions, you will soon convince yourself that those very talents are only a curse of heaven; but you will find them again as blessings, if you can still believe in the perfectibility of the mind, if you can grasp new relationships between ideas and feelings, if you keep deepening your knowledge of men, if you can add a single degree of strength to morality, if you can flatter yourself that you use your eloquence to unite all the various opinions of the friends of noble truth.

ON TASTE AND CIVILIZED MANNERS AND THEIR LITERARY AND POLITICAL INFLUENCE (2.2)

For some time people in France have been convinced that they really should also have a literary revolution, so as to give the rules of taste the widest possible latitude in every genre. Nothing could be more opposed to the progress of literature, which is so good at spreading philosophical understanding and maintaining liberty. Nothing could be more fatal to the improvement of manners, which should be one of the goals of republican institutions. The exaggerated delicacies of the old regime may be irrelevant to the real and ever-reasonable principles of taste, but it would have been perfectly possible to abolish a few conventional rules without overturning the barriers defining the path of genius and maintaining written and spoken dignity and decorum.

The despotic hold of the aristocratic classes on taste and manners is the only motive anyone suggests for this sweeping change in the tone and forms that maintain respect and consideration. It is useful, then, for us to set forth the characteristic faults we may find in some of the pretentions, tricks, and arbitrary demands of the old regime, so as to show with even greater force the horrible literary and political effects of the boundless audacity, graceless gaiety, and degrading vulgarity introduced during several periods of the Revolution. By opposing these two extremes—the artificial notions of the ancien régime and the grossness of certain people's ideas during the Revolution—we will be able to reflect accurately about the noble simplicity that should characterize the speech, writing, and manners of a republic.

The French nation was too civilized in some respects; its institutions and social customs had taken the place of natural affections. In Greek and Roman republics, especially Lacedaemonia, the laws took over the individual character of each citizen, forming everyone according to the same model; political feelings absorbed every other kind of sentiment. Lycurgus used laws to encourage the republican spirit; the French monarchy achieved the same thing by using the authority of its prejudices to encourage the vanity of social rank.[12]

Such vanity was the sole occupation of almost every social class: man lived simply to make an impression on his surroundings, to obtain some arbitrary superiority over his immediate rival, to arouse an envy it would soon be his turn to feel. From person to person, class to class, poor vanity found peace and quiet nowhere but on the throne: everywhere else, from the highest position to the lowest, people spent their lives comparing themselves with their equals or superiors. Instead of finding any sense of self-worth within himself, each person looked into the eyes of the others to see the idea they had concocted of the importance he had gained among his peers.

This intellectual rivalry about things that would have been absolutely trivial if not for their influence on happiness—this craving for success—this fear of disapproval: all these often contaminated and distorted the principles of natural taste. There was the taste of the day; there was the taste of some special class; there was the taste which arose from the general state of mind created by such relationships. Social groups existed capable of celebrating familiar devices and outlawing simple beauties by allusions to their own habits, interests, and even caprices. Whoever showed himself outside these social patterns categorized himself as lower class; and to be lower class is bad taste in countries where classes exist. Until they have received the education of liberty, the common people make fun of themselves: anyone trying to break away from the tone dictated by upper-class influence in France simply would have looked silly, even if he had had the best of ideas.

This tyranny of opinion went too far, and may have ended by damaging genuine talent. The rules of politeness and taste grew subtler every day; manners kept moving farther and farther away from impressions of nature. Ease of manner did not imply any surrender of sentiment. Politeness divided people into classes instead of uniting them. The unself-consciousness and simplicity essential to perfect grace could not keep people from watching with unswerving attention or apparent absentmindedness for the observance of the slightest signs of social distinctions.

At the same time, people were aiming for a sort of equality, the kind that brings all minds and characters down to the same level, weighs down the distinguished and comforts the envious second-rate. You had to talk like everybody else, keep quiet like everybody else, know what was being done to avoid doing anything original, and risk nothing. Only by long imitation of the accepted manners could one acquire the right to claim a reputation of one's own. The art of avoiding the pitfalls of cleverness was the only occupation of wit; and these shackles of etiquette often made real talent feel oppressed. This kind of taste, which feels injured by an original attempt, a burst of gossip, or energetic language, is effeminate rather than delicate; it stopped the flight of the mind. Genius cannot deal with artificial considerations. Glory is tempestuous, and the stormy waves of its popular following will break open such flimsy dikes as these.

Through pointless relationships, a system of respect without order, and a theater in which recognition had nothing to do with real merit, French society had created a power of ridicule that the best of men could not defy. Satire is the most powerful of all weapons to discourage emulation of great characters. A shrewd, accurate glimpse of the petty side to a great mind disturbs the self-confidence necessary to genius; the lightest sting of cool, indifferent banter can kill off the lively hopes encouraging a great heart to feel enthusiasm for glory and virtue.

Nature has provided remedies for the major miseries of human life. Genius is a match for adversity, ambition for danger, virtue for calumny. But ridicule is capable of insinuating itself into our lives, fastening onto virtues themselves and undermining them silently and unawares.

Contemptuous carelessness wields great power over the purest enthusiasm; even pain loses its natural eloquence when it comes up against biting wit. Energetic language, an unself-conscious tone, great actions are all inspired by a kind of confidence in the feelings of those around us. An icy joke can freeze it.

The spirit of satire attacks anyone who gives real value to anything at all in the world; it makes fun of everyone who is serious about life and still believes in real feelings and important interests. This discouraging frame of mind is not without a kind of philosophy, in a sense, but it stops the movement of the soul which inclines us to devote ourselves; it embarrasses even indignation, and withers the hopes of youth. The only thing beyond the range of its shots is insolent vice, and in fact this is an attack satire rarely tries to make, tempted to respect what it cannot hurt.

The tyranny of ridicule characterized the last years of the ancien régime; it began by refining taste, but it ended by exhausting strength: literature must have felt the effects of it. To make the written word more uplifted and human beings more energetic, we should make taste independent of the elegant, affected habits of aristocratic societies, however famous for perfect grace they may happen to be. Their despotic power must entail serious handicaps for liberty, political equality, and even the best literature.

On the other hand, how could there not be an opposition between gross bad taste and literary renown, morality, everything good and noble in men's relationships with one another?

Since the Revolution, a revolting vulgarity in manners is often combined with the exercise of any kind of authority. The faults of power are contagious. Power, especially in France, almost seems to affect not only actions and speech but the intimate thoughts of the sycophants surrounding the powerful. Courtiers of all regimes imitate those they praise, filling themselves with respect for anyone whose help they need and forgetting that even self-interest requires only external demonstrations, and that there is no need to falsify one's own judgment in making the desired appearance.

Bad taste of the kind that ruled for some years during the Revolution is harmful to morality, as well as to social relations and to literature. People let themselves joke about their own crudeness and vices, admitting them shamelessly and making fun of timid souls still averse to such degrading gaiety. These new freethinkers boast about their shame, and consider themselves clever in direct proportion to the astonishment they arouse in everyone around them.

In the long run, the coarse or cruel words which those in

power often allowed themselves in conversation ended up by depraving them and reacting on their listeners' morals.

An excellent English custom forbids the judicial bench to anyone whose profession involves shedding the blood of animals. There exists a morality of natural instinct, of unpremeditated, irresistible impressions, independent of the morality founded on reason. Someone who is so used to seeing animals suffer that he has managed to conquer the revulsion of his own senses at the sight of it becomes much less susceptible to pity, even for human beings; at least, he no longer feels involuntary sensations of pity. Vulgar, savage words create the same effect as the sight of blood in some ways. As we get used to speaking such words, the ideas they are retracing become more familiar. In wartime, men excite themselves to the furious emotions they need to arouse them by a constant use of the grossest possible language. The justice and impartiality necessary for the administration of civil justice oblige us to use forms and language which calm both speaker and listener.

Good taste in the language and manners of those in power inspires respect, making violent measures less necessary. A judge whose tone revolts the souls of his listeners has to resort to persecution to obtain obedience.

Kings are environed by a mist of illusions and memories; elected officials command in the name of their own personal superiority, and need all the external signs of it. What clearer sign of it is there than good taste, present in all one's words, one's gestures, one's accents, one's very actions, proclaiming a dignified, untroubled soul that always makes the necessary connections and never loses either a sense of itself nor the respect due to others? This is how good taste exerts real political influence.

People generally believe that the republican spirit requires a change in the character of literature. I believe this is true—but not in the sense they mean. The republican spirit demands more severity in the good taste associated with good customs. It may also allow literature to include a more energetic beauty, a more philosophical, more touching tableau of the great events of life. Montesquieu, Rousseau, and Condillac, republicans ahead of their time, began this desirable revolution in French writing; we must finish it.[13] As the Republic necessarily develops stronger passions, the art of painting should grow along with its subjects. Oddly enough, though, the way that authors have tried to take advantage of their supposed newfound freedom has been in ribald and frivolous writing.

Everyone remembered the reputation for gaiety France had earned throughout Europe, and thought it could be preserved by giving in to the very things forbidden by good taste and delicacy. I discussed the causes of French grace earlier in this book. Not one of them still exists today; not one of them could be revived, if we assume that the proposed scheme would allow for liberty and political equality.

The graceful models our language provides could serve as guides for the French, but only as they would for foreign nations. What kept that spirit of gaiety alive in France was the tone and manners of so-called good company. In a free country, people in society will be much more concerned with political questions than with the amenities of form and the charm of wit. Where there is political equality, all worthwhile genres will be allowed, and there will be no exclusive society devoted to the perfection of society wit, and concentrating all the influence of money and power in its own hands. Without such a tribunal, however, young writers cannot develop the delicate tact and subtle, accurate shading necessary to give light writing the conventional grace and the merit of taste so admired in French writers, particularly in the fugitive pieces of Voltaire.

Literature will be completely lost in France if we keep turning out these so-called graceful attempts which are only making us look ridiculous. Real gaiety can still be found in good comedy, but as for that playfulness we were accused of practically in the middle of all our misfortunes, it is gone. Except for a few people who still remember times gone by, all the recent attempts at it are just corrupting French literary taste and putting us well beneath the level of all the serious nations of Europe.

Before the Revolution, people often observed that a Frenchman unfamiliar with upper-class society would be unmasked as soon as he tried to make a joke, whereas it was much harder to tell an Englishman's rank by listening to him speak, because he would have the same serious, simple manners. Despite the differences which will remain between the two nations for many years, French comic writers will soon have to recognize that they no longer have their former resources for pleasantry. Far from giving them more latitude in this respect, the Revolution means that they must pay more attention than ever to good taste: society and all societies, confused after a revolution, offer very few good models and inspire none of the everyday habits which make grace and taste part of one's own nature without the reminder of reflection.

The rules of good taste as applied to republican literature are simpler than those adopted by writers in Louis XIV's time, but no less strict. Under the monarchy, a host of customs sometimes let the tone of propriety stand in for reason. In a republic, however, taste can only consist in a perfect awareness of true and lasting relationships, so that to lack the principles of taste is to remain ignorant of the real nature of things.

Under the monarchy rash criticism often had to be disguised and new opinions veiled under accepted prejudices; the taste needed for such devices required a good deal of subtlety. But in a free country the ornamentation of truth is in harmony with truth itself. Expression must come from the same source as feeling.

In a free country no one has to be locked into the same circle of opinions forever. Variety of form is not needed to hide intellectual monotony. The interest in progress still exists, since the career of thought is not limited by prejudice; but the mind becomes simpler when it does not have to struggle against boredom, reviving our attention by risking affectations condemned by natural taste.

A rather tricky tour de force under the old regime was the art of being morally offensive without bad taste, playing with morality by using delicate language to express proportionately indecent ideas. This talent is fortunately completely unsuited to republican virtues and the republican frame of mind. As soon as one barrier was broken, none would be respected; what sacred ties do not restrain cannot be stopped by social relations.

Besides that, one has to have an unusually subtle mind to succeed in this dangerous genre, a combination of formal grace and depraved feelings. Such subtlety is lost in the rather rough use of one's abilities appropriate to a republic. One needs a delicate touch to give immorality the grace without which the portrait and principles of vice would disgust even the most corrupt of men.

Some other time I will discuss the comic gaiety that comes from an understanding of the human heart; but it does seem likely to me that the French will stop being famous for this pleasing, elegant, lighthearted wit that so enchanted the court. Time will dispose of the men who still provide models of this genre, and its memory will fade;

books are not enough to remind us. Only habit can teach us what is lighter than thought. When the society which inspired this kind of instinct and quick tact is destroyed, the tact and the instinct die too. When a particular way of life ceases to exist, we must give up everything that can only be learned in its context, rather than from general theories.

A clever man once said that happiness was serious business. We might say as much of liberty. A citizen's dignity is more important than a subject's, because every talented person is one more obstacle to political usurpation. Our own conscience makes us take on this mission of honor; only nobility of character can give it strength.

There used to be people who combined elegant manners with almost habitual joking, but this combination presupposes perfect taste and delicacy and a feeling of one's own superiority, power, and even rank. Such things are not developed by an egalitarian education. This lighthearted but imposing gracefulness does not suit republican manners: it distinguishes the habits of great fortune and high rank far too clearly. Thought is more democratic; it grows at random among all men independent enough to have a little leisure time. Thought is therefore what we have to encourage, by less literary indulgence in subjects limited to formal grace.

The terrible side of our destiny makes us think: if national misfortunes do make men grow, it must be by correcting what was frivolous in them, and concentrating their scattered wits through the terrible power of pain.

As for taste in literature, it will have to be devoted to the ornamentation of ideas. It will still be useful, because deep ideas and noble feelings make no effect if obvious errors of taste distract your attention, break your chain of thoughts, or disrupt the sequence of emotion which leads your mind to great results and your soul toward lasting impressions.

People may complain about the frailty of the human mind, sticking at a misplaced word instead of concentrating on what is really important. But in the middle of life's most violent situations, even in the moment of death, we often see some silly incident distract men from their own misfortunes. How can we hope that ideas or a book will capture any reader's interest so strongly that his attention will not be distracted by inappropriate language?

One of the miracles of talent is the ability to tear your listeners or readers out of their own egotism; but if errors in taste give your judges (whoever they are) the chance to show off their own wit by criticizing you, they invariably make the most of the opportunity, thinking no more about the author's ideas or feelings.

The taste required for both serious and imaginative republican literature is not a separate talent, but the pinnacle of all talents. It does not oppose itself in any way to deep feelings or energetic expressions: its simplicity and naturalness are the only decorations suitable to strength.

Civilized manners, like the good taste they are part of, have great literary and political importance. Literature frees itself from the authority of socially acceptable style much more easily in a republic than in a monarchy, but the models for most imaginative works still have to be taken in the examples that pass in front of our eyes as a matter of habit. And what would become of writings imprinted by custom if the vulgar manners that highlight everyone's faults and drawbacks continued to prevail?

French writers would still have classical writings to imbibe, but their imagination would not be inspired by their environment. Imagination would be nourished by reading, rather than by the impressions the writers themselves were experiencing. Writers would find it almost impossible to combine direct observation and grand sentiment; they would have to push their memories aside instead of using them. It would scarcely be possible for even the soul's contemplation to give any idea of the real picture.

Some may say that politeness is such a slight advantage that it can be omitted with no loss to the great and real virtues which constitute strength and elevation of character. If politeness is defined as the gallant manners of the time of Louis XIV, the men of early classical times certainly had no notion of it, and they are still the most impressive models offered to the admiration of the ages by history and even by imagination. If politeness is the proper standard of men's relationships among themselves, however, if it shows what one believes oneself to be and what one is, if it shows other people what they are or what one thinks of them, then it involves a great number of thoughts and feelings.

Manners may vary according to character, and the same kindness express itself gently or brusquely; but a philosophical discussion about the importance of politeness must consider the widest possible meaning of the word, and not be sidetracked by the differences created by individual characters.

Politeness is the bond established by society between men who are strangers to one another. Virtues attach us to family, friends, and people less fortunate than ourselves; but in every relationship which we do not characterize as a duty, civilized manners prepare the way for affections, make belief easier, and preserve for each man the position his merit should give him in the world. They mark the degree of respect to which each individual is entitled, thus awarding the prize and goal of a lifetime's endeavors. We shall now examine the disastrous results of gross manners, and the politeness appropriate to the republican spirit.

The only thoughts and feelings which resound in the soul are those of women, great men, love, and glory. But how can we find a pure and proud image of woman in a land where social relations are not supervised by strict decency? If women, those independent judges of life's trials, let their fine instinct for lofty sentiments wither, where are we to find the model for virtues? A woman loses her charm by what she hears and by what people dare to say in her presence, as well as by any indelicate words she may permit herself. Modesty and simplicity are enough to maintain the respect woman needs in her family; but more is needed in society. The elegance of her language and the nobility of her manners are part of her dignity, and they are what is effective in commanding respect.

Under the monarchy, the spirit of chivalry, the pomp of rank and the magnificence of fortune—all things that strike the imagination—made up for real merit to a certain degree. In a republic, however, women are nothing if they cannot make an impression on others by whatever will distinguish their natural elevation. Whenever you strip away an illusion, you have to put something real in its place; when you destroy an ancient prejudice you need a new virtue. Instead of there being more freedom in daily social relationships in a republic, one has to be much more careful to avoid any kind of mistake, since all distinctions are founded on personal qualities alone. If one scratches one's reputation the least little bit, one can no longer rebuild one's life through rank or birth or any advantages foreign to one's own worth.

Everything I have said about women is almost equally true for men who play a brilliant role in society. They too will have to watch over their reputations much more closely than they did when aristocratic dignity was enough to guarantee its possessor the respect of the multitude. These ways of existing in the opinion of others undergo a process of daily attack and defense under a republic, which gives enormous weight to everything that can act on people's minds or imaginations.

If we turn from the favors of opinion to the maintenance of legal power, we shall see that authority itself is a weight that the governed can hardly bear. Minds which are not created for slavery feel an initial bias against power. If this prejudice is increased by the coarse manners of the man in power, it turns into real hatred. Every man of taste and some measure of high-mindedness inevitably feels a need to ask forgiveness for the power he possesses. Political authority is the necessary drawback of a great good—order and security; but the person who holds this authority always has to justify himself for having it, in a sense, by his manners as well as by his actions.

In the course of the last ten years, we have often seen enlightened men governed by ignorant ones whose arrogant tone and vulgar manners were even more revolting than their limited minds. Republican opinions get confused in some people's heads with the rude words and repellent jokes of certain republicans, and their irrational feelings naturally turn away from the republic.

Manners bring men together or separate them by a force even stronger than opinion—I could almost say than feelings. With a liberal mind, one can live comfortably in a social circle belonging to a different political party. One can even forget about serious wrongdoing, about fears inspired (perhaps rightly) by someone's immorality, if his noble language creates an illusion as to the purity of his soul. But what is impossible to bear is the coarse education betrayed by every word, every move, the tone of voice, the position of the body, all the involuntary signs of the habits of life.

I am not talking here about deliberate respect, but about involuntary impressions, born again every minute. In great emergencies we know each other by the feelings that come from the heart. In the petty relationships of society, however, we understand each other by our manners, and there is a point beyond which vulgarity makes both witness and object feel unbearable embarrassment and even shame.

By great good fortune, life almost never calls on us to endure a combination of vulgar manners and lofty sentiments. Strict integrity inspires such noble confidence and pure calm that it usually makes an upright man in any walk of life guess everything he would have learned from a good education. The coarseness victimizing us is almost always composed of vicious sentiments: audacity, cruelty, and insolence in their most hateful forms.

Social conventions are the image of moral life, presupposing it in any circumstances which do not give a chance of proving it; they keep men in the habit of respecting each other's opinions. If a state's leaders damage or despise these conventions, they themselves will no longer be able to inspire this respect, the elements of which they themselves have destroyed.

Another kind of impoliteness also characterizes men in power: not coarseness, but a sort of political fatuity, the importance one gives to one's own office, the effect that this office produces on oneself and that one wants to make others share. We have been forced to watch many examples of this since the Revolution. Under the old regime the only people who were called to high office were those accustomed from childhood to the privileges and advantages of superior rank; power made hardly any changes in their habits. During the Revolution, however, important state offices were filled by men of low condition, and without naturally lofty characters: humble about their personal merit and vain about their power, these men thought themselves obliged to adopt new manners along with their new employment. Nothing is further from this result of vanity than the affection and respect that republican judges ought to have. Affection and respect are related to individual character, and the man who thinks he has become another person because he has been named to high office is only showing you that your interest and respect should pass on to his successor if he loses it.

Is there a better way for a person to make himself known to his fellow man than through such dignity of manners and simplicity of expression? Transferred to the stage or told in history books, do they not inspire almost the enthusiasm of great actions? Coincidence may permit a man to attract attention for a few outstanding deeds without his being particularly talented or heroic, but there is no mistaking the way the words, tone of voice, and manners we use toward those around us distinguish true greatness: it is the only inimitable way.

It has been suggested that we substitute coldness and dignity for the once-warm French way of greeting people. The first citizens of a free state should certainly behave more seriously than the toadies of a monarch; but exaggerated coldness would check the flow of every generous impulse. A man with cool manners always looks impressive, because he is letting you know how unimportant he thinks you are. But this painful feeling he arouses in you leads to nothing useful, nothing fruitful. Such coldness torments goodness, high-mindedness, real superiority, without affecting insolent familiarity. Perfect manners encourage whatever is distinguished in every person, inhibiting nothing but his faults.

Let us make no mistake about the external signs of respect. Stifling noble feelings and drying up the fountain of thoughts is just the result of fear. The art of inspiring respect consists in raising the souls of other people to one's own level, giving intelligence its true value, creating the confidence all generous beings feel in each other.

It is extremely important to create social links in France, bringing political parties together: civilized manners are one efficient means of achieving this goal. Every enlightened man would rally to the cause, and this united class could form a tribunal of opinion, distributing blame and praise with some degree of justice.

This tribunal would also have an influence on literature; writers would know where to look for a national taste and wit, and could work to reflect and increase it. It would be disastrously confusing to have a national taste and wit that was nothing but a mélange of all levels of education, distinguishing nothing but political parties.

What difference can it make whether or not we share the same political opinions, if we differ in mind and feelings? What a wretched result of our civil troubles—for us to give more importance to some view of public affairs than to all the relationships of soul and thought, the only indissoluble brotherhood!

Civilized manners are the only thing that can soften the harshness of political party spirit. They permit people to see each other for a while before loving each other, and to talk together for a time before coming to an agreement. Step by step, the deep hatred we may have felt for someone we have never spoken to grows weaker and weaker through the relationship of conversation—of consideration—of attentiveness, giving sympathy new life and making us find someone like ourselves in the person we thought our enemy.

ON WOMEN WRITERS (2.4)

Unhappiness is like the black mountain of Bember, at the edge of the blazing kingdom of Lahor. As long as you are climbing it, you see nothing
ahead of you but sterile rocks; but once you are at the peak, heaven is at
your head, and at your feet the kingdom of Cashmere.
                            —*The Indian Hut*, by Bernadin de Saint-Pierre[14]

The existence of women in society is still uncertain in many ways. A
desire to please excites their minds; reason recommends obscurity; and
their triumphs and failures are equally and completely arbitrary.

I believe a day will come when philosophical legislators will
give serious attention to the education of women, to the laws protecting
them, to the duties which should be imposed on them, to the happiness
which can be guaranteed them. At present, however, most women
belong neither to the natural nor to the social order. What succeeds for
some women is the ruin of others; their good points may do them harm,
their faults may prove useful. One minute they are everything, the next
nothing. Their destiny resembles that of freedmen under the emperors: if
they try to gain any influence, this unofficial power is called criminal,
while if they remain slaves their destiny is crushed.

It would no doubt be generally preferable for women to
devote themselves entirely to the domestic virtues, but the peculiar thing
about men's judgments of women is that they are much likelier to forgive
women for neglecting these duties than for attracting attention by unusual talent. Men are quite willing to tolerate women's degradation of
the heart, so long as it is accompanied by mediocrity of mind. The best
behavior in the world can scarcely obtain forgiveness for real superiority.

I am now going to discuss the various causes of this peculiar
phenomenon, beginning with the condition of women writers in monarchies, then in republics. I am interested in the differences these political situations make in the destinies of women who set their minds upon
literary celebrity; I will then consider more generally the sort of happiness fame can promise these women.

In monarchies, women have ridicule to fear; in republics,
hatred.

In a monarchy, the sense of the right and proper is so acute
that any unusual act or impulse to change one's situation looks

ridiculous right away. Anything your rank or position forces you to do finds a thousand admirers; everything you invent spontaneously, with no obligation, is judged severely and in advance. The jealousy natural to all men calms down only if you can apologize for success under cover of some obligation. Unless you cover fame itself with the excuse of your situation and practical interests, if people think your only motive is a need to distinguish yourself, you will annoy those whom ambition is leading in the same direction as yourself.

Men can always hide their vanity or their craving for applause under the appearance or reality of stronger, nobler passions; but women who write are generally assumed to be primarily inspired by a wish to show off their wit. As a result, the public is very reluctant to grant its approval, and the public's sense that women cannot do without this approval is precisely what tempts it to deny it. In every walk of life, as soon as a man sees your obvious need of him, his feelings for you almost always cool down. A woman publishing a book makes herself so dependent on public opinion that those who mete it out make her harshly aware of their power.

These general causes, acting more or less uniformly in all countries, are reinforced by various circumstances peculiar to the French monarchy. The spirit of chivalry, still lingering on in France, was opposed in some respects to the overeager cultivation of letters even by men; it must have aroused all the more dislike for women concentrating on literary studies and turning their thoughts away from their primary concern, the sentiments of the heart. The niceties of the code of honor might well make men averse from submitting themselves to the motley criticism attracted by publicity. How much more must they have disliked seeing the creatures entrusted to their protection—their wives, sisters, daughters—running the gauntlet of public criticism, or even giving the public the right to make a habit of talking about them!

Great talent could triumph over all these considerations, but it was still hard for women to bear reputations as authors nobly, simultaneously combining them with the independence of high rank and keeping up the dignity, grace, ease, and unself-consciousness that were supposed to distinguish their habitual style and manners.

Women were certainly allowed to sacrifice household occupations to a love of society and its pleasures; serious study, however, was condemned as pedantic. If from the very first moment one did not rise above the teasing which went on from all sides, this teasing would end by discouraging talent and poisoning the well of confidence and exaltation.

Some of these disadvantages are not found in republics, especially if one of the goals of the republic is the encouragement of enlightenment. It might perhaps be natural for literature to become women's portion in such a state, and for men to devote themselves entirely to higher philosophy.

The education of women has always followed the spirit of the constitutions established in free countries. In Sparta, women were accustomed to the exercises of war; in Rome, they were expected to have austere and patriotic virtues. If we want the moving principle of the French Republic to be the emulation of enlightenment and philosophy, it is only reasonable to encourage women to cultivate their minds, so that men can talk with them about ideas that would hold their interest.

Nevertheless, ever since the Revolution men have deemed it politically and morally useful to reduce women to a state of the most absurd mediocrity. They have addressed women only in a wretched language with no more delicacy than wit. Women have no longer any motive to develop their minds. This has been no improvement in manners or morality. By limiting the scope of ideas we have not succeeded in bringing back the simplicity of primitive life: the only result of less wit has been less delicacy, less respect for public opinion, fewer ways to endure solitude. And this applies to everything else in the current intellectual climate too: people invariably think that enlightenment is the cause of whatever is going wrong, and they want to make up for it by making reason go backward. Either morality is a false concept, or the more enlightened we are the more attached to morality we become.

If Frenchmen could give their wives all the virtues of Englishwomen, including retiring habits and a taste for solitude, they would do very well to prefer such virtues to the gifts of brilliant wit. All the French will manage to do this way, however, is to make their women read nothing, know nothing, and become incapable of carrying on a conversation with an interesting idea, or an apt expression, or eloquent language. Far from being kept at home by this happy ignorance, Frenchwomen unable to direct their children's education would become less fond of them. Society would become more necessary to these women—and also more dangerous, because no one could talk to them of anything but love, and this love would not even have the delicacy that can stand in for morality.

If such an attempt to make women completely insipid and frivolous ever succeeded, there would be several important losses to national morality and happiness. Women would have fewer ways to calm men's furious passions. They would no longer have any useful influence over opinion—and women are the ones at the heart of everything relating to humanity, generosity, delicacy. Women are the only human beings outside the realm of political interest and the career of ambition, able to pour scorn on base actions, point out ingratitude, and honor even disgrace if that disgrace is caused by noble sentiments. The opinion of society would no longer have any power over men's actions at all if there were no women left in France enlightened enough to make their judgments count, and imposing enough to inspire genuine respect.

I firmly believe that under the ancien régime, when opinion exerted such wholesome authority, this authority was the work of women distinguished by character and wit. Their eloquence was often quoted when they were inspired by some generous scheme or defending the unfortunate; if the expression of some sentiment demanded courage because it would offend those in power.

These are the same women who gave the strongest possible proofs of devotion and energy during the course of the Revolution.

Men in France will never be republican enough to manage without the independence and pride that comes naturally to women. Women may indeed have had too much influence on public affairs under the ancien régime; but they are no less dangerous when bereft of enlightenment, and therefore of reason. Their influence then turns to an inordinate craving for luxury, undiscerning choices, indelicate recommendations. Such women debase the men they love, instead of exalting them. And is the state the better off for it? Should the very limited risk of meeting a woman whose superiority is out of line with the destiny of her sex deprive the republic of France's reputation for the art of pleasing and living in society? Without any women, society can be neither agreeable nor amusing; with women bereft of wit, or the kind of conversational grace which requires the best education, society is spoiled rather than embellished. Such women introduce a kind of idiotic chatter and cliquish gossip into the conversation, alienating all the superior men and reducing brilliant Parisian gatherings to young men with nothing to do and young women with nothing to say.

We can find disadvantages to everything in life. There are probably disadvantages to women's superiority—and to men's; to the vanity of clever people; to the ambition of heroes; to the imprudence of kind hearts, the irritability of independent minds, the recklessness of courage, and so forth. But does that mean we should use all our energy to fight natural gifts, and direct our social institutions toward humbling our abilities? It is hardly as if there were some guarantee that such degradation would promote familial or governmental authority. Women without the wit for conversation or writing are usually just that much more skillful at escaping their duties. Unenlightened countries may not understand how to be free, but they are able to change their masters with some frequency.

Enlightening, teaching, and perfecting women together with men on the national and individual level: this must be the secret for the achievement of every reasonable goal, as well as the establishment of any permanent social or political relationships.

The only reason to fear women's wit would be some sort of scrupulous anxiety about their happiness. And indeed, by developing their rational minds one might well be enlightening them as to the misfortunes often connected with their fate; but that same reasoning would apply to the effect of enlightenment on the happiness of the human race in general, a question which seems to me to have been decided once and for all.

If the situation of women in civil society is so imperfect, what we must work toward is the improvement of their lot, not the degradation of their minds. For women to pay attention to the development of mind and reason would promote both enlightenment and the happiness of society in general. The cultivated education they deserve could have only one really unfortunate result: if some few of them were to acquire abilities distinguished enough to make them hungry for glory. Even this risk, however, would do society no harm, and would only be unfortunate for the very limited number of women whom nature might dedicate to the torture of useless superiority.

And if there were to be some woman seduced by intellectual celebrity and insistent on achieving it! How easy it would be to

divert her, if she were caught in time! She could be shown the dreadful
destiny to which she was on the verge of committing herself. Examine
the social order, she would be told; you will soon see it up in arms against
any woman trying to raise herself to the height of masculine reputation.

As soon as any woman is pointed out as a person of distinction, the general public is prejudiced against her. The common people
judge according to a few common rules which can be followed without
taking any risks. Whatever goes beyond the habitual immediately offends
people who consider daily routine the safeguard of mediocrity. A superior man is enough to startle them; a superior woman, straying even
farther from the beaten track, must surprise and annoy them even more.
A distinguished man almost always has some important career as his field
of action, so his talents may turn out to be useful to the interests of even
those who least value the delights of the mind. The man of genius may
become a man of power, so envious and silly people humor him. But a
clever woman is only called upon to offer them new ideas and lofty sentiments, about which they could not care less; her celebrity seems to
them much ado about nothing.

Even glory can be a source of reproach to a woman, because
it contrasts with her natural destiny. Strict virtue condemns the celebrity
even of something which is good in itself, because it damages the perfection of modesty. Men of wit are so astounded by the existence of women
rivals that they cannot judge them with either an adversary's generosity
or a protector's indulgence. This is a new kind of combat, in which men
follow the laws of neither kindness nor honor.

Suppose, as a crowning misfortune, a woman were to ac-
quire celebrity in a time of political dissension. People would think her
influence unbounded, even if she had no influence at all; accuse her of
all her friends' actions; and hate her for everything she loved. It is far
preferable to attack a defenseless target than a dangerous one.

Nothing lends itself more quickly to vague assumptions
than the dubious life of a woman with a famous name and an obscure career. An empty-witted man may inspire ridicule, a man of bad character
may drop under the weight of contempt, a mediocre man may be cast
aside—but everyone would much rather attack the unknown power
they call a woman. When the plans of the ancients did not work out,
they used to convince themselves that fate had thwarted them. Our
modern vanity also prefers to attribute its failures to secret causes instead

of to itself; in time of need, what stands in for fatality is the supposed power of famous women.

Women have no way to show the truth, no way to throw light on their lives. The public hears the lie; only their intimate friends can judge the truth. What real way is there for a woman to disprove slanderous accusations? A man who had been slandered lets his actions answer the universe, saying, "My life is a witness: it too must be heard."[15] But where can a woman find any such witness? A few private virtues, hidden favors, feelings locked into the narrow circle of her situation, writings which may make her known in places where she does not live, in times when she will no longer exist.

A man can refute calumny in his work itself, but self-defense is an additional handicap for women. For a woman to justify herself is a new topic for gossip. Women feel there is something pure and delicate in their nature, quickly withered by the very gaze of the public. Wit, talent, passion in the soul may make them emerge from this mist which should always be surrounding them, but they will always yearn for it as their true refuge.

However distinguished women may be, the sight of ill will makes them tremble. Courageous in misfortune, they are cowards against dislike; thought uplifts them, but their character is still weak and sensitive. Most women whose superior abilities make them want renown are like Erminia dressed in armor.[16] Warriors see the helmet, the lance, the bright plume of feathers, and think they are up against strength, so they attack with violence; with the very first blows, they have struck at the heart.

Such injustices can not only spoil a woman's happiness and peace of mind, but also alienate even the most important objects of her affection. Who can be sure that a libelous portrayal will not strike at the truth of memory? Who knows whether or not slanderers, having wreaked havoc with life, will rob death itself of the tender, regretful feelings that should be associated with the memory of a beloved woman?

So far I have portrayed only the unfairness of men: but what about the threat of injustice from other women? Do not women secretly arouse the malevolence of men? Do women ever form an alliance with a famous woman, sustaining her, defending her, supporting her faltering steps?

And that is still not all. Public opinion seems to release men from every duty toward a recognizably superior woman. Men can be ungrateful to her, unfaithful, even wicked, without making public opinion responsible for avenging her. "Is she not an extraordinary woman?" That says it all; she is abandoned to her own strength, and left to struggle with misery. She lacks both the sympathy inspired by a woman and the power protecting a man. Like the pariahs of India, such a woman parades her peculiar existence among classes she cannot belong to, which consider her as destined to exist on her own, the object of curiosity and perhaps a little envy: what she deserves, in fact, is pity.

6.

Delphine

DELPHINE TO MLLE. D'ALBÉMAR (1.23)

I have seen him again, sister, seen him again! and what I feel for him is no longer pity, but respect—attraction—everything that would have guaranteed me a lifetime of happiness. Oh! what have I done? I've tied myself down with such chains of trust and friendship—and he, what does he think? What does he want? Because when it comes right down to it, if he weren't in love with my cousin could he be forced into anything, if . . . Look at the empty arguments I am using. Wouldn't it still be for my sake that he would be breaking this engagement? I would look as if I had made the marriage possible with my gifts, and then broken it up with what people would call my attractions. I am richer than Matilde: they would say I had taken advantage of that; and I would strike Mme. de Vernon to the heart. She would accuse me of lacking delicacy—and I need her to respect me so much! But what is the point of all these rationalizations? Does Léonce love me? Would he ever get out of a promise his mother had made? You be the judge: these are the elusive signs by which I guess at his passion. Ah! Today was too happy! the beginning and end, perhaps, of a charmed life I shared for a few short hours through the magical powers of feeling.

I was at Mme. de Vernon's yesterday when M. de Mondoville was announced. He was not so pale as the first time I had seen him, but his face still had the appealing charm that had touched me so keenly, and his noble, serious expression was even more remarkable because he had recovered his strength. He bowed first to me; I felt proud of this mark of interest, as if the least little signs of his interest were assigning everyone there his station in life. Mme. de Vernon introduced him to Matilde, who blushed. I thought Matilde looked very beautiful; all the same, Louise, I am positive he observed her with no real warmth, and that his eyes did not show their natural sensibility until he turned to me. M. Barton was sitting next to me on the garden terrace; Léonce sat down next to him. Mme. de Vernon suggested that he stay for the evening, and he agreed.

All of a sudden I felt deliciously serene. I had three hours ahead of me in which I was sure of seeing him; I was not worried about his health anymore, and the only thing bothering me was an overintense feeling of happiness. For a long time I chatted with him—in front of him—for him: my pleasure in this conversation was quite new to me. Until then I had just thought of conversation as a way to show the range of my knowledge or any wit I might have, but with Léonce I was trying to find topics closer to the heart. We talked about one novel after the other, going through the few that reveal the intimate sorrows of sensitive characters. There was a kind of internal emotion within me giving life to everything I said. My heart kept pounding away, even when the discussion was purely literary. My mind kept its ease and fluency, but my soul felt disturbed, as it does at the most important times in one's life. That night I could not convince myself that something extraordinary had not happened.

My admiration and respect for Léonce increased with every word he spoke. His speech was terse, but energetic; even when he used strong, eloquent expressions, he was obviously saying only half he thought, and one could glimpse treasures of feeling and passion in his heart which he was not spending all at one time. How quickly he understood me! he took such an interest in hearing me speak! No! I cannot imagine a sweeter situation: one's thoughts aroused by the soul's emotions, vanity's triumphs transformed into heartfelt pleasures—oh what happy moments! Imagine life without them!

In the meantime I noticed Matilde's face and gestures showing a good deal of temper. Mme. de Vernon, who usually likes to chat with me, was talking to her neighbor without showing the slightest interest in our conversation. At last she took Mme. du Marset's arm, saying loudly enough for me to hear: "Would you like to play cards, madame?

The conversation here is too grand for us." At these words I blushed deeply and got up, saying I wanted to be included in the game; Léonce reproached me with a look. M. Barton came up to me, saying with touching kindness: "I would have thought I was listening to you for the first time today, madame; the charm of your conversation has never struck me so strongly." Oh, how sweet it was to be praised in front of Léonce! He gave a sigh, leaning on the back of the chair I had been sitting on. M. Barton whispered to him: "Don't you want to approach Mlle. de Vernon?" "Leave me here, for heaven's sake," answered Léonce. Those are the words I heard, Louise; his tone of voice was unforgettable.

When the game was set up, Léonce was left almost alone with Matilde, and went to speak to her; the conversation looked cold and stilted. I could not concentrate on the game. Mme. du Marset was annoyed with me, but Mme. de Vernon excused my mistakes with enchanting kindness. She was completely gracious to me throughout the whole game, and I was so touched by this that I did not go near Léonce again; I felt Mme. de Vernon's sweetness required no less of me. She wanted to keep me with her for a private chat, which I refused. I do not want to hide my feelings from her: let her guess them; I am willing, more than willing—but I cannot bring myself to bring up the subject. Wouldn't that be pointing out the sacrifice I want her to make? I would feel more comfortable with her if I were the one who should be grateful. Then I would admit my folly and leave everything to her generosity— but I am afraid of taking advantage of the service I have done her.

Rely on your natural delicacy, sister, not your unfair prejudice against Mme. de Vernon. Tell me what I should do if he loved me, if he thought he was free. Alas, this advice may prove unnecessary— Léonce may spare me the conflicts I am so frightened of!

DELPHINE TO MLLE. D'ALBÉMAR (1.25)

My dear, he spoke to me—and with interest, with intimacy—good God, I felt so honored! Listen carefully—the decision about my fate may come very soon because of what happened today.

I had been dining at Mme. de Vernon's with Mme. du Mar-
set and her inseparable friend, M. de Fierville. By some chance, just at the
moment when Léonce usually makes his appearance, Mme. de Vernon
happened to direct the conversation toward politics. Mme. du Marset
broke out against everything noble and grand about the love of liberty;
to hear her talk, she might have been discussing the unfortunate consequences of revolution. I let her go on for some little time, but then I was
annoyed by M. de Fierville's teasing an English guest who was opposed to
the absurd things she was saying. M. de Fierville always supports his
friend's irrationality by ridiculing whatever serious attention anyone pays
to anything; he frightens people who have no confidence in their own
wit by making them think that the only proof against pedantry is sarcasm.
The Englishman, newly arrived in France, was intimidated by this trick,
and I was eager to rescue him: I joined the discussion in spite of
myself.

Mme. du Marset has memorized some insulting remarks
about Rousseau that she can be made to recite on cue.[1] Mme. de Vernon
set her off; I answered rather contemptuously. Mme. du Marset, stung,
turned toward Mme. de Vernon and said: "All the same, madame, my
opinions are not so ridiculous, whatever your niece may say. I was writing
again to Mme. de Mondoville only last night about the things going on in
France, and she absolutely agrees with me."

When I heard that Mme. du Marset corresponded with
Mme. de Mondoville, I realized immediately that she might have told her
about me—that she might even tell her about this conversation—and
that she would describe me as a madwoman to Léonce's mother, whose
hatred for the French Revolution goes to singularly exaggerated extremes. I was so stunned by this thought that I could not utter
another word.

Mme. du Marset went on, with the laugh characteristic of
vanity imitating confidence: "Well, madame! No answer? Is there any
chance I could be right? Have I reduced that great mind of yours to
silence?" Léonce was announced; how I prayed for this disastrous conversation to end! But Mme. de Vernon called him over pitilessly, asking,
"Is it true your mother hates Rousseau? Mme. d'Albémar is most enthusiastic about both his writings and his political ideas, and she is
defending them against Mme. du Marset, who relies on your mother's opinions."

I trembled as she spoke, and waited breathlessly for Léonce's reply. He had turned toward Mme. du Marset when her name was mentioned: I could not see his face, but something in the tilt of his head bespoke a certain contempt for her, and at first I found this reassuring. Mme. du Marset, who was facing him, must have been disturbed by it; she managed to utter these words: "Yes, your mother agrees with me completely, sir. She has written to me a number of times saying so."

"I don't know what my mother writes to you," answered Léonce in a tone I had never heard him use, filling me with respect and fear. "However, I would prefer to remain in ignorance of what you say back to her."

"Do let's leave all that alone," said Mme. de Vernon rather sharply. "We can go and take a walk in the garden."

I was very eager to have some explanation of what Léonce had said; delighted as I was to hope that his anger was all on my behalf, I needed him to tell me so himself. It was quite natural for me to stay a few steps behind the others as we walked; for a moment I thought I saw him hesitate, but he plucked a leaf from the same tree I was gathering from, so I started the conversation.

"I think I owe you some sort of thanks for rescuing me," I began.

"I will always be glad to defend you, madame, even if I do not approve of you."

"But what did I do wrong?" I cried, with some emotion.

"Lovely Delphine! Why on earth do you voice opinions which arouse such passionate hatred? opinions which are—perhaps rightly—so repellent to people of your class?"

LÉONCE TO M. BARTON (1.27)

Dear tutor: my fate is decided. No one but Delphine will ever rule my heart. She came very close to compromising herself for me yesterday at the ball. I am so grateful to her for putting me in her debt! I have no more doubts—I just have to put my decision into practice. What I need from you is advice on how to do it.

On July 4 I will be at Mondoville; we must decide what I should write to my mother. Mme. de Vernon has still said nothing so far to me about wedding plans, and when I come back from Mondoville I will bring the subject up myself. Mme. de Vernon is an intelligent woman, and a friend of Delphine's; she will help, once she understands that my decision is final. The only thing that frightens me is the force of the marriage contracts, and since my mother has avoided answering my questions on this topic she must not think her honor is at stake. If she had thought her scrupulous sense of right could be compromised by my disobedience, she would have given me my orders right away, and in no uncertain terms. Her letters only concentrate on the supposed failings of Mme. d'Albémar. People have convinced her that Delphine is light and careless—that she continually compromises her reputation and misses no opportunity to express opinions directly opposed to everything one should love and respect. Your job, Barton, will be to make my mother understand Mme. d'Albémar; she will sooner believe you than me.

Delphine certainly does have too much confidence in her own abilities, and she pays far too little attention to the impression her behavior may be making on other people. She needs to direct her mind toward an understanding of the social world, and protect herself from her own indifference to a public opinion influenced at least as much by mediocre people as by their betters. Our faults may be diametrically opposed, but I now believe that this may increase both our happiness and our virtues. I am convinced Delphine will subordinate her actions to my wishes; her way of thinking may liberate mine. At the very least she will calm down that burning vulnerability which has already hurt me so badly. Everything will be all right once I am her husband, my friend. Everything will be fine.

Yesterday—how can I tell you about yesterday? That would be to throw myself back into a trouble which is driving me crazy. Love is an amazing feeling—a whole differerent life within life. There are memories and thoughts so alive with happiness in my heart that I can feel the joy of living with every breath I take. My enemy would have harmed me so much by killing me! My wound now makes me anxious; sometimes I am afraid it will reopen. If you can believe this, I am disturbed by such passionate impulses that I am afraid of dying before tomorrow comes, before an hour passes, before the instant when I see Delphine again.

Please don't think I am talking about a youthful love—the sort of love to which a wise friend would object. You do want my mother to prefer Mme. d'Albémar to Matilde, even though you have forced yourself not to oppose her opinions. Your logic is in harmony with your pupil's decision. Do not resist it! If you only knew how much more it makes me love you!

Before going to Mme. de Vernon's ball, I got your letter about M. de Serbellane, agreeing that he was the man Mme. d'Albémar had always seemed to favor. You were trying to calm me down, but your letter actually renewed my anxiety. I arrived at the ball in a rather sad mood. Matilde had dressed up in a Spanish outfit, an excellent setting for the beauty of her face and figure. She has never shown me any special favor, but I felt that her choice of this outfit was meant to show good will toward me. I wanted to talk to her, and after she agreed to go nearer the entrance door, so that I could keep an eye on it, I sat down with her. I was so wildly impatient to see Delphine that I could not follow my ballroom conversation with Matilde, usually no great effort.

All of a sudden I felt the air was filled with perfume, and trembled at recognizing the scent of Delphine's flowers. She came into the room without seeing me, and at first I did not go near her, enjoying the fact that we were both in the same place, taking voluptuous delight in prolonging the pleasure of the happiest day of my life. I let her circulate through the ballroom before going near her; I could see she was still looking for someone, even though everybody was crowding around. She was wearing a simple white gown, her beautiful hair knotted with no ornament but her inimitable grace and originality. Looking at her, how ungrateful I became for Matilde's outfit! Delphine's was the one to choose. What do reminders of Spain mean to me? I remember nothing before the day I first saw Mme. d'Albémar.

Delphine caught sight of me in a window alcove where I was standing to watch her; her thrill of delight did not escape me. She then noticed Matilde, whose costume struck her with such force that she stood stock-still in front of her, silent and lost in a trance. A pretty young Italian woman named Mme. d'Ervins approached and invited Delphine into the adjoining room. She hesitated—so as to speak to me, no doubt; but Mme. d'Ervins seemed hurt by this reluctance, and Delphine hesitated no longer.

Delphine's conversation with Mme. d'Ervins was a rather long one, and by the time she returned I was growing impatient. "It may be foolish of me to report my actions to you without knowing if you take any interest in them," she said. "But even if you think this is an imprudent step to take, you will think no worse of me than you already do, and at least you will not suspect me unfairly. I have to talk to M. de Serbellane alone, for a reason I cannot explain. My motives have nothing to do with my own feelings. I would be deeply mistaken about Léonce if he were unable to recognize the voice of truth, and if I were not sure of convincing him of my sincerity when I call on his respect for me as my witness."

The dignity and sincerity of this speech made a deep impression on me. Oh Delphine! if you were lying—it would be such a betrayal of your charms, apparently meant for enhancing spontaneity and involuntary affection, combining elegant social graces and natural feelings in one and the same woman!

Delphine came back to the ball after her conversation with M. de Serbellane was over, and was asked to dance by M. d'Orsan. This is a nephew of Mme. du Marset's; he has to keep his talents busy all the time, because he uses them instead of a brain. He was asking her to dance a polonaise which they had both been taught by a Russian; everyone at the ball was extremely curious to see it.[2] M. d'Orsan was so insistent that Delphine was forced to give in, but there was something very appealing in the glances she threw my way. She had complained to me about how boring M. d'Orsan was; our mutual understanding was spontaneous, her smile included me in her gently malicious observations.

Men and women alike had climbed up on the benches to watch Delphine dance. I could feel my heart beat violently now; all eyes were upon her; the harmony between their thoughts and mine was painful to me. I would have been happier watching her by myself.

Grace and beauty have never made a more astounding effect on a large group of people. The polonaise is a foreign dance with a magic suggested by nothing we have ever seen—a mixture of indolence and vivacity, melancholy and Asiatic gaiety. Sometimes the music grew gentle, and Delphine would take a few steps with her head down and arms crossed, as if memories or regrets had suddenly tainted the brilliance of the fete; but soon she would go on with her light and lively dance, wrapping herself in an Indian shawl which outlined her body and hung with her long hair down her back, making her whole self into an irresistible tableau.

This expressive, even inspired dance has great power over the imagination; it retraces poetic ideas and feelings which the most beautiful poetry of the Orient can hardly describe.

Such eager applause broke out when Delphine stopped dancing that for a moment it seemed as if every man there was in love with her, and every woman her slave.

I am still weak, and have been forbidden to take any exercise which might heat the blood, but I could not resist the temptation of an English country dance with Delphine. A set was forming the length of the gallery; I asked her to go down it with me.

"Can you do that without any risk of injury?" she asked.

"Have no fear for me," I replied. "I will be holding your hand."

The dance began; several times my arms were around that bewitchingly light, supple figure. Once as we spun around I felt her heart beat beneath my hand. Could that heart, endowed by all the powers of heaven, be alive with some softer emotion for me?

I was so carried away by happiness that I insisted on starting the same country dance all over again. The music was captivating: two melodious harps accompanying the wind instruments in a lively but touching melody. Delphine's dancing grew more animated little by little, her glances toward me more expressive; when the steps of the dance drew us close together, it was as if her arms were involuntarily opening to welcome me back, as if she were taking pleasure in leaning on me, despite her absolute dexterity. These intoxicating pleasures made me forget that my wound had still not healed. At the end of the set, as we reached the last couple, I felt my knees give way in a wave of weakness. With one last burst of strength I drew her even closer, whispering, "Delphine! Delphine, if I were to die like this, would you feel sorry for me?"

"My God!" she interrupted, her voice touched by emotion. "My God, what is the matter with you?" The way my face had changed was a shock to her. We had finished the dance; I leaned against the mantle, unconsciously holding my hand to my wound, which was very painful. Delphine could not master her distress; she gave in to it so much that despite my weakness I could see every eye fixed upon her. The fear of compromising her gave me strength, and I insisted on going into the next room. We had to walk some little distance; Delphine took no heed of anything but my condition, and crossed the whole ballroom without bowing to a soul, following behind me and, when she saw me stumble, coming to my side to support me. Useless to say I was feeling better, or that the fresh air would cure me! She thought only of my danger, and let the whole world see her undue distress and eager interest.

Oh Delphine! I swore I would be your husband at that moment exactly as if we had been at the altar. You gave me your faith and the gift of your innocent fate: you had tarnished your reputation for me!

As soon as I reached an open window, I felt completely better. Suddenly realizing what had happened, Delphine said tearfully, "I have just behaved in a most extraordinary way! and it is your imprudence that has put my heart to this cruel test. Léonce, Léonce, did you have to make me suffer to understand me?"

"Can you possibly suspect me of wanting to show other people something I hardly dare receive lovingly and respectfully in my own heart? If you are afraid of being blamed by society, I—"

"I am not afraid of being blamed by society," Delphine replied with an unusually tart expression. "But everyone will know my secret before I have told it to my friends. You have no idea how guilty such behavior makes me!" She was about to continue, when we heard something from the salon; the name "Mme. d'Ervins" was being repeated. Delphine immediately left me to find out what was the matter.

"Mme d'Ervins has fainted," said M. de Fierville. "Her husband has ordered that she be taken away in her carriage; he does not want her cared for anywhere but at home."

He had hardly finished speaking before Delphine flew down the staircase, caught up with M. d'Ervins, climbed into his carriage without so much as a word to him, and was driven off: that was all I saw. She was carried away by the quick impulse of passionate kindness. I was left alone in the middle of the fete, now unrecognizable to me. I tried to find the pleasures I associate with love, but in vain; I was pierced by the tender, serious feeling that fills the heart of an honest man when he has given his life and taken on the responsibility for another person's happiness.

I don't know whether or not telling you my feelings is taking advantage of your friendship. But why should your respectable age and character keep me from portraying this pure love, guiding me in the choice of my life's companion? Surely the story of your pupil's happiness will give you pleasure. Reminders of your youth cannot be bitter to you, since your own memories are all bound up with virtue.

I am going to wait for my mother's answer before I give Mme. d'Albémar a complete explanation. I will be near you at Mondoville in a few days, since you need me there. I want us to write to my mother together, from the place where she spent her early married life and my childhood; those memories will make her feel favorably disposed toward me.

DELPHINE TO MLLE. D'ALBÉMAR (1.30)

I have spent a very restless day, Louise dear, and I still have not managed to speak to Mme. de Vernon. In spite of a few pleasant moments, the whole day has left me with feelings of acute anxiety. I wrote to Mme. de Vernon as soon as I woke up, asking her to see me alone at breakfast time; I may not have told her in so many words exactly what I wanted to talk about, but I think I gave some pretty clear indications. She made my servant wait for two hours, and finally sent him away with a letter apologizing for not being able to accept my offer. The letter finished with these remarkable words: "I can read into your heart as well as you do, my dear Delphine, but I don't think the time is right for us to talk to one another yet."

I have been reflecting on this sentence for some time, and I still can't understand it. Why is she trying to avoid this interview? She told me herself two days ago that she had not yet spoken to Léonce about the marriage plans—can she possibly have guessed my feelings for him? Could she be generous enough, sensitive enough, to want to break this engagement for my sake, without a word to me? How I would blush at such a sacrifice! What have I done to deserve it? On the other hand, if she had any notion of such a thing, how could she let Matilde go on seeing Léonce every day? In a state of unbearable indecision, I finally made up my mind to go to see her and force her to listen to me.

But what did I have to say to her? That I loved Léonce; that I wanted to stand in the way of her daughter's happiness, and upset all our plans! Louise, you are much too encouraging about this weakness of mine. I will not let myself hope until Mme. de Vernon has heard me out and decided my fate.

I was just leaving the house when M. de Serbellane arrived. I was sorry to see the change in his face; I could see he was suffering. "I read Thérèse's letter," he said. "It was painful—I had hoped to live my life without harming anyone, and here I have been the downfall of the most sensitive of women. Let us see what can be done, though," he went on, regaining his self-control. "I agree to go away, since she wants me to, though I can hardly bear to look as if I were giving in to M. d'Ervins. I am not afraid of anyone's thinking I was trying to save my own life. You have given me so many proofs of angelic goodness, madame, that I must ask you one last favor. You must let Thérèse and me come to your house tomorrow night. I am going to pretend to be leaving this morning; M. d'Ervins will think I am on my way to Portugal. He has to go to Saint-Germain on business, and Thérèse and I will come here in secret while he is away. I realize that an ordinary woman would refuse this request, and a light woman would grant it without thinking twice; I will be allowed it because of your sensitivity. I may not always have been as impetuous as Thérèse, but I need this farewell today as much as she does. These last events have made more of an impression on me than I would have believed possible, and I want her to hear what I have to say about her situation."

M. de Serbellane paused here, astounded by my silence. I felt more averse than ever to any further steps because of what had happened yesterday with M. de Fierville: calumny or gossip can doom me in Léonce's eyes. All the same, I did not have the courage to turn M. de Serbellane down. What reason could I give him? I would have blushed to invent a moral scruple when the cause of my hesitation was not really morality. Eternal shame is the lot of those who try to usurp respect on false grounds.

I am not sure whether or not M. de Serbellane noticed these

struggles. Taking my hand, however, he said with the serenity which always seems to have right on its side: "You promised this to Thérèse. Can you deceive her trust in you? Can you possibly have become hardened to her despair?"

"No," said I. "I will not hurt her like that, whatever happens. Use this interview to calm her mind and bring her back to the duties fate has imposed on her; then, even if the effect on me is some great misfortune, I will never have been hard-hearted toward another human being, and I will be entitled to pity."

"What a generous friend!"cried M. de Serbellane. "You will be fortunate with your emotions—I have guessed them, I venture to approve of them. All I want is for you to be happy. I swear to be so prudent and secretive about this interview that any possible inconvenience to you will be avoided. I will use these last hours to strengthen Thérèse's mind; the only words spoken in your house will be worthy of you. The next night I am leaving—leaving, perhaps forever, a woman who has loved me more than anyone else has ever done—and I leave you, madame, so noble, so sensitive, so sincere."

This was the first time M. de Serbellane had ever expressed his respect for me this keenly, and I was deeply touched. The man has a knack for making his slightest words move you; he inspired enough courage in me to keep me going for several minutes. As soon as he had left, however, I was overcome by great sorrow at the thought of the many risks involved in the promise I had made.

Léonce would surely have disapproved of me if I had been able to consult him, don't you think? He would not want his wife to let herself act so weakly; I am sure of that at least. If only my conduct until now had been what he would demand of a wife! But hadn't I already promised? Could I bear to be the cause of such racking pain, and of my own free will? No. All the same, I wish this day were over.

Distracted as I was by this promise, I was in no condition to speak to Mme. de Vernon, but I followed my plan of going to see her. I found her with Léonce; he was going to spend a few days at Mondoville, and had come to say goodbye. He apologized for not having come to see me, speaking so sweetly about my devotion to friendship that I could only hope he loved me the more for it. He took part in our conversation with a very easy mind; it seemed to me as I watched him that his decision had already been made. Before he had seemed carried away, but not resolute; seeing him so calm made me hope for great things. He could never have looked at me so serenely if he had given me up.

Mme. de Vernon was going to the Tuileries to pay court to the Queen, and asked me to go with her; Léonce said he would go too. I went back home to dress, and Léonce and Mme. de Vernon came to get me a quarter of an hour later.

We were waiting for the Queen in an antechamber with forty of the most distinguished women in Paris, when Mme. de R. arrived. Mme. de R. is an extremely irresponsible woman who has lost her reputation through real errors and incredible flightiness. I have seen her three or four times visiting her aunt, Mme. d'Artenas, and have always been careful to avoid any relationship with her—but I do sometimes notice something basically sweet and good about the things she says. I don't know how she can have been foolish enough to appear at the Tuileries without her aunt; she must be well aware of the fact that no woman wants to speak to her in public. Mme. de Sainte-Albe and Mme. de Tesin were there when she came into the salon; these ladies take a good deal of pleasure in summary justice, and are happy to satisfy their natural arrogance in the name of virtue. Their seats were on the same side of the room as Mme. de R's, and they stood up; all the other women got up at the same time too, whether out of society manners or fear I do not know, and came to the other end of the room near Mme. de Vernon, Mme. du Marset, and me. Soon all the men had followed this example: men may seduce women but they like to keep the right to punish them for being seduced.

Mme. de R. was left alone, the object of every eye, seeing the circle draw back with every step she took to approach it, and incapable of hiding her confusion. It was almost time for the Queen to have us enter her room, or else come out herself and receive us. I could see that the scene would become even more cruel at that point. Mme. de R.'s eyes were filled with tears; she was looking at us as if to beg for the help of one woman. I could not resist such unhappiness. The fear of displeasing Léonce still held me back—it is always with me—but a last look at Mme. de R. touched me so keenly that I crossed the room and sat down next to her. Yes, I said to myself. Society's rules are once again contrary to the real will of the soul: let them be sacrificed once more.

Mme. de R. greeted me as if I had brought her back to life,

which is indeed what it feels like to be relieved of the tortures inflicted by a society's merciless exercise of its power. I had scarcely begun to speak to her before feeling I had to look at Léonce; I could see embarrassment on his face, but not displeasure. It seemed to me that his anxious eyes were scanning the assembly to see the impression I had made, but that his own impression was favorable!

Mme. de Vernon kept on talking to M. de Fierville, apparently oblivious to what was going on, and I managed the embarrassments of my self-imposed role fairly well until the end. As we left the Queen's apartment, Mme. de R. said, with a burst of feeling that repaid me many times over for my sacrifice: "Generous Delphine! You have taught me the only lesson that could have made any impression on me. You have made me love virtue, its courage, its influence. You will realize in a few years that from this day forward there will be a change in me. It will be a long time before I feel worthy of coming to see you, but that is the goal I will give myself; that is the hope that will keep me going." At these last words I took her hand and gave it an affectionate squeeze. A wry smile from Mme. du Marset and a look from M. de Fierville were proof of their disapproval; they were both speaking with Léonce, who seemed painfully affected by what he was hearing. I looked around for Mme. de Vernon, but she was still with the Queen. During this moment of uncertainty, Léonce came up to me and asked very seriously if he could see me alone after taking Mme. de Vernon back. I nodded my consent, too disturbed to speak.

I went back home and tried to read while I waited for Léonce. By the time the clock struck three, I was convinced that Mme. de Vernon had kept him, that he had reached an understanding with her, that she had made him think he should keep his mother's promises by appealing to his scruples, and that he was going to write to me saying he could not come. A servant entered at this point; he had a letter in his hand, and I had no doubt that it was his excuse. I took it, but I could not see; a cloud covered my eyes. When I saw Thérèse's signature a feeling of intense happiness came over me. She was asking me to come to her house that evening. I agreed very eagerly—I must have been grateful to her for being the person who had written to me.

I sat down again more calmly; in a little while, however, my anxiety came back. For the last hour I had been able to single out the sounds of individual carriages: I could tell right away which ones were coming from Mme. de Vernon's direction. As the carriages drew near, I would stop breathing so as to hear them better; as soon as they passed my door I would sink into the most painful depression. One stops at last—a knocking at the carriage door—the door opens—and it is the familiar blue carriage of Léonce. I was then terribly ashamed of the state I was in; I felt Léonce would be able to guess it, and I quickly grabbed a book, pretending to receive as an ordinary caller, according to social conventions, a man who was making my heart beat so strongly that my gown rose and fell on my breast.

Léonce appeared at last, and the air grew light and fresh. He began by saying that Mme. de Vernon had insisted on keeping him with her in a most peculiar way, without anything to say, continually asking him to perform the most meaningless tasks. "She must have been trying everything she could think of to keep you in her power," I said, making an effort to control myself. "That can hardly surprise you."

"Mme. de Vernon is not in control of my fate," said Léonce, a little sadly. "You are the only person who has that power. I just don't know whether you are going to use it to make me happy." I kept silent, astounded by his doubt, and he went on: "If I had the honor of pleasing you, wouldn't you think of excuses for me? You provide excuses enough for the wicked. Would you forget my mother's character? and the obstacles . . . " He stopped, leaning his head on his hand.

"What are you accusing me of, Léonce?" I asked him. "I want to hear that before trying to justify myself."

"Your intimate relationship with Mme. de R. Is that a friend for Mme. d'Albémar to pick?"

"This is the third time I have seen Mme. de R. since coming to Paris," I answered. "I have never been to her house, and she has never come to mine."

"What!" cried Léonce. "And Mme. du Marset had the gall to say—"

"You listened. You are much more guilty than she is. And there's more to it," I went on. "You disapproved of my taking a place next to her, didn't you?"

"No," Léonce answered. "I was suffering, but I did not blame you."

"Suffering!" I said hotly. "When I was giving in to a generous impulse! Oh Léonce! That unfortunate woman's misery was what should have hurt you, not my good luck in having a chance to help her! Mme. de R. has certainly degraded herself, but how can we possibly understand all the circumstances that made her a lost woman? Was her husband a protector, or a man who did not deserve to be loved? Did her parents take care of her education? Did her first choice treat her gently, or blight every hope of love, every sense of delicacy? Oh! Women's fate depends on men in so many ways! But I can hardly boast of thinking about Mme. de R.'s conduct today, or of any indulgence she may deserve. I was drawn toward her by a completely unpremeditated impulse of pity. I was not her judge—and one would have to be more than her judge to refuse her comfort for the torture of public humiliation. Do you think those women who were insulting her would have avoided her if they had met her alone in the country? No. They would have spoken to her. Their virtuous indignation would not have been aroused, because it would have gone unwitnessed. There is such petty vanity and cold cruelty in that kind of ostentatious virtue: the sacrifice of a human being, not to morality, but to pride.

"Listen to me, Léonce," I cried with enthusiasm. "I love you. You know that—and I wouldn't try to hide it from you if by some chance you were unaware of it. Far be it from me to play around with the heart—even the most innocent tricks! But I hope I will never sacrifice to that omnipotent passion the good qualities given me by the dear friends who raised me. I will face what is the greatest of dangers for me, the fear of displeasing you—yes, I will face even that, if there is any question of bringing some unhappy creature consolation."

The expression on Léonce's face had told me long before I finished speaking that I had conquered his tendency toward severity. He was enjoying listening to me, though, so I had gone on, encouraged by his glances. "Delphine, heavenly Delphine," he now said, taking my hand, "I cannot resist you any longer. What difference does it make whether or not our characters always agree? There is no other woman like you in the whole world. No one else's face bears the divine stamp of heaven. You can never be compared with another woman. Your soul, your voice, your gaze have taken hold of my whole being. I don't know what my fate will be with you—but without you there is nothing for me on this earth but faded colors, blurred images, wandering shades. Nothing exists if you are not there; nothing is alive. Be my life's companion," he cried, throwing himself at my feet, "my guardian angel throughout the years ahead of me. I entrust you with my happiness as well as my life; take care of it. Treat my faults gently: they come from the same passionate nature as my love. And ask heaven on our wedding day to let me die young and beloved by you, without the least chill in the touching affection your heart has been kind enough to grant me."

Oh Louise! The feelings I had! I took both his hands in mine, I wept, I was afraid to say anything that might interrupt those intoxicating words!

Léonce said he would be writing to his mother in Spain to tell her his intentions, and asked me to promise to marry him as soon as he got an answer, whatever that answer might be. I was overjoyed, and began agreeing to be happy for life, when I suddenly realized that this request was contrary to my decision to tell Mme. de Vernon about my secret before making any engagement. My delicate scruples forbade me to give any definite answer before I had spoken to her. I did not want to tell Léonce about this decision, for fear of annoying him, so I asked him not to insist on my promising anything before he came back. Astounded, he flinched at these words, and his face grew dark.

I was about to reassure him when the door flew open, and I saw Mme. de Vernon, her daughter, and M. de Fierville enter the room. I was terribly disturbed by their presence, and overwhelmingly sorry that I had not had time to explain to Léonce about my wounding rejection. Mme. de Vernon paid no attention to me, and sat down with no further ado, announcing that she had come to fetch me for dinner. Matilde was surprised for a moment when she saw Léonce at my house, but the moment passed without arousing her suspicions: her mind is so slow and her ideas so rigid that she runs no risk of jealousy.

"By the way," Mme. de Vernon began, "is it true that M. de Serbellane is leaving for Portugal the day after tomorrow?"

I turned very red at this, afraid of compromising Thérèse, and said hastily that he had left that very morning. Léonce looked at me sharply and then became lost in thought. I was once again aware of my disastrous secret, and began to tremble as if my destiny were in great danger.

Mme. de Vernon suggested that we leave, pressing Léonce to join us in a halfhearted way. He refused; M. Barton was waiting for him. As I was getting into the carriage, he said to me in low, solemn tones: "Never forget that with someone like me, any wrongdoing of the heart, any dissimulation, would destroy my happiness and my trust simultaneously and forever." With the others all around me, I could not speak: I gazed at him so that he would pity me. He understood, shook my hand, and went away.

Since that moment, however, I have been weighed down by painful depression. It has finally been arranged that Mme. de Vernon will see me alone tomorrow night. Before then, Thérèse and her lover will have had their meeting at my house—that is too much for one day. I saw Thérèse tonight. M. de Serbellane had sent her a note telling her about my promise; I would not have known how to persuade her I was capable of taking it back, even if I had wanted to. Her husband thinks M. de Serbellane is on his way already; he will be going to Saint-Germain tomorrow. It has all been irrevocably arranged—I am tied with so many knots—but I hope at least that this will be the last secret there will ever be between Léonce and me. I have told you everything, dearest sister; think of me. My fate will be decided very soon.

DELPHINE TO MLLE. D'ALBÉMAR (2.2)

Yes, I will come to be with you—and forever—but why do you say that he never loved me? I know I have no more future, but you must leave me the past.

He loved me at the concert; at the ball; the last time I saw him—I am sure of it! For twelve days now I have done nothing but go over the same memories again and again; I have recalled words, looks, accents I had not enjoyed enough, but which must convince me of his affection. He loved me, I was free, and he is another woman's husband: you must not think that my thoughts will ever get out of this cruel circle drawn around me by regret. Ever since that day when I should have died, I have lived alone. I see no one but Thérèse; I have not answered Mme. de Vernon's letters, I have sent messages that I could not see her. You yourself could have done nothing for me.

I will be able to regain some self-control—but as for happi-

ness! Even your rational mind will tell you there is no more happiness for
me. You surely do not think I will ever love any man but Léonce, or that I
can ever forget the irresistible charm that inspired the first love of my life.
Well, a woman's fate is over and done with when she has not married the
man she loves. Society has left women's fate only one hope: when the
lottery is drawn and lost, it's all over. We can make vain attempts, we
often even degrade our characters by flattering ourselves that we can
repair an irreparable misfortune. But this useless struggle against fate just
upsets the days of youth, and deprives our last years of virtuous
memories, the only glory of old age and the grave.

What is there to do, therefore, when something—whether
unknown or deserved—has taken away from you the supreme good:
love in marriage? What is there to do, when you are condemned never to
know it? Extinguish your feelings, make yourself dry up, like so many
people who say they manage perfectly well that way? Stifle those heartfelt
impulses which call for happiness and dash themselves against necessity?
I have almost succeeded in that—at the expense of my good qualities, I
realize, but what does it matter? For whose sake would I be preserving
them now?

I am less tender with Thérèse. There is something forced
about the way I speak, in my air, which makes me dislike myself. These
faults suit me: didn't Léonce think I was unworthy of him? Why
shouldn't I believe he was right? You want me to come back to you,
Louise dear. But will you recognize me? I have worked some peculiar
changes in myself and everything lovable about me. I had to harden my
soul to bear what I am suffering, didn't I? To be awake without hope, to
drag through every minute of a long day as if it were a heavy burden, to
find no more interest or life in one's usual occupations, to look at nature
without pleasure and the future without delight—good heavens, what a
destiny! And if I abandon myself to my misery, do you know what notion, what unworthy notion takes hold of me? The need for some explanation with Léonce.

I feel as if I would tell him things that would avenge me—
but what use would there be in vengeance? Only pride can preserve
whatever remains of his respect for me. But can he avoid seeing me? I am
the one who can refuse to see him, I must do that and I want to. Louise:
what ruined me was a lack of restraint in my character. I feel within me a
certain admiration for good and even bad qualities which keep one from

being influenced by other people. I love and respect coldness, disdain, resentment—Léonce will see whether or not I too can be like that— what will he see? He no longer looks at me. I upset myself, and he is at peace. My life plays no part in his; he goes on his way, and leaves me behind after watching me fall from the chariot which carries him along.

You talk to me of retirement! I hate the thought of society; but solitude is painful to me too. In the silence around me, I am pursued by the thought that no one on earth cares about me. No one! forgive me—I was thinking only of Léonce. What a disastrous feeling: it makes the heart a wasteland, leaving alive none of the sweet affections that once filled it! It is for you, for you alone, sister, that I am trying to live. Mme. de Vernon, whom I once loved so much, is nothing but a painful thought to me now; in the depths of my heart I reproach her bitterly. Alas! Léonce may be the only one who deserves reproaches; I want to keep myself from injustice, the foremost fault of the miserable. I will receive Mme. de Vernon, since she wants to see me. She writes that my refusal makes her unhappy—oh! I do not want to make her unhappy. Perhaps seeing her again will make me feel her charm once more.

I am begging for something to interest me, some pleasant moment, as one would invoke life's most wonderful boon. I feel as if it were impossible to stop suffering, as if there were nothing left in the world but pain.

MME. DE VERNON'S STORY (2.41)

You are the only person who has ever loved me in my whole life. A lot of people have found me attractive, and wanted to be with me, but you are the only one who has ever done anything for me without hope of personal gain or some goal other than the satisfaction of your friendship and generosity. And in spite of this, you are the person I have wronged more than anyone in the world! the only one, perhaps, who really has the right to blame me. How can I explain such conduct to you—or to myself? I will not paint it in rosy colors, at any rate; I will forbid myself, for once,

the help of anything but the truth. I appeal to your intelligence in this accurate portrayal of my character; I will not take advantage of my situation
to win my pardon by any possible effect on your emotions.[3]

My natural temperament was originally sweet and pliant,
but the circumstances determining my education changed it, and not for
the better; I do think it could have been encouraged to grow in a happier
direction. No one took much notice of me in my childhood, when shaping my heart toward confidence and affection would have been easy. My
mother and father both died before I was three, and the people who
brought me up did not deserve any affection from me. My guardian was a
very distant, very careless relative who provided me with all sorts of
tutors and no attention at all to my health or morals. He was willing to be
kind to me, but his heart gave him no indication of how to do it; as a
result, his conduct varied according to his memory and his mood.
Beyond that, he considered women as toys when they were children and
more or less pretty mistresses when they were young ladies, without anything to say on rational issues at any time.

I soon realized that all the feelings I expressed were being
ridiculed, and that my mind was being forced into silence, as if it were an
unsuitable thing for a woman to have. The result was that I locked my
feelings within myself, learned very young the fine art of lying, and stifled
the sensibility nature had given me. The only one of my natural qualities
to escape from my attempts to imprison them all was pride. When I was
caught in a lie, I would keep silent and refuse to give any reason for it; but
I did think it unfair that the same people who counted women for
nothing, allowing them no rights and almost no abilities, were the very
same ones who insisted on women's being frank and sincere—the virtues
of strength and independence.

As I had no money, my guardian grew tired of me, and one
morning he came and told me I had to marry M. de Vernon. M. de Vernon was a man I had met for the first time the evening before, and I
found him absolutely repellent. I resisted quite vehemently, giving in to
the one and only unpremeditated impulse I have ever shown in my life.
My guardian threatened to lock me up in a convent for the rest of my
days if I turned M. de Vernon down; I had no hope of liberating myself
from his tyranny, because I had no earthly possessions whatsoever. I examined my situation, and realized I was powerless. Useless struggle
seemed to me the behavior of a child. I gave it up—but with a feeling of

hatred for a society which would not defend me, and left me no resource but lying. Ever since then, my mind was irrevocably made up: I would lie whenever I might think I had to. I firmly believed that women's fate doomed them to falsehood; I confirmed my childhood notion that my sex and poverty made me an unhappy slave allowed to play all sorts of tricks on her tyrannical owner. I never thought about morality—I thought morality was irrelevant to the oppressed. I was not stifling my conscience, because to tell the truth, my conscience never reproached me until the day I lied to you.

M. de Vernon was not an easygoing soul like my tutor, but it was always a temptation to deceive him because he was so frightened of being dominated and so likely to be fooled. It was so easy—and there was always such a bother when he was told the most innocent truth that I swear it would have taken some sort of chivalry to talk with a man like him sincerely. During the last fifteen years I have made it my habit to owe my pleasures to nothing but the art of concealing my tastes and in-clinations. I have made this art into a principle, so to speak, seeing in it women's only means of defense against the injustice of their masters.

I did such a good job of getting M. de Vernon to spend a few years in Paris that he thought we were going against my will. I loved lux-ury; I don't know anyone who needs a lot of money more than I do, thanks to a combination of personality, fantasies, and spendthrift habits. M. de Vernon had become rich by economizing, but I aroused his vanity so thoroughly that by the time of his death he was almost ruined, and greatly in debt to Léonce's family, as you know. I had M. de Vernon in my power, though he treated me harshly. He had no idea at all that I was influencing his actions, but he spoke roughly to me anyway, just to prove to himself that he was my lord and master.

Often my pride would secretly rebel against the things I had to do to show my servile condition. I would have been poor again if I had left M. de Vernon, however, and I was convinced that the greatest humiliation anyone could bear was a lack of fortune in the middle of society, and the dependency involved in such deprivation.

Pretty and clever though I was, I never wanted to take lovers. I was frightened of the power of love, and I felt it could not be combined with the necessity for lying. Then too, I had become so used to restraining myself that no involuntary affection could arise in my heart. I was sharply aware of the inconveniences of flirtation, and I decided to keep my reputation intact right there in the middle of Paris, since I did not have the virtues that provide an excuse for being swept away. I think no one has ever been a better judge than I am of the value and ingredients of this sort of public respect; but are the bonds of love any better, such as they exist in our society? I think not.

At first I thought I would bring my daughter up according to my own ideas, and give her my character too; but teaching another person to lie is nauseating, and I was repelled by the process of giving lessons in my philosophy. My daughter was rather fond of me as a child, and I was unwilling either to tell her my secret or to deceive her. Nevertheless, I was (and am) convinced that women are doomed to misery if they abandon themselves to their feelings or lose control over themselves in any way at all, since they are the victims of all social institutions. As I have told you, Matilde showed from the start every sign of having a bitter character, so I decided to give her Catholicism as a restraint; I congratulated myself on having found a way to subject her to the yoke of feminine destiny without contaminating her natural sincerity. You can tell from all this that I did not like my way of life, though I was convinced it was necessary to survive.

M. de Vernon died, and the state of his fortune made it impossible for me to stay in Paris. This gave me great pain; I love society; or, more precisely, I have no love for solitude. I have never given myself the habit of any steady occupation, and I lack the imagination to find amusement in retirement, or variety in any thoughts of my own. I like society—gambling—all that. I enjoy everything that offers distraction from without; I hate inner upheaval; I am incapable of intense pleasure, which is why I have a hatred of pain. I have avoided pain with constant care and unshakable resolution.

I went to Montpellier.[4] That was six years ago, when I met you; you were sixteen, and I almost forty. M. d'Albémar, who had brought you up, was to marry you the following year, despite the fact that he was almost sixty. This engagement annoyed me very much, as it deprived me of any hope of inheriting anything from him, and ending the money troubles which were so peculiarly hateful to me. At first I was prejudiced against you—but after all these painful confessions I have earned the right to be believed when I swear that I always found you extremely attractive, and took fresh pleasure in every conversation I had with you during the three years I spent in Montpellier. But my soul was no longer accessible to feelings strong enough to change me. In order to be loved by someone like you, I had to hide my own character; I studied yours, to make mine look as if it conformed to it. This pretense may have been aimed at pleasing you, but it contaminated the charm of the friendship. Your husband died. I had told you I wanted my daughter's education to be finished in Paris; you offered to come with me, lending me the forty thousand pounds I needed to set up an establishment there. I accepted the favor: and that is what started to deprave my fondness for you.

Until that time, I had thought of you as a pleasure in my life, because you were so young and lively; from that moment on, I realized you could be useful to me, and I examined your character from that angle. I soon saw that you were dominated by your good qualities— kindness, generosity, trust—as other people are by passions. Your virtues might be unpremeditated, but they were almost as hard for you to resist as other people's vices were for them. Your independent opinions and romantic way of acting and seeing things were in striking contrast to the society in which your tastes, triumphs, rank, and riches would place you. I could easily see that your attractions and advantages might arouse passionate feelings in your favor; but they would make you enemies as well. And I thought I would have no difficulty influencing you in the struggle you were destined to wage against jealousy and love.

I swear that at the time my only intention was to use this in-fluence for our mutual happiness. Léonce's feelings for you changed my mind, however. His marriage to my daughter was very important to me. I have already explained my reasons to you; they were such that even your generosity could not lessen their influence over my destiny. Without this marriage, I would be held responsible for M. de Vernon's fortune, and I would have no way to give my daughter a suitable way of life. Nor could I have kept up my position in Paris.

I had a few debts that I had not admitted to you, among which was a debt to M. de Clarimin. I was sure he would keep quiet—I had no idea he was capable of the conduct he has shown toward me. I have known him since I was a child, and he is the only man who has ever deceived me; I thought he was hiding nothing because of the way he has always shown himself to me as completely immoral. One day, despite my customary caution, I wrote him a rather sharp letter, hurting his feelings.*

*This letter has not been found.

The habit of lying does have the disadvantage that a single fault can destroy the fruits of one's greatest efforts. Natural characters carry the remedy for their own mistakes within them; made-up characters may support themselves, but they never recover from a fall.

I had a grudge against you for trying to take Léonce away from my daughter, since we had agreed on this marriage together. You would probably have been able to justify yourself if I had spoken frankly to you, but I have a particular hatred of explanations. Having determined not to show what I think, I hate those moments when everyone is meant to tell everything. I kept my anger at you alive, then, and it grew even more bitter for being contained.

I nearly told you everything going on inside me the day of M. d'Ervins' death—you showed such confidence in me at the denouement of that tragic tale, just when I was all ready to oppose your marriage. But this impulse ran so contrary to my nature and my habits that I felt a kind of stiffness inside me preventing me from giving in to it. Innumerable coincidences favored my plans. A letter from Léonce's mother, solemnly opposing his marriage to you, arrived the night before I was to talk to him. The public was convinced that M. de Serbellane was in love with you, and that this was why he was so annoyed by M. d'Ervins' rudeness to you. Your letter to Léonce was vague enough to agree with anything one might choose to imply or omit. The efforts you made to save Mme. d'Ervins' reputation were inevitably compromising. I saw myself surrounded by the kind of disastrously easy things that end by dragging one down in the struggle between self-interest and honorable behavior.

I still hesitated, though—I swear I did. Twice I asked for the horses to take me to Bellerive. Finally, on the very morning of Léonce's return, I had a conversation with my daughter in which she told me that she loved him, and that her life's happiness was involved in marrying him. Then I made up my mind; I told myself that I had formed a contractual obligation to Matilde to marry her to Léonce by giving her hopes of it, and by letting her see such a remarkable young man day after day; and that I was only performing my duties as a mother in using every possible means to make him marry her.

This self-interest was reinforced by an opinion which cannot excuse me in your eyes, but is still quite convincing to me: I do not believe Léonce's character would ever have made you happy. I know that

his virtues may be points of similarity between you, but I realize something else too: that even in the interview when I earned my misfortunes
by betraying your trust—even then, what was acting on Léonce was not
simple jealousy. When I told him that general opinion was against you,
and that people would blame him for choosing a woman who had compromised herself in public, I was wielding enormous influence over the
way his mind worked. Every time I tried to make him reach a decision by
appealing to what he owed his reputation, I made him get red and anxious in a way that would not be completely soothed even if it had been
proved to him that only appearances were against you.

You now have an explanation of my conduct, though not an
excuse. The worst thing I did was to force Léonce's consent, and carry
him off to church before the two of you could see each other again. I
have been punished for it; this unfortunate marriage has given me
nothing but grief. My daughter has withdrawn from me and refuses to do
anything I want. I have thrown myself into all the distracting activities
that hold anxiety at bay; I have been gambling and staying up all night
every night; I felt I was cutting short my life, and I rather liked the
idea.

I was always afraid that some stroke of chance would allow
you and Léonce to clear things up between you. If I tried so hard to keep
that from happening, it was mostly in the hope of keeping your
friendship—stealing it, rather, as I no longer deserved it. The marriage I
wanted had taken place, but I needed Léonce's absence to give me time
to make you forget him. You might even have formed other ties, which
would have made you care less about the way your breakup with M. de
Mondoville had been managed. I was deathly afraid of an explanation,
and in order to prevent one I made sure I knew everything the two of
you did for two months while Léonce was delaying his trip. Your character and his made that easier. You were busy with M. de Serbellane on
Mme. d'Ervins' behalf, with no notion that at your age you might be
seriously damaging your reputation. As for Léonce, he is not only
jealous, but very sensitive to the way a woman may be doing him wrong,
or look to other people as if she is doing so, and it is easy to take advantage of this by making him angry against the very woman he loves. Finally
Léonce left for Spain, and you invited me to come to Montpellier with
you. I was confident of being able to keep your friendship now that
Léonce was away, so I came back to you with all my heart, with the

keenest friendship I have ever felt for anyone. In accepting a favor from you, I was worthy of it. I believed in happiness more than I ever had before. My health grew stronger, and my withered soul was refreshed by the hope of spending the rest of my life with you. That is when Mme. d'Ervins' daughter uncovered the world's best-kept secret; and it's a fitting punishment for a woman who thought herself good at lying because she fooled grown men, to have her game spoiled by a child.

This is the thing that has killed me, the cause of my fatal illness. You were right to be angry about my behavior when you were shown the truth; but I tried to avoid painful scenes, since our relationship was over in any case. The more guilty I felt, the more I suffered, the more I wanted to hide it from you. I did not try to soften your heart, though you could have doomed me as far as Léonce went. I could count on your generosity, true—but please don't reject the one good thing I can say for myself: I swear that the reason I could not beg to you is that I loved you.

As long as I was still in society, it did not suit me for people to know the real cause of our quarrel. I found myself committed to keeping up my character and putting up a skillful defense. My character was experiencing a good deal of change from within, but after forty years one's habits are still in control even if they are no longer in tune with one's feelings. One needs either lengthy reflections or severe shocks to correct the faults of a lifetime; a few days of repentance are not enough.

Such a sharp, deep wave of feeling went through me the other day when I saw you leaving, and saw the gentle, tender look you gave me! it has hastened the end of my life. At that moment I would have liked to keep you with me and tell you my secrets, but I needed to be at death's door to have the confidence to talk about myself. I am timid, in spite of my apparent presence of mind; proud by nature, in spite of my deceptively simple behavior. There is some kind of opposition within me I do not understand; it has often kept me from giving in to whatever good impulses I may have had.

At last I am going to die; this whole life of struggling and plotting is over. I once thought myself the only person in the world who really understood life; I thought everyone who spoke to me about feelings of devotion and high virtue must be a fake or a fool. Since knowing you I have had other thoughts now and then, but I am still not sure that my dry theory was altogether wrong. With anyone but you, the only reasonable relationships may well be calculated friendships.

Whatever the truth of all this, I do not consider myself wicked. I had a very low opinion of men, and I armed myself ahead of time against their evil intentions. I had no bitterness: I made all my inferiors and dependents quite happy, and even when I deceived people who had claims on me it was by making their lives pleasanter. Toward you I have acted wrongly, Delphine—you whom I have loved more than anything else in the world. That is so incomprehensible! so strange! Why couldn't I let myself go, and abandon myself to the impression you were making on me? I fought it like a madness, like a weakness disturbing a diplomatically well-organized life, whereas actually it was a feeling that would have contributed to my interests as well as my happiness.

I have told everything in this letter, without exaggerating any motives that might have excused me. I have given just weight to my feelings for my daughter and my own personal calculations. Believe me, then, about the only interest left to me: believe I die loving you.

I have lived my life filled with deep distrust for men, and great skepticism as to virtue and affection. You are the only person I have ever found who was both superior and natural, unaffected in manners, generous in sacrifice, constant, passionate, witty like clever people, and trusting like the best—in all, such a good, tender creature that you are the only person I hope will shed a few tears on my grave, in spite of all these unforgivable confessions, and keep something of tenderness in your memory of me.

SOPHIE DE VERNON

FRAGMENT (5.3)
SOME PAGES WRITTEN BY DELPHINE
ON HER VOYAGE

I am quite weak; I take pity on myself. So many men and even women walk steadily along the path traced before them, capable of finding contentment in those regular, monotonous days nature lavishes on anyone who wants them—and as for me! I drag through the days second after second, racking my brain to find the art to avoid the sensation of life and keep myself from reflecting on myself, as if I were guilty, and remorse were lying in wait for me within my heart.

I have tried to read; I sought my favorite tragedies and novels. I used to find a charm in the emotion caused by these works; the only sorrow I knew was in those tableaux sketched by the imagination, and the feeling of tenderness that came over me was one of my sweetest pleasures. Now I cannot read a single one of those words, put down at random perhaps by the writer; I cannot do it without a bitter impression. Unhappiness is no longer the touching adornment of love and beauty to me, but a burning, dry sensation; it is nature's exterminator, withering all the seeds of hope which are developing within us.

How few writings there are which tell you everything there is to fear in suffering! Oh! how frightened people would be, if there were a book that really unveiled unhappiness—a book showing what every-one has always been afraid to represent: the weaknesses and miseries which drag along in the wake of great misfortunes; anxieties for which despair is no cure; distaste which the bitterness of suffering cannot deaden; pettiness side by side with the noblest sorrows; and all these contrasts, all these irrelevancies working together only to do harm, tear-ing the heart by every kind of pain all at one time! In plays, you see only one side of the unhappy being, from a noble point of view, always in-teresting, always proud, always full of feeling. But I, I sense moments in the weariness of prolonged unhappiness when the soul gets tired of ex-altation, and seeks more poison in minute memories and hitherto un-noticed details—it does seem as if the least misfortune could do for us would be to set us free of those.

Ah! I lost happiness too soon. I am still too young—my soul has not had the time to prepare itself to suffer. One year, one happy year! Is that enough? Oh my God! man's desires always outdistance what you give him, but I can imagine nothing, in my enthusiasm, beyond the felicity I have tasted. I have no sense that there is anything beyond love! Give it back to me—unhappy woman! Isn't such a prayer blasphemous? Shouldn't I be taking it back before it reaches heaven?

THE REASONS WHY LÉONTINE DE TERNAN DECIDED TO BECOME A NUN (5.11)

I was once a very beautiful woman, and I am now fifty years old.[5] These two absolutely ordinary things have been the cause of everything I have ever felt in life. I don't know if I have been less reasonable than the average woman, or if my mind was more observant, more penetrating, less likely to preserve its own illusions. What I do know is that when I lost my youth, I found nothing in the world to fill my life. All the ties that connected me to the world loosened, as if spontaneously, until not one remained that I could really be sorry to lose. That was the point at which I felt I had to abandon the world.

I was clever then—perhaps I still am clever, but it is hard to judge, because that wit developed as it did through the confidence I had in my face. I was imaginative and lighthearted, I told stimulating stories, I could get angry with grace. Confident of attracting everyone as soon as I appeared, I felt a lively desire to please and the sweet certainty of success. This confidence inspired in me a host of ideas and expressions which I have never been able to find again since.

I had married a good, reasonable man who was madly in love with me. I was faithful to him—more out of pride than virtue, I must admit. I wanted to be cared for, followed, adored, without giving any one man the special preference they were all trying for. I was not guilty of wronging my husband, then, but I thought about him very little. He gradually developed the habit of interesting himself keenly in business affairs, distracting himself from the feelings which had absorbed him for several years. I had two children, a son and a daughter: I made them very happy when they were young. I saw to their pleasures, I gave them all the most famous tutors, and I enjoyed their affection until the boy was eighteen and the girl sixteen. That was when my life took on a new perspective, growing darker until it ended in ending the way I live now, which is as much like death as possible.

My face held its own for rather longer than usual; all the same, as soon as I turned thirty I began to think about the short time I had left. I was astounded by a novel sensation: I was frightened of the future instead of longing for it, I stopped making plans, I held the days back instead of hurrying them past. I tried to become more considerate to my friends—they noticed, and were no fonder of me. I became capricious and unpredictable again; people were no readier for that. No one around me was aware of the slightest change in the way he felt about me, but I could already see changes that nobody else yet suspected.

It occurred to me that I could make some new friends to re-fresh my life and mind. But I did not have it in me to love anyone I had not known in my first youth. My feelings may never have been very deep, but there was still an enormous difference between the new affections I was asking myself to feel and the involuntary affections which had deter-mined my first friendships. With peculiar precision, I would repeat the same things I had said in earlier days, in order to see if I could produce the same effect. I kept thinking I was meeting different characters, totally altered situations—whereas everything was really the same except myself. What I had lost was not yet the charm of youth, but the lively, undefined hopefulness that brings with it all the charm associated with the overwhelming odds of a long future.

None of my friendships held firm. Nothing worked out spontaneously. All my relationships were artificial, and needed constant care—I was doing too much or too little for other people—I had no sense of proportion about anything, because there was no proportion at all between my aims and my means. Finally, after seven or eight years of vain attempts to make life give me the impossible, a day came when I realized that I had really changed. I was at a ball: no man complimented me on my face all night long, and people even began to speak tactfully to me about beautiful young women, and turn the conversation to more serious topics when I was there. I felt as if judgment had been pro-nounced. Other people had finally discovered what I had predicted. There was no point in fighting it; I was too proud to cling to the few petty triumphs I might still have had by working very hard.

At this point I was still only middle-aged, and I could see nothing ahead of me, no hopes or goals that could involve my whole being. A man my age could have begun some new career. Until the last year of a long, long life, a man can hope for some moment of glory, and glory is a delightful illusion like love—a happiness which is not made up of sacrifices and efforts such as pure reason offers us. But women! Good God, women! How sad their destiny is! Halfway through life, they have nothing left but insipid days, growing paler year by year—as boring as material life and as painful as morality.

And your children? one might ask. Your children?

Nature is prodigal toward youth, restricting motherhood's sweetest pleasures to the same time of life that allows us the joys of love. We are the primary object of our children's affection at an age when we can still be an adoring husband's or lover's. When our youth is finished, however, our children's youth is beginning, and the attractions of life take them away from us just when we would most need to rely upon their feelings.

I tried to come back to my husband. He was kind to me. When I asked him, however, for the care—the sustained interest—in short the love I had inspired in him twenty years earlier, he did not refuse it to me, but he had completely lost any memory of it, as he had of the most trivial childhood games. What pleasure can you find in the company of a man to whom you are not necessary in some essential way? a man who could live with you or without you, and takes less interest in your existence than you do yourself?

When other people no longer care about you spontaneously, there is a good deal of temptation to make demands on them, and to reconquer with one's faults the control one can no longer expect from one's charms. The less love I inspired, the more I wanted my children's affection for me to have all the enthusiasm and idolatry I had cherished in the homage that had been paid me. The less interest and pleasure I took in society, the more I needed steady sweet companionship at home. But the more we come to need any feeling, pleasure, or goal, the harder it is to get. Nature and society both follow the well-known maxim of the Evangelist: "Unto every one that hath shall be given."[6] The losers, however, undergo a quick succession of contagious misfortunes.

I tried to keep myself busy, but nothing really interested me. My children were already educated, and my husband was busy with his own concerns, taking me for granted in a way that did not allow me to make changes in our relationship. What motive could I have for taking any action? Everything was all the same to me. It took me whole hours to come to a decision about the simplest actions of daily life, because no particular action was more imperative, more agreeable, or more useful than the next.

My husband died. We had not been living very tenderly together, but I felt as if his loss deprived my life of any remaining charm or dignity. My children had been married, one in Spain, one in Holland:

there was no longer any necessary relationship between myself and anyone else. When we are young, the links of family relationships are a
bother, and all we want is to surround ourselves with people drawn to us
by mutual attraction. When we are old women, though, we wish there
were nothing arbitrary about our lives any longer—we wish our feelings
and the relationships that arise from them were all foreordained. We
build no hopes on chance or choice.

I could no longer understand how to get through the end-
less days I might still have left. I could foresee no interests, variety, or
pleasures to fill them—nothing but a frivolous murmur of insipid
notions that could not even sing me sweetly to sleep in my grave. Vanity
has a great and inevitable influence on women's fate. Women have no
private or public business, no obligatory occupations, so they concentrate on what concerns them. They see life in terms of details—but life is
more interesting when one takes a larger view than it is through day-to-
day observations. So I was experiencing a painful inner restlessness,
noticing everything, wounded by everything, enjoying nothing. There
was a steady source of pain within me, adding to my miseries and cutting
into my pleasures. Even in my best moments, the fact that my life was
fading gained on me every day.

In the end I went to see one of my friends, a nun who enjoyed perfect peace. She had no trouble persuading me to adopt her profession. What did I have to lose? Was I not already under the control of
death? Dying begins as soon as the first love withers, the first feeling
grows cold, the first charm disappears! Its harbingers are all marked on
our faces ahead of time. Little by little we see ourselves deprived of the
means of expressing our feelings. The soul loses its interpreter, our eyes
stop portraying our experiences; our hearts' impressions, locked up
within us, no longer have glances or countenances with which to communicate. Then we have to lead a serious life, and wear on our defeated
faces the sadness of old age, the tribute it pays to tyrannical nature.

Everyone talks about the timidity of youth; how sweet that
is! It comes from the anxiety of hope. The timidity of old age, however, is
the bitterest sensation imaginable, composed of the cruelest possible experiences: a suffering that can no longer fancy it inspires the slightest interest, and a pride afraid of exposing itself to ridicule. The only goal of
this sort of negative pride is invisibility. You feel dimly ashamed of still
being alive when your place in the world is already taken and you are one

of life's supernumeraries, surrounded by people who are in control of life and possess it in all its vigor.

I wanted the convent I lived in to be far from Paris: the sound of society is painful in even the happiest solitude. Someone suggested an abbey a few leagues from Zurich. I came here three years ago. Since then, I have at least been hiding from view the slow, cruel spectacle of the deterioration of old age. Instead of fighting my sadness, I have adopted a way of living that consecrates it as the unique occupation of my life. Sadness can be very good company, as soon as one stops trying to distract one's attention. And in the end, what else can I say? I had to live, and this is how I have tried to manage.

7.

Corinne, or, Italy

—Udrallo il bel paese,
Ch' Appenin parte, e 'l mar circonda e l'Alpe.
—Petrarch[1]

OSWALD LEAVES ENGLAND FOR ITALY

(1.1)

Oswald, Lord Nelvil, left Edinburgh for Italy during the winter of 1794.[2] He was a Scottish nobleman with a handsome, aristocratic face, a good deal of wit, a great name, and an independent fortune, but his health had been weakened by intense sorrow, and the doctors had prescribed Southern air, fearing for his chest. Lord Nelvil followed their advice, though he took very little interest in prolonging his life. He hoped, at least, that he might find some distraction in the things he would be seeing. The cause of his illness was that most intimate sorrow, the loss of a father; his regret was embittered by harsh circumstances, intensified by scrupulous remorse, and mingled with the phantoms of imagination. It is not hard to convince ourselves that we are guilty when we are suffering; violent grief distresses conscience itself.

At twenty-five, Oswald was discouraged with life. His mind judged everything in advance, and his wounded emotions no longer enjoyed the illusions of the heart. He was most obliging and devoted to his friends, when he could be of use; but nothing, not even the good he was doing, gave him any pleasure. He always sacrificed his preferences to those of other people, which was not hard for him; but this complete sacrifice of self-interest could not be explained by simple generosity. Very often, it was attributable to a kind of unhappiness which no longer allowed him to take an interest in his own destiny. People who did not care about him enjoyed his character, finding it full of grace and charm; but those who loved him felt that he was concerned with other people's happiness like a man who no longer hoped for his own, and were almost hurt by the way he made them happy without their being able to give him any happiness in return.

Oswald had a mobile, sensitive, passionate nature, a combination of everything that can involve others and oneself, but misery and repentance had made him fearful of destiny; he thought he could disarm fate by making no demands on it. He was hoping to protect himself against the pain that tears at the soul through strict devotion to his duties, and renunciation of intense pleasure: his experiences had frightened him, and nothing in the world seemed worth the chance of such misery. If one is capable of this kind of pain, however, where can one find a way of life to protect one from it?

Lord Nelvil flattered himself that he could leave Scotland without regret, since his presence there gave him no pleasure; but this is not the way the fatal imagination of sensitive people works. He had no suspicion of the bonds tying him to the most painful places, and to his father's house. In those rooms there were places he could not go without trembling; when he decided to leave them, though, he felt even more alone. Something dry and barren took hold of his heart. He could no longer cry when he was unhappy, or bring back all the little local details that touched him so deeply. His memories were no longer living; he was no longer connected to the things around him. He did not think less about the person he missed, but it became harder to retrace his presence.

Sometimes too, Oswald reproached himself for having left the places where his father had lived. "Who knows?" he wondered. "Perhaps the shadows of the dead cannot go everywhere with those they love! Perhaps they can only wander near their graves! Perhaps my father is missing me right now and is not strong enough to call me from so far

away! When he was alive, alas, a combination of incredible events must
have convinced him that I had betrayed his love, that I was a traitor to
my fatherland and my father's wishes—to everything sacred on the face
of the earth!" These memories made Lord Nelvil so unbearably unhappy
that not only would he have been unable to confide them to someone
else, but he was afraid of going into them himself. It is so easy to hurt
one's self with one's own reflections!

Leaving one's fatherland is much more painful when it involves a sea crossing; a trip that begins with the ocean is a very solemn
one. An abyss seems to open up behind you, as if it might be impossible
to go back. Besides, the spectacle of the sea invariably makes a deep impression; the sea is the image of the infinite, always an attraction to the
mind, which is constantly on the verge of getting lost in it. Leaning on the
helm, his gaze fixed on the waves, Oswald was apparently calm; his pride
and shyness usually prevented him from showing his emotions even to
his friends. Painful inner feelings were disturbing him, however. He was
remembering the time when, as a young man, he had been aroused by
the sight of the sea, by the desire to swim through the waves, measuring
his strength against the current. "Why should I always abandon myself to
this reflection?" he wondered with bitter regret. "There is so much
pleasure in active life, in the kind of violent exercise that makes us feel
the energy of living! Then even death looks like nothing but an event,
glorious perhaps, sudden at least, and with no foretaste of decay. But the
kind of death that comes unsought by courage, this death of the
shadows, which takes away in the night all you hold dear, which despises
your mourning and rejects your open arms, pitilessly making you face the
eternal laws of time and nature—this death makes one despise human
destiny and the impotence of pain, all those vain attempts about to crash
against necessity."

Such were the feelings tormenting Oswald. His unfortunate
situation was a combination of the vivacity of youth and thoughts appropriate to a different time of life. He identified himself with the ideas
that must have concerned his father in the last stages of life, bringing the
eagerness of twenty-five to the melancholy reflections of old age. He was
tired of everything, but he missed being happy exactly as if he still had illusions. This antithesis disorganized him to the depths of his soul,
because it was in total opposition to the intentions of nature, which in-
situtes wholeness and gradual process in the nature of things. From the

outside, however, Oswald's manners still looked gentle and harmonious; instead of making him ill-tempered, his sadness made him even kinder and more thoughtful of others.

Two or three times during the crossing from Harwich to Emden, the sea threatened to be stormy.[3] Lord Nelvil advised the sailors, reassured the passengers, and, when he took the helm himself, taking the pilot's place for a moment, showed a strength and skill that should not be considered as simple physical litheness or agility: the soul partakes in everything we do.

When the time came to part, everyone on board gathered around to say goodbye to Oswald, thanking him for a thousand little favors he had done and forgotten. Once it was a child who had taken a good deal of his time; more frequently an old man whom he had helped to walk when the wind was rocking the boat. No one had ever seen such unselfishness; every day had gone by without his devoting a single moment to himself. He had abandoned each moment to other people, out of melancholy and kindness. As they left him, the crew cried out almost in unison: "May you be happier, my lord!" Oswald had never once expressed his sorrow, and these men of another class had not said a word about it to him as they made the crossing together. But the common people, in whom their superiors rarely confide, are used to discovering feelings without the help of words; they pity you when you are suffering even if they do not know the cause of it, and their spontaneous pity is unadulterated by either blame or advice.

1.5

Oswald traveled to Rome through the marches of Ancona and the Ecclesiastical State[4] without seeing anything, or taking any interest; this was due both to his melancholy disposition and to a certain natural laziness, from which nothing but strong emotion could pry him loose. He had developed as yet no taste for the arts, having lived only in France, where society is everything, and in London, where political interests are almost everything. His imagination took no delight in either natural marvels or artistic masterpieces, as it was concentrating on its own pain.

The Count d'Erfeuil went through every town guidebook

in hand, with the double joy of passing his time in seeing everything and
of assuring everyone that he had seen nothing to be admired by anybody
familiar with France. The Count's boredom discouraged Oswald, who
was in any case prejudiced against Italy and the Italians. He had not yet
penetrated the mystery of that country and its people—a mystery that
has to be understood through the imagination rather than the kind of
judgment developed by English education.

The Italians are much more remarkable for what they have
been and could be than for what they are now. The desert surrounding
the city of Rome is exhausted by glory; it seems too proud to produce; to
anyone who looks at it from a utilitarian point of view, it is nothing but
uncultivated, neglected land. Oswald had been brought up accustomed
to the love of order and public prosperity, and he was at first unfavorably
impressed as he crossed the abandoned plains that herald the approach
to the city once queen of the world. He blamed the laziness of the inhabitants and their leaders. Lord Nelvil judged Italy as an enlightened ad-
ministrator; the Count d'Erfeuil, as a man of the world. Whether
through reason or frivolity, therefore, neither of them experienced the
effect the Roman *campagna* produces on the imagination when one has
filled oneself with memories and regrets, with the natural beauties and
famous misfortunes that spread an indefinable charm throughout that
countryside.

The Count d'Erfeuil would make comic speeches complaining about the surroundings of Rome. "No country houses!" he
cried, "no carriages, nothing indicating that a great city is nearby! Good
God, how depressing!" As they approached Rome, the postilions cried
out, "Look, look! The dome of St. Peter's!" That is the way Vesuvius is
pointed out by the Neapolitans, and the sea by the people who live near
the shore. "Anyone would think we were looking at the dome of the Invalides,"[5] exclaimed the Count d'Erfeuil. This comparison—less accurate than patriotic—destroyed any effect the sight of that magnificent
miracle of human creation might have made on Oswald. Their entrance
to Rome was made not in beautiful daylight or on some lovely night, but
on a cloudy evening, in the sort of dull weather that tarnishes and con-
fuses everything. They crossed the Tiber without noticing, entering
Rome by the Porto del Popolo, which leads straight to the Corso, the
biggest street of the most modern part of town, but also the part of town

with the least originality, the one that looks most like other European cities.

There were crowds strolling through the streets; marionettes and charlatans were attracting groups of people around the column of Antoninus. Oswald's attention was completely captured by the things closest to him. The name of Rome still had no resonance in his soul; he felt nothing but the deep isolation that takes hold of your heart when you enter a foreign city and see a multitude of people completely unaware of your existence, and who have nothing in common with you. In the huge caravansary of Rome, everything is foreign—even the Romans themselves, who seem to live there not as foreigners, "but as pilgrims resting at the side of the ruins."* Oswald, oppressed by painful feelings, went to his room, and did not go out to see the town. He was very far from thinking that this town, which he had entered with such feelings of depression and sorrow, would soon be the source of so many new ideas and pleasures for him.

CORINNE AT THE CAPITOL: IMPROVISATION AND CROWNING

(2.1)

Oswald awoke in Rome. As he opened his eyes he was struck by a brilliant Italian sun, and his soul was filled with love and gratitude for the heaven which seemed to be showing itself through its beautiful rays of light. He heard the many church bells of the city ring; cannon shots, relayed from point to point, were heralding some solemn occasion. On inquiring what was going on, he was told that the most famous woman in

---

*This reflection is taken from an epistle on Rome by M. de Humboldt, the Prussian minister to Rome and brother of the famous traveler. It is hard to find a man whose conversation and writing imply so much knowledge and so many ideas.[6]

Italy—Corinne, poet, writer, improvisator, and one of the most beautiful women in Rome—was to be crowned on the Capitol that very morning. Oswald asked about this ceremony, hallowed by the names of Petrarch and Tasso, and became more curious with everything he was told.[7]

Nothing is further from an Englishman's habits and opinions than this kind of great publicity given to the destiny of a woman. Foreigners find the Italian enthusiasm for all imaginative talents contagious, however, at least for the moment; it is easy to forget even one's own national prejudices when surrounded by a nation that expresses its feelings so vividly. In Rome ordinary people understand the arts and show some taste when they talk about statues, because paintings, monuments, ancient ruins, and a certain degree of literary merit are among their national interests.

Oswald went out into the public square, and heard people talking about Corinne—her talent, her genius. They had decorated the streets through which she was to pass. The masses who usually gather only in the wake of fortune or power were almost in an uproar to see someone whose mind was her only merit. In the current political situation, the glory of the fine arts is the only glory Italians are allowed, so they are sensitive to this kind of genius with an eagerness which would certainly produce many great men if applause were enough to produce greatness—if it did not take a strong life, large-scale interests, and an independent existence to nourish the mind.[8]

Oswald wandered through the streets of Rome, waiting for Corinne to arrive. Every moment someone spoke her name, or told some new story which illustrated a captivating range of talents. One said that her voice was the most touching in all Italy; another, that no one was as good at tragic acting; a third, that she danced like a nymph, and sketched gracefully and with originality. All agreed that no one had ever written or improvised such beautiful poetry, and that her daily conversation was graceful one moment, eloquent the next, in a way that enchanted all her listeners. Some quarreling went on as to the Italian town which had been her birthplace, but the Romans insisted that to speak Italian with such a pure accent one had to be born in Rome. Her family name was unknown. Her first work had appeared in print five years earlier, and had borne only the name Corinne. No one knew where she had lived before that time, or how. Lord Nelvil found this combination of mystery and publicity, a woman everyone talked about without know-

ing her real name, one of the marvels of the extraordinary country he had
come to see. In England he would have judged such a woman most
severely, but here in Italy he did not apply any social conventions, and he
looked forward to the crowning of Corinne with the interest he might
have felt for an anecdote from Ariosto.[9]

A burst of beautiful music proclaimed the triumphal pro-
cession. Any event, no matter what it is, arouses emotion if it is heralded
by music. A number of Roman noblemen and some foreigners preceded
Corinne's chariot. "That is the retinue of her suitors," said one Roman.
"Yes, everyone offers her incense," agreed another, "but she does not
favor anyone; she is rich, and independent. They say she is a woman of illustrious birth who prefers to remain incognito—she certainly has the
look of it." "In any case," continued a third man, "she is a goddess, surrounded by clouds." Oswald looked at the man who had said this; everything about him marked him as coming from the depths of society, but in
the Mediterranean everyone uses poetic expressions quite naturally, as if
they were breathed in with the air and inspired by the sun.

At last the four white horses drawing Corinne's chariot
made their way into the middle of the crowd. On this chariot, which had
been designed in the classical style, sat Corinne, with young girls dressed
in white walking on either side. Wherever she went, people were throwing perfumed flowers through the air; everyone came to the windows to
see her, and these windows had been decorated with flowerpots and
scarlet rugs. "Long live Corinne!" everyone cried. "Long live genius! long
live beauty!" The emotion was universal. Lord Nelvil, however, did not
share it yet. He had been telling himself that if he wanted to be a judge of
all this he would have to put aside English reserve and Gallic wit, but he
was still unable to surrender to the festivities, when at last he caught sight
of Corinne.

Corinne was dressed like Domenichino's sibyl, her beautiful
black hair intertwined with an Indian shawl wound around her head; her
gown was white, with a blue scarf fastened under the bosom in a picturesque costume close enough to ordinary dress not to seem affected.[10]
Her attitude on the chariot was both noble and modest—she was obviously glad to be admired, but a feeling of timidity mingled with her joy
and seemed to ask forgiveness for her triumph. The expression of her
face, her eyes, her smile, all aroused one's interest, and her first glance
made Lord Nelvil her friend, even before he was conquered by a more

vivid impression. Her arms were quite beautiful; her tall, though rather full figure bore the energetic stamp of youth and happiness, like Greek statues; her gaze was inspired. Her way of bowing and giving thanks for the applause had a natural quality that set off the brilliance of her extraordinary situation. She gave the impression of a priestess of Apollo moving toward the Temple of the Sun, and at the same time of a perfectly ordinary woman in the daily relationships of life. Whatever she did had a charm arousing interest and curiosity, astonishment and affection.

As Corinne drew closer to the Capitol, so rich in memories, the admiration of the crowd increased. The beautiful sky, the enthusiastic Romans, and Corinne herself electrified Oswald's imagination. He had often seen statesmen borne in triumph by the people in his own country, but this was the first time he had witnessed such honors given to a woman, a woman famous for her genius alone. Her triumphant chariot had cost no one's tears; no fear or regret prevented anyone from admiring nature's finest gifts: imagination, feeling, and intellect.

Oswald was so absorbed in his reflections, so busy with these new ideas, that he did not notice the ancient and famous places through which Corinne's chariot was passing. When it stopped at the foot of the staircase leading to the Capitol, all Corinne's friends rushed to offer her their hands. She chose to take the hand of Castel-Forte, the Roman lord with the greatest reputation for intelligence and good character. Everyone approved of this choice, and Corinne ascended the Capitol staircase, whose imposing majesty seemed to welcome the light steps of a woman. When she reached the top, there was a burst of music, and the triumphant sibyl entered the palace which had been made ready for her.

At the end of the reception room stood the senator waiting to crown her and the Conservators of the Senate; at one side were all the cardinals and the most distinguished women of the country, at the other the men of letters of the Academy of Rome.[11] The other end of the room was filled by part of the enormous crowd that had followed Corinne. The chair destined for her was on a lower level of of the platform than the senator's. The custom was for her to kneel down on the first step before sitting down in the presence of this august assembly. Corinne did this with such nobility and modesty, such sweetness and dignity, that Lord Nelvil felt his eyes fill with tears. His own emotion amazed him, but it seemed to him that in the middle of all this brilliance, all this triumph,

Corinne's glances had been begging for the protection of a friend—the protection a woman can never do without, no matter how superior she may be. And he thought to himself how sweet it would be to support a woman who needed his support only because of her sensibility.

After Corinne was seated, the Roman poets began to read the sonnets and odes they had written in her honor. All praised her to the skies, but their praises were not about her personally any more than about any other woman of superior genius. It was a pleasant combination of mythological allusions and images that could have been addressed throughout the ages, to every woman famous for her literary talent from Sappho's time to ours.[12]

This way of praising Corinne disturbed Lord Nelvil. He already felt that just by looking at her he could have given a truer, more accurate, more detailed portrait, a portrait that could have belonged only to Corinne.

2.2

Prince Castel-Forte began to speak about Corinne, and what he had to say drew everyone's attention. He was a man of fifty, measured and dignified in his speech and manner. Lord Nelvil's interest in his portrait of Corinne was unmixed with any other emotion, because of the Prince's age and everyone's assurances that he and Corinne were no more than friends. Without these reasons for security, Oswald would already have been capable of feeling vaguely jealous.

The Prince read a few pages in prose, unpretentious, but especially appropriate for an understanding of Corinne. He first showed the special merit of her work, saying that it consisted partly in the deep study she had made of foreign literature; she was able to combine to a very great degree the Mediterranean imagination, tableaux, brilliance of life, with the understanding and observation of the human heart which seems the share of countries where external objects arouse less interest.

He praised Corinne's grace and gaiety, which were not mocking, but lively in spirit and imaginatively fresh; he tried to praise her sensitivity, but it was easy to see that some personal regret was mingled with what he was saying about this. He regretted the difficulty experi-

enced by a superior woman in finding an object for her affections, as she
has already made herself an ideal image of it, arrayed with all the gifts her
heart and genius could desire. He took pleasure, nevertheless, in portraying the passionate feeling that inspired Corinne's poetry, and her art of
seizing on touching relationships between natural beauty and the most
intimate impressions of the soul. He pointed out the originality of Corinne's expressions, which came from her own character and way of feeling, without any nuance of affectation to mar a charm that was not only
natural but involuntary.

He spoke of her eloquence as of an overpowering force that
captivated its listeners in proportion to their own intelligence and true
sensitivity. "Corinne is certainly the most famous woman in our country," he continued, "but only her friends can portray her. The soul's true
qualities must always be guessed at; fame can keep us from recognizing
them just as much as obscurity, if some sort of sympathy does not come
to our aid." He spoke of her talent for improvisation, which was very different from what is generally called improvisation in Italy.[12] "It must be
attributed not only to her fertile mind," he added, "but to the deep emotion inspired in her by all generous thoughts; as soon as she speaks about
them, she is aroused and inspired by enthusiasm, the inexhaustible
source of feelings and ideas." Prince Castel-Forte also made his listeners
feel the charm of a style that was always pure and harmonious. "Corinne's poetry," he said, "is an intellectual melody uniquely capable of expressing the charm of extremely fugitive, delicate impressions."

He praised Corinne's conversation; it was easy to see that he
had enjoyed its delights. "A combination of imagination and simplicity,
accuracy and exaltation, strength and sweetness in one person, offering
constant variety in all the pleasures of the mind. That charming verse of
Petrarch could be applied to her:

> Il parlar che nell' anima si sente
> The language one hears in the soul.[14]

I think she must have something of that boasted grace and Oriental
charm the ancients attributed to Cleopatra.

"My imaginary universe is composed of the places I have
been with her, the music we have heard together, the pictures she has
made me see, the books she has made me understand. In all these things

there is some spark of her life; and if I had to exist far away from her, I would at least try to surround myself with them, sure as I might be that I could never find the trace of fire she had left in them, the trace of herself in fact. Yes," he continued, his eyes happening to fall on Oswald, "look at Corinne if you can spend your life with her, if the double existence she will give you can be guaranteed for some time; but do not look at her if you are condemned to leave her. As long as you lived, you would be looking for this creative soul capable of sharing and multiplying your thoughts and feelings: and you would never find it again."

Oswald trembled at these words; his eyes were fixed on Corinne, who was listening with an emotion born not of pride, but of more pleasing, touching sentiments. Prince Castel-Forte began again, after a momentary wave of tenderness; he talked about Corinne's talent for painting, music, declamation, dance; he said that in all these talents, Corinne was always herself, never following any style or rule too rigidly, but expressing through various languages the same power of the imagination, the same magic of the fine arts in their different forms.

"I do not flatter myself," Prince Castel-Forte said in conclusion, "that I have painted a picture of someone whom one cannot understand without having heard her; but her presence is for us in Rome like one of the blessings of our brilliant sky, our inspired nature. Corinne is the link among all her friends; she is the movement and interest of our life; we count on her kindness; we are proud of her genius; we tell strangers, 'Look at her, she is the image of our beautiful Italy. She is what we would be without the ignorance, envy, discord, and indolence to which our fate has condemned us.' We take pleasure in contemplating her as a wonderful production of our climate and fine arts, as a descendant of the past, as a prophecy of the future; and when strangers insult this country, out of which came the light that illuminated all Europe, when they are pitiless about our wrongs, which come from our misfortunes, we tell them: 'Look at Corinne.' Yes, we would follow in her footsteps, we would be men as she is a woman, if men could create a world within their hearts as women can; and if our genius, necessarily dependent on social relationships and external circumstances, could catch fire from the torch of poetry alone."

The moment Prince Castel-Forte stopped speaking, everyone broke into applause; even though the end of his speech implied an indirect censure of the current condition of the Italian people, all the great statesmen approved of it, which only goes to show the kind of liberal attitude there is in Italy. Such liberality may not change institutions, but it does make superior minds pardon a peaceful opposition to existing prejudices.

The reputation of Prince Castel-Forte was very high in Rome. He spoke with unusual sagacity, a remarkable talent in a country where people are even cleverer in their conduct than in their speech. He lacked the shrewdness in affairs of business that often distinguishes Italians, but he took pleasure in thinking, and was not afraid of the fatigue of meditation. The lucky inhabitants of the sunny South tend to avoid this fatigue, flattering themselves that they can intuit everything through their imaginations, as their fertile earth gives forth fruit without any cultivation, by the simple grace and favor of the heavens.

2.3

Corinne arose after the Prince had finished speaking; she thanked him with a gentle, noble bow that showed both modesty and a very natural joy in being praised just as she would have secretly wished. It was customary for the poet crowned on the Capitol to improvise or recite a poem, before the laurel wreath was placed on his head. Corinne had her lyre brought to her; this was her favorite instrument, something like the harp, but with a more classical shape and simpler sound. She felt very shy as she tuned it, and asked in a trembling voice what subject was to be imposed on her. "The glory and happiness of Italy!" cried everyone around her unanimously. "Very well," replied Corinne, already feeling the support of her talent, "the glory and happiness of Italy!" And she made herself heard in enchanting verses inspired by a love of her country; prose can give no idea of it. [. . .]

She was interrupted by several moments of wild applause. Oswald was the only one who was not involved in these noisy outbursts. When Corinne had said, "Here one is consoled for even heartache," he had leaned his head on his hand, and he had not lifted it again since then. Corinne noticed this, and quickly recognized him as an Englishman by his features, his hair, his clothes, his height, his manner. She was struck by his sad face and the fact that he was in mourning. His glance, fixed on her at that moment, looked mildly reproachful; she guessed the thoughts in his mind, and felt a need to satisfy him by speaking of happiness with less assurance, and devoting a few lines to death in the midst of the celebration. With this in mind, she took up her lyre once again, silenced everyone by striking a few long, solemn sounds, and began again.[15]

Oswald was so enchanted by these last strophes that he expressed his admiration in the most vivid way; this time even the Italians' ecstasy was no match for his. Indeed, this second improvisation of Corinne's had been aimed at him rather than at the Romans.

Most Italians speak in a sort of monotonous chant called *cantilena* when they read poetry.* However different the words, one's impression is always the same, because the accent—which is much more immediate than words—almost never changes. But Corinne recited with a range of tone which did not destroy the sustained magic of the harmony; it was as if different melodies were all being played by some celestial instrument.

Corinne's touching, sensitive voice as she spoke in Italian, a ceremonious, sonorous language, had an altogether novel effect on Oswald. English prosody is uniform and hidden; its natural beauties are all melancholy. Its colors have been shaped by clouds, and its modulation by the sound of waves. But when Italian words, brilliant as a feast day, resonant as the instruments of victory people compare to the color scarlet—when Italian words, still stamped with the pleasures a glorious climate offers every heart, are pronounced by a voice touched with emotion, their muted luster and concentrated force cause an intense, unexpected wave of emotion. Nature's intention seems frustrated, its kindness futile, its offers rejected; and the expression of pain in the middle of such enjoyment is much more astounding and deeply moving than when sung in Northern languages, which seem inspired by sorrow.

2.4

The senator took the crown of myrtle and laurel to place it on Corinne's head. She loosened the scarf around her forehead, and her ebony-black

*From this blame as to the Italian way of reciting poetry we must make an exception for the famous Monti, who speaks poetry just as he writes it. One of the greatest dramatic pleasures one can have is to hear him recite the episodes of Ugolino, Francesca da Rimini, the death of Clorinda, etc.[16]

hair fell in curls to her shoulders. She came forward bareheaded, her glance alive with a feeling of pleasure and gratitude which she made no attempt to conceal. She knelt again to receive the crown, but she seemed less disturbed, less shaky than at first: she had just spoken, just filled her soul with the noblest thoughts, and enthusiasm had won out over timidity. She was no longer a fearful woman, but an inspired priestess, joyously devoting herself to the cult of genius.

When the crown had been placed on Corinne's head, all the instruments rang out, playing the sort of triumphal airs that lift the soul in a powerful, sublime way. The sound of timpani and the flourish of trumpets touched Corinne again; her eyes filled with tears, and she sat down for a moment, covering her face with her handkerchief. Greatly moved, Oswald came forward out of the crowd, and stepped forward to speak to her, but was too embarrassed to do so. Corinne watched him for some time, though she was very careful not to let him see her paying attention to him; when Prince Castel-Forte came to take her hand so as to take her from the Capitol to her chariot, she let herself be led away, though absentmindedly, turning her head back several times on one excuse or another so as to see Oswald.

Oswald followed her; as she was descending the staircase, accompanied by her cortege, she turned back to see him once again, and the movement made her crown fall. He rushed to pick it up and give it back to her, pronouncing a few words in Italian to the effect that humble mortals put at the gods' feet the crown they dare not place on their heads.* Corinne thanked Lord Nelvil in English, with that pure, insular national accent which can hardly ever be imitated on the Continent. Oswald was absolutely astounded to hear her. He stayed stock-still for a moment, and then, distressed, leaned on one of the basalt lions at the foot of the Capitol staircase. Struck by his emotion, Corinne gazed at him again; but they were sweeping her away to her chariot, and the whole crowd disappeared long before Oswald regained his strength and presence of mind.

Until now, Corinne had charmed him as an enchanting foreigner, one of the marvels of the country he intended to visit. Her English accent brought back memories of his country, however, naturalizing

---

*Lord Oswald seems to be alluding to this beautiful distich of Propertius:

> Ut caput in magnis ubi non est ponere signis,
> Ponitur hic imos ante corona pedes.[17]

her charms. Was she English? had she spent part of her life in England? He could not guess: but she could not have learned to speak that way from study alone; she and Lord Nelvil must have lived in the same country. Who knew if their families might not have been connected? Perhaps he had even seen her in her childhood! We often have a sort of innate image of the beloved in our heart that convinces us we are recognizing something we are actually seeing for the first time.

Oswald had many prejudices against Italian women; he thought them passionate, but fickle, incapable of deep and lasting emotions. Corinne's words on the Capitol had already given him a very different impression; what would it be if he could find memories of his country once again, receiving a new life through the imagination, reborn for the future without breaking with the past!

In the middle of these reveries, Oswald found himself on the Sant'Angelo bridge leading to the castle of the same name: it is Hadrian's tomb, which has been converted into a fortress.[18] The silence of the place, the pale ripples of the Tiber, the rays of the moon lighting the statues set on the bridge and turning them into white shadows staring fixedly at the flow of the waves and of time, no longer their concern—all these things brought him back to his usual ideas. He put his hand on his breast, felt the portrait of his father, which he always wore, and took it off to look at it. The recent moment of happiness he had just experienced, and its cause, brought back his former feelings of guilt toward his father all too strongly. This reflection rekindled his remorse.

"Eternal memory of my life!" he cried. "My friend! greatly offended, yet so generous! Could I have believed that a feeling of pleasure would enter my heart so soon? You are not reproaching me: best and most indulgent of men, you want me to be happy, you still want it in spite of all my sins; but at least let me recognize your voice if you speak to me from heaven, as I did when you were on earth!"

CORINNE PERFORMS ON THE MISENO

(13.3)

During the week-long delay she had requested, Corinne decided to give a fete for Lord Nelvil. This notion of a festive occasion was mixed with some very melancholy feelings, however. As she examined Oswald's character, it was impossible for her not to be anxious about the impression that the things she was going to tell him would be making on him. In order to forgive Corinne for sacrificing her rank, her family, and her name to an enthusiasm for talent and the fine arts, he would have to judge her as a poet and an artist. Lord Nelvil was certainly bright enough to admire imagination and genius, but he believed that social relations came first, that the primary aim of women (and men too for that matter) was not the exercise of intellectual faculties, but the accomplishment of individual obligations. His bitter remorse at straying from his projected path had only strengthened his strict inner principles of morality. He was tightly bound in many ways by English customs—the habits and opinions of a country in which people are so comfortable with a scrupulous respect for their duties and the law; besides, the discouragement following deep sorrow predisposes one to whatever is in the natural order of things, whatever can be taken for granted, whatever requires no new resolution or decision contrary to the circumstances marked out for us by fate.

Oswald's love for Corinne had changed his way of feeling completely; but love never completely changes one's character, and Corinne could see this character through the passion that had triumphed over it. It may even have been that Lord Nelvil's charm itself had a good deal to do with this opposition between his nature and his feelings, which gave a greater value to all his proofs of affection. But the moment was coming when her life would be determined by the passing anxieties she had been pushing aside, so that they had disturbed her happiness only lightly and as if in a dream. This soul born to be happy, used to the changing sensations of talent and poetry, was astounded by the bitterness and fixity of sorrow. Her whole being was shaken by a trembling unknown to women long resigned to suffering.

Meanwhile, in all this cruel anxiety, she was secretly preparing one last brilliant day with Oswald. Her imagination and sensibility combined in a romantic way. She invited the English who were in Naples, along with some Neapolitans whose society gave her pleasure. On the morning she had chosen for the fete, the day before the confession which might destroy her happiness forever, a peculiar distress animated her face, giving it an altogether new expression. An inattentive observer might have mistaken this liveliness for joy, but Corinne's agitated, restless movements, her glances which focused on nothing, made Lord Nelvil see only too clearly what was going on in her mind. In vain he tried to calm her with tender protestations. "You will tell me that in two days," she kept answering, "if you still believe it; right now those sweet words give me nothing but pain." And she would go away from him.

The carriages for Corinne's guests arrived at the end of the day, when the sea breeze rises and refreshes the air, so that man may contemplate nature. The first break in their journey was Virgil's tomb, where Corinne and her party stopped before crossing the grotto of Pausilipo. Virgil's tomb is placed in the most beautiful place in the world, with a view of the Bay of Naples in the background. There is so much peace and grandeur in this view that anyone would think Virgil himself had chosen it; these simple lines of the *Georgics* might have been his epitaph:

Illo Virgilium me tempore dulcis alebat
Parthenope . . .

Then sweet Parthenope welcomed me, Virgil.[19]

His ashes still rest there, and the memory of his name attracts the homage of the whole world to this place. That is all man can snatch from death on this earth.

Petrarch planted a laurel on this grave; Petrarch is no more, and the laurel is dying. The strangers who come in droves to honor Virgil's memory have written their names on the walls around the urn. These unknown names are a nuisance; the only reason they seem to be there is to disturb the peaceful solitude inspired by this place. Petrarch alone deserved to leave some lasting trace of his journey to Virgil's tomb. From that sanctuary of glory we descend in silence, remembering the thoughts and images consecrated forever by the poet's talent. What a wonderful conversation with future generations, continued and renewed by the art of writing! What then are the shadows of death? For a man's ideas, feelings, and expressions to remain, and for his very self to be gone! In nature, such contradiction is impossible.

"Oswald," said Corinne to Lord Nelvil, "the impressions you have just been feeling are no preparation for a fete. How many fetes have taken place by tombstones, though!" she added, with a good deal of exaltation in her glance.

"Dearest friend," replied Oswald, "what is this secret sorrow that disturbs you? Confide in me. I owe you the six happiest months of my life, and perhaps during that time I may have made yours a little sweeter. Who could be impious toward happiness? or deny himself the supreme pleasure of being kind to a soul like yours? Alas—to feel necessary to the humblest of mortals is already a good deal—but to be necessary to Corinne! Believe me, that is so much glory and pleasure that no one would give it up."

"I believe your promises," Corinne answered. "But aren't you aware of moments when something violent and strange grips the heart, quickening its beats in painful agitation?" They crossed the grotto of Pausilipo with torches—that is the way to do it, even at noon, because it's a tunnel under the mountain, almost a quarter of a league long; when you are in the middle, you can scarcely see daylight at the ends. You hear an extraordinary echo inside: the horses' tread and the cries of the drivers make a single deafening sound that leaves your mind no consecutive thought. Corinne's horses were going amazingly fast, but she was still not satisfied, saying to Lord Nelvil, "Oswald dear, they are going so slowly! Make them hurry." "Why are you so impatient, Corinne?" he answered. "When we used to be together, you did not want to make the time go faster; you enjoyed it." "But now," said Corinne, "everything must be decided. Everything has to be finished, and I feel a need to hurry everything, even if it ends in my death!"

On leaving the grotto one has a lively sensation of pleasure in finding daylight and nature again—and what nature offers itself to one's eyes! What Italian landscape often lacks are trees; here there are trees in abundance. Besides, the ground is covered with so many flowers that one could easily do without the kind of forest that is the greatest natural beauty of every other country. The heat is so great in Naples that one cannot take a walk in the daytime, even in the shade; but in the eve-

ning, this sheltered country, surrounded by sea and sky, is entirely open
to view, and one breathes fresh air everywhere. The transparent air, the
variety of places, and the picturesque shapes of the mountains are so
characteristic of the views of the kingdom of Naples that artists prefer to
draw its landscapes above any others. Nature has a power and originality
in this country that is impossible to explain by any of the charms one
looks for elsewhere.

"I am taking you along the shore of the lake Averno near
the Phlegeton; you see before you the temple of the Cumaean Sibyl.[20]
We are crossing a place famous under the name of the pleasures of Baiae,
but I am not suggesting that we stop here. We will recall the historical
and poetical memories around us here when we have come to a place
where we can see all of them at once."

The Cape Miseno was where Corinne had prepared the
music and dancing.[21] The arrangement of the fete was most picturesque.
The Baian sailors were dressed in vivid, contrasting colors, and a few
Orientals from an Eastern boat in harbor were dancing with peasant girls
from the nearby islands of Ischia and Procida, whose costume still bears
some resemblance to the Greek. Voices in perfect tune could be heard in
the distance, and instruments answered each other behind the rocks,
from echo to echo, as if the sounds were about to be lost in the sea. The
air was delightful, filling the soul with a feeling of joy which gave new life
to everyone around, even Corinne. Someone suggested that she join the
peasant dance, and at first she agreed with pleasure; but she had hardly
begun when gloomy feelings made her hate the merriment she was part
of. Drawing quickly away from the music and dancing, she went to sit
down at the very end of the cape, on the edge of the sea. Oswald hurried
after her, but as he reached her, the company caught up with him, begging Corinne to improvise in this lovely place. Her distress at that moment was so great that she let herself be led, incapable of reflecting on
what they wanted from her, to the little hill on which they had placed her
lyre.

13.4

Corinne wanted Oswald to hear her one more time, however, as he had
heard her that day at the Capitol, with all the talent heaven had given

her; if that talent were to be lost forever, she wanted its last rays to shine for the man she loved. This desire gave her the inspiration she needed, despite her agitation. Her friends, seated in an enclosure, were all eager to hear her; even the common people—ordinary people whose Southern imagination made them excellent judges of poetry—gathered silently around, their lively Neapolitan faces showing eager attention. The moon rose on the horizon, though the last rays of the day still gave out some pale light. Vesuvius, the Gulf of Naples with all its scattered islands, and the countryside from Naples to Gaete—the landscape in the universe where volcanoes, history, and poetry have left the strongest imprint— could all be seen from the top of the little hill jutting out into the sea to form Cape Miseno. Corinne's friends turned to her in unison, asking her to take "the memories these places retrace" as the subject of the poetry she was about to chant. She tuned her lyre and began in a faltering voice. The expression in her eyes was beautiful, but anyone who knew her as Oswald did could see heartfelt anxiety in her gaze. Nevertheless, she tried to contain her sorrow and rise above her personal situation, if only for a moment.

Corinne's Improvisation in the Campagna of Naples

"Nature, poetry, and history are equal rivals here; we see here all at once the wonders of the ages.

"I see the lake of Averno, a dead volcano whose flow once aroused terror; the Acheron and Phlegeton, bubbling with underground fire, are the rivers of Hades visited by Aeneas.

"Fire—that all-consuming life which creates and devours the world—was more terrifying when its laws were less understood. Nature used to reveal her secrets to poetry alone.

"The town of Cuma, the retreat of the sibyl, Apollo's temple, were all on this hill. Here is the woods where the Golden Bough was gathered.[22] The land of the *Aeneid* is all around you. Fictions consecrated by genius have become memories, whose traces we still seek.

"Into these waves a Triton threw the foolhardy Trojan who dared defy the gods of the sea with his songs; these hollow, echoing rocks are as Virgil described them.[23] If imagination is omnipotent, it is faithful.

When man feels nature, his genius is creative; it is imitative when he thinks he is inventing it.

"Amid these terrifying masses, ancient witnesses of the creation of the earth, we see a new mountain which comes from the volcano. Here the earth becomes stormy like the sea, but without going peacefully back to its original limits. Once raised by the trembling of the abyss, this heavy element digs valleys, raises mountains, and bears witness with its petrified waves to the storms that tear at its breast.

"If you strike this earth, the underground vault resounds as though the inhabited world were nothing but a surface, ready to split open. The countryside of Naples is the image of the human passions: sulfurous and fertile, its dangers and pleasures both seem to come from these fiery volcanoes which give the air so much charm and make the thunder rumble under our feet.

"Pliny studied nature, the better to admire Italy; he boasted of his country as the most beautiful of countrysides when he had run out of titles to honor it.[24] In search of science as a warrior seeks conquest, he left from this promontory to observe Vesuvius through the flames that devoured him.

"O memory, noble power, your empire is here in these places! From age to age, strange destiny! man complains of what he has lost. It is as if times gone by all contain some happiness that is no more; and while the mind grows proud of its progress and looks forward, the soul seems homesick for some former homeland whose past draws near to her once more.

"We envy the Romans' splendor; but did they not envy their ancestors' masculine simplicity? They once despised this voluptuous countryside, whose delights conquered only their enemies. Look in the distance at Capua, which conquered the warrior whose inflexible soul resisted Rome longer than all the universe.[25]

"The Romans lived here in their turn; when their strength of soul was good for nothing but shame and misery, they grew weak without regret. At Baiae, they wrested a beach for their palaces from the sea. The mountains were hollowed out to provide columns, and the masters of the world, now slaves, conquered nature to console themselves for having been conquered.

"It was near the promontory of Gaeta over there that Cicero lost his life.[26] The triumvirate, with no respect for posterity, deprived it of whatever thoughts that great man might have had. Their crime still goes on, only now it is being committed against us.

"Cicero succumbed to the dagger of tyrants. Scipio, less fortunate, was banished by his country while it was still free.[27] He ended his days not far from this shore; the ruins of his tomb are called the Tower of the Fatherland. What a touching allusion to the memory that possessed him!

"Marius fled in the Minturn marshes, near Scipio's home.[28] Thus through the ages great men have been persecuted by their countries; but their apotheosis consoles them, and the heavens, which the Romans thought they controlled, receive Romulus, Numa, and Caesar among its stars—new luminaries, blending the rays of glory, in our eyes, with those of heavenly light.

"As if misfortunes were not enough, here too is the trace of every kind of crime. There, at the end of the gulf, is the isle of Capri; there old age disarmed Tiberius, whose cruel, voluptuous, violent, weary soul grew bored with crime itself, and wanted to dive into even lower pleasures, as if tyranny had not degraded him enough already.[29]

"Agrippina's tomb is on these shores, facing Capri; it was built only after Nero's death, since the man who killed his own mother also forbade her interment.[30] He lived for a long time at Baiae, surrounded by the memories of his deed. What monsters chance brings together for us to see—Tiberius and Nero staring at each other!

"These islands served the crimes of the ancient world almost as soon as the volcanoes had brought them forth from the sea. The unfortunate beings condemned to these lonely rocks amid the waves contemplated their homeland from afar, trying to breathe its perfumes in the air; sometimes, after a lengthy exile, a death sentence told them that at least their enemies had not forgotten them.

"O earth! However bathed in blood and tears, you keep producing flowers and fruit. Have you no pity, then, for man? Does your maternal breast not tremble at the return of his ashes?"

At this point Corinne stopped to rest for a few moments. Everyone at the fete threw branches of myrtle and laurel at her feet. The gentle, pure moonlight made her face look more beautiful, and the fresh sea breeze tossed her hair in a picturesque way, as if nature was taking pleasure in adorning her. Meanwhile Corinne was caught up in an irresistible wave of tenderness, thinking about these enchanting places, the intoxicating evening, Oswald there now, but perhaps not forever; tears streamed from her eyes. Even the common people who had just applauded her so noisily respected her emotion, and everyone waited silently for her words to share her feelings. She played a prelude on her lyre for some time, and then abandoned herself to an uninterrupted flow of poetry no longer divided into stanzas.

"Your tears are also claimed by the heart's memories, and the names of women. Here at Miseno, Cornelia, Pompey's widow, mourned him nobly until she died herself. Agrippina wept for Germanicus on these shores until the same assassin who took her husband thought her worthy to follow in his footsteps. The island of Nisida witnessed the farewells of Brutus and Portia.[31]

"So the hero's lover has had to watch him die. She may follow him for a while, but in vain; the day comes when she must leave him. Portia kills herself; Cornelia presses to her breast the sacred urn which never answers her cries; Agrippina deliberately provokes her husband's murderer for many years in vain. Wandering like ghosts on the ruined beaches of the eternal river, these unfortunate creatures are sighing to get to the other shore. In their long solitude, they interrogate silence, and ask all of nature, this starry sky, this deep sea, to give them back that beloved voice, that sound and accent they will hear no more.

"Love, supreme power of the heart! Mysterious enthusiasm, a combination of poetry, heroism, and religion! What happens when destiny separates us from the one who possessed the secret of our soul, and gave us heavenly life, the life of the heart? What happens when absence or death leaves a woman alone on this earth? She languishes and falls. How many times have the rocks around us offered their cold support to these abandoned widows, who once leaned against a friend's breast, or on a hero's arm!

"You see Sorrento before you. Tasso's sister lived there when he came to her as a pilgrim, asking from the humble woman asylum from the injustice of princes.[32] His long misery had almost disturbed his mind; he had nothing left but genius, nothing but the understanding of divine things. All his images of the earth were distorted. This is how talent, terrified by the desert around it, wanders through the universe without finding anything that resembles it. Nature no longer provides him with an echo—and ordinary people think that the malaise of a soul which does not have enough air, enthusiasm, or hope in this world is madness.

"And fate," continued Corinne with growing emotion, "fate pursues exalted souls, poets whose imagination is linked to the power to love and to suffer. They are exiles from another land, and the universal goodness must not have ordered everything for the few chosen and condemned. What can the ancients have meant, when they spoke of destiny with such terror? What power does destiny have on common, peaceful beings? They follow the seasons, they run the ordinary race of life. But the priestess who delivered the oracles felt stirred by some cruel power. Some involuntary force I do not understand makes genius hurry toward disaster; it hears the sound of the spheres which ordinary ears cannot perceive; it penetrates the mysteries of feeling unknown to other men, and its soul harbors a God it cannot contain!

"Sublime Creator of this beautiful world, protect us! Our impulses are weak, our hopes deluded. The passions have a stormy, tyrannical hold over us, leaving us neither liberty nor peace. What we do tomorrow may decide our fate; on the other hand, something we said yesterday may have been an irrevocable error. When our mind rises to the highest thoughts, we feel a dizziness blurring everything before our eyes as if we were at the top of a tall building. Even then, however, dread sorrow is not lost in the clouds: it cleaves them; it parts them—oh God! What is it trying to tell us?"

At these words, Corinne's face turned deathly pale; her eyes closed, and she would have fallen to the ground if Lord Nelvil had not immediately been there, supporting her.

13.5

Corinne regained consciousness, and was able to regain a little calm at the sight of Oswald, who was looking at her with a touching expression of concern and anxiety. The Neapolitans were commenting in some surprise on the somber note in Corinne's poetry. They admired the harmonious beauty of her language, but all the same they would have liked her verses to be inspired by a happier frame of mind, as they believe that the fine arts, especially poetry, are a way to distract us from the sorrows of life, not to dig deeper into its terrible secrets.

But the English people who had heard Corinne were filled with admiration. They were delighted by this way of expressing melancholy feelings with Italian imagination. The lovely Corinne, whose animated features and lively glance were made to paint happiness—a daughter of the sun, attacked by secret sorrow—was like a flower still fresh and brilliant, but threatened by early death because of some black spot of fatal blight.

The entire company embarked for the return to Naples. The warm, calm evening made everyone keenly aware of the pleasure of being at sea. In a delightful romance, Goethe painted the fondness people feel for the water in hot weather. A river nymph praises the charm of her waves to a fisherman; she invites him to refresh himself and, seduced little by little, he plunges in at last.[33] This magic power of the wave bears some resemblance to the serpent's gaze, which attracts through fear. The wave, which rises in the distance and grows bigger as it approaches the shore more and more rapidly, seems to correspond to some secret desire of the heart, beginning gently and becoming irresistible.

Corinne grew calmer; the delights of the beautiful weather made her more sure of herself. She put up her hair to take advantage of the air around her, looking more charming than ever. The wind instruments, following in another boat, created an enchanting effect in harmony with the sea, the stars, and the intoxicating sweetness of an Italian evening; and they aroused an even more touching emotion, as of the voice of heaven in the middle of nature.

"Beloved friend," said Oswald in a low voice, "friend of my heart, I will never forget this day. Could any day be happier?" As he spoke, his eyes were full of tears. One of Oswald's strongest attractions was this sort of emotion—easy, but restrained, often filling his eyes with involuntary tears. At such times, he had an irresistible expression in his eyes. Sometimes he would be visibly shaken by some secret wave of tenderness mingling with his gaiety, and giving him a sort of noble charm.

"Alas, no!" answered Corinne. "I cannot hope for another day like this one. Let it be blessed, at least, as the last day of my life, if it isn't—if it cannot be the dawn of a lasting happiness."

THE HISTORY OF CORINNE

(14.1)

Oswald—I am going to begin by making the confession which will decide my fate. If you do not think you can forgive me after reading that far, cast me away from you without finishing the letter. If everything is not over between us when you realize the name and destiny I have renounced, though, you may find some excuse for me in what you learn.

My father was Lord Edgermond. I was born in Italy to his first wife, a Roman; Lucile Edgermond, the girl they destined for you, is my half-sister, the fruit of my father's second marriage to an English-woman.

Now hear me. I was born and raised in Italy, and lost my mother when I was ten years old. She had made a fervent last wish on her deathbed that I finish my education before going to England, however; so my father left me with one of her aunts in Florence until I was fifteen.[34] My talents, my tastes, even my character had been formed by the time my great-aunt's death made my father decide to send for me, so that I could be with him again. He now lived in a little town in Northumberland which I suppose may not give any real idea of England, but it was all I knew of England during the six years I spent there.[35] My mother had told me all through my childhood how dreadful it would be not to live in Italy anymore, and my aunt had often repeated that this fear of leaving her country had made my mother die of a broken heart. My good aunt was also convinced that a Catholic woman was damned if she lived in a Protestant country. I did not share this fear, but the idea of going to England filled me with terror.

I left Italy with a feeling of inexpressible melancholy. The servant who had come to fetch me spoke no Italian. My poor Theresina had agreed to follow me, despite constant tears at leaving her country, and I could still speak a little Italian with her in secret, but I was forced to break my habit of those harmonious sounds which give pleasure even to strangers, and whose spell over me was combined with all the memories of childhood. I made my way north—a sad, somber feeling that I experienced without really understanding why.

It was five years since I had last seen my father when I arrived at his house. I had trouble recognizing him—it seemed to me that his face looked more solemn. He greeted me with tender concern, however, telling me over and over again how much I resembled my mother. My little sister, then three years old, was brought to meet me: the fairest face, the blondest, silkiest hair I had ever seen. I was astounded at the sight of her—we have hardly any faces like that in Italy—but from that moment on I took a great interest in her. That very day I took some of her hair to make a bracelet, and I have treasured it ever since. At last my stepmother appeared, making a first impression on me that grew stronger and deeper throughout the six years I spent in her company.

Lady Edgermond loved nothing but the county in which she had been born, and my father, who was dominated by her, had given up as a sacrifice to her any possibility of living in London or Edinburgh.[36] She was a cold, dignified, silent woman, whose eyes might be tender when she was looking at her daughter but who otherwise had something so set about her face and speech that it seemed impossible to make her understand a new idea, or even a new word, to which her mind was not already accustomed. She received me politely enough, but I could easily see that my whole way of acting was a surprise to her, and that she was promising herself that she would change it if she could.

No one spoke a word during dinner, though several neighbors had been invited. I was so bored by this silence that halfway through the meal I tried to talk a little to an old man sitting next to me. In the conversation I quoted a few lines of Italian poetry—very pure and delicate, but something to do with love. My stepmother, who knew a little Italian, looked at me, blushed, and signaled to the ladies to withdraw for tea even earlier than usual, leaving the men alone at table for dessert. I understood nothing about this custom. It is a custom that amazes everyone in Italy, where no one can imagine any pleasure in society without women, and for one moment I thought my stepmother was so angry at me that she did not want to remain in the same room with me. I reassured myself, though, because she indicated that I should follow her, and did not reproach me even once during the whole three hours we spent in the drawing room, waiting for the men to come and join us.

At supper, my stepmother spoke to me, telling me very sweetly that it was not the custom in England for young ladies to talk, and it was especially unsuitable for them to quote poetry in which the word "love" was mentioned. "You must try to forget everything to do with Italy, Miss Edgermond," she went on. "That is a country one can only wish that you had never known."

I cried all night, my heart weighed down with misery. In the morning I went to take a walk. It was terribly foggy—I could not even catch sight of the sun, which might at least have reminded me of my own country. As I was walking I saw my father, who came up to me, saying: "My dear child! Everything is different from Italy here. Women have no vocation among us, other than their domestic duties. Your talents will relieve your boredom when you are alone, and perhaps you will have a husband who will enjoy them. In a little town like this, though, everything that attracts attention arouses envy; you would never find a husband at all if people thought you had foreign tastes. One's way of life has to follow the hallowed customs of this isolated, provincial place. I spent twelve years in Italy with your mother—twelve years whose memory is very sweet to me. I was young then; novelty pleased me. I have come back to my own little cell now, and I find myself the better for it. A regular, somewhat monotonous life makes the time go by without one's even noticing. And there is never any point in fighting the customs of the country one lives in. One always suffers for it. Everything gets known in a town as small as ours; everything gets repeated. There may be no room for emulation, but there is plenty for jealousy, and it is much better to suffer with a little boredom than to keep meeting people with surprised and hostile faces, asking you every minute why you are doing everything you do."

No, Oswald—you can have no idea how much pain I felt at hearing my father talk like this. I remembered him as I had seen him in my childhood, full of grace and vivacity; I saw him now bowed down under the cloak of lead described by Dante in the *Inferno*, which mediocrity throws across the shoulders of those who bend under her yoke.[37] Enthusiasm for nature, for the arts, for feelings—everything was disappearing from my sight. My soul tormented me like a useless flame, devouring my own being when it could find no more nourishment in the world outside. I am a gentle person by nature, so my stepmother had nothing to complain about in the way I behaved toward her; my father even less, because I loved him dearly, and could still find some pleasure in my conversations with him. He was resigned to his lot—but he was aware of his own resignation, whereas most of our country gentlemen, drinking, hunting, and sleeping, thought they were leading the sanest, most beautiful life in the world.

These people's contentment disturbed me to such a point that I began to ask myself it if was not my way of thinking that was mad. Perhaps my own way of life was really not as good as this totally solid existence, which escaped from both unhappiness and thought, both feeling and reverie. But what could I have done with that depressing conclusion? Mourn for my talents as if for a misfortune, whereas in Italy they had passed for a gift from heaven!

Among the people we saw, there were a few who did not lack for wit, but they blotted it out like an annoying ray of light, and by the time they were forty this little nod of the head was usually paralyzed along with all their other movements. Toward the end of the autumn my father went hunting, and we sometimes waited up for him until midnight. In his absence, I stayed in my room most of the day cultivating my talents, which made my stepmother furious. "What good is all that stuff?" she would ask. "Will it make you any happier?" And that word drove me to despair. "'What is happiness, then," I would ask myself, "if not the development of our abilities? Isn't moral suicide as bad as physically killing oneself? And if I do have to smother my mind and my soul, what is the point of preserving the miserable remains of my life, which arouse me to no purpose?"

I was very careful not to talk this way to my stepmother, though. I had tried it once or twice: she replied that a woman was made to take care of her husband's household and her children's health. Any other pretensions could do nothing but harm, and her best advice would be to hide them if I had them. This perfectly ordinary advice left me absolutely unable to find any answer at all. Emulation and enthusiasm, the driving forces of genius and the soul, all have a special need of encouragement; under a sad and frozen sky they wither away like flowers.

It is the easiest thing in the world to make oneself look virtuous while condemning everything to do with an exalted soul. Mankind's noblest goal, duty, can be distorted like any other idea, becoming an offensive weapon used by narrow minds—mediocre people happy with their mediocrity—to silence talent and get rid of enthusiasm, genius, all their enemies. Anybody who listened to them would think that duty consisted in the sacrifice of whatever distinguished abilities one may possess, and that intelligence was a crime one could expiate only by leading exactly the same life as people who have none at all. But can it be true that people of different characters are obliged to follow the same rules? Aren't great thoughts and generous feelings a sort of debt that human beings capable of them should pay on their earth? Shouldn't every woman, like every man, blaze her own trail according to her own character and talents? Do we have to be like bees, whose swarms follow one after the other without progress and without variety?

No, Oswald. Forgive Corinne her pride. I thought I was created for some other destiny. I feel as submissive to the man I love as those women who would not let their minds judge or their hearts desire anything; if you were pleased to live your life in the depths of Scotland, I would be happy to live and die there with you. Instead of abdicating my imagination, however, I would use it to help me take more pleasure in nature. The wider I could stretch my mind, the more glory and happiness I would find in declaring you its master.

My stepmother was almost as disturbed by my ideas as by my actions. My living the same life she did was not enough: I had also to do it for the same reasons. She wanted the faculties she lacked to be considered merely as some sort of sickness—nothing more. We lived rather near the sea, and the north wind often made itself felt in the castle. At night I would listen to it blow down the long corridors, and by day it was amazingly good at fostering silence when we gathered together in a group. I never went outside without some painful experience, as the weather was cold and damp. Nature had a hostile quality about her there which made me bitterly aware of the loss of her gentle Italian sweetness.

During the winter we went back to town—if "town" is the word for a place that has no theater, architecture, music, or paintings— nothing but a collection of little bits of gossip, a concatenation of boring things which manage to keep on being monotonous even when they change.

In our society birth, marriage, and death were all that ever happened, and they bore more resemblance to each other there than elsewhere. Try to imagine what it was like for an Italian woman like me, seated around a tea table after dinner with my stepmother's company for several hours a day. There would be a group of seven women, the most heavy-going in the county. Two were old maids of fifty, as timid as if they were fifteen, but not so lively. One would say to the other, "Do you think the water has boiled long enough to make the tea, dear?"

"It might be too soon, I think, dear," the other would answer, "because the gentlemen are not yet ready to join us."

"Will they stay at table long today?" a third would ask. "What do you think, dear?"

"I don't know," the fourth would answer. "It seems to me that the election for Parliament must be next week, and they might want to stay at table so they could discuss it."

"No," a fifth would counter. "I rather think they are talking about the fox hunt that kept them so busy last week. It is starting up again on Monday. All the same, it seems to me dinner will be over before long."

"Ah! that is more than I dare hope for, " the sixth would sigh. And the silence would begin all over again. In Italy I had been in convents which seemed full of life to me compared with this circle, and I did not know what to make of myself.

Every fifteen minutes a voice would be raised, asking extremely insipid questions, and getting extremely cold answers, and then the boredom which had lifted from these women for an instant settled back down on them with more weight than ever; one might have called them unhappy women, if habits instilled from childhood on the mind did not make it capable of bearing anything. At last "the gentlemen" would come back, but this long-awaited moment never brought any change in the women's existence. The men would continue their conversation around the fireplace; the women stayed in the middle of the room, distributing teacups. When it was time to leave, off they went with their husbands, ready to start in the morning all over again on a life which differed from today's only by the date in the almanac—and by the trace of the years which would leave their mark on the faces of these women in the end, exactly as if they had been alive all that time.

I still cannot imagine how my talent escaped that killing frost. There are two sides to everything, of course. Enthusiasm can be either praised or blamed; movement and stillness, variety and monotony can be either attacked or defended. One can plead for life, but there are also things to be said in favor of death, or what comes close to it. And it's not really true that one can just ignore what ordinary people say. Ordinary people can see into the recesses of your mind in spite of you; they lie in wait for you at moments when your superiority has got you into trouble and they say, very quietly, "Oh well!"—a remark apparently made with great restraint, but the harshest you could hear, nonetheless. Envy is only bearable when it is aroused by admiration of talent. What could be worse than to live in a place where the only thing superiority arouses is jealousy, inspiring no enthusiasm whatsoever? a place where one is hated just as if one were powerful, while one is actually weaker than any nonentity? Such was my situation. In those narrow confines my speech was only noise, a nuisance to almost everyone. I had no chance (as I might have had in London or Edinburgh) of meeting any of those great men who are capable of learning and judging, and could have found some charm in talking to a foreign woman, even if she did not always conform to their strict local etiquette, because they crave the inexhaustible pleasures of the mind and conversation.

I would sometimes spend whole days in my stepmother's circle without hearing a single word related to an idea or an emotion. We were not even allowed to gesture as we spoke. On the girls' faces were the most beautiful bloom, the loveliest colors, and the most absolute immobility imaginable; quite a contrast between nature and society! Old and young, they all enjoyed the same pleasures. They took tea, they played whist, and they grew old still doing the same things, still staying in the same place. The passing of time could not have missed these women; they were far too easy to find.

In the smallest towns in Italy there are theaters and music, improvisators, enthusiasm for poetry and the arts, lovely sunshine. You feel you are alive. I was beginning to forget all this, however, in the country where I lived. Instead of going out myself, I think I could have sent a doll, improved by some slight mechanization, to fulfill my social functions very nicely. Men can always find good ways to use their leisure time in England, no matter where they live, because even in the provinces there are various kinds of interests which do honor to humanity; but the existence of women in that corner of the world was flat indeed. There were a few women whose wits were developed by nature and reflection, and I occasionally unearthed an unusual tone of voice, look, or whisper, but the small talk of a small town, omnipotent in that little circle, soon destroyed such seeds. A woman who began to speak or show herself in any way would have looked like a rebel or a lady of uncertain virtue. Even worse, she would have gained no advantage from it.

In the beginning, I tried to wake this sleepy society up. I would suggest a poetry reading, or a musicale. Once we did agree upon a date; but suddenly one woman remembered that she had promised three weeks ago to have dinner with her aunt; another, that she was in mourning for some old cousin she had never met, who had died months before; a third, that she had household arrangements to make at home. All this was well and good, but what was always sacrificed were the pleasures of the imagination and the mind. I heard them say "That isn't done" often enough to think that the best negative of all, among so many, might be not to live.

After struggling for some time, I myself gave up these pointless efforts. Not that my father forbade me to try: he even made my stepmother promise not to torment me. But I was kept from moving by all the insinuations, all the sly glances while I was speaking, a thousand little hurts like the pygmies' chains tying Gulliver down.[38] I ended up acting like the others on the surface and dying inwardly of boredom, impatience, and disgust. Four years I spent like this, four of the most tedious years you can imagine. What hurt most of all was that I could feel my talent beginning to grow cold. My mind was filling itself with trivialities, and there was nothing I could do about it. When no one in a society takes the slightest interest in science, literature, painting, music, where no one cares about the imagination, conversations have to deal with petty details and minute criticisms. Minds which are foreign to activity and meditation are so narrow, vulnerable, and constrained that social relations become difficult as well as dull.

The only pleasure to be found in a situation like that is in a certain methodical regularity, very convenient for those who would really like to destroy superiority and bring the whole world down to their level. Such conformity is a steady, habitual torture to people whose natures call them to some destiny of their own. I was at once bitterly conscious of the ill will I was arousing in spite of myself, and depressed by the emptiness that made me unable to breathe. There is no point in telling oneself, "That man is not fit to judge me—that woman cannot understand me." The human face has great power over the human heart: whenever you read a sign of hidden disapproval on someone's face it disturbs you in spite of yourself. In the end, the circle surrounding you always manages to hide the rest of the world, just as the smallest object is able to hide the sun if it is right before your eyes. Neither Europe nor posterity can keep us from hearing quarrels in the house next door: anyone who wants to be happy and develop his inborn genius would do well to be very careful about the choice of his immediate environment.

14.2

I had no diversions except the education of my little sister. My stepmother did not want Lucile to learn music, but she gave me permission to teach her drawing and Italian, and I am sure she has not forgotten them—I must do her the justice of saying that she showed considerable intelligence at the time. Oh Oswald! if it is for your happiness that I took all that trouble, I still applaud myself for it! I would applaud myself for that in my grave.

By then I was almost twenty years of age, and my father wanted to arrange a marriage for me. This is the point at which my fatal destiny starts unfolding. My father was a close friend of yours, Oswald, and you were the man he thought of for my husband. If only we had known each other then—and you had loved me! There would have been no cloud over either of our fates. I do not know whether it was pride or presentiment, but I had heard such panegryrics about you that I was greatly flattered by the idea of marrying you. You were too young for me by eighteen months, but everyone said your mind and studious tastes were ahead of your age. I made up so enchanting a notion of life spent in the company of someone with a character such as yours was painted that this hope made my prejudices against the life women led in England vanish completely. Besides, I knew that you wanted to settle in Edinburgh and London, and I was confident of finding distinguished society in either of those cities. I kept telling myself what I still believe today—that the only thing wrong with my situation was living in a small town buried in the provincial North. Big cities are the only places for people who leave the beaten track, if they want to live in society at all. Where life is varied, novelty is welcome; in places where monotony is a comfort-

able habit, people do not want to be amused every so often only to discover that they are bored all the rest of the time.

Let me repeat this, Oswald, because I take pleasure in saying
it: I felt real anxiety as I waited for your father's arrival. He was to spend a
week with us. My anxiety can only have been a sign foretelling my future,
because there was so little reason for it at that time. When Lord Nelvil
arrived, I wanted to please him—wanted it too much, perhaps, as I took
such unnecessary trouble to make sure of it, dancing, singing, improvis-
ing. My mind had been repressed for so long that it may indeed have
broken its chains with too much force. In the last seven years, experience
has calmed me down. I do not need to show off so much; I am more accustomed to myself, and I have learned how to wait. I may have less confidence in other people's goodwill, but I am also much less eager for their
applause. At that time, however, there could certainly have been something strange about me. There is so much fire in the very young—so
much imprudence! We throw ourselves into life so eagerly! However
bright we may be, there is no substitute for time; this brightness may
allow us to speak about mankind as if we knew what we were talking
about, but we never act on our own insights. A kind of fever in our
minds prevents us from making our behavior follow our own logical
arguments.

I do not know for certain, but I think Lord Nelvil found me
too lively a young lady. He was courteous and friendly to me, but after
his week with us was over he left the house and wrote to my father saying
that, all things considered, he thought his son too young for this
marriage. How important do you think this confession is, Oswald? I
could have kept these details from you—I could have lied. Can it
possibly condemn me in your eyes? I have improved in these seven
years—I know I have. Would your father have been able to see my tenderness and eagerness for you without being touched himself? He loved
you, Oswald! He and I would have understood each other.

My stepmother made up her mind to marry me off to the
son of her older brother, who had an estate in the neighborhood. Mr.
Maclinson was a man of thirty, rich, handsome, wellborn, decent, and
gentlemanly. He was also, however, so completely convinced of the
authority of husband over wife and of the foreordained submission and
domestication of women, that he would have been just as shocked by

any doubt on the subject as if one had dared to put honor or honesty in question. Mr. Maclinson liked me very much; what everyone in town said of my lively wit and peculiar character did not bother him in the least. It would have been impossible for anyone to make any changes in his house: it was all so orderly, so well regulated, everything always happened at the same time and in the same way. No one could have done anything on any given day differently from the way it had been done the day before—not the two old aunts who ran the household, not the servants, not even the horses. As for the furniture which had witnessed this way of life for three generations, it would no doubt have begun to move around by itself if anything new had happened in its presence. So Mr. Maclinson was quite right: he had nothing to fear from my going there. Any little liberties of mine might have amused him for fifteen minutes a week, but they could never have had any real results; the force of habit was too strong.

Mr. Maclinson was a good man, incapable of hurting anyone. However, if I had talked to him about the countless worries that can torment an active, feeling mind, he would have thought I had the vapors and suggested I go out riding and get some fresh air. He wanted to marry me precisely because he had no notion of the needs of the mind and the imagination—because he found me attractive without understanding me. If he had had the slightest idea of what a distinguished woman really is, and of her possible advantages and handicaps, he would have been afraid that he might not please me. But this anxiety never so much as entered his mind. Imagine my disgust for such a marriage! I absolutely refused. My father supported me; my stepmother became deeply resentful of me. She was a tyrant at heart, though her timidity often kept her from openly expressing her wishes. When people did not guess what she wanted, she got angry at them—and if one resisted after she had taken the trouble to express herself, she was even less forgiving because of what it had cost her to break out of her usual reserve.

The whole town blamed me in no uncertain terms. Such a suitable match! they cried. Such a tidy fortune! such a worthy man! such a respected name! I tried to explain why this suitable match did not suit me; I was wasting my time. Sometimes while I was speaking I could make myself understood, but what I had said would leave no trace as soon as I left the room: my listeners' usual ideas came right back into their minds, and were received with fresh delight as old acquaintances whom I had been trying to keep away from them.

There was one woman who was much brighter than the others, though she had made her life conform to the common run. One day when I had been speaking even more eagerly than usual, this woman took me aside. Her words made a deep impression on me: "You are going to a great deal of trouble, my dear, and to absolutely no effect. You will never change the nature of things. A little town up north, out of touch with the rest of the world and with no taste for the arts and letters, is unable to be anything except what it is. If you must live here, resign yourself; get away if you can. Those are your only two choices." This reasoning was only too clear. I felt a respect for this woman I did not have for myself: her tastes were rather like my own, but she had managed to resign herself to a fate I could not stand. With all her love of poetry and spiritual pleasures, she was a better judge of the force of things and the stubbornness of men. I tried hard to see her, but although her mind may have ranged far beyond the confines of her social circle, her life was locked into it. And I think she was even a little afraid that our conversations might reawaken her natural superiority: what use would it have been to her?

14.3

I would have spent my whole life in this wretched situation, in spite of everything, though, if I had not lost my father. A sudden accident took him away from me; I lost in him my protector, my friend, the only person in that living desert who understood me. I was so desperate that I could not put up any more resistance to my own feelings. I was twenty years old, and with no support or relations except my stepmother, a woman with whom I had become no more intimate during our five years of living together than on the day we met. My stepmother began to talk to me about Mr. Maclinson again. She had no real right to order me to marry him, perhaps, but he was the only eligible man received at the house, and she told me quite plainly that she would favor no other marriage. This was not so much because she really liked Mr. Maclinson, nephew or not,

as because she thought I was getting above myself in turning him down;
she was joining forces with him more in defense of mediocrity than out
of any real family pride.

My situation became more hateful with every passing day. I
felt myself gripped by the most acute pain that can possess the soul:
homesickness. For lively, sensitive people, exile can be a torture worse
than death. Your imagination begins to hate everything around you—
climate, countryside, language, customs, life as a whole, life in its smallest
details. Our native country gives us a thousand habitual pleasures we are
not even conscious of until we have lost them:

> La favella, i costumi,
> L'aria, i tronchi, il terren, le mura, i sassi!
>
> the language, the customs,
> the air, the trees, the earth, the walls, the stones!
> Metastasio[39]

It is agony enough to be unable to see the places where one has spent
one's childhood: there is some peculiar magic by which memories of that
age keep one's heart young and nevertheless sweeten the thought of
death. When the grave is near the cradle, one's whole life seems to be
spent in the shade of the same tree. Years spent on foreign soil are root-
less. The older generation there has not witnessed your birth: it does not
function, for you, as the protective generation of your parents. The many
interests you hold in common with your compatriots mean nothing to
strangers; you have to explain everything, comment on everything, tell
everything instead of the easy communication, the pouring forth of
thoughts, that starts up as soon as you find your own countrymen. Every
time I remembered the way people spoke in my country, so full of good
will, I felt deeply touched. "Cara, carissima, dear girl, darling girl," I
would sometimes murmur on my solitary walks, imitating to myself the
friendly welcome of Italian men and women. And then I would compare
this welcome with the one I was getting.

I wandered through the countryside every day. In Italy I was
used to hearing harmonious melodies sung by voices in perfect pitch:
here nothing echoed through the clouds but the cries of crows. Fogs had
replaced my country's beautiful sunshine and pleasant air; fruit scarcely
ripened; I could hardly find any vines at all. Flowers did not grow well,

and grew far apart; fir trees covered the mountains like a black cloak all year round. One ancient building—even a painting, one beautiful painting—would have lightened my heart; but within thirty miles I would have sought such a thing in vain. Everything around me was colorless and dismal; what few dwellings and their inhabitants there were only took away the poetic horror of solitude which sends such a delightful little shiver through one's soul. Instead of that, we had an easy life, some social intercourse, and a little bit of culture, just enough for people to say, "You lack for nothing, so you ought to be a happy girl." What a stupid judgment, dealing with the facade of life, when the heart of both happiness and misery is in the most intimate, secret sanctuary of the self!

At the age of twenty-one, I naturally came into my inheritance: my mother's fortune and a legacy from my father. It did once occur to me in my solitary daydreaming that since I was of age, and an orphan, I could go back to Italy and lead an independent life completely dedicated to the arts. This project made me drunk with joy once it had entered my mind, and at first the possibility of an objection did not even occur to me. When the fever of hope had calmed down a little, though, I was afraid of making such an irrevocable decision; imagining what everyone I knew would think of it, I found this apparently easy plan completely impractical. All the same, though, the image of a life among reminders of antiquity, the arts, and music had come to me in such enchanting detail that I felt a new loathing for my own tedious existence.

The talent I had been afraid of losing had in fact been enhanced by my systematic study of English literature. The deep thinking and feeling characteristic of your poets had strengthened my mind and soul without making me lose the lively imagination peculiar to the Italian countryside. I could therefore believe myself destined to unusual advantages, because of the special circumstances giving me a double education and two different nationalities, so to speak. I remembered the approval my first attempts at poetry had been awarded by some good judges in Florence, and I grew very excited about the success I might be able to achieve now. In a word, I had great expectations for myself: is that not the first and greatest of youth's illusions?

It seemed to me as if I would come into possession of the universe as soon as I could no longer feel the searing breath of bitter mediocrity. When it came to making up my mind to run away, however,

I felt public opinion stand in my way. Public opinion mattered much more to me in England than in Italy; I may not have liked the little town in which I lived, but I did respect the country of which it was a part. If my stepmother had condescended to take me to London or Edinburgh—if she had dreamed of marrying me to a man with enough intelligence to appreciate mine, I would never have given up my name and way of life, even to go home. And even so, however harsh my stepmother's rule had been for me, I might never have had the strength to change my situation, if not for a number of circumstances that joined forces as if to make up my mind for me.

I had Theresina, my maid, still with me. You know her. She is a Tuscan woman; her mind has not been cultivated in any way, but she speaks the noble, harmonious language that gives the most trivial conversation of our people so much grace. She was the only person with whom I could speak my language, and this link bound me close to her. I often saw her look sad, though I did not dare ask her why, suspecting that she was homesick like me, and afraid of being unable to restrain my own feelings any longer if another woman's stirred them up. Some sorrows grow lighter when they are communicated, but the sicknesses of the imagination grow greater if they are shared, especially if we see in another person a grief like our own. Then the evil we are suffering seems invincible, and we stop trying to fight it. My poor Theresina suddenly fell seriously ill; I could hear her groaning night and day, and I decided to ask her what was giving her so much pain. How amazed I was to hear her tell me almost everything I had been feeling myself! She had not reflected so much on the cause of her misery; she blamed local circumstances and individual people more. But she felt it all without knowing why—the bleakness of the natural world, the insipidity of our town, the coldness of its inhabitants, the constraint of their customs. She kept crying out, "Oh my country! Shall I never see you again?" And then she would add that she did not want to leave me, and weep, with a bitterness that tore my heart, at being unable to reconcile her fondness for me with her beautiful Italian sky and the joy of hearing her maternal language.

Nothing could have made more impression on me than seeing my own feelings reflected this way in a person of ordinary birth who had kept her naturally lively Italian character and tastes. I promised that she would see Italy again. "With you?" she asked. I kept silent. Then she tore her hair, swearing that nothing would take her from me; she looked ready to die before my eyes at these words. At last something escaped my lips to the effect that I too would go back. This remark was merely intended to calm her down, but it became serious because it gave her such inexpressible pleasure, and because she trusted it. From that day on, without a word to me, she got to know a number of the businessmen in town, and would tell me exactly when a ship was leaving from the nearby port for Genoa or Leghorn.[40] I would listen to her without answering; she imitated my silence, but her eyes would fill with tears. Every day my health suffered more and more from the climate and my inner pain; as I have often told you, my mind needs movement and gaiety. Real grief would kill me; too much in me is at war with grief. One must be capable of submitting to sorrow if one is not to die of it.

I often came back to the idea that had been preoccupying me since my father's death. But I loved Lucile very much—she was nine years old then, and I had taken care of her since she was six. It occurred to me one day that by running away like that I would damage my reputation so much that my sister's might suffer too. For some time this fear made me give up my plans. One evening, though, I was more upset than usual by my anguished relationships with my stepmother and society. I found myself alone at supper with Lady Edgermond. After an hour's silence, I was in such pain at her imperturbable coldness that I began complaining about the life I led. At first I was speaking more to force her into conversation than to lead her into any conclusion about me; then, growing warmer, I suddenly suggested the possibility of someone in a situation like mine leaving England forever.

My stepmother was no whit distressed. Cool and collected—I will never forget it as long as I live—she said to me: "Miss Edgermond, you are twenty-one years old. Your mother's fortune is your own; so is the one your father left you. You are, therefore, your own mistress, and may do as you like. But you do owe it to your family to change your name if your choice dishonors you in public opinion, so that you pass for dead." When I heard these words I stood up impetuously, and left the room with no reply.

My stepmother's contemptuous harshness made me very angry. For a moment, I was possessed by a desire for vengeance quite foreign to my nature; these impulses calmed down, but my conviction that no one cared about my happiness broke the bonds still tying me to the house where I had last seen my father. Lady Edgermond had not appealed to me, but I had not felt toward her the indifference she had shown toward me. I had been touched by her tenderness to her daughter; I thought I had interested her through the care I had taken of the girl. Perhaps, though, this very case had aroused her jealousy; the more she forced herself to make sacrifices in general, the more passionate she became in the only affection she allowed herself. Everything living and ardent in the human heart, under my stepmother's rational control in her other relationships, could be seen cropping up in her personality again as soon as her daughter was at stake.

In the midst of the resentment I felt at this conversation with Lady Edgermond, I heard from Theresina, greatly excited, that a ship from Leghorn had just come into port only a few leagues away, and that on this ship there were some extremely respectable businessmen. "They are all Italians!" she wept, "they speak nothing but Italian. They are reembarking again in a week, and going straight to Italy, and if madame had decided . . . "

"You go with them, good Theresina," said I.

"No, madame! I would rather die here!" And she left my room. I stayed there, reflecting on my duty to my stepmother. It was quite clear to me that my stepmother no longer wanted me to live with her. My influence on Lucile displeased her; she was afraid that my reputation as an extraordinary person might someday injure her daughter's chances. She had, in fact, let me see what was in her heart when she had suggested that I make myself pass for dead—bitter advice which had revolted me at first, but which began to look quite reasonable when I thought about it.

"Of course!" I would cry. "Let me pass for dead here, where my life is nothing but restless sleep. I will live again with nature—with the sun—with the arts! The cold letters of my name, engraved on an empty tomb, will take my place perfectly well in this lifeless land."

And yet these brief flights toward liberty still did not give me the force of definite resolution. There are times when we think we have the strength to do as we wish, and others when the usual order of things seems to win out over all the feelings of the soul. That was my state of indecision—and it could have lasted forever, since nothing outside me was forcing me to make up my mind. Then, toward evening on the following Sunday, I heard some singers under my window—Italians who had come from Leghorn on the ship. Theresina had drawn them there as a pleasant surprise. I cannot express what I felt. Floods of tears rained down on my face; all my memories were born again. Nothing retraces the past like music—more than retraces it. When music evokes the past it seems like the ghosts of those we loved, covered by a veil of melancholy and mystery. The musicians sang those delicious lines written by Monti in his exile:

> Bella Italia, amate sponde,
> Pur vi torno a riveder.
> Trema in petto e si confonde
> L'alma oppressa dal piacer.
> Beautiful Italy! Beloved shores!
> I come again to see thee
> My soul fainting with pleasure
> Trembling and stunned within me.[41]

I was intoxicated. I felt for Italy everything we feel when we are in love—desire, enthusiasm, longing—I was not my own mistress. My whole soul was drawn toward my native land. I needed to see it, to breathe it, to hear it; every beat of my heart called me to my beautiful home, my smiling countryside. The dead in their graves could be no more impatient to raise their tombstones and live again than I was to throw away my winding sheets and take possession of my imagination, my genius, and my nature once more. In the middle of all the excitement caused by this music, my feelings were too confused for me to understand them clearly, and I was still very far from making any decision when my stepmother entered the room. I was to stop the singing, she asked, because it was a scandal to listen to music on Sunday. I tried to insist— the Italians were leaving in the morning, I had not enjoyed such pleasure for six years. My stepmother did not listen to me. Respect for the customs of the country one lived in was more important than anything else, she said; going to the window, she ordered her servants to send my poor compatriots away. They made their departure, singing from time to time an adieu that struck me to the heart.

My feelings overflowed. The ship was to leave in the morning; just in case, and without a word, Theresina had prepared everything for my departure. Lucile was visiting one of her mother's relatives for the week. My father's ashes were not buried here in the country house, but in the tomb he had arranged on his estate in Scotland. In the end I went without warning my stepmother, leaving a letter to inform her of my decision. I went in one of those moments when one gives oneself to destiny, when anything seems better than slavery, disgust, and boredom; when thoughtless youth trusts to the future, and sees it in the skies like a brilliant star, promising a happy ending.

14.4

More anxious thoughts took hold of me once I lost sight of England, but as soon as we landed in Leghorn I was quickly consoled by the charm of Italy, since I had left no strong attachment behind me. Keeping my promise to my stepmother, I told no one my real name, and simply called myself Corinne, a name the story of the Greek Corinna, a poet and friend of Pindar, had made me love.[42] My appearance had changed so much as I grew up that I was sure no one would recognize me. I had lived a very quiet life in Florence, and I had to count on what has in fact happened: no one in Rome has ever known who I was. My stepmother wrote, saying she had spread a rumor that I had been under doctor's orders to go south for my health, and had died on the way. Her letter contained no further reflection. She sent me my whole fortune, which is substantial, promptly and accurately, and never wrote to me again.

Five years passed from that time until the moment I met you, five years in which I tasted a good deal of happiness. I came to Rome to establish myself, and my reputation has grown. The fine arts and literature have given me great public success and even greater pleasure in private. I had no idea before I met you of the tremendous power our feelings have over us. My imagination sometimes made my dreams brighter and dimmer, but without hurting me; I had never been ruled by passion. My mind had never been captured by admiration, respect, or love; even when I did love, I could imagine more good qualities and charms than I had seen. I remained above my own impressions instead of being their slave.

Do not make me tell you about the two men who filled my life until I met you; their passion for me has been only too much in the public eye. At this moment it would be a violation of my deepest feelings to believe that anyone but you could ever have interested me; and I am equally sad and sorry that it was so. All I can say is what my friends have already told you: I liked my independent existence so much that after a lot of indecision and painful scenes I broke two engagements; I had contracted them out of a need to love, and I could not make myself fulfill them. One was a great German nobleman who wanted to marry me and take me to his country, where his rank and fortune obliged him to live; the other was an Italian prince who offered me a life of great brilliance in Rome itself. I liked the German because he inspired great respect in me, but as time passed I noticed that his mind had no inner resources. I had to take so much trouble to keep the conversation going when we were alone, and to hide from him what he had missed! I did not dare show him what I can do in light conversation; I was afraid of making him uncomfortable. I could see that his feeling for me would decrease as soon as I stopped humoring him, and it is hard to keep on being enthusiastic about people one is humoring. It always implies more pity than love when a woman has to be careful about how she handles a man's inferiority, and the kind of calculation and forethought involved in such care shrivels the heavenly quality of spontaneous emotion. As for the Italian prince, he had a graceful, active mind. He wanted to live in Rome, he shared all my tastes, he liked my way of life. I noticed, however, that he lacked strength of mind on an important occasion, and I could see that in life's difficulties it would always be I who was giving strength and support to him. That was it for love; women need support, and nothing casts such a pall over them as the necessity of providing that support themselves. And so I was disillusioned twice: not by mistakes or misfortunes, but by my own observant mind uncovering what my imagination had hidden from me.

I believed myself destined never to love anyone with my whole soul. This was sometimes a painful idea; more often, I would applaud my own freedom. I was afraid of my own capacity for suffering, this passionate nature which is a threat to my happiness and my life; but I would reassure myself, thinking that my judgment was not easily overwhelmed, and that it was unlikely for anyone ever to fulfill my ideas of the character and spirit of a man. I always tried to escape the absolute power of an emotional tie by noticing a few faults in what might have become the beloved object. I had no conception of the fact that love can actually be increased by the anxiety that faults inspire. Your discouraging melancholy and indecision and your strict opinions disturb my peace of mind, Oswald, but they do not cool my emotions. It often occurs to me that these feelings will not make me happy, but then it is myself I am judging, and never you.

You now know the story of my life. I have hidden nothing: how I left England, how I changed my name, my inconstant heart. You may well think that my imagination has often misled me. What would there be in my life to keep you from loving me, though, if women were not tied down by society with all kinds of chains from which men are free? Have I ever deceived anyone? Have I ever done anything wrong? ever been tainted by vulgar interests? Sincerity, goodness, self-respect— could God ask anything more of an orphan girl alone in the universe? Happy the woman who meets the love of a lifetime when they are both taking their first steps in life! But do I deserve him less because I met him too late?

I will tell you this, anyway, my lord, and with a frankness you can trust: despite the loss of great happiness and a glory I prize above any other kind, it seems to me that I would not want us to marry, if there were any way I could spend my life near you without marrying you. This marriage may be a sacrifice for you. Someday you may regret not having married my lovely sister Lucile, as your father intended. She is twelve years younger than I am, and her name is as spotless as the first flowers of spring. We would have to make my name bloom again in England, where it has already crossed into the country of the dead. If I can make a judgment based on a knowledge of her as a child, Lucile has a gentle, innocent soul; she may be capable of understanding you, as well as loving you. You are free, Oswald. Your ring will be returned to you whenever you like.

Before you make your decision, you may want to know what I will go through if you leave me. I have no idea. Violent waves of emotion do rise up in my soul sometimes, and if they made life unbearable to me it would not be my fault. On the other hand, I have a great capacity for happiness. I sometimes feel a kind of fever of thought within me, making my blood circulate faster. I get interested in everything— speak with pleasure—delight in other people's wit, in their interest in me, in nature's miracles, in works of art untainted by affectation. Would it still be within my power to go on living if I could not see you? That is for you to judge, Oswald. You know me better than I know myself. I am not responsible for what I might experience; it is up to the person who plunges in the dagger to know if the wound he is making is mortal. And even if it were, Oswald, I would have to forgive you.

My happiness is completely dependent on the feeling you have shown for me in the last six months. I would defy all your willpower and tact to deceive me as to the smallest change in that feeling. Cast aside any notion of duty on this score; I do not recognize promises or guarantees in love. Once the wind has withered a flower, nothing but heaven can make it bloom again. A tone of voice or a glance from you would be enough to tell me that your heart has changed, and I would hate anything you could offer me instead of your love—that divine ray of light, my heavenly radiance. Be free now, Oswald, free every day, still free even if you were my husband, for if you stopped loving me I would free you from the indissoluble ties that bound you by my death.

I want to see you again as soon as you finish this letter. My impatience will lead me to you, and I will know my fate when I catch sight of you. Disaster strikes quickly; the heart may be weak, but it is never mistaken in the deadly signs of irrevocable fate. Adieu.

8.

On Germany

ON THE APPEARANCE OF GERMANY (1.1)

Many vast forests are the sign of a new civilization: the ancient land of the South has almost no more trees, and the sun falls straight down on earth ravaged by men. Germany still offers some traces of uninhabited nature. From the Alps to the sea, between the Rhine and the Danube, you see a countryside covered with chestnut and fir trees, crisscrossed by impressively beautiful rivers, and cut across by picturesque mountains; but at first your soul is filled with sadness by vast moors, sands, neglected roads, and a severe climate. Only after some time do you discover what is captivating about being here.

The south of Germany is well cultivated; but even the most beautiful landscapes of this country have something serious about them that makes you think of work rather than pleasure, of the inhabitants' virtues rather than nature's delights.

The ruined castles one glimpses on mountaintops, the houses built of earth, the narrow window, the snow that buries the plains in winter all give a harsh impression. There is something silent about both men and nature here which grips at the heart. Time seems to go more slowly than elsewhere, vegetation seems no quicker to take hold in the earth than ideas in men's heads, and the even furrows of the laborer seem as if they were traced into a heavier earth.

All the same, once you have overcome these unreflecting sensations, the country and its inhabitants offer your observant mind something interesting and poetic: you can feel that gentle souls and imaginations have made these countrysides beautiful. The high roads are planted with fruit trees, placed so as to refresh the traveler. The landscapes on either side of the Rhine are almost always superb: this river might be called the tutelary genius of Germany, with pure, rapid, majestic currents like the life of an ancient hero. The Danube is divided into several branches; the Elbe and Spree rivers are easily troubled by storms; only the Rhine is almost unchanging. The landscapes it crosses through seem so serious and various, so fertile and solitaire all at once, that you could almost believe the river itself had cultivated them, without any help from modern man. This river relates in passing the noble deeds of times gone by, and the ghost of Arminius still seems to wander on these steep riverbanks.

Gothic monuments are the only remarkable buildings in Germany. These recall the age of chivalry, which has left its traces in almost every city and public museum. The Northerners, conquerors of the world, seem to have left memories of themselves in leaving Germany, and the whole country looks like the dwelling place of a great people, long gone. Most of the arsenals of German cities contained painted wooden figures of knights in armor, with helmets, bucklers, cuisses, and spurs all strictly according to ancient usage; you stroll among these upright dead, whose raised arms seem ready to strike at the enemy, rigidly holding their lances. The fixed image of once-lively actions gives a painful impression. This is the way buried men were discovered after earthquakes, still maintaining the last gesture of their last idea.

There is no modern architecture in Germany worth quoting. The cities are generally well built, however, and the proprietors decorate them with good-natured care. In several towns the houses are painted in many colors: there are figures of saints and all sorts of ornaments, certainly not in perfect taste but giving variety to the outside of the buildings and indicative of a well-disposed desire to give pleasure to fellow citizens and strangers alike. The brilliance and splendor of a palace serve the vanity of its owner; but the careful decoration and good intentions of these little dwellings are rather hospitable in their way.

The gardens in some parts of Germany are almost as beautiful as English gardens; luxurious gardens always imply a love of nature. In England, simple houses are built in the midde of magnificent parks; the owner neglects his home and takes great care of the landscape. This combination of magnificence and simplicity certainly does not exist in Germany to the same degree. Nevertheless, despite feudal pride and a lack of wealth, there is everywhere a certain love of beauty which has to result in taste and grace sooner or later, since it is the true source of it. Often in the center of the superb gardens of German princes Aeolian harps are placed near grottoes surrounded with flowers, so that the wind can carry through the air both sounds and perfumes. The imagination of these Northerners is attempting to create an Italian nature; and there are some brilliant afternoons of the short summer when you manage to forget the difference.

ON WOMEN (1.3)

Nature and society make women quite accustomed to suffering, and I think it is clear that most women today are better than men. In an age when the universal malady is egoism, men are necessarily less generous and sensitive than women: all practical interests relate to them. Women are related to life only by the ties of the heart; even when women go astray, they are misled by sentiment. Their personality is always double, whereas the only goal of men's personality is that personality itself. Women may be worshiped with the affection they inspire, but the affections they grant are usually sacrifices. The most beautiful virtue, devotion, is women's pleasure as well as their destiny: no happiness exists for them except through the reflected glory and reflected good fortune of someone else. In the end, living outside oneself—whether through ideas, feelings, or virtues—makes the soul accustomed to a sense of elevation.

In countries where men are called upon by political institutions to exercise the military and civil virtues inspired by patriotism, they regain their own superiority and take back their rights as lords of the universe. When they are somehow condemned to idleness or servitude, however, they fall that much lower. The destiny of women always stays the same, created by women's souls alone, untouched by the influence of political circumstances. When men do not know how to use their lives in a noble and worthy way, or are unable to do so, nature takes her revenge for the very talents she has given them. Physical strength is good for nothing but mental inertia, moral force becomes coarseness, and the day goes by in vulgar exercise and amusements—horses, hunting, banquets—which are quite suitable as diversions but brutalizing as occupations. All this time, the women are cultivating their minds, while sentiment and reverie are keeping the image of everything noble and beautiful alive in their souls.

German women have their own special charm—an appealing tone of voice, blonde hair, brilliant complexions. They are modest, but not as timid as Englishwomen. They have obviously not been so accustomed to meeting men who are superior to them, and they also have less to fear from the harshness of public opinion. They try to please through sensibility, to arouse interest through imagination. They are familiar with the language of poetry and the fine arts: they flirt enthusiastically, as in France one flirts with wit and teasing. The absolute loyalty characteristic of Germans makes love less of a threat to the happiness of their women. Perhaps they approach it with more confidence because it is clothed in romantic colors, and because they have less to fear from disdain and infidelity.

Love is a religion in Germany—a poetic religion, too tolerant of anything that can be excused by sensibility. There is no denying that easy divorces in Protestant countries damage the sanctity of marriage. People change their spouses in such countries as calmly as if they were putting together the plot of a drama. Men's and women's natural good nature ensures that these facile ruptures are not contaminated by bitterness, and as Germans have more imagination than real passion, the strangest things happen in this country with peculiar placidity. But manners and character lose all stability this way: the spirit of paradox shakes the most sacrosanct institutions, and there are no reasonably fixed rules about anything at all.

It would be no mistake to make fun of some German women, who push uplift to affectation; their sugary language dissolves anything striking or strong-minded about their minds and characters. These women are neither sincere nor deceitful—it is just that they are incapable of seeing or judging accurately. Real events pass before their eyes like fantasies. Should they happen to be unfaithful, they still maintain the tone of sentimentality associated in their country with honor. A

German woman spoke with a melancholy expression when she said, "Out of sight, out of mind—I really can't explain the reason why." A Frenchwoman might easily have said the same thing, but she would have been speaking lightly.

Such absurdities are exceptions; despite them, there are many German women with sincere feelings and unaffected manners. Their careful education and natural purity of soul make them wield a gentle, steady power. They interest you more and more every day in things that are great and grand, and make you more and more confident in every kind of hope. They understand how to reject the dry irony that breathes death on the pleasures of the heart. Nevertheless, German women rarely show the quick spirit which makes conversation live and ideas move. This kind of pleasure can only be found in the wittiest, most piquant Parisian society. You need the elite of a French capital for such rare entertainment—all you find elsewhere is public eloquence and private charm. Conversation as talent exists only in France. In other countries, conversation provides politeness, discussion, and friendship; in France, it is an art for which imagination and soul are certainly very welcome, but which can also provide its own secret remedies to compensate you for the absence of either or both, if you so desire.

GOETHE (2.7)

What Klopstock lacked was creative imagination: he could put great thoughts and noble feeling into verse, but he was not what anyone would call an artist.[1] The things he imagines are weak, and he dresses them up in colors that rarely have the strength we like to find in poetry—and in all the arts which are supposed to give fiction the energy and originality we find in nature. Klopstock gets lost in the ideal. But Goethe never loses touch with the earth, even when he is dwelling on the most sublime ideas. His mind has a vigor undiluted by sensibility. We could take Goethe as representative of the whole of German literature—not that there are no writers superior to him, in some respects, but no one else can be so clearly identified as having a kind of imagination to which the Italians, English, and French cannot lay the slightest claim.

Goethe has written in every genre, and we will examine his work in a number of the following chapters; but perhaps a personal understanding of the man who has had so much influence on his country's literature will help us to understand it.

Goethe is a man whose conversation is incredibly witty—and despite what people say to the contrary, wit should be capable of light conversation. There are a few examples of silent genius, caused by timidity, unhappiness, contempt, or boredom, but far-ranging ideas and a soul on fire usually inspire one to communicate with others. Those who do not want to be judged by what they say may very well not deserve our interest in what they think. If Goethe can be made to talk, he is admirable; his eloquence is nourished by his ideas, and his jesting is full of philosophy and grace. Goethe's imagination is struck by external objects in the same way as the imagination of the artists of ancient times, though his rational mind has only too much modern maturity. Nothing disturbs his willpower, and the very drawbacks of his character—bad temper, awkwardness, constraint—pass like clouds at the foothills of the mountain while his genius stands at the peak.

What we are told of Diderot's conversation might give us some notion of Goethe's; if we judge according to his writings, however, the distance between the two men becomes infinitely great.[2] Diderot is a slave to his own wit; Goethe controls his talent. Trying to create an effect, Diderot becomes affected, whereas we see Goethe despise success in a way we find oddly pleasing, even when we find his negligence annoying. Diderot needs philanthropy to compensate for his lack of religious feeling. Goethe is more likely to be bitter than sugary, but what he is more than anything else is natural; and without that quality, what is there in any human being that can interest any other?

Goethe no longer has the lively ardor that inspired him to write *Werther*, but the heart of his thoughts still stimulates everything around him. It is as if he were not touched by life, and describes it only as an artist. He now values the tableaux he shows us more than the emotions he experiences: time has made him a spectator. When he still played an active part in passionate scenes, and his heart suffered more, his writings made a more vivid impression.

As we always cut our poetical theories to suit our talent, Goethe now maintains that the author must keep calm even when he is composing a passionate work, and that the artist should work in cold blood to act more strongly on his readers' imagination. When he was young, he may well have thought differently. Perhaps then he was possessed by his genius, instead of mastering it; perhaps then he was aware that since the sublime and divine are only transitory in the human heart, the poet is inferior to the inspiration that moves him, and cannot judge it without losing it.

At first we are amazed to find coldness, even stiffness, in the author of *Werther*. When we put Goethe at his ease, however, the play of his imagination dissipates our initial awkwardness. He is a man whose mind is universal, and its universality makes it impartial; but this impartiality has nothing to do with indifference. It is a double existence, a double force, a double light that illuminates both sides of every question simultaneously. When it comes to thinking, nothing stops him—not the age he lives in, not his habits, not his personal relationships. His eagle eye drops straight down on what he sees. If Goethe had had a political career, if his soul had been developed through action, his character might have been firmer, more decided and patriotic, but his mind would not soar as freely above all points of view; passion or self-interest would have planned a practical path for him.

Goethe takes pleasure in breaking the threads he has woven, in his writings as well as his conversation, thwarting the emotions he has aroused and toppling the statues he has made us admire. Whenever he interests us in a fictional character, he shows us absurdities that must detach us from him. He disposes of the poetic world as a conqueror does of the real world, believing himself, like nature, strong enough to introduce destructive genius in his own works. If he were not such a good man, we might be afraid of a superiority rising above everything to degrade and elevate, touch and tease, affirm and doubt successively and successfully.

As I have already said, Goethe was a remarkable combination of the major traits of the German genius: great profundity of ideas; the grace born of imagination, more original than the gracefulness that comes from society wit; and a sensibility which may sometimes have been fantastic but was all the more capable of interesting readers who are looking in books for something to vary their monotonous destiny, and want poetry to take the place of real events. If Goethe were French, people would make him talk from morning to night. Diderot's contemporaries used to go and draw ideas from his conversation for their writings, and gave him the habitual pleasure of inspiring admiration. In

Germany people do not know how to spend their talents in conversation: so few people, even among the most distinguished, are in the habit of asking and answering questions that society counts for almost nothing there. But this does not make Goethe's influence less extraordinary. There are a lot of men in Germany who would find genius in the address on a letter, if Goethe had put it there. Admiration for Goethe is a kind of fraternity whose passwords permit the initiates to recognize one another. If strangers trying to join in the admiration show any mental reservations indicating that they have allowed themselves to scrutinize works which gain greatly from being closely examined, they are rejected contemptuously. No man can arouse such fanaticism without having great capability for good and for evil: only power, in some form, frightens men enough to make them love it that way.

CLASSICAL AND ROMANTIC POETRY (2.11)

The name "Romantic" was recently introduced in Germany to designate the poetry originating with the troubadours' chants, born of chivalry and Christianity. We have to postulate that the realm of literature is divided between paganism and Christianity, North and South, antiquity and the Middle Ages, chivalry and Greek and Roman institutions, if we are to judge ancient or modern taste from a philosophical point of view.

The word "classical" is sometimes taken as synonymous with classic perfection. I am using it in another sense here, calling the poetry of the ancient Greeks and Romans "classical," and the poetry which is somehow related to the traditions of chivalry "Romantic." This dichotomy also refers to the two eras of the world—the age before the establishment of Christianity and the era following it.

Some German writers also compare ancient Greek and Roman poetry to sculpture, and Romantic poetry to painting; in fact, the progress of the human mind has been described in a lot of different ways, such as going from materialistic to spiritualistic religions, or from nature to Divinity.

France, the most cultivated of Latin nations, is inclined toward classical poetry, imitated from the Greeks and Romans. England, the most illustrious Germanic nation, loves Romantic and chivalrous poetry, and is proud of her masterpieces in this genre. I am not trying to discuss here which kind of poetry is better, but only to show the derivation of this difference of tastes from the primary sources of thought and imagination, as well as from accidental causes.

In epic poems and ancient Greek and Roman tragedies, there is a kind of simplicity coming from the way people then identified themselves with nature, and believed that they depended on fate just as nature depends on necessity. Reflecting very little, man would relate the action of his soul to the outside world. Consciousness itself was represented by external objects, and the torches of the Furies showered remorse on the heads of the guilty.[3] In ancient times, the event was all-important; in modern times, character has become more important. The anxious reflection eating away at us like Prometheus' vulture would have looked insane among the clear, distinct relationships of the civil and social state in ancient times.[4]

When sculpture began in Greece, only single statues were made; groups were composed later on. We could say the same of all the arts. There were no groups: the objects represented followed one after the other as if in bas-reliefs, without any kind of combination or complication. Man personified nature: nymphs peopled the waters, hamadryads the forests. Then it was nature's turn to take possession of man. We could almost say that man became like the torrent, the thunder, the volcano—he acted so much by involuntary impulse and so little as a result of the effects of reflection on the motives or consequences of his actions. The ancients had a corporeal soul, so to speak; its feelings were strong, direct, and consecutive. This is not true of the human heart developed by Christianity: modern men have drawn from Christian repentance the habit of turning continually inward upon themselves.

To manifest this internalized existence, however, the infinite nuances of what is going on within the soul must be presented by a variety of events in every form. If the arts today were limited to the simplicity of ancient times, we would lose the intimate multiple emotions of which our own souls are capable without achieving their characteristic primitive force. Artistic simplicity would soon turn into frigidity and abstraction today, whereas ancient simplicity was full of life. The feelings which distinguish chivalrous Christianity are honor and love, bravery and pity; these inclinations can only be shown by dangers, adventures, love affairs, misfortunes, and the whole Romantic interest that gives the tableaux continual variety. The origins of artistic effects of classical and Romantic poetry are thus very different. One is ruled by fate; the other by Providence. Fate takes no account of men's feelings, while Providence judges actions according to feelings alone. How could poetry *not* create a completely different world, depending on whether it is portraying the work of a blind and deaf destiny in constant struggle with mortal beings, or an intelligible order presided over by an Eternal Being, answering the interrogation of our hearts?

Pagan poetry has to be simple and striking like external objects; Christian poetry needs the thousand colors of the rainbow if it is not to get lost in the clouds. Ancient Greek and Roman poetry is purer as art; modern poetry makes us shed more tears. It is not a question of judging between classical and Romantic poetry, however, but of deciding whether to imitate one or be inspired by the other. For moderns, ancient literature is a transplanted literature. Romantic or chivalrous literature is native to us, and our own religions and institutions have made it blossom. Writers who imitate the ancient Greeks and Romans follow very strict rules of taste. Unable to consult either their nature or their memories, they have to conform to the laws of how to adapt ancient masterpieces to suit our taste, although all the political and religious circumstances that gave birth to those masterpieces have changed. Such "antique" poetry is rarely popular, even if it is very well done, because it has no connection with anything national in modern times.

French poetry—the most classical of all modern poetry—is the only modern poetry that has not spread among the common people. Venetian gondoliers sing the stanzas of Tasso; Spaniards and Portuguese of all social classes know the verses of Calderón and Camoëns by heart.[5] Shakespeare is admired in England by the people as much as by the upper class. Poems of Goethe and Bürger have been set to music, and you hear them over and over from the banks of the Rhine to the Baltic.[6] Our French poets are admired by every cultured mind at home and through Europe, but they remain completely unknown to the common people and even the urban bourgeoisie, because the arts in France are not native to the very country in which their beauties are developing.

French critics claim that German literature is still in its infancy. This opinion is completely wrong. The Germanic nations know more than anyone else in the world about ancient Greek and Roman languages and works of art, and are certainly not ignorant of the advantages and disadvantages of the genres they adopt or reject; but their character, habits, and reasoned analysis have led them to prefer a literature founded on the memory of chivalry and medieval miracles rather than one based on Greek mythology. Romantic literature is the only literature still capable of being brought to perfection. Rooted in our own soil, it is the only one that can still grow and find new life. It expresses our religion; it recalls our history. Its origin is ancient, but not antique.

Classical poetry must pass through the memories of paganism before it can reach us: Germanic poetry is the Christian era of the arts. Such poetry uses our own personal impressions to move us: the genius inspiring it speaks straight to our hearts. It seems to evoke our life itself as a phantom—the most powerful, terrifying phantom of all.

KANT (3.6)

Kant lived to a very advanced age without ever leaving Koenigsberg. He spent his whole life there in the frozen North, meditating on the laws of human intelligence. An insatiable appetite for study led him to acquire all sorts of knowledge: he was familiar with the sciences, with languages, with everything. He was not looking for glory, either; that came very late to him, and when he finally heard in his old age some rumor of his renown, he was happy with the silent pleasure of reflection. Alone in his meditation, he contemplated his own soul. The examination of his own mind provided him with new support for virtue; though he was never involved with men's burning passions himself, he was able to forge weapons for those called upon to struggle with them.

This rigorously philosophical life is almost unequaled except among the Greeks, and seems to answer in advance for the writer's good faith. To this pure good faith we must add a discriminating and accurate mind, capable of criticizing genius when it goes too far. That is enough, I think, to make us judge the persevering work of a man like this with impartiality, if nothing more.

Kant's first publications were various writings on the physical sciences. He showed such sagacity in this work that he was the first to predict the existence of the planet Uranus, as Herschel himself recognized after discovering it. *The Critique of Pure Reason*, his treatise on the nature of human understanding, appeared almost thirty years ago.[7] This work remained unknown for some time, but when its treasure of ideas was finally discovered it created such a sensation in Germany that almost everything done since then in literature as well as philosophy comes from the momentum provided by it.

This treatise on human understanding was followed by *The Critique of Practical Reason*, about moral judgment, and *The Critique of Judgment*, on aesthetics. The same theory is the foundation of all three treatises, which include the laws of intelligence, the principles of virtue, and the contemplation of the beauties of nature and the arts.

I am going to try to give some insight into the principal ideas of this doctrine. Whatever care I take to explain it clearly, I cannot deny even from myself that understanding it will still demand a good deal of attention. A prince learning mathematics once grew impatient at the work it required. "Your Highness has to take the trouble of studying in order to learn," said his teacher. "There is no royal road to mathematics."[8] I am hoping that the French public, with many reasons to believe itself a prince, will allow me to tell it that there is no royal road to metaphysics either, and that if one wants to achieve some understanding of any theory, one has to go through the intermediate stages by which the author himself has reached the results he presents.

Materialist philosophy had abandoned human understanding to the realm of external objects; morality to self-interest; and the beautiful to the pleasing. Kant wanted to reestablish first principles and spontaneous activity in the soul, conscience in morality, and the ideal in the arts. Let us see how he achieved these goals.

When *The Critique of Pure Reason* was published, there were only two theories of human understanding current among serious thinkers. The first, Locke's, attributed all our ideas to our sensations.[9] The second, that of Descartes and Leibnitz, tried to prove the spirituality and activity of the soul, free will, and the whole idealistic doctrine.[10] However, these two philosophers supported their doctrine with purely speculative proofs. In the preceding chapter I tried to show the disadvantages of such attempts at abstraction, which stop the blood from circulating in our veins in order to give our intellectual faculties complete control over us. The algebraic method leaves no imprint on our minds when it is applied to things we cannot grasp by simple reasoning. While reading these treatises on lofty philosophical notions, we think we understand them; we think we believe them; but the very arguments that seemed most convincing very soon escape our memory.

If man tires of these efforts, and limits himself to what he knows through the senses, his soul will find nothing but pain. How can he have any idea of immortality, when the signs of destruction are so deeply etched on the faces of mortals, and living nature crumbles steadily away into dust? When all our senses speak to us of death, what feeble hope would talk to us about being born again? If we consulted nothing but our sensations, what notion of divine goodness could we possibly have? Our life is a battleground for so many sorrows, nature is disgraced by so much ugliness, that the unhappy creature curses life a thousand times before a final convulsion snatches it away. If man rejects the evidence of his senses, how is he to guide himself on this earth? If he believes nothing *but* the senses, though, what enthusiasm, morality, or religion could resist the assaults of pain and pleasure, one after the other, over and over again?

Reflective thought was wandering in this vast uncertainty when Kant first tried to trace the limits of the two realms of the senses and the soul, external and intellectual nature. The meditative power and wisdom with which he marked these limits were unprecedented. He did not get lost in new theories about the creation of the universe; he recognized the limits imposed by the eternal mysteries on the human mind; and it may surprise people who have only heard about Kant at second hand to learn that in many respects there has never been a philosopher so opposed to metaphysics. The only reason he went so deeply into metaphysics was to use its own means to show its inadequacy. He is like a new Curtius, trying to fill up the abyss of abstract thought by throwing himself into it.[11]

Locke had fought and won against the doctrine of innate ideas by representing them as part of man's experimental knowledge. The study of pure reason, of the primary faculties constituting the mind, did not attract his attention. Leibnitz, as we have seen, pronounced this sublime axiom: "There is nothing intelligence does not get from the senses, except intelligence itself." Kant recognized, with Locke, that there are no innate ideas, but he set himself the task of exploring the meaning of Leibnitz's axiom, examining the laws and feelings constituting the essence of the human soul, independent of all experience. *The Critique of Pure Reason* tries to show these laws and the things subject to them.

Skepticism, the almost inevitable result of materialism, had gone so far that Hume finally shook the foundation of reasoning itself in his search for arguments against the axiom "There is no effect without a cause."[12] Human nature is so unstable that if we do not put the principle of belief at the center of our souls, the incredulity which begins by attacking the existence of the moral world will also destroy the material world, originally so useful in overthrowing the other.

Kant wanted to know if the human mind was capable of absolute certainty, and he found it only in necessary ideas: that is, in the laws of our understanding, the nature of which prevents us from imagining anything otherwise than the way these laws represent it to us.

The primary imperative forms of our minds are space and time. Kant proves that all our perceptions follow these two forms: he concludes that they are in us and not in the objects, and that in this respect our understanding is imposing laws on external nature instead of receiving them from her. Geometry, measuring space, and arithmetic, dividing time, are sciences of complete evidence, because they depend on the necessary notions of our understanding.

The truths we acquire through experience never carry this absolute conviction. When we say "The sun rises every day," or "All men are mortal," the imagination could invent an exception to these truths, which only experience makes us consider unquestionable. But even imagination itself cannot suppose anything outside space and time, so we cannot consider these forms of our thought, imposed on things by us, as a result of habit, the constant repetition of identical phenomena. The sensations may be questionable, but the prism across which we receive them is unchanging.

We must add the principles of our reasoning process to this primary intuition of space and time—or rather we must base this intuition on the principles of reasoning, the laws of our intelligence, without

which we could understand nothing: connection between cause and effect, unity, plurality, totality, possibility, reality, necessity, etc.* Kant considers all of these necessary ideas; he considers the only true sciences to
be those founded immediately on them, as they are the only notions in
which there can be certainty. The forms of reasoning have results only
when we apply them to judging external objects. They are subject to
error in this application, they are still necessary in themselves: we cannot
do without them in any of our thoughts. It is impossible for us to imagine
anything outside the relation of cause to effect, possibility, quantity,
etc.—and all these notions are as inherent to our way of conceiving
things as time and space. We perceive things only through the immutable
laws of our way of reasoning. These laws, then, are also within ourselves
rather than outside us.

In German philosophy, subjective ideas are those which
come from the nature of our intelligence and its faculties, and objective
ideas are those which are aroused by sensations. Whatever names we
may adopt for them, I think the study of our minds will agree with Kant's
main idea, his distinction between the forms of our understanding and
the objects we understand according to these forms. Whether he confines himself to abstract ideas or appeals—in religion and morality—to
feelings he also considers independent of experience, nothing is more
luminous than the line of demarcation he traces between what comes to
us through sensation and what belongs to the spontaneous action of
our souls.

Some words of Kant's doctrine have been misinterpreted,
so that people claim he believed in *a priori* knowledge, in things imprinted in our minds before learning.

Other German philosophers closer to the Platonic system
believed in the existence of some model of the world within the human
mind, thinking that man would not be able to conceive of the universe if
he did not already have an innate image of it within himself. But there is
no question of this doctrine in Kant, who reduces the number of intellectual sciences to three: logic, metaphysics, and mathematics. Logic
teaches nothing by itself, but there can be no doubt about its principles,
taken in the abstract, because they are based on the laws of our understanding. This science can only lead us to wisdom in its application to

*Kant calls the various ideas necessary to understanding "categories," and gives a table of them.

ideas and things: its principles are innate, its application is experimental. As for metaphysics, Kant denies its existence, claiming that reasoning can take place only within the sphere of experience. Mathematics alone seem to him to depend on the notion of space and time—the laws of our understanding prior to experience. He tries to prove that mathematics are not a simple process of analysis, but a synthetic science, positive, creative, and certain in itself, with no need of recourse to experience to prove its truth. In Kant's book we can study the argument with which he supports this point of view. But it is clear, at least, that there is no one more opposed to what people call the philosophy of dreamers, and that he would be more inclined toward a dry, didactic way of thinking—although his doctrine is aiming at uplifting the human race, now degraded by materialism.

Far from rejecting experience, Kant considers the work of life as nothing other than the action of our innate faculties on the knowledge that comes to us from the outside world. He believes that without the laws of understanding, experience would be mere chaos, but that the laws of understanding have as their sole object the elements given by experience. The result is that beyond its limits metaphysics itself has nothing to teach us, and that we must attribute prescience and our belief in everything beyond the visible world to sentiment.

When we try to use reason alone to establish religious truths, it becomes an instrument that can be bent in any direction, either to attack or to defend them, because in this respect experience offers us no support. Kant draws two parallel lines on which he puts the arguments for and against the liberty of man, the immortality of the soul, the passing or eternal duration of the world—and he appeals to sentiment to tip the scales, as the metaphysical proofs seem equal to him on both sides.* He may have been wrong to push the skepticism of reasoning this far, but he does so only to eliminate skepticism, by removing from certain questions the abstract discussions encouraging it.

It would be unfair to suspect the sincerity of Kant's religious faith simply because he maintained that there was a parity between the pro and con arguments of the great questions of transcendental metaphysics. On the contrary, there seems to me to be a good deal of candid innocence in that admission. Very few minds are capable of understand-

---

*Kant calls these opposing arguments on the great metaphysical questions "antinomies."

ing such arguments, and those few are so prone to fight among themselves that anyone who banishes from metaphysics all questions relating to God's existence, free will, or the origin of good and evil is doing religious faith a great favor.

Various respectable people have said that no weapon should be neglected, and that metaphysical arguments should be used as well to persuade those on whom they make some effect; but such arguments lead to discussion, and from discussion to doubt, on any topic whatsoever.

The golden ages of the human race, in every period, have been those in which truths of a certain order were never contested in either speech or writing. Passions might have led to guilty acts, but no one cast doubt on religion even if he disobeyed it. Sophisms and the abuse of a certain kind of philosophy have destroyed this noble firmness of belief, the source of heroic devotion, in various countries at different times. Isn't it beautiful to see a philosopher deny his own science admission to the sanctuary, and use all the force of abstract reasoning to prove that there are places from which it should be banished?

There have been despots and fanatics who tried to forbid human reason to study certain subjects, and reason has always freed itself from these unfair shackles. But limits imposed by reason on herself do not enslave her; on the contrary, they give her the new strength that always comes from the authority of laws which have the free consent of those who are governed by them.

A deaf-mute might be profoundly convinced of the existence of the Divinity even without having been educated by the Abbé Sicard.[13] The primary truths fall within the realm of feeling, which is why they can be experienced by many people who are as far from being deep thinkers as deaf-mutes are from those who can hear and speak.

Doctors recognize in the study of physical man the animating principle keeping him alive, but no one knows what life is. If we started in with rational argument, we could easily prove to people that they are not living—various Greek philosophers have done so. The same is true of God, and conscience, and free will. We have to believe in them because we feel them: any argument will necessarily be on a level lower than this fact.

You cannot practice anatomy on a living body without destroying it. When analysis tries to work on indivisible truths, it affects their unity and distorts them for the same reason. In order to let half of our self observe the other half, we must divide our soul in two. However this division takes place, it deprives our being of the sublime identity we need for the strength to believe the things only conscience can assert.

Get a great number of men together in a theater or public square, and tell them some truth of rational argument—or any general idea at all. You will immediately see before you almost as many different opinions as people. But if you tell them a few details about someone's greatness of heart, in accents of generous feeling, you will know right away from the unanimous waves of emotion that you have touched the instinct of the soul, which is as keen and powerful in our being as the instinct for self-preservation.

In attributing the knowledge of transcendent truths to feeling, which does not admit of any doubt, and trying to prove that reasoning is only valid within the sphere of sensations, Kant is very far from considering this power of feeling to be an illusion. On the contrary, he gives it the highest rank in human nature; he makes conscience the innate principle of our moral existence, and the sentiment of the just and unjust is for him the primitive law of the heart, as space and time are the first law of intelligence.

Has not man denied the existence of free will, thanks to reasoning? Yet he is so convinced of it, so convinced that all creatures are capable of spontaneous choice between good and evil, that he surprises himself by feeling respect or contempt even for animals!

Feeling is what assures us of our freedom, and this freedom is the foundation of the doctrine of duty. If man is free, he must create his own all-powerful motives to fight the influence of the outside world, and disengage our will from egoism. Duty is the proof and guarantee of man's metaphysical independence.

In the following chapters we will examine Kant's arguments against a morality founded on self-interest, and the sublime theory he puts forth instead of this perverse and hypocritical sophistry. There may be more than one way of looking at Kant's first work, *The Critique of Pure Reason*; he must have expected people to use reason against him, because he saw it as inadequate and contradictory. But I think no one can read his *Critique of Practical Reason* and the various things he has written on morality without respecting them.

Not only are the principles of Kant's morality austere and

pure, as might be expected of a philosopher's inflexibility, but he is always bringing in the evidence of the heart to support the evidence of the understanding. He takes a peculiar pleasure in using his abstract theory on the nature of the intelligence to support the simplest, strongest feelings.

A conscience acquired through sensations can be destroyed by them; we degrade the dignity of duty by making it depend on external objects. This is why Kant insists on showing us over and over that the necessary precondition of our moral being, the law by which it exists, is a deep feeling of this dignity. The notion of good and evil within us can no more be destroyed by the realm of sensations and the evil actions they inspire than by any errors we might make in applying the notions of space and time. In any situation, there is always a force of reaction against circumstances, which comes from the depths of the soul. We feel strongly that neither the laws of understanding, nor moral liberty, nor conscience, come to us from experience.

In *The Critique of Judgment*, his treatise on the sublime and the beautiful, Kant applies to the pleasures of the imagination the same system which gave him such fruitful results in the realm of intelligence and feeling. Or perhaps I should say that he is examining the same soul, now manifesting itself in the sciences, morality, and fine arts. In poetry and in the arts able to portray feelings through images as poetry does, Kant maintains that there are two kinds of beauty: one connected to time and this life, the other to eternity and the infinite.

Let no one object that eternity and the infinite are unintelligible; it is finite, temporal things that often look more like illusions. The mind cannot set limits to anything; being cannot conceive of nothingness. Even the exact sciences cannot be studied in depth without coming up against the notions of infinity and eternity, and the most positive things belong to this infinity and eternity as much as feeling and imagination, in some respects.

From this application of the feeling of the infinite to the fine arts comes the ideal: the beautiful considered as the realized image of what our soul imagines, not a collection or imitation of the best things in nature. Materialist philosophers judge the beautiful according to the agreeable impression it makes on us, thus placing it in the domain of sensations. Spiritualist philosophers, who relate everything to reason, equate the beautiful with the perfect, and find some analogy with the good and the useful, the first degrees of perfection. Kant rejected both these explanations.

To consider the beautiful simply as the agreeable is to limit it to the sphere of sensations, and therefore to a difference of individual taste, so that it never deserves the universal consent which is the true hallmark of beauty. To define beauty as perfection requires a sort of judgment resembling the foundation of esteem. The enthusiasm inspired by the beautiful has nothing to do with either sensation or judgment. It is an innate disposition, like the feeling of duty and the notions necessary to understanding; we recognize beauty when we see it because it is the external image of the ideal whose model exists in our intelligence. A difference of taste may apply to the agreeable, since the source of this kind of pleasure is sensation. But all men must admire what is beautiful, whether in the arts or in nature, because in their souls they have heaven-sent feelings which beauty awakens and makes them enjoy.

Kant goes from the theory of the beautiful to the sublime, and this second part of his *Critique of Judgment* is even more remarkable. According to him, the sublime consists in the conflict between moral freedom and destiny or nature. Unlimited power frightens us, grandeur crushes us, but through the strength of our will we escape the feeling of our physical weakness. Destiny's power and nature's immensity are in infinite opposition to the miserable dependency of any earthly creature—but a spark of the sacred fire within our breast conquers the universe, because that spark is enough to resist everything the forces of the world could possibly demand of us.

The first effect of the sublime is to crush man, the second is to restore him. At first, even if no personal harm can happen to us, we are terrified by contemplating the sight of the storm, raising the waves of the sea as if it threatened both heaven and earth. When the clouds gather and nature's fury shows its full strength, however, man feels in himself an energy capable of freeing him from his fears through will or resignation, through the exercise or abdication of his moral freedom; and this self-consciousness gives him new life and encouragement.

When we hear about a brave, generous action, or learn that men have suffered incredible pain to stay faithful to the slightest nuances of their opinions, our minds are initially stunned by the image of the tortures they have suffered. Little by little, though, we regain our strength, and the sympathy we feel for greatness of soul makes us hope that we too would be capable of conquering the miserable sensations of this life, so as to remain true, noble, and proud to the last day of it.

In any case, no one can define the high point in our existence. "We are too exalted to understand ourselves," as Augustine says.[14] Anyone who thinks he can exhaust the contemplation of even a simple flower has a very poor imagination; how is it possible, then, for us to understand everything involved in the idea of the sublime?

I certainly do not flatter myself that these few pages have given any real account of a theory that has occupied all the thinkers of Germany for the last twenty years; but I hope to have said enough about it to show the general spirit of Kant's philosophy, and to be able to explain its influence on literature, science, and ethics.

In reconciling experimental and idealistic philosophies, Kant did not subordinate either one to the other. Instead, he was able to strengthen each of them. Germany was then threatened by a dry-as-dust doctrine that treated all enthusiasm as error and relegated all the comforting feelings of life to the rank of prejudice. It was a keen satisfaction for men who were both philosophers and poets, capable of both study and exaltation, to see the soul's most beautiful affections defended with the rigor of the most abstract reasoning. The mind's energy can never be negative for long: it can never consist primarily in what we don't believe, what we don't understand, what we despise. We need a philosophy of belief, of enthusiasm—a philosophy which confirms, through reason, the revelations of feeling.

Kant's adversaries have accused him of simply repeating the arguments of the ancient idealists, claiming that his doctrine is merely an old system in new language. There is no basis for this complaint. Kant's doctrine has not only new ideas but an unusual character.

Kant's doctrine feels the effects of the eighteenth-century philosophy it is meant to refute, but that is because it is human nature to come to terms with the spirit of one's times, even if one is fighting it. Plato's philosophy is more poetical than Kant's, Malebranche's is more religious;[15] but Kant's great virtue was to restore moral dignity by founding everything beautiful within the heart on a strictly reasoned theoretical basis. The opposition that people were trying to make between reason and sentiment turns reason toward egoism and sentiment into madness. Kant, called to settle all the great intellectual treaties of alliance, made the heart a single hearth at which all human faculties are in harmony.

The polemical part of Kant's work, his attack on materialism, would be a masterpiece all by itself. Materialism has become so deeply rooted in our minds, with such consequences of irreligion and egotism, that we should consider those still fighting this system by a simple revival of the thought of Plato, Descartes, and Leibnitz as national benefactors. But the philosophy of the new German school has a swarm of ideas of its own. It is founded on enormous scientific knowledge, growing greater every day, and on a peculiarly abstract and logical way of reasoning. Kant may blame the use of such reasoning in the examination of truths beyond the realm of experience, but in his writings he shows a metaphysical strength that puts him in the first rank of thinkers.

We must admit that Kant's style in *The Critique of Pure Reason* deserves most of his adversaries' complaints. His terminology is very difficult to understand, involving the most irritating neologisms. Kant lived alone with his thoughts, and he convinced himself that he needed new words for new ideas. There are already words for everything, however.

Kant often takes an obscure metaphysics as his guide in perfectly clear matters. He carries a luminous torch only in the dark shadows of the mind, reminding us of the Israelites, who were led by a pillar of fire at night and a pillar of cloud during the day.[16]

In France no one would have taken the trouble to study works so loaded with difficulties, but Kant was dealing with patient and persevering readers. That was certainly no excuse for taking advantage of them. All the same, perhaps Kant would not have delved so deeply into the knowledge of human understanding if he had put more importance on the expressions he was using to explain it. The ancient philosophers used to divide their doctrine into two distinct parts, one reserved for the initiated and one they professed in public. Kant's way of writing about theory is very different from the way he writes about the application of that theory.

Kant takes words for ciphers in his metaphysical treatises, giving them whatever value he wishes without worrying about their meaning in common usage. This seems to me a serious mistake. The reader's attention is exhausted in the comprehension of the language, and never gets to the ideas; the known never serves as a step toward the unknown.

When Kant abandons his scientific language, however, we must do him justice even as a writer. When he is talking about the arts or morality, above all, his style is almost always perfectly clear, energetic, and simple. His doctrine looks so wonderful then! How well he expresses the sense of the beautiful and the love of duty! He distinguishes them both with such force from any calculations of self-interest or utility! He ennobles actions by considering their origin, rather than their outcome; and what moral grandeur he is able to give man, whether he is examining him in himself or in relation to the outside world! Man, that exile from heaven, that prisoner on earth—so great an exile, such a miserable captive!

We could extract a lot of brilliant ideas on all kinds of topics from Kant's writings. In fact, his doctrine may well be the only one from which we can get ingenious new insights nowadays, since the materialist perspective no longer offers us anything interesting or original on any topic. The cream of the jest about serious, noble, divine topics has been skimmed, and the only way for us to make the human race young again is by returning through philosophy to religion, and through reason to sentiment.

ON THE ROMANTIC DISPOSITION IN AFFAIRS OF THE HEART (3.18)

The English philosophers' system of putting moral sentiment—or moral sense—at the foundation of virtue has nothing to do with the sentimental morality we will be discussing here. Sentimental morality hardly exists outside of Germany, either as a name or as a notion, and there is nothing philosophical about it. It simply makes a duty of sensibility, and makes us likely to underestimate people who have none.

The power to love must be very close to morality and religion. Our repugnance for cold, hard souls is perhaps a sublime instinct warning us that even when such creatures are behaving irreproachably, they are still acting mechanically and calculating their own best interests. There can be no sympathy between them and us. In Germany, where people like to make precepts out of their impressions, everything that is not sensitive and even romantic[17] is considered immoral. *Werther* made exalted feelings so fashionable that hardly anyone was brave enough to be dry and cold even if that was his natural character.[18] This is where we get that obligatory enthusiasm for the moon, forests, countryside, and solitude—as well as the nervous ailments, the affected voices, the looks that insist on being looked at, the whole apparatus of sensibility so despised by those whose souls are strong and sincere.

The author of *Werther* was the first to make fun of these affectations. All countries have something ridiculous about them, however, and it may be better for the absurdity to consist in the foolish exaggeration of something good than in an elegant claim to something bad. The need for success is unconquerable in men, and even more unconquerable in women, so the pretensions of ordinary people are a sure sign of the ruling taste at a given time in a given society. The same people who made themselves "sentimental" in Germany would have been fickle and fastidious somewhere else.

The great susceptibility of the German character is one of the main reasons for the importance Germans attach to the least nuances of sentiment. This susceptibility is often related to the sincerity of one's affections. It is easy to be constant if one is not sensitive. All you need then is courage: *well-organized discipline begins at home.* When our happiness is greatly influenced by the signs of interest granted or denied us by other people, however, we are clearly more sensitive than someone who exploits his friends like a piece of land, trying to make a profit on them.

We should nevertheless avoid the many subtle, finespun codes of emotions filling the novels of many German writers. Germans are not always completely natural, there is no doubt about that. They are so sure of their faithfulness and sincerity in all the real relationships of life that they are tempted to look on the affectation of the beautiful as a cult of the good, and to let themselves make disastrous exaggerations in their novels.

This competition for sensibility on the part of a number of German women and German writers would be quite harmless if not for the fact that making fun of affectation throws sincerity itself into disrepute. Cold, egotistical men take particular pleasure in ridiculing passionate attachments, and would like to make everything they do not feel themselves look artificial. There are even people of real sensitivity whose own feelings are weakened by sugary exaggeration, people who grow blasé through a surfeit of sentiment, as one could become bored by religion through boring sermons and superstitious practices.

It is a mistake to apply our positive ideas about good and evil to the delicate nuances of sensibility. Accusing a person of his shortcomings in this respect is like making it a criminal offense not to be a poet. People who think rather than act have a natural sensitivity which may make them unfair to those who are different from them. It takes imagination to guess at the sufferings the heart can cause. The best people alive are often slow and stupid at this: they trample down sentiments as if they were walking on flowers, absolutely amazed to see them wither. Are there not human beings indifferent to Raphael, unmoved by music, bored by the ocean and the heavens? How could such men possibly understand the tempests within the soul?

Aren't the most sensitive people alive sometimes discouraged? Suddenly dried up inside, as if the Divinity were withdrawing from them? They still stay faithful to their affections; but there is no more incense in the temple, no more music in the sanctuary, no more emotion in the heart. Our unhappiness sometimes makes us silence the voice of feeling inside us—a voice that can sound harmonious or excruciating, depending on whether or not it is in tune with fate. There is no way to make a duty of sensibility, because those who feel it often suffer from it enough to have both the right to repress it and the desire to do so.

In hot-blooded countries, sensibility is never mentioned without terror; peaceful, dreamy nations think they have nothing to fear by encouraging it. No one has ever written about it with perfect sincerity, however, because everyone wants to glorify his own experiences or the feelings he arouses in others. Women try to present themselves like a novel, and men like a history book. But the most intimate relationships of the human heart have still not been explored—far from it. Someday perhaps someone will speak with absolute sincerity about all the things he has felt, and the world will be astounded to find that most of its maxims and observations are mistaken, and that there is an unknown soul at the center of that soul about which all the stories are told.

LOVE WITHIN MARRIAGE (3.19)

In marriage, sensibility becomes an obligation. Virtue is enough for any other relationship, but in marriage, where destinies are intertwined and two hearts beat as one, deep affection would seem to be an almost necessary link. Infidelity creates so much trouble between husband and wife that eighteenth-century moralists usually related all the heart's delights to parental love, ending by considering marriage as little more than the necessary precondition for the joy of having children. That is false as morality, and even falser as a statement about happiness.

Being kind to our children is so easy that we should claim no great merit for it. In their earliest years, children cannot have any wishes other than those of their parents, and as soon as they become young people they exist on their own. Fairness and kindness are the main duties of a relationship which nature makes so easy. It is far different with this other half of ourselves, able to find happiness or misery in the least of our actions, looks, and thoughts. This is where morality has scope for action; this is also where the true source of happiness can be found.

Knowing you have a friend of your own age, with whom you are to live and die, whose interests are your own, whose prospects you share, including the prospect of death—this is the feeling that keeps destiny at bay. It may happen that your children, or more often your parents, become your companions through life; but this rare and sublime pleasure goes against the laws of nature, whereas the partnership of marriage is in harmony with the whole of human existence.

Why, then, is this sacred partnership so often profaned? I will risk the truth: we must attack the inequality social opinion gives to the duties of the two spouses. Christianity has brought women out of a condition very much like slavery. The basis of this admirable religion is equality before God, so it tends to maintain the equality of rights on earth: divine justice, the only perfect justice, admits no privilege of any kind, and the privilege of force less than any other. A number of prejudices from the days of women's slavery still exist, however, and in combination with the great freedom given women by modern society, these prejudices give rise to many evils.

It is right to exclude women from political and civil affairs: anything that puts women in competition with men goes against their natural vocation. Fame itself is only a brilliant way to bury the happiness of a woman. However, if women's destiny is to be one continuous act of devotion to conjugal love, the reward of this devotion will have to be the scrupulous fidelity of any man who is the object of it.

Religion may not make any distinction between the obligations of husband and wife, but the world certainly does. Women's trickery and men's resentment are both born of this distinction. Where is the heart capable of giving itself without wanting another in return? Who would accept friendship in good faith as a reward for love? Who can sincerely promise to be faithful to a person who does not want to be faithful himself? Fidelity may certainly be required by religion, because religion knows the secret path to the mysterious land where sacrifice turns into pleasure. But the bargain man wants to impose on his companion is so unfair!

"I will love you passionately for two or three years," says the man. "Then, at the end of that time, I will talk sense with you." And what men call sense is disillusionment about life. "I will be cold and bored at home, and try to be pleasant elsewhere. As for you, who are usually more imaginative and sensitive than I am, and have no career or distraction such as the world offers me—you who live for me alone, while I have a thousand other things to think about—you will be satisfied with the second-rate, frigid, part-time affection it suits me to give you, and despise any homage that might express higher, more tender feelings."

This is such an unfair arrangement! Every human feeling refuses to have anything to do with it. There is a peculiar contrast between the forms of respect toward women introduced throughout Europe by chivalry and the tyrannical liberty men have awarded themselves. This contrast creates all the miseries of sentiment: illegitimate attachments, betrayals, neglect, and despair. Germanic countries have been less struck than others by these disastrous results, but they must fear the influence of modern civilization in the long run. It would be better to lock women up like slaves, awakening neither their minds nor their imaginations, than to launch them in the middle of the social world and develop their faculties, only to refuse them the happiness these very faculties require.

In an unhappy marriage, suffering is a power that goes far beyond all the other pain of this world. The whole soul of a woman depends on conjugal attachment. To struggle against fate alone, moving toward your coffin without a friend to support or mourn you—that is a form of isolation beside which the Arabian desert pales. And when the whole treasure of your youth has been given in vain, and you can no longer hope to see the reflection of those first rays at the end of your life, when the dusk has nothing to recall the dawn, and is faded like a livid ghost foretelling night—then your heart rebels, and it seems as if you have been deprived of God's gifts on this earth. And if you still love the man who treats you as a slave, since he does not belong to you and has you in his power, despair takes hold of all your abilities and consciousness itself grows dim with misery.

Women might recite these two lines of a fable to husbands who treat them lightly:

A game for thee,
But death for me.

And as long as there is no intellectual revolution to change men's minds about the fidelity required by their marriage vows, there will always be a war between the sexes—a secret, constant, tricky, perfidious war which damages the morals of both.

In Germany there is hardly any inequality between the two sexes, but that is because women break their sacred ties just as often as men. Easy divorce gives family relationship a kind of anarchy which leaves nothing standing in its original truth and strength. If anything sacred is to remain on earth, it is still better to have one slave in marriage than two freethinkers.

A woman's first glory is purity of soul and conduct. How degraded she would be without them! It is possible, however, that the general happiness and dignity of the human race could benefit just as much from the fidelity of men within marriage. Is there anything in the whole moral system finer than a young man who respects this great bond? Public opinion does not require it of him. Society leaves him free. A sort of barbaric teasing would have stifled the moans of the heart he had wounded, because blame is always ready to turn against the victim.

Such a man is his own master, but he imposes duties on himself. His mistakes cannot inconvenience him in any way, but he fears the harm he may do the woman who has entrusted herself to him: generosity binds him all the more closely because society sets him free.

Women are commanded to be faithful for a thousand different reasons: they may well fear the dangers and humiliations that are the inevitable results of a mistake. But the voice of conscience is the only voice raised to men: man knows he is making someone suffer, knows that by being unfaithful he is destroying a feeling which should last until death and renew itself in heaven. Alone with himself, alone in the middle of every kind of seduction, such a man stays pure as an angel—and if angels are not portrayed with women's features, it is because this combination of strength and purity is even more divinely beautiful than the absolute modesty of the weak.

Unless memory holds us back, imagination will detach us from what we do have, beautify what we fear we cannot have, and make sentiment look like a problem that has already been solved. In life as in the arts, however, problems that have been solved do not demand any real genius. In affairs of the heart, what we need is the security to feel the kind of affections that are proof of eternity, since they alone can give us any idea of infinite duration.

A faithful lover seems to choose his beloved afresh every day for the first time. Nature has given him limitless independence, and he cannot foresee the dark days of life, for a long time at any rate. His horse can carry him to the ends of the earth. War, which he loves, gives him at least a temporary freedom from domestic relationships, and seems to reduce the whole question of existence to victory or death. The earth belongs to him, all pleasures are offered him, no fatigue can frighten him, no intimate connection is necessary to him. He shakes the hand of a comrade in arms, and forges the only bond he needs. A time will no doubt come when destiny will tell him its terrible secrets, but he has still no suspicion of that. Doesn't every generation, on taking possession of its new world, believe that all its ancestors' misfortunes were caused by their own weakness? That they were born as shaky and feeble as they are today? Well, starting from the heart of such illusions, a man must be truly virtuous and sensitive to devote himself to one long love, the link between this life and the next! A proud male glance that is also modest and pure is really beautiful, radiant with the modesty that can fly from the crown of the virgin saints to adorn even a warrior's brow.

Should this young man want to share the sunny days of his youth with one object of his affections, he is sure to find skeptical contemporaries to call him the dreaded name of dupe, the terror of today's youth. But he is the only truly beloved man: is he really such a dupe? The fears and pleasures of pride are the stuff of frivolous, deceitful affections. Is a man a dupe if he does not enjoy tricking others to be tricked in his turn, more broken perhaps than his victim? Is he a dupe if instead of looking for happiness in the miserable schemes of vanity, he seeks them in the eternal beauties of nature, which tell us of constancy, duration, and depth?

No. God has created man the first, the noblest of creatures—and the noblest creature is the one with the most obligations to fulfill. Using one's natural superiority to free oneself from the most sacred of ties is a singular abuse of it. Real superiority consists in the force of the soul: and the force of the soul is virtue.

THE INFLUENCE OF ENTHUSIASM ON THE ENLIGHTENMENT (4.11)

This chapter is a resumé of my whole book, in some respects: since enthusiasm is the distinguishing characteristic of the German nation, its influence on enlightenment can be judged according to German intellectual progress. Enthusiasm lends life to invisible things, and interest to things without immediate bearing on our worldly prosperity. That's why this feeling is characteristic of the quest for abstract truths, which are cultivated in Germany with remarkable ardor and loyalty.

While philosophers inspired by enthusiasm may do the most accurate and patient work, they are also the last ones to aim at brilliance. They love knowledge for itself, and do not take themselves into account when the object of their cult is at stake. Physical nature follows its unvarying course through the destruction of individuals; man's thought becomes sublime when he succeeds in thinking of himself from a universal point of view. He then quietly contributes to the triumph of truth: truth, like nature, is a force that acts only through progressive and regular development.

It would be no mistake to say that enthusiasm makes people tend toward systematic theories; anyone who is very much attached to his own ideas wants to relate everything else to them too. All the same, though, it is usually easier to deal with sincere opinions than with opinions adopted out of vanity. We would have no trouble reaching an understanding in human relationships if we had to deal only with what people really think; the discord comes from what they pretend to be thinking.

Enthusiasm is often accused of leading to error, but superficial interest can be much more misleading. To reach the heart of things, we need some impulse arousing us to get eagerly involved. Considering the human destiny in general, I think we can say that we come across the truth only when our souls are elevated; anything that tends to put us down is a lie. Error, despite everything people say, is on the side of vulgar emotions.

Let me repeat: enthusiasm has nothing to do with fanaticism, and cannot lead people astray. Enthusiasm is tolerant—not out of indifference, but because it makes us feel the interest and beauty of everything. Reason does not replace the happiness it takes away from us; enthusiasm finds in the heart's reverie and the mind's whole range of thought what fanaticism and passion concentrate in a single idea, a single object. The universality of this feeling is precisely what makes it favorable to thought and imagination.

Society develops the mind, but only contemplation can form genius. In countries dominated by vanity, vanity is the moving force, and it leads inexorably to mockery, which kills enthusiasm.

Who can deny the fun of noticing ridiculous things, and sketching them in a lively, graceful way? It might be better to refuse to give in to such pleasure; but this is not a threatening kind of mockery. Really disastrous mockery is the kind that focuses on ideas and sentiments, infiltrating the source of strong, devoted affections. Man has great power over his fellow man, and the greatest harm he can do him is to interpose the phantom of ridicule between his generous impulses and the actions they might inspire.

Love, genius, talent—even pain: these sacred things are all exposed to irony, and no one can calculate how far the power of that irony may extend. There is something piquant about wickedness, something feeble about truth. Admiration for great things can be upset by joking: anyone who attaches no importance to anything looks as if he were above everything. If enthusiasm does not protect our hearts and minds, therefore, they may be assaulted by a sort of denigration of the beautiful, combining insolence and gaiety.

Our social minds are constructed so that we often command ourselves to laugh, and are even more frequently ashamed to cry. Why? Because vanity feels more secure with jest than with emotion. We have to be able to count on our own minds if we are to face mockery seriously; we need a lot of strength to show sentiments vulnerable to ridicule. As Fontenelle said: "I am eighty years old; I am a Frenchman; and in my whole life I have never ridiculed the least little virtue in the least little way."[19] This saying implies a deep understanding of society. Fontenelle was not a man of feeling, but he was a man of wit, and whoever is endowed with any sort of superiority always senses human nature's need to be serious. Only mediocre people want everything to be built on sand, so that no one can leave a trace of himself on earth more durable than their own.

Germans do not have to struggle against the enemies of enthusiasm, and this removes one great obstacle for men of distinction. The mind sharpens itself in combat, but talent needs confidence. To experience the inspiration of genius one must believe in admiration, glory, and immortality. The difference between centuries does not come from nature, always free with her gifts, but from the ruling opinion of the time. If this opinion tends toward enthusiasm, great men rise up everywhere. If discouragement is proclaimed instead of the call to noble efforts, nothing will be left of literature but judges of times past.

The terrible events we have witnessed have left us with souls blasé; everything related to thought pales beside the omnipotence of action. Varying circumstances have led people to change their minds on a given question again and again, so no one believes in ideas anymore—or at least thinks of them as anything more than means to an end. Belief does not seem a thing of our time: when a man says he has an opinion people take it for a delicate way of saying that he has some particular interest.

The most decent men then invent a system transforming their laziness into dignity; they say nothing can be accomplished; they agree with Shakespeare's Hermit of Prague: "That that is, is";[20] they say that theories have no influence on the world. In the end such men make what they are saying come true, because with such a way of thinking it is impossible to act on other people. If wit consisted only in seeing the pros and cons of everything, it would make everything spin around us so much that we would be unable to walk firmly on such shaky ground.

We also see young people, eager to seem disillusioned of enthusiasm, affecting a considered contempt for exalted feelings. They think they are showing precocious strength of mind: they are actually boasting about premature decadence. As for talent, they are like the old man asking if people still fell in love. The mind deprived of imagination would be quite willing to despise nature itself, if nature were not the stronger.

People still aroused by noble desires are certainly hurt by the constant barrage of arguments that would disturb even the most confident hope. Good faith must not be discouraged by this, though, because it is concerned with what men really are, not what they seem to be. Whatever the surrounding atmosphere, a sincere word is never completely lost; success may have its day, but there are centuries for the good that can be done by truth.

Each of the inhabitants of Mexico carries a little stone along the main highway to add to the great pyramid they are building in the middle of their country. It will bear no one's name, but every one of them will have contributed to a monument that will last longer than them all.[21]

9.

The Mannequin
A Dramatic Proverb
in Two Acts

Cast of Characters

The Count d'Erville, French gentleman
M. de la Morlière, member of a refugee family living in Berlin*

Sophie, his daughter
M. Frederic Hoffman, German painter

The scene is in Berlin, at the home of M. de la Morlière.

ACT I

Scene 1. M. de la Morlière, Sophie

LA MORLIÈRE: No, no! Love of country means more to me than anything else in the world.

SOPHIE: Your family left France a hundred years ago, Papa, and you have never set foot in it yourself.

---

*The part of M. de la Morlière should be played with a German accent.

LA MORLIÈRE: My grandfather may have been forced to take refuge in Germany because of the revocation of the Edict of Nantes—indeed—but we have always kept our French heart—French blood—French tastes.[1]

SOPHIE: Not exactly a French accent, though, Papa, do admit.

LA MORLIÈRE: I may be so unfortunate as to pronounce a word with a bit of a gutteral now and again, but you do not have to be so mean as to point it out. Anyway, if my language is no longer graceful, that's exactly the problem: it's happened because I've been living with these damned Germans. That is the very reason why I want a French son-in-law. A French son-in-law will correct my pronunciation, and make everything look French around here, and tell me stories of the good old days of Louis XIV. When I was a boy my grandfather always used to tell me about Louis XIV.

SOPHIE: The man you want me to marry, Papa, the Count d'Erville, is the least likely man in the world to tell you anything interesting about any of that. I like Frenchmen as much as you do, but that particular Frenchman is a caricature of French faults—French virtues, if that sounds any better. He claims he is here to go to the reviews of our great King Frederic.[2] Has he the least notion of what he has been seeing? I ask you. Did he or did he not watch a whole army march by through his opera glasses? What has he been thinking about, except himself? He travels to show off, not to learn. It is hard to overlook his ignorance too, because he has something to say about everything and ideas about nothing. That is not really a Frenchman, Papa. We have Germans much worthier of being called French than the Count d'Erville.

LA MORLIÈRE: The Count d'Erville is the bearer of a very distinguished name.

SOPHIE: They would never let him in the Almanach de Gotha.[3]

LA MORLIÈRE: The great names of France may not have the thirty-two quarters Germans are so proud of,[4] but there is more sparkle to French nobility. More style. More grace.

SOPHIE: Grace, when it comes to genealogy! What a combination! I know how fond you are of the word "graceful." I agree—it is the Frenchest word in the world. But do you really think the Count d'Erville *is* graceful? For one thing, he never listens to what other people are saying.

LA MORLIÈRE: No one talks as well as he does.

SOPHIE: He never *stops* talking!

LA MORLIÈRE: What else do we have to do, besides listen?

SOPHIE: He doesn't know anything.

LA MORLIÈRE: He guesses.

SOPHIE: Only the other day the King was making fun of the stupid way he was talking about military strategy, which he claims to have been studying all his life.

LA MORLIÈRE: Well. No. He is strongest on literature.

SOPHIE: Literature! M. de Voltaire made mincemeat of him yesterday for the idiotic things he was conceited enough to say; and in front of the cleverest man in France, no less.

LA MORLIÈRE: M. de Voltaire is certainly clever. No one is trying to take that away from him. He is not a nobleman, however. To be a really accomplished Frenchman one must combine book learning with a knowledge of the world.

SOPHIE: Absolutely right, Papa, one must have both those things,—but is it enough to lay claim to them?

LA MORLIÈRE: You are not being fair to M. d'Erville.

SOPHIE: And is being unfair to M. d'Erville a good reason for me to marry him?

LA MORLIÈRE: In France, people who marry make marriages of convenience.

SOPHIE: Well, we are in Germany, so I would like to be able to include a little bit of love as well.

LA MORLIÈRE: If I leave it to you, you would marry that painter, Frederic Hoffman, a young man who has never been out of Berlin and knows nothing about anything but art.

SOPHIE: Frederic is unaffected, naturally sincere, proud, and modest. His gracefulness comes from the superiority of his mind and soul, and it belongs to all ranks and nations.

LA MORLIÈRE: Well, he would be no credit to us in France, all the same. Wouldn't it be nice to go back home—just once—full of the glory we had when we left?

SOPHIE: You would be willing to leave the place where you were born?

LA MORLIÈRE: I may have happened to be born here, but birth is an accident; it counts for nothing in the life of a man. My real country is France. France— France! I am bored everywhere else.

SOPHIE: Are you seriously considering doing this, Papa? You've never gone back before.

LA MORLIÈRE: Supposing I admit that. What difference does it make? I always think of myself as having spent my life there.

SOPHIE: Think about this instead: if I marry M. d'Erville, I will have to leave you. I know you—you talk of traveling, but you will never do it.

LA MORLIÈRE: Too true. My imagination travels, and my feet have the gout. Don't betray me, Sophie. Here at home I like a fire, some beer, and my pipe.

SOPHIE: All three of those things are terribly German, Papa, you do realize?

LA MORLIÈRE: Bad habits we don't discuss in public, that's all. But when I know you are in France—when I can say "My daughter, the Countess d'Erville, writes me that they have performed this new play—or published that book—or that the King has appointed so-and-so to office!" Then I'll believe I am where my ancestors were. I will feel a hundred years younger.

SOPHIE: A hundred years younger, Papa! You would never have lived at all. You are sacrificing your own happiness to such moonshine! Alas!

LA MORLIÈRE: M. d'Erville will be here in a minute. Stay with us for a while, so I can make you see . . .

SOPHIE: And there's something else you don't know, Papa. M. d'Erville doesn't like me.

LA MORLIÈRE: How can you say that, my child? You, whom I have brought up in the French tradition? And educated in the German? M. d'Erville is so fond of wit!

SOPHIE: Fond of his own. He doesn't like other people's, and he certainly wouldn't like his wife's.

LA MORLIÈRE: All women are piquant and attractive in France, you know.

SOPHIE: When you say all women, you say a mouthful. M. d'Erville will never stand for any woman attracting a fraction of the attention he wants himself. The qualities in my conversation you are kind enough to praise don't give him anywhere near as much pleasure as my silence—I've seen it ten times if I've seen it once.

LA MORLIÈRE: This is crazy. Do not tease me again about this marriage. I have given my word. I am a German and a Frenchman, daughter; you know whether or not I can break it.

SOPHIE: I can see M. d'Erville coming, Father; I leave you to him.

LA MORLIÈRE: Don't go. He's so eager to see you!

SOPHIE: Eager to see me! You really understand the man.

LA MORLIÈRE: Be frank. Do you think there is another woman he prefers, here or elsewhere?

SOPHIE: Certainly not. He is in love with no one but himself. That rivalry is as good as any other, however, and no woman has ever had the better of it. *[Exit]*

Scene 2. Enter the Count d'Erville

COUNT: Good day, good father-in-law—a name I am happy to call you. My heart belongs to you, just as if the knot were already tied.

LA MORLIÈRE: How wonderful it is to hear you talk like that! Germans take years to form close friendships, and we are already the best friends in the world, even though I have only known you for two weeks.

COUNT: You are so right! Whatever interests you interests me. Personally, as it were.

LA MORLIÈRE: Did you get to speak to the Minister about that post my brother wanted?

COUNT: Brother? You have a brother?

LA MORLIÈRE: Do I have a brother? I have been talking to you about him for at least two hours a day all week long.

COUNT: Time flies when you are speaking to me . . . .

LA MORLIÈRE: And when you are not listening. Never mind. French vivacity is its own excuse. But I will give you the details now.

COUNT: Won't be necessary. Your brother is German, I understand?

LA MORLIÈRE: German! No, since I am French; an émigré. Can you possibly have forgotten that? I would have thought my pronunciation—

COUNT: Delightful. And tell me, how good is your comprehension?

LA MORLIÈRE: My comprehension! Of French? But I hardly know any German. I speak German only for business matters.

COUNT: Quite right too. French is the only language for polite society. Foreign languages are not polite—that's why I don't know any. My tutor tried to teach me, but I was afraid of spoiling my French.

LA MORLIÈRE: Very true. I cannot prevent myself from knowing a little German, but I'm doing my best to forget it.

COUNT: Right. Because what good is it?

LA MORLIÈRE: It can be useful in Germany, from time to time.

COUNT: That makes sense. I have always managed very well without it, though.

LA MORLIÈRE: Tell me the truth. Do I have an accent?

COUNT: An accent? Gascon? Picard? Normand?

LA MORLIÈRE: No . . . an accent . . . of this country . . . if you make me say it . . . a German accent.

COUNT: Haven't really paid much attention. Now that you mention it, though, I do think . . .

LA MORLIÈRE: Go on. Go on.

COUNT: There are some words you pronounce . . .

LA MORLIÈRE: Yes?

COUNT: A little too well.

LA MORLIÈRE: What?

COUNT: A little too loudly.

LA MORLIÈRE: Good God! It's the truth! My grandfather used to warn me. I'm so eager to be speaking French that I'm afraid of not being understood.

COUNT: Only natural. After we spend some time together, though, your speech will be light and quick like mine. Can you believe it? The King of Prussia, Frederick the Great himself, does not speak like a Frenchman. What he says is all very well, but there is no ease in his expressions. He talks slowly. Anyone would say he thinks while he speaks, which is terribly ungraceful.

LA MORLIÈRE: What about M. de Voltaire, who is at court now? What do you think of him?

COUNT: Frankly, I really wasn't listening to him. I was all ready to tell about Paris—I had just left Paris—everyone was wild to hear all about Paris. There will always be another chance to talk to M. de Voltaire.

LA MORLIÈRE: But they say he's leaving tomorrow.

COUNT: Ah! So sorry to hear it. However, he appears in print so often that I am free to read him whenever I like. The people whose words are absolutely not to miss are the ones who only speak. Plenty of time to get to know the ones who write.

LA MORLIÈRE: What do you think of my daughter's wit? Be perfectly frank with me.

COUNT: Frankly—since you wish me to be frank—it is my way to be frank, and it has been so successful that I never worry about it—Sophie is a clever girl, very clever; but she puts herself forward. She makes a little too much noise in a room.

LA MORLIÈRE: I thought my daughter's innocent liveliness would be just right for French taste.

COUNT: No doubt. As for me, though—I don't know if you agree with me or not—I like women who talk very little. I like a smile of approval or encouragement a thousand times more than Sophie's way of monopolizing the conversation. Much more suitable . . .

LA MORLIÈRE: Sir?

COUNT: Your daughter—charming. I adore her. I already told you that. But I don't know . . . there is something more French about your manners than hers.

LA MORLIÈRE: Well, that's easy to understand. I have always paid more attention to the mother country than she has.

COUNT: When I am your son-in-law, you will think you live there. You do know my affairs are not quite in order, by the way. I have not concealed it from you; I have vast estates which have been in my family for generations, but I do also have debts. A lot of debts, unfortunately.

LA MORLIÈRE: That is the custom in France, is it?

COUNT: Absolutely.

LA MORLIÈRE: We must follow the custom. But you are not intending to ruin yourself or my daughter, I hope?

COUNT: Certainly not. That is completely out of date. People no longer ruin themselves. They have realized how necessary money is for elegance itself, and they try to be as rich as they can. Money is graceful.

LA MORLIÈRE: Of course—I am only sorry I have so little ready cash in hand.

COUNT: A pity. Ready cash is the best kind. I wish you could watch me spend money, you know. The way I do it would give you such pleasure.

LA MORLIÈRE: If it was your money, yes, though with my own . . .

COUNT: For a man like you, is there any difference? The manner is what counts.

LA MORLIÈRE: So true. I am entirely French in this regard. Long live manners! Manners are the only thing that gives us pleasure. I have prepared a surprise for you, by the way! I hope you like it. You know Frederic Hoffman, the talented German painter?

COUNT: I catch your meaning. You want me to have my portrait painted for your daughter. So kind. But I have forestalled your wishes; here it is.

LA MORLIÈRE: Not at all—I was thinking of my daughter's portrait.

COUNT: Good thinking. Absolutely right. Of course I wanted hers too, but I did not dare . . .

LA MORLIÈRE: I would have thought it took more confidence to offer one's own portrait than to receive one of the woman one loves.

COUNT: *[looking at his own portrait]:* Too kind.

LA MORLIÈRE: You are not answering what I am saying to you.

COUNT: Pardon me. I was distracted. There is something about my features which is missing from this portrait. Artists can never quite catch it.

LA MORLIÈRE: have Frederic touch it up. Frederic is very clever. You say nothing. Are you jealous, by any chance?

COUNT: Jealous? Me? Jealous? Why?

LA MORLIÈRE: Because everyone says he's in love with my daughter.

COUNT: Good God! It never occurred to me. It's not in my nature to be jealous. I have a little bit of faith in my lucky star—my lucky star has always done right by me. Anyway, frankly, an artist . . .

LA MORLIÈRE: Of course. All the same, Frederic is wellborn and witty, and I have not seen too many Germans who speak French as well as he does.

COUNT: Only outside France does speaking French well look like a virtue; we take that advantage rather for granted. Certain ways of speaking are noticed even among us, though. Do you think your daughter is capable of feeling such nuances?

LA MORLIÈRE: Have you any doubt of it?

COUNT: She was listening to me very poorly yesterday. Being a good listener is a great talent in a woman. *You* have that talent. Speaking to you gives one a great deal of pleasure.

LA MORLIÈRE: Ah! that's because I am nearer to the moment when my grandfather left France. The French tradition is getting weaker with each generation.

COUNT: What do you mean, each generation? A month's absence is enough to make one rusty. When one gets back to Paris one will need time to recover—to be, in a word, everything one should be.

LA MORLIÈRE: If that is the case, we'd better hurry up with the wedding. Tomorrow. Tonight—I would not care to have a rusty son-in-law, not for anything in the world. I can feel myself how sad it would be. I don't know how to describe what one is like, when one is ignorant of how one is in Paris. One speaks quite at random, one does not even know if one is right in feeling what one feels. In short, one can be certain of nothing.

COUNT: Count on me to put you in the know.

LA MORLIÈRE: Please wait here for the painter; he is going to bring you Sophie's portrait. It is time for me to go to my brother's This is rather familiar behavior, leaving you here in my house, but I want to say goodbye in the French style, without making apologies. That's the way they do it in Paris, isn't it? [Bows several times] Please don't think I am ignorant of the respect I owe you, my lord. I am going away on tiptoe. Without a word. Without one single bow. Lightly, as my grandfather would have done. In short, as a true Frenchman. No, no, do not bow to me. I am going. I have gone. [Exit]

Scene 3. Count

COUNT: And he calls that saying nothing! He spent so much time asking permission to leave I thought he'd never get on with it. All the same, I wish his daughter were more like him, such as he is. She is a shrewd little thing—I don't like it, I don't like it at all.

Scene 4. Count, Frederic

COUNT: Good afternoon, M. Frederic. I'm so terribly sorry not to have had my portrait painted *chez vous*. I know you would have done a better job than that M. Schiehle . . . Schlihles . . . I can't pronounce German names.[5]

FREDERIC: The same thing happens to us with French names.

COUNT: Can that be possible?

FREDERIC: Very. We are all foreigners to one another.

COUNT: Foreigners! Frenchmen! Are you serious?

FREDERIC: Not in France; but in Germany.

COUNT: True; though that state of affairs will not last much longer. My future father-in-law, M. de la Morlière, told me you were to deliver a portrait of his daughter, Mlle. Sophie, to me.

FREDERIC: I did not realize it was intended for you, monsieur.

COUNT: And for whom did you think it *was* intended?

FREDERIC: *[aside]*: Alas!—Here it is, monsieur. Do you think it looks like her?

COUNT: There is some likeness, yes, but it is much prettier than she is.

FREDERIC: I would have thought that impossible.

COUNT: Ah! An illusion, my good man. A nice-looking girl, Sophie, but your portrait is a thousand times better-looking.

FREDERIC: I am very far from agreeing with you.

COUNT: That's simple: you are in love with Sophie. Which I know; the father-in-law told me.

FREDERIC: Monsieur—

COUNT: And it doesn't bother me one single bit, because I'm not. I'm thirty years old. I've already been in love lots of times, and lots of people have been in love with me. I don't fool myself with illusions about anything anymore.

FREDERIC: You surprise me, monsieur. You are marrying a woman whom many men envy you, and I would have thought you could be a little more aware of your good fortune.

COUNT: I bet you read a lot of novels. Come on. Make a bet.

FREDERIC: Yes. Granted. But I still think what I just said is no exaggeration.

COUNT: Everything that goes beyond the limits of reason is romantic story-book stuff.

FREDERIC: And where do you set the limits of reason?

COUNT: In everyday usage. It is fitting for a man like me to marry a rich girl of somewhat inferior birth. If not, I can assure you I would be quite willing to hand Mlle. Sophie over to you.

FREDERIC: Monsieur, I would like you to refrain from speaking to me of my personal matters.

COUNT: Why? I am willing to talk about mine, myself.

FREDERIC: To each his own.

COUNT: True. I don't blame you. But let me point out that it's the father-in-law who took a fancy to me; this marriage of mine is not my idea. Far from it. Mlle.

Sophie has her own notions about everything. She frequently contradicts me, and that is not a way to get to know me. I keep quiet when people start debating—it is such a bore. People have to learn how to appreciate me from the very beginning, or they may as well give it up. Would you believe it? What I really like is English manners—English shyness. Yesterday at the Minister's there was . . .

FREDERIC: Lady Berwick.

COUNT: Just so; I thought whe was the wittiest woman in the world.

FREDERIC: How do you know she is witty? She does not speak a single word of French.

COUNT: She understands it perfectly—and as for her eyes—

FREDERIC: She was enchanted with you.

COUNT: I noticed that. I would like to give her a copy of this portrait before leaving here. If you are willing to make one, touching it up according to my instructions . . .

FREDERIC: Monsieur, let me keep the portrait of Mlle. Sophie and I will make you two copies of yours, exactly as you wish.

COUNT: Sophie's portrait? But can we do that? I ask nothing better, myself, because—and I can have a better one made in France. Though the father-in-law might be angry.

FREDERIC: I will take care of that.

COUNT: But Sophie!

FREDERIC: But the English lady who listens so nicely! And looks at you so nicely!

COUNT: Ah! true; there is no woman who has such a graceful way of talking—I mean not talking, of course. Well, do whatever seems best to you—I would not want a gallant chap like yourself to be angry with me. Listen, I think the eyes are not quite right . . . .

FREDERIC: In Mlle. Sophie's portrait?

COUNT: No, in mine. But don't make them look the way I do today—I am so depressed. So sad. It's annoying not to be marrying for love. Not that I would want to make an imprudent match, but it would be so nice to have everything. You Germans think you are the only melancholy people in the world, but we have our own moments of reverie. To get *this* look for my portrait. This lost look. Good, isn't it? Adieu. [Exit]

Scene 5. Sophie, Frederic

SOPHIE: Frederic darling! I've been lying in wait for M. d'Erville to leave, so as to see you alone for a moment.

FREDERIC: Sophie! Can you possibly marry a man like him? You do realize he doesn't love you?

SOPHIE: Do you think it would take me this long to notice that?

FREDERIC: Would you believe he has given me your portrait, in exchange for my making him two copies of his own?

SOPHIE: That is a bit much, I admit. But what can I do? My father has given his word, and nothing will make him break it.

FREDERIC: How can you answer with such indifference? Have you taken on the character of the man you are going to marry already? Flighty, insensitive, ruled by vanity in this, the most important circumstance in your life? Forgive me, Sophie. That isn't the way you have been toward me. But how can I talk politely about my misery and yours? The Count d'Erville is not for you. Even if you didn't care about my love, even if you didn't regret someone who has loved you so much, your soul is much too noble and profound to be understood by a man like that.

SOPHIE: Frederic, I have made a mistake. I have plans I haven't told you about. I wanted to keep them from you until after I had spoken to my father one more time, but you are so sincere that I cannot hide anything in my heart from you.

FREDERIC: What plans, for heaven's sake?

SOPHIE: I know my father. He will never ask to be released from his promise if M. d'Erville does not take the initiative.

FREDERIC: What hope is there of that?

SOPHIE: I have been trying to displease M. d'Erville; that has been a success, thank goodness. All I have to do for that is deprive him of the ability to shine. The problem is that I gain nothing by being disagreeable to him, because he isn't marrying me for love.

FREDERIC: Then what are you hoping to gain?

SOPHIE: I am hoping to lay a little trap for him.

FREDERIC: Sophie! Trap a Frenchman! No German has ever managed that.

SOPHIE: Not frequently, I must admit. But M. d'Erville is so very full of himself that he pays very little attention to anything else. Vanity is a very good handle, and M. d'Erville has so much of it that I flatter myself I can lead him around by it without his even noticing. Besides, he is extremely fond of money—all he wants to do with it is spend it, but it is still a taste that is always a little common, and we can use it to get rid of him. Darling Frederic, I am so eager to escape this horrible fate and keep myself for you that I would be willing to try anything.

FREDERIC: Oh Sophie! I cannot dare to hope for so much happiness.

SOPHIE: Frederic dear, we have done no one any harm. Why shouldn't fate be on our side? Look, here comes my father—leave me alone with him.

[Frederic exits.]

Scene 6. Sophie, M. de la Morlière

LA MORLIÈRE: I thought you were with M. d'Erville.

SOPHIE: He left some time ago. You know what he thinks of me?

LA MORLIÈRE: I suppose I do, since he is marrying you.

SOPHIE: Good reasoning! The Count does not quite realize that it takes two to get married.

LA MORLIÈRE: You have a grudge against him. I don't quite like that.

SOPHIE: Father, I am right. I swear to you.

LA MORLIÈRE: I would be really annoyed. Let me tell you one more time: I have given my word.

SOPHIE: Suppose I made M d'Erville himself release you?

LA MORLIÈRE: Then I would be free . . . though I would still resent your breaking up this marriage, which—

SOPHIE: Father, before you blame me, do me this favor: come with me to see my uncle. He knows M. d'Erville better than you do. He can tell you—

LA MORLIÈRE: Your uncle does not know a single word of French. He makes Germans of us all. He forgets his ancestry, his country, his—

SOPHIE: Even so, Papa, you love my uncle very much.

LA MORLIÈRE: True.

SOPHIE: Well, with him there I will tell you what I am hoping for—

LA MORLIÈRE: Hoping?

SOPHIE: That M. d'Erville will ask you for the hand of your niece in marriage.

LA MORLIÈRE: Niece? What niece? I have no niece. Do you want to make a liar of me?

SOPHIE: Certainly not. I prefer to take that on myself.

LA MORLIÈRE: You would let yourself stoop to deceit?

SOPHIE: An innocent trick. You will approve of it yourself.

LA MORLIÈRE: What I want to know—

SOPHIE: You will know very soon. Follow me to my uncle's. If M. d'Erville does not release you from your promise, I agree to obey you.

LA MORLIÈRE: Very well, let's be off. I will go with you. But nothing good will come of it, so far as I can see.

ACT II

Scene 1. M. de la Morlière, Sophie

LA MORLIÈRE: But you are crazy, child. The idea may make me laugh—it *is* funny. But it cannot possibly work.

SOPHIE: You'll see.

LA MORLIÈRE: That M. d'Erville would take an artist's mannequin for my niece?

SOPHIE: I'll put it over there behind that curtain, where I draw when Frederic comes to help me copy your bust.

LA MORLIÈRE: Over there? Let's see . . . but there's someone there already. Who is that? *[He bows. Sophie bows.]* How can you invite visitors here at a time like this? I could have been overheard.

SOPHIE: No, Papa, I swear it.

LA MORLIÈRE: And she looks most unhappy at having been made to wait.

SOPHIE: A very peaceable lady, Papa. We will soon make it up.

LA MORLIÈRE: Madame, have you something to say to my daughter? What the devil! She won't answer. Go and talk to her. You're laughing! What can you be thinking of? What are you driving at?

SOPHIE: Well, you see for yourself, Papa: it has a chance of fooling M. d'Erville.

LA MORLIÈRE: Hm! Is that the mannequin?

SOPHIE: Yes, Papa.

LA MORLIÈRE: Good grief! It's unbelievable.—And when my "niece" refuses to speak?

SOPHIE: He will take her silence for admiration.

LA MORLIÈRE: And when he wants to know if he is loved in return?

SOPHIE: He will do both question and answer all by himself.

LA MORLIÈRE: And if he takes her hand, won't he realize that it's made of papier-mâché?

SOPHIE: That would be something else again . . . . My cousin's reserve will delay that moment, though, and as I'm going to be there myself at the interview I think I'll be able to manage. You will be released from your promise, and I may do what I wish with my heart.

LA MORLIÈRE: Well, if my future son-in-law turns out to be that much of a fool, I will have to agree he is no Frenchman. A Frenchman is the most perceptive of men.

SOPHIE: Tell the truth, Papa. Do you *want* to give your daughter to someone who would prefer a mannequin?

LA MORLIÈRE: Well, no. Certainly not. Do you really believe him so insensitive to the charm of your conversation? My grandfather used to tell me such stories of Mme. de Sévigné and Mme. de La Fayette,[6] women who—

SOPHIE: M. d'Erville would like to reduce women to the role of ciphers.

LA MORLIÈRE: Harsh words for a lighthearted man.

SOPHIE: Vanity is harder than virtue in some ways.

LA MORLIÈRE: Well, I will not interfere. If he comes to ask my niece's hand in marriage, enough said, you can marry your artist. If not, however, you sign your contract with M. d'Erville tonight.[7]

SOPHIE: Tonight!

LA MORLIÈRE: Goodbye. I will see you later. *[Exit]*

Scene 2. Sophie, Frederic

SOPHIE: So! Has my uncle spoken to M. d'Erville?

FREDERIC: Yes, he has, Sophie darling. You can't imagine how easily he swallowed the bait. Would anyone have believed that a man who has seen you—

SOPHIE: Enough flattery, my friend. You don't know how much pleasure you give me in proving that he isn't in love with me.

FREDERIC: Your uncle told M. d'Erville all about his only daughter—much richer than you, but not out in society because she spoke no French and was so shy. "I like shy women," said he. "I am good-natured, and I enjoy reassuring them." Your uncle added that your "cousin" had seen M. d'Erville ride by on horseback, and that from then on her head had been turned. "Poor little thing!" answered he. "That must be because I ride so well, and she has seen no one else who—" He meant that there was no one in this country as graceful as himself, but modesty held him back. I thought it would be only polite to finish his sentence; he did not protest. Your uncle cannot stand the man, so he was taking a good deal of joy in telling him over and over how jealous you were of your cousin. You let her visit you only in the morning, so no other visitors can see her. M. d'Erville will be here any minute; he thinks he will be surprising you. I told him I would go for your cousin right away, and bring her to your closet.[8] Let us draw the curtain shut, and do not open it until I come back. I will give you enough time to arouse his curiosity by refusing to let him see her.... Darling Sophie! I see you feel uncomfortable about deceiving even someone who wants to marry you for your money. I am too; but I think, just for once, that we can let ourselves abandon the role of dupes, which we are usually so proud to play.

SOPHIE: You are right, Frederic, that's what was bothering me. But look, here comes M. d'Erville! His self-confidence makes mincemeat of my scruples. Let's be clever at playing our roles; hasn't he been play-acting all day long?

Scene 3. Sophie, Frederic, Count d'Erville

COUNT [to Frederic, aside]: Are you going to get her?

FREDERIC: In a minute.

COUNT: Hurry! I am getting impatient!

FREDERIC: Calm down. You interest me.

COUNT: My imagination is so easily aroused!

[Frederic exits.]

Scene 4. Sophie, Count d'Erville

SOPHIE *[enters]*: Ah! Welcome, monsieur. *[She curtsies.]* I have not seen you all day. Did you go out this morning? Have you been to the museum to see the new exhibition of paintings? I was thrilled with it myself. For shades of color, delicacy of line, intensity of composition . . .

COUNT *[aside]*: What chatter! *[Aloud]* No, mademoiselle; I have been busy with something else.

SOPHIE: Should I flatter myself it was with thoughts of me?

COUNT: The thought of you is certainly capable of occupying my mind, but I must admit people have been making me curious about something else.

SOPHIE: What is that, may I ask?

COUNT: They say you have a most agreeable cousin.

SOPHIE: Agreeable! She never utters a word.

COUNT: Exquisite taste, though.

SOPHIE: Who told you that?

COUNT: Her father for one, and then a man whose judgment you respect: M. Frederic.

SOPHIE: Aha! Can't you see? What he wants is for you to give me up and marry my cousin instead.

COUNT: Mademoiselle, could you possibly believe . . . and besides, your cousin would never be willing.

SOPHIE: Who knows? My cousin is a person of whom one may make what one will. She has no ideas or wishes of her own at all: where you put her, there she stays.

COUNT: I can tell you I am very fond of docility in women.

SOPHIE: Anyone would have to agree that my cousin is docile. But with her you would never enjoy your favorite pleasure: the pleasure of understanding another person, answering each other, communicating your feelings and thoughts to each other.

COUNT: I am more willing to give up that particular pleasure than you imagine. What I need more anything else is to be understood. As for the rest, I am not demanding. I do not need other people to tell me their own concerns. I respect their secrets.

SOPHIE: Indifference is often a help to discretion. All in all, monsieur, I see my cousin suits you much better than I do. I have noticed for some little time that my uncle would be glad to have you for a son-in-law. But do not make me introduce you to the woman for whom you are rejecting me! And in my own house!

COUNT: Dear Sophie, I am touched by your pain, and I imagine what it must be. But that German artist is in love with you! He is far better suited to you than I am. He is romantic, like you; I am reason, pure and simple. Your cousin's mind will be much more like my own.

SOPHIE: You are quite sure of that?

COUNT: I will be, as soon as I have seen her.

SOPHIE: And her fortune *is* so much more substantial . . .

COUNT: Ah! You have just said the only thing in the world that could have kept me from releasing your father from his promise.

SOPHIE [aside]: Good heavens, what was I doing! [Aloud] You are far too generous, monsieur. My cousin's substantial dowry, which is to be paid in cash, should hardly be a reason why your delicacy should keep you from asking for her hand in marriage. I could only marry you if I were sure of having your whole heart. Please do not marry me if you do not feel enough passion for me to make you happy in misery and solitude. Do not do it. Do not marry me.

COUNT: Misery! Solitude! Have you any idea how horrible that sounds? Have you, by any chance, any passing notion that such a thing could happen to us? Speak to me quite openly.

SOPHIE: People who love each other always have to suppose things like that.

COUNT: What on earth are you saying? Does your cousin suppose things like that too?

SOPHIE: Good Lord, no. My cousin is—well, she is a person of whom no evil can be spoken.

COUNT: Such praise is worth a good deal, coming from a rival.

SOPHIE: Rival! A rather strong expression. You may find in future that the rivalry is not so bitter as you think.

COUNT: Come, come. No bitterness, I beg you. Try to show your characteristic generosity instead. You Germans have novels full of such admirable sacrifices . . . .

SOPHIE: Which you are advising me to make on your behalf.

Scene 5. Count, Sophie, Frederic

Enter Frederic

COUNT: Ah! Frederic. Is mademoiselle's cousin here?

FREDERIC: Yes, monsieur, in that dressing room over there.

COUNT: Let me see her.

SOPHIE: Take it easy. She would be terribly frightened if you went up to her so suddenly. You sit down here with M. Frederic, and my cousin and I will sit on the sofa behind that curtain.

COUNT: You will at least open the curtain, I hope.

SOPHIE: As long as you keep your distance.

COUNT: The very idea!

SOPHIE: That's the way I want it. Will you give me your word?

COUNT [to Frederic]: Women's jealousy is so demanding! I suffer from it all the time. [To Sophie] Very well. Your wish is my command.

SOPHIE: I'm counting on that. I'll be right back. [Exit]

Scene 6. Count, Frederic

COUNT: Have you any notion how unhappy poor Sophie is feeling? It gives me such pain. I must say I did not realize that she had become so attached to me. Forgive me for mentioning it to you, since you are in love with her. It's not very tactful of me.

FREDERIC: We must each suffer our fate with courage.

COUNT: So true—especially since she will be much more likely to appreciate you better when she sees me determined to marry her cousin. She will no doubt miss me in the beginning, but you are so agreeable that she will have to forget me after that. Besides, you can say I am ungrateful—unfaithful—whatever you like. So long as you help me succeed with the beautiful cousin, I'll be perfectly happy.

FREDERIC: You can count on me to do my best.

Scene 7. Count, Frederic, Sophie

SOPHIE [opens the door to the dressing room]: My cousin commands me to tell you that she is very eager to hear your voice, monsieur, after having had the pleasure of seeing you.

COUNT [to Frederic]: Good-looking, don't you think? Her hat hides her face a little, but it seems to me she has a real Greek profile.

FREDERIC: Absolutely.

COUNT: The line from forehead to nose is perfectly straight.

FREDERIC: Not a hair's-breadth short.

COUNT: Which is very rare. [To the mannequin] I had no idea that you were standing at the window when I rode by, mademoiselle. If I had had any way of knowing, I would have certainly stopped.

FREDERIC: She shows good taste by not answering that, don't you think?

COUNT: Oh yes. It shows she is deeply moved. I've always liked making that effect on women.

SOPHIE: My cousin says that before she heard you speak she thought that she knew French, but your flowing tongue is so intimidating that she wants to learn your language all over again before daring to speak it with you.

COUNT: Very true! I do speak quickly—foreigners are often embarrassed. A fault, but I have never been able to correct it. Might I venture to give you a few questions to translate into German for your cousin?

SOPHIE: That is such a cruel thing to ask me to do!

COUNT: Oh well, if it distresses you. I will just have to give up, and—

SOPHIE: No, no. Stay here. I insist. I only hope my generosity makes you happy.

COUNT: Does the young lady enjoy reading?

SOPHIE: My cousin says she has never bothered much about reading.

COUNT [to Frederic]: I'm sure you don't like the sound of that; you are, as they say in Germany, a "cultured" man. Well, as for me, I like the frankness of that answer. Let my wife read the letters I write her, and I won't insist on any other literature. . . . Do you like drawing, mademoiselle?

SOPHIE: My cousin doesn't think it is quite right for a woman to draw.

COUNT [to Frederic]: Do you understand why?

FREDERIC: I suppose she only wants to know the face of the man she loves.

COUNT: Enchanting! Simply enchanting! I'm always bored by amateur sketching. It's all really so pretentious. . . . And does the young lady enjoy music?

SOPHIE: My cousin says she has no voice at all.

COUNT: So much the better. Musicians are such terrible company, and you can never speak a word in the room where they are playing. . . . And does the young lady enjoy dancing?

SOPHIE: My cousin says she has never danced, and she is none the worse for that.

COUNT [rising]: A truly accomplished woman.

SOPHIE: Ah! how easy it is to please other people with the things one doesn't know.

COUNT: I see what you mean. You want a woman to have wit. And talent.

SOPHIE: Yes, monsieur, I admit it.

COUNT: Well, I do not care about any of that in the least.

SOPHIE: Flattering for my cousin.

COUNT: No need to be malicious, please. Don't make me offend this lovely young creature—her angelic sweetness deserves affection. I'm sorry to say this to you, but a woman is not supposed to shine compared with men, let alone to make us fade with her brilliance. A woman is supposed to support us, to comfort us in the shadows.

SOPHIE: My cousin will be the same in sunshine and in shadow.

COUNT: Would she be willing to follow me to France?

SOPHIE: She says she will be equally happy wherever you put her.

COUNT: So delightfully accommodating!

FREDERIC: Don't you wish her mind were just a little bit more lively?

COUNT: A little, I admit. But Paris will give her that.

FREDERIC: Paris can work miracles.

COUNT: Then I have only one more question for your lovely cousin: the most important question of all. Have I been lucky enough to please her? Have the goodness to ask.

SOPHIE [upsets the mannequin as she turns around; it almost falls]: Good heavens!

COUNT: What? Has she been taken ill?

FREDERIC [apart]: Careful, Sophie. —No, it's nothing.

SOPHIE: My cousin was trying to hide her feelings—I mean to explain them— but she got so excited that she almost fell down.

COUNT: Almost fell down! What sensitivity! I would have to have a heart of stone to resist such sincere proof of her affection . . .

FREDERIC: Her affections will never change; I will answer for that.

COUNT: Mademoiselle, I see your father coming. Will you permit me—

SOPHIE: Whatever you like, monsieur.

COUNT: Forgive me. But the sympathy that beats between two hearts conquers all. You know that.

Scene 8. Count, Frederic, Sophie, M. de la Morlière

COUNT: I throw myself on your mercy, monsieur. I thought myself in love with your daughter; I was bowled over by her brilliant talents. Quite rightly; but I do feel the happiness comes from kinship of soul. Since I came to Germany I have become more serious, and I agree with the philosophers: one ought to marry for love.

LA MORLIÈRE: Good for you, my lord. You have released me from my word. I hold myself a free man, and my daughter a free woman.

COUNT: Certainly. But that's not all. I want you to help me win your adorable niece.

LA MORLIÈRE: What niece?

COUNT: Right there in front of you. Her delightful modesty keeps her still. Don't embarrass her, for heaven's sake!

LA MORLIÈRE: My adorable niece is at your command. Take her away; take her wherever you like.

COUNT: Ah! Mademoiselle. *[Approaches the mannequin]* Good God, what's this? A mannequin! You have all been making fun of me! Mademoiselle Sophie?

SOPHIE: Forgive me for having wanted to find out if you really loved me. I played this trick on you because I was afraid of not really pleasing you enough.

COUNT *[to Frederic]*: And you?

FREDERIC: I stand ready to defend my conduct.[9]

SOPHIE: My lord, do not make a simple joke into something horrible. I was annoyed at you for thinking so little of women's wit, and for blaming women who attract attention in society. You must admit that you have exercised your talent for satire against women like me over and over again.

COUNT: I admit it.

SOPHIE: Well, I wanted to show you a woman who would not put forward her own opinion about anything, and broke none of the rules of etiquette: a real cardboard doll, just like all those living dolls. Forgive me for this petty vengeance. You have made such fun of my country and its inhabitants that perhaps you will let a German woman succeed in making fun of you, just for once; it will never happen again. And it is a matter of no importance. I love Frederic, and I do not suit you in any way. If you still want to have anything to do with me, however, I will not consider myself free. I am ready to keep the promise from which you have released my father. So it all depends on you. You are really noble and generous, I know you are. I put my fate in you hands.

COUNT: Mademoiselle, since you are leaving it up to me, I bow to your wishes. Let me hope, however, that somewhere in the world there are women less malicious than you, who are not, for all that, mannequins.

10.

Reflections on Suicide

Unhappy people are the ones to write for. People who have the good things of this world learn only from their own experience, and consider abstract ideas on any topic nothing but wasted time. Sufferers are different: reflection is their safest refuge. Isolated from the distractions of society by misfortune, they examine themselves like an invalid tossing on his bed of pain, seeking the least agonizing position they can find.

Inordinate misery makes people think about suicide. We need not be afraid of devoting too much time to this subject—it is at the heart of mankind's whole moral organization. I flatter myself that I can offer a few new insights into the motives that lead us to suicide, and those that should turn us away from it. I will talk without malice or exaltation. We must not hate people who are unhappy enough to detest life, but neither should we praise the ones who give way under an overload: if they could keep going, their moral strength would be all the greater.*

Most people who condemn suicide, conscious of being on the solid ground of reason and duty, support themselves with contemptuous language which may wound their adversaries; they may also combine the blame appropriate to guilty actions with an unfair attack on enthusiasm in general. But I believe that the simplest way to show the superiority of resignation to rebellion against destiny is through the principles of true enthusiasm and love of moral beauty.

I propose to present the question of suicide in three different ways. I will first examine the effects of suffering on the human

---

*In my work on the influence of the passions I praised the act of suicide, and I have always been sorry for this thoughtless statement. I was full of the pride and vivacity of my first youth at the time. But what would be the point of living, if not in the hope of improving?[1]

soul; second, the laws of Christianity on suicide; and finally the greatest moral dignity of mankind on this earth.

THE EFFECTS OF SUFFERING ON THE HUMAN SOUL (1.1)

We cannot hide it from ourselves: individuals vary as much in the impressions pain makes on them as they do in genius and character. Not only circumstances but their ways of feeling these circumstances differ so greatly that people whose opinions we respect on every other subject cannot agree on this one. Of all the limits of the mind, this is still the most unbearable, the ultimate boundary that keeps us from understanding other human beings.

I believe that happiness consists in having a destiny in keeping with our abilities. Our desires are things of the moment, often harmful even to ourselves; but our abilities are permanent, and their demands never cease. The conquest of the world may have been as much of a necessity to Alexander as the possession of a cottage to a shepherd. It need not follow that the human race should lend itself to providing fodder for Alexander's colossal abilities; but we may say that, given his nature, this was the only way he could be happy.

Any way of life is pleasant for some people and miserable for others; it all depends on one's ability to love, the quickness of one's mind, the importance one attaches to public opinion. The inflexible law of duty is the same for everybody; moral strength depends on the individual. Only profound understanding of the human heart can give any sort of philosophical equity to our judgments about the happiness or unhappiness of people who do not resemble us in the least.

It seems to me, therefore, that one cannot argue about individual experiences. Our advice is limited to conduct and the spiritual strength invariably prescribed by virtue and religion. There is as much variation in the causes and intensity of unhappiness as in circumstances and individuals. Analyzing all the possible combinations of fate and

character would be like trying to count the waves of the sea. Consciousness is the only thing that exists in us as a constant from which we can get
the peace of mind we crave. Most men resemble each other in what they
can do, not in what they do; anyone capable of reflection must admit that
when we commit faults against morality we always feel capable of avoiding them. Once we recognize that man is ordained to suffer misery on
this earth, we cannot excuse ourselves either by the violence of this pain
or by the acuteness of our reaction to it. Everyone has within himself the
means of doing his duty. What is amazing in the moral world, as in the
physical, is the degree to which what is necessary is evenly distributed,
whereas the superfluous varies in thousands of ways.

Physical suffering and moral suffering are one and the same
thing in their action on the soul. Sickness is mental sorrow as well as
bodily affliction, but while physical pain usually destroys the body, moral
suffering serves to regenerate the soul.

It is not enough to believe that pain is not an evil, like the
Stoics: in order to be resigned to pain, we have to believe it is a good.
The slightest pain would be insufferable if we thought it was just an accident. Given the influence of individual irritability on our way of feeling,
we would have no more right to blame a man who killed himself for a
pinprick than for an attack of gout—for a mishap no more than for a misfortune. If the slightest feeling of suffering does not tend to perfect the
soul, it will inspire rebellion, because there is more injustice in a useless
minor evil than in the greatest suffering tending toward some noble goal.

This is not the place to go back to the great metaphysical
question of the origin of evil, which has kept philosophers so busy to so
little effect. We cannot imagine human freedom without the possibility
of evil. We cannot imagine virtue without human liberty, or life everlast-
ing without virtue; we must consider this chain the necessary condition
of our existence, including its first incomprehensible, indispensable link.
If reflection and feeling lead us to think that there is always some
justice—hidden or manifest—in the workings of Providence, we cannot
consider suffering either accidental or arbitrary. If man thought that
Divinity could give a creature limitless qualities or capabilities, and infinity along with them, he would have as much right to complain about
one fewer joy as about one more sorrow. Why shouldn't man be as angry
about not having always been alive as about having to stop being alive?
What can his complaints be based on? Is he rebelling against the system

of the universe, or against the part he plays in a whole subject to invariable laws?

Suffering is a necessary element in our ability to be happy—we cannot imagine one without the other. The sharpness of our desires is related to the difficulties they encounter; the agitation of our pleasures to the fear of losing them; the acuteness of our affections to the dangers threatening our beloved. No mortal being has ever been able to untie the Gordian knot of pain or pleasure except by the slash of the knife which cuts off life itself.

"Yes," unhappy people may reply, "we are willing to submit to the balance of good and evil in the ordinary run of things. When fate treats us as enemies, though, it is only fair for us to escape its blows." But the scale regulating the result of this weighing procedure is in ourselves alone: the same way of life that throws one person into despair would delight someone with more modest hopes. This does not contradict my statement that we should take individual ways of feeling into consideration. One man's happiness may certainly be out of harmony with another's character—but resignation befits us all. In physical nature there are two opposing forces making the world move: momentum and gravitation. The two poles of moral existence may also be seen as the need to act and the need to submit: willpower and resignation. The mind has to get its balance between them.

Most men understand only two forces in life capable of influencing their own destiny: fate and their own will. This is why they go back and forth between pride and irritation. When irritated, they curse destiny like children hitting the table they run into. When satisfied with what is going on in their lives however, they attribute these events to themselves alone, and are proud of the means they have used to control them; they consider these means the only source of their happiness. Both ways of seeing things are wrong.

Man's will usually acts together with destiny. When destiny turns into necessity, however, and is stamped as irrevocable, it is the manifestation of the plans Providence has for us. A wise man once called necessity a tonic. Adopting this maxim unreservedly would involve rising to great heights, but we do have to have some sort of respect for fate. Sometimes quick, sometimes slow, sometimes anticipated, sometimes unforeseen, fate is a power that takes hold of life at a given moment and determines its course. It is far from blind, as people like to suppose; anyone would think it knew us very well, because it always attacks our most intimate weaknesses. It is the secret tribunal judging us, and when it seems unfair, we may be the only ones who know what it wants to tell us and what it is forcing us to do.

We certainly come through the trial of adversity far better for the experience if we submit to it with quiet resolution. The soul's greatest virtues develop only through suffering, and in time this process of self-perfection makes us happy. The circle closes and brings us back to the innocent days before we did wrong. Killing ourselves because we are unhappy is a withdrawal from virtue, therefore, and a withdrawal from the pleasures this virtue would have given us after we had triumphed over our pain with its help. The Platonic philosophers said that the soul needed a period of life on earth to purge itself of guilty passions.[2] It almost seems as if the goal of life were the renunciation of life. Physical nature accomplishes this through decay, moral nature by sacrifice. Human existence consists in abdicating personality in order to be reabsorbed in the universal order. Children understand nothing but themselves; young people understand themselves and the friends that are part of themselves; but as soon as the first signs of decay appear, we must either console ourselves with general considerations or abandon ourselves to the many terrors that accompany the last half of life, because happy or unhappy circumstances count for very little compared with the inflexible laws of nature. What should make men desperate is old age and death, not their individual frustrations—but we submit easily to the universal human condition, and rebel only against our own share in it. We do not reflect that the universal condition is found in everyone's portion, and that the differences are more apparent than real.

In discussing the moral dignity of man, I make a clear distinction between suicide and devotion—that is, between sacrificing one's self to others or to virtue (which is the same thing) and renouncing existence because it is a burden to us. The motives determining one to kill oneself change the nature of this action completely. A person who gives up life to do good to his fellow men is immolating his body to his soul, whereas someone who kills himself out of impatience with pain is almost always sacrificing his conscience to his passions.

Those who claim that suicide is an act of cowardice are wrong: this far-fetched assertion has not convinced anybody. But we do have to distinguish bravery from strength of mind. To kill oneself, one cannot be afraid of death; but there is a lack of strength in not knowing how to suffer. Some kind of anger is needed to conquer one's own will to survive, if the sacrifice is not required by religious feelings. Most people who have attempted suicide and failed do not try again, because in suicide—as in all reckless acts of the will—there is a sort of madness that quiets down when it gets too close to its own goal. Unhappiness is almost never absolute: its relations with our hopes or memories are often the greatest part of it. When a severe, acute shock takes place within us, our unhappiness shows itself to our imagination in a very different light.

Look back after ten years on someone undergoing a great loss of any kind, and you will find that he is suffering and enjoying himself for very different reasons than the original loss that constituted his happiness ten years ago. This is not to say that happiness has come back to him. Hope and fear have taken other paths in it, however; and our moral life is composed of the activity of those two feelings.

There is one cause of suicide that appeals to the heart of almost every woman: love. The great fascination of this passion must be the main cause of error in the way we judge self-slaughter. Everyone insists that love overpowers the greatest abilities of the soul, and that nothing can be stronger than love. Now that every sort of enthusiasm has undergone the attack of satirical skepticism, novels maintain the prestige of feeling in the few countries of the world where good faith still survives. It seems to me, however, that there is only one misery of love against which the soul's energy will shatter, and that is the death of a beloved person who loves us in return.

When the heart with which our own existence was merged lies cold in the grave, an inner trembling makes the whole natural world grow dim. Some moralists think that this pain is easier to bear than those involving injured pride; on the contrary, it may be the only one which goes beyond our God-given strength to resist suffering. The heart is certainly wounded by our loved one's infidelity, but that wound is contaminated by the passions of vanity. Something nobler than vanity is tearing at us when we have to abandon our beloved, with nothing left of such great enthusiasm but our memory of the empty appearances that aroused it. But we must tell ourselves this harsh verdict: from the moment anyone is untruthful or unfaithful in the intimate, sincere liaison two pure, true beings ought to have, it is because he did not deserve the feelings he was inspiring in the first place. In this reasoning I am not trying to imitate scholars who reduce the miseries of life to syllogisms. We suffer in thousand ways, through different, opposed, and contradictory feelings. None of us should try to deny anyone else's pain. But wanting to kill oneself because of any grief involving vanity is crazy as well as wrong: everything connected with vanity passes. We should not give such passing things the right to hurl us into eternity.

The only motive for suicide would be some kind of unhappiness entirely free from every impulse of pride. Such unhappiness would consist in pure feeling. But religion softens this bitterness. Providence wants the soul's wounds to be curable, and comes to the help of anyone she has struck beyond his strength. The palm of the angel of peace often shelters us at such a time—and who knows? this angel may be the very person we were mourning, touched by our tears and endowed by heaven with the right to watch over us.

Any pain that is not sharpened by vanity is necessarily modified by time; these uncontaminated sufferings inspire a religious frame of mind that leads to resignation.

The most common cause of suicide in modern times are ruin and dishonor. As our society is organized, such reversals cause great anguish in a thousand different ways. The cruelest of these is the loss of one's position in the world. Imagination acts on the past as well as on the future, and we connect ourselves with our worldly goods in a way that is hard to break. After a while, though, new situations offer most people new perspectives. Happiness is composed of relative sensations to such a degree that what acts on the imagination is not the thing in itself, but its relationship to yesterday or tomorrow. If a man fears some degree of pain because of fate or a master's threats, and he learns that half his fears have been spared him, his impression will be quite different from what he would have felt if he had never experienced that terror. It is as if fate bargains with the unfortunate, repenting, like every other ruler, after the damage is done.

Decreasing the painful effect opinion has on most people is very hard: the phrase "I am dishonored" completely clouds the mind of social man. Nor can we keep ourselves from feeling sorry for anyone who succumbs under the weight of this misfortune. His resentment may well mean that he did not deserve it. And there are two main classifications of the causes of dishonor: those relating to the faults with which our consciences reproach us, and those arising from involuntary errors, which are not criminal in any way.

Remorse is necessarily related to our notion of divine justice, since we would never feel anything stronger than regret if we did not compare our actions with this supreme example of equity. There are only two ways to think about existence. Either it is a game of chance in which winning or losing stakes are the goods of this world, or it is a novitiate for immortality.[3] If we keep to the idea of the game of chance, we see nothing in our conduct but the results of good or bad reasoning; if we take the life to come as our goal, our conscience clings to the intention. Someone limited to earthly interests may have regrets, but only the religious man can feel remorse. Being religious is enough to make us feel that our primary obligation is expiation, and that conscience orders us to suffer the consequences of our wrongdoings, so as to make amends for them, if possible, by doing good. The religious man feels rightful dishonor as a just punishment from which he has no right to escape, because while there are many human actions more perverse than suicide, no others seem to snatch us so irrevocably away from God's protection.

Passions lead us on to guilty acts whose goal is happiness. In committing suicide, however, we renounce all help from above, and that cannot be reconciled with any kind of pious disposition.

Anyone who is really remorseful will cry aloud with the prodigal son: "I will arise and go to my father, and will say unto him, Father, I have sinned against heaven, and before thee, and am no more worthy to be called thy son."[4]*

Undeserved dishonor never lasts—I believe we can say that much. The influence of the truth on the public is so strong that if we wait long enough we will be put in our rightful place. Time is a sacred thing that seems to act independently even of events taking place in time. It is the help of the helpless and unfortunate, one of the mysterious ways in which the Divine manifests itself to us. The public is a very different

---

*A religious person expresses himself with this touching resignation: the more criminal he thinks himself, the less likely he is to give himself the right to end his life, since he has not done what the God who gave it to him wanted him to do with it. As for guilty people with no faith in a future life and no reputation in this one, the only drawback to suicide for them is that it keeps them from the good things that might still happen to them, and each can estimate the chances of this for himself, according to probability calculations.

thing from each individual in some respects. The public is intelligent, though made up of so many stupid beings; the public is noble, although an infinite number of commonplace things are done by the people who constitute it; this public always rallies to justice in the end, as soon as the prevailing temporary circumstances disappear. "In your patience possess ye your souls," says the Evangelist.[5] The advice of piety is here the advice of reason also. When we reflect on the Scriptures, we find a wonderful collection of good advice on how to do without success in this world, as well as on how to achieve it.

The misery involved in bodily existence—physical pain, incurable disease—would seem to be among the most plausible causes of suicide. In modern times, however, this is rarely what leads people to kill themselves. The miseries in the ordinary course of things may overwhelm us, but they do not lead us to revolt. Before we abandon ourselves to anger against fate, wanting to be free of it or revenged on it as an oppressor, we have to feel irritated as well. Most people make a strange mistake when they think about their destiny—a mistake well worth examining from all sides, because of its great influence on the impressions of the soul. It seems all we need is a sufficient number of companions in misfortune to resign ourselves to whatever events take place; we see injustice only in the misfortunes that happen to us as individuals. But most of these differences are evened out in the long run, like the resemblances—and do not all of them fall equally within the laws of nature?

I will not dwell on the ordinary consolation of the hope of a change in circumstances, because some kinds of pain are not amenable to such consolation. But I do believe we can say with some confidence that hard, steady work has comforted most of those who have devoted themselves to it. There is a future in every form of occupation, and what man needs at every moment is a future. When our abilities find no scope for action outside ourselves, they devour us like the vulture of Prometheus.[6] Work exercises and directs these abilities. When one has some imagination—and most people who suffer have a good deal—one can always take new pleasure in the study of the greatest works of the human mind, either as an amateur or as an artist. A clever woman once remarked that there is a little boredom in all suffering; a profound reflection. Real boredom, the boredom of active minds, consists in a lack of interest in everything around us, combined with abilities which make such an interest necessary—thirst with no chance of anything to drink. Tantalus is a fair enough image of the soul in that condition.[7] Employment gives existence back its flavor. The fine arts have both the originality of individual objects and the greatness of abstract ideas. They keep us in touch with nature: it is possible to love nature without these pleasant intermediaries, but they do help us enjoy it better.

Whatever the depths of misery to which we sink, we should not despise the Creator's first gifts, life and nature. Social man puts far too much importance on the web of circumstances making up his personal life. Existence is a wonderful thing in itself. People who are sick often beg for nothing more. Savages are happy just to be alive; prisoners think of open air as the supreme good; the blind would give all they possess to see external objects once more. Tropical climates, where colors are brighter and perfumes stronger, create an impression difficult to describe in words; the pleasure caused by the sight of the earth and sky has much more power over us than philosophical consolations. Among all our ways of finding happiness, then, the power of contemplation is the one we should foster. We are so shut up in our own selves, so disturbed and wounded by so many things, that we need to immerse ourselves constantly in that limitless sea of thoughts. We should make ourselves invulnerable in it, as in the Styx—or, at any rate, resigned.[8]

No one is foolhardy enough to say he can bear anything in this world; no one dares depend on his own strength enough to answer for it. Very few people of superior abilities have not been attacked more than once by despair. Life often seems like one long shipwreck, with friendship, fame, and love as the flotsam and jetsam. The riverbanks of time gone by in our own generation are littered with them; but if we have salvaged our inner harmony from the wreck, we may be able to enter in communication with the works of the Divine Being nevertheless.

The harmonies of the Creation are heavenly mercy, death's repose, a few great constant ideas, and a beauty in the universe which is there to foretell better days, not to torment man. When we grow accustomed to understanding them, they bring us peace. These are the same sources from which the hero and the poet draw their inspirations. What keeps us from thinking that a few drops of the cup that lifts them above humanity would not be good for us all?

We call fate malignant because it always strikes us in our most sensitive spot. What we should blame, however, is not the malignancy of fate, but our own impetuous desires, hurling us against the obstacles we meet like soldiers impaling themselves on their opponents' swords. The things we have to learn through suffering are necessarily related to the part of our character most in need of being repressed. We cannot allow a belief in God without supposing that He directs the way destiny acts upon man, so we cannot consider this destiny a blind force. We must still decide whether He who governs it has given man liberty for submitting to it or for escaping it. [. . .]

11.

Considerations
on the Main Events
of the French Revolution

THE OPENING OF THE ESTATES GENERAL, MAY 1789 (1.16)

I will never forget the moment when we saw the twelve hundred deputies of France march solemnly to church for mass, the night before the opening of the Estates General. It was a most impressive spectacle, and new to the French: every inhabitant of the city of Versailles had turned out to stare at the procession, joined by some curious Parisians. The nature and strength of this new kind of authority within the state were still unknown, and its very existence was a shock to nearly everyone who had not been thinking about the rights of nations.

   The upper clergy had lost a certain amount of public respect; many prelates had not been any too regular in their habits, and an even greater number cared about nothing but politics. The people are as severe toward the clergy as toward women; they want to see absolute devotion to duty from both. Similarly, public respect for the nobility is founded on military glory, and this too was a thing of the past. A long period of peace had meant that any nobles who might have felt eager to reincarnate their ancestors had had no chance to do so, and that the great lords of France were just famous nobodies. As for the minor aristocracy, their chances of distinguishing themselves had been no better, because the government had not permitted gentlemen to follow any career but the military. Many new creations could be seen among the rows of noblemen, wearing their swords and feathers a little awkwardly. Everyone was wondering what these men were doing among the First Estate, simply because they had obtained the unfair privilege of not paying their share of public taxes—a good question, since this was the beginning and end of their political rights.

The nobility had fallen from splendor, then, thanks to all this idle flattery, contamination by parvenus, and the long peace, while the clergy had lost the intellectual advantage of medieval times. As a result, the Third Estate had increased in importance. Their black suits and coats, confident glances, and impressive number attracted attention; they included men of letters, merchants, and a great number of lawyers. A few nobles had had themselves named deputies of the Third: the most remarkable of these was the Count Mirabeau.[1] Strange to say, the high opinion people had of Mirabeau's intelligence was increased by fear of his immorality, despite the fact that this very immorality was what had diminished the influence his astounding abilities should have won for him. It was hard not to stare, once you had caught sight of him. His great mass of hair alone set him apart from the others, as if his strength depended on it, like Samson's; the ugliness of his face made it the more expressive. His whole person gave the impression of an anomalous power—the kind of power, all the same, that one could imagine in a popular tribune.

None of the other six hundred deputies of the Third had yet made a name for himself. Among them were honorable men, but also men to be afraid of. Party spirit was beginning to hang over France, and nothing but wisdom or power could eliminate it. Power had already been undermined by public opinion; what could be done, then without wisdom?

I had found a place by the window next to Mme. de Montmorin, wife of the Minister of Foreign Affairs.[2] At the sight of these representatives of the whole nation, assembled for the first time in France, I must confess I abandoned myself to some very lively hopes. Mme. de Montmorin was a woman of no intellectual distinction whatsoever, but the determination in her voice made some effect on me. "You are wrong to celebrate," she said. "Great disasters will come of this—disasters for

France, disasters for ourselves." This unhappy woman died on the scaffold, along with one of her sons. The other son drowned; her husband was killed in the massacre on September 2 of that year; her older daughter died in a prison hospital; and her younger daughter, Mme. de Beaumont, an intelligent, generous woman, was crushed by the weight of her sorrow before she reached the age of thirty. Niobe's family was not struck harder than this poor mother's, and that day it was as if she had a premonition of it.[3]

The opening of the Estates General took place the next day. A large one-room building had been hastily erected on the Avenue de Versailles to receive the deputies. Many spectators were admitted to the ceremony. A platform had been built for the King's throne, the armchair of the Queen, and the chairs of the rest of the family.[4] On the proscenium of this theater sat the Chancellor, M. de Barentin. The three orders were in the orchestra pit, the clergy on the right, the nobility on the left, and the deputies of the Third facing the stage. The Third Estate had announced ahead of time that its members would not kneel at the King's entrance in accordance with the ancient custom, which had been followed the last time the Estates General had been assembled. In 1789, everyone—even the purest aristocrats—would have found it ridiculous and out of tune with the spirit of the times for the members of the Third Estate to go down on their knees.

A murmur ran through the assembly at Mirabeau's appearance; he understood its meaning very well. As he proudly crossed the room to take his place, however, he looked ready to make enough trouble in the state to overturn the hierarchy of esteem along with every other kind of rank. M. Necker was wildly applauded as soon as he entered.[5] His popularity was still intact, and the King could use him without betraying the system whose fundamental principles he had adopted.

When the King came into the middle of this assembly to take the throne, I felt frightened for the first time. For one thing, I could see that the Queen was greatly moved. She came late, and the color of her complexion was altered. The King spoke with his usual simplicity, but his face showed less energy than the faces of the deputies. This was a disturbing contrast, because in these circumstances strength was needed on both sides: nothing was settled yet.

All three speeches—the King's, the Chancellor's, and M.

Necker's—were about achieving financial recovery. M. Necker's speech presented all the improvements the administration could make, but hardly touched on constitutional questions. He limited himself to warning the assembly about its inclination to haste, in an expression that has become proverbial: "Never be jealous of time." After the meeting, the popular party—a majority of the Third, a minority of the nobility, and a few of the clergy—complained that M. Necker had treated the Estates General like a provincial administration, talking about nothing but how to guarantee the national debt and improve the taxation system. The principal aim of the Estates General was to make a constitution. Of course that was perfectly true: but did they really expect the King's minister to be the first to bring up issues that could be proposed only by the people's representatives?

As for the aristocrats, as soon as they heard M. Necker say that in eight months he had restored finances enough to be in a position to levy new taxes, they began to blame him for having convoked the Estates General at all, since financial need did not make this absolutely obligatory. They seemed to forget that a promise to call the Estates General had been made before he had been recalled to power. Now, as almost always, M. Necker was treading a path between two extremes. He certainly did not want to tell the people's representatives to concentrate exclusively on the Constitution. However, he did not want to fall back into arbitrary high-handedness either, content with temporary resources which would not have guaranteed the creditors of the state in any way, or answered to the people for the use being made of its sacrifices.

ON POLITICAL FANATICISM (3.15)

Until this point, the events we have been recalling have been only the kind of history we can find examples of elsewhere. Now, however, a chasm will be opening under our feet; we discover no path in the abyss, and our mind leaps in fear from disaster to disaster, until hope and consolation are both gone. We will pass as quickly as possible over this

dreadful crisis, in which no one man can hold our attention, no individual circumstance arouse our interest. Everything is all the same,
though all extraordinary—all monotonous, though horrible. It would
almost be shameful to be able to look at such gross atrocities closely
enough to describe them in detail. Let us look carefully, however, at the
principle underlying these monstrous phenomena: political fanaticism.

Worldly passions have always played some part in religious
fanaticism, and a genuine belief in abstract ideas is often food for political
fanaticism. This is a universal mixture; but its proportions are what constitute good and evil. The social order itself is a most peculiar structure,
impossible to imagine as other than what it is. To ensure its continued
existence, all the same, we are forced to make concessions that torment
the sympathy of high-minded souls, flatter the vanity of various others,
and arouse the irritation and cravings of the great majority. The political
fanaticism we have witnessed in France must be attributed to this state of
things, more or less pronounced in individual cases, more or less softened by manners and education. A sort of fury took hold of the poor in
the presence of the rich; as the jealousy inspired by property was reinforced by aristocratic distinctions, the people grew proud of their own
numbers. Everything constituting the power and brilliance of the
minority seemed to them simple usurpation. The seeds of this sentiment
have always been there, but we have felt human society shaken to its
foundation only during the French Reign of Terror. We should not be
surprised at the deep scars this abominable scourge has left on people's
minds. The only reflection we can allow ourselves to make—confirmed,
I hope, by the rest of this work—is that the remedy for popular passion
lies in the rule of law rather than in despotism.

Religious fanaticism may set no limits to an indefinite future
that arouses imaginary hopes, but the pleasures of this life seem unlimited to anyone who has not tasted them. The Old Man of the Mountain sent his subjects to their deaths by granting them earthly pleasures,
and we ourselves often see men risk death for the chance of a better life.[6]
And vanity exalts itself in the defense of its own superior advantages; it
looks less guilty than the attackers, because some notion of property
clings even to injustices when they have existed for a long time. But the
two elements of religious and political fanaticism still subsist: the will to
dominate felt by those riding on top of the wheel of fortune, the eagerness to make it turn felt by those riding on the bottom. This is the princi-

ple underlying every kind of violence. The pretext changes, but the cause remains; and the reciprocal relentlessness is the same. The quarrels between patricians and plebeians, the war of the slaves, the peasants' war, the struggle still going on between nobles and bourgeois—they all originate in the difficulty of maintaining human society without disorder or injustice. Modern men could not exist either separately or together without some notion of respect for law in their minds: all crimes would come from the very society that is supposed to prevent crime. The abstract power of representative government does not irritate men's pride; it is therefore through this institution that the torches of the furies can be extinguished. They were lighted in a country where the only thing that mattered was self-love; and once self-love is aroused among the people, it bears no resemblance to our fleeting nuances. It is the need to kill.

Massacres just as dreadful as the Reign of Terror have been committed in the name of religion; the human race exhausted itself for centuries in pointless attempts to force all men into the same beliefs. No one could achieve this goal. William Penn's simple idea of tolerance banished from North America the fanaticism so horribly staged in Mediterranean countries. The same is true of political fanaticism: it can be calmed only by liberty. After a while, a few uncontested truths will still remain, and people will talk about the old institutions as we do about outdated scientific theories, completely effaced by the evidence of the facts.

Mutual antipathy was stronger in France than elsewhere because there was almost no connection among the different classes of society. If one knows someone personally, even the most criminal of men, one cannot hate him in quite the same way as if one were imagining him. Pride had set up barriers everywhere, and limits nowhere. There was no country in the world where gentlemen were such strangers to the rest of the nation; they touched the second class only to offend it. In other countries, men of different legal standing mix together more, thanks to a spirit of hail-fellow-well-met, sometimes even of vulgarity. But the elegance of the French nobility increased the envy it inspired. Its manners were as hard to imitate as its prerogatives were to gain. And the same scene was repeated on every step of the scale. The irritability of an ultrasensitive nation made everyone jealous of his neighbor, of his superior, of his master. Not content with domination, all those individuals humiliated each other. Multiplying the political connections between the different classes, and giving them ways to be useful to each other, is the only way we will ever be able to appease that most dreadful of passions: the hatred of human beings for their fellow men, the mutual aversion of creatures whose remains must all be buried in the same earth, and be reborn together on the last day.

ON THE GOVERNMENT CALLED THE REIGN OF TERROR (3.16)

I hardly know how to approach the fourteen months after May 31, 1793, when the Gironde was condemned. It is like Dante's Hell—one keeps on going down and down, from circle to circle.[7] The relentless attack on nobles and priests becomes an inflamed anger at the existence of land-owners; then at talent of any kind; then even at beauty: in the end, at anything great or generous still in the possession of human nature. The facts about this period tend to merge into each other, and I am afraid it is impossible to begin such a story without staining one's imagination in-eradicably in blood. We are thus forced into a philosophical considera-tion of events that would otherwise exhaust the eloquence of our in-dignation without satisfying the feelings they arouse within us.

Once the people were freed from their harness there is no doubt that they were in a position to commit any kind of crime. But how can we explain their depravity? The government we are now supposed to miss so sorely had had plenty of time to form this guilty nation. The priests whose teaching, example, and wealth were supposed to be so good for us had supervised the childhood of the generation that broke out against them. The class that revolted in 1789 must have been accus-tomed to the privileges of feudal nobility which, as we are also assured, are so peculiarly agreeable to those on whom they weigh. How does it happen, then, that the seed of so many vices was sown under the ancient institutions? No one should claim that any other nation of our time would have done the same if it had had a revolution. The French influence aroused rebellions in Holland and Switzerland, but nothing like Jacobinism took place there. During the forty years of English history that we put in the same category in so many respects, there was nothing comparable to the fourteen months of the Terror. What can we conclude from this, then?—That no people had been as unhappy for the preceding century as the French. If the Negroes of Saint-Domingue have committed even greater atrocities, it is because they had been even more greatly oppressed.[8]

These reflections certainly do not make us hate the crimes of the Terror any the less. After twenty years, however, we must combine our acute contemporary indignation with an enlightened examination that may serve as a guide for the future. The English revolution was set off by religious quarrels. The Puritans were also affected by love of equality, the underground volcano of France, but the English were genuinely religious—and religious Protestants, which makes people more moderate as well as more austere. Although England, like France, is stained by the murder of Charles I and the despotism of Cromwell, the Reign of Terror is a horrible and unique phenomenon whose weight must be borne throughout history by France alone. But no one can be observing civil disorder as a thinker if he is ignorant of the fact that every action is equal to its own reaction. The furies of rebellions allow us to measure the vices of institutions; we must blame a nation's moral condition on the government it has had for so long, not the government it is hoping for. Where did the disorderly tendencies of the early years of the Revolution come from, after all, if not from a hundred years of superstition and arbitrary rule?

In 1793 it seemed as if France had no room for any more revolutions. Everything had already been overthrown—Crown, nobility, clergy—and the success of the Revolutionary armies made peace throughout Europe something to hope for.[9] This is just when popular tyrannies do arise, though: as soon as the danger is past. The worst of men control themselves as long as there are obstacles and fears; after they have won, their repressed passions know no bounds.

After the death of the King, the Girondins tried vainly to put some sort of laws into effect—any laws. But they could not force people to accept any social organization whatsoever; an instinct for savagery rejected them all. Hérault de Séchelles proposed a scrupulously democratic constitution; this was duly accepted by the Assembly, but suspended for the duration of the war.[10] The Jacobin party wanted to wield despotic power—it is completely inaccurate to call their form of government anarchy. Authority stronger than theirs has never ruled in France. Theirs was a peculiar sort of power, however; derived from popular fanaticism, it inspired terror even in the men who ruled in its name, who all lived in constant fear of being condemned in turn by others who might take the audacity of persecution one step further. At this time the only man who lived fearless was Marat. Marat's face was so coarse, his emotions so frantic, his opinions so bloodthirsty that he was convinced no one could plunge deeper than he into the abyss of crime. Robespierre himself did not achieve this hellish sense of security.[11]

The only remaining men of this time still worthy of taking their place in history are the Girondins. In their heart of hearts the Girondins must have been bitterly sorry for the means they had used to overthrow the throne. When these same means were used against them, and they recognized their own weapons in their wounds, they must have reflected on the swift justice of revolutions, condensing centuries of events into instants.

The Girondins fought with intrepid eloquence every hour of every day against speeches sharp as daggers, that held death in every word. The murderous traps closing in on these condemned men could not detract in any way from their admirable presence of mind; this is what shows the true value of the orator's talents.

When M. de Condorcet was condemned he wrote a book on the perfectibility of the human mind; this book may contain errors, but its general theory is inspired by a hope for men's happiness. Condorcet kept this hope alive even under the executioner's blade, at the very moment when his own fate was lost forever.[12] Twenty-two republican deputies were summoned before the Revolutionary tribunal: their courage did not fail for an instant. When the sentence of death was pronounced, one of them, Valaze, fell from his seat. The deputy next to him, also condemned, and thinking his colleague was frightened, picked him up roughly and reproached him. He picked him up dead. Valaze had buried a dagger in his heart with so firm a hand that he did not breathe an instant after he had struck himself down. Party spirit is so inflexible that these men, defending whatever decent people still remained in France, had no hope of gaining any influence. They struggled, went under, and died without any premonitory whisper of history promising them the least reward. Even the constitutional royalists were insane enough to want the terrorists to triumph, so that they themselves would be revenged on the republicans. Their knowledge that the terrorists would condemn them too was useless; angry pride swept everything before it. Abandoning themselves to their resentment, the constitutional royalists forgot the one essential rule of politics: support the least evil of your adversaries, even if that party is still very far from your own point of view.

The three great resources of the Committee of Public Safety were the scarcity of basic foods, the abundance of worthless assignats, and the enthusiasm aroused by the war.[13] The Committee frightened the people, or paid them, or made them march to the border, all at its own convenience. "We must continue the war," as one of the deputies of the Convention said, "so that the convulsions of liberty will be stronger." No one can tell whether or not these twelve members of the Committee of Public Safety had the slightest notion in their minds of any kind of government at all. Except for the war, the direction of national concerns was nothing but a mélange of coarseness and savagery in which the only apparent plan was to make one-half the nation massacre the other half. The Jacobins included people among the condemned aristocracy with such facility that half the inhabitants of France were running the risk of suspicion, and suspicion was enough to lead anyone to his death.

The assassinations of the Queen and Madame Elisabeth may have aroused even more astonishment and horror than the murder of the King, because there is no way to think these terrible crimes had any other aim than that of inspiring fear. The condemnations of M. de Malesherbes, M. de Bailly, M. de Condorcet, and M. de Lavoisier deprived France of a tithe of its glory. Eighty people a day were sacrificed, as if the massacre of Saint Bartholomew's Day had begun again, drop by drop.[14] This government—if we can call it a government—faced one great difficulty: it had to use the resources of civilization to wage war, and the violence of savagery to arouse passions. This misfortune of the upper classes did not affect the people, or even the bourgeoisie. Parisians promenaded through the streets like Turks during the plague, with the difference that it was fairly easy for people who were not well known to protect themselves from danger. In the very presence of the tortures, the theaters were crowded as usual. The novels being published were called A New Sentimental Journey, Dangerous Friendship, Ursula and Sophie.[15]

The triviality and frivolity of life went on side by side with its darkest furies.

We have not tried to conceal things that men cannot erase from their memories, but in another chapter we will try to recall the virtues that continued to do honor to France, even in this most dreadful epoch of her history.

ON EXILE (4.8)

The power to exile without appeal is one of the attributes of authority that predispose it most strongly toward tyranny. The monarchy's use of *lettres de cachet* was certainly a major cause of the French Revolution, as has often been said;[16] but now it was Bonaparte, elected by the people and trampling on all the principles for which the people had revolted, who assumed the power of exiling anyone who displeased him a little, and of imprisoning without benefit of trial anyone who displeased him more than that. I can well understand how most of the former courtiers rallied to Bonaparte's political system. A change of ruler was the only concession they had to make. But the republicans, who must have felt hurt by every word Napoleon's government spoke—every act—every decree: how could they lend themselves to his tyranny?

Many men and women with a variety of opinions have suffered these decrees of exile, giving the sovereign of the state even more absolute authority than he would get from illegal imprisonments; it is harder to use violent measures than a kind of power which is technically benign, however terrible in fact. Insurmountable obstacles always attract the imagination; exile was a source of deep unhappiness to great men like Themistocles, Cicero, and Bolingbroke—especially Bolingbroke, who writes that he finds death itself less terrifying.[17]

To call sending a man or woman away from Paris "sending them off for some country air," as the expression went, is to talk about real suffering with such sweet words that the pain is easy for political flatterers to treat lightly. And yet the simple fear of such exile is enough to bring the entire population of the empire's capital to its knees. Scaffolds may awaken courage sooner or later, but the everyday domestic annoyances of banishment just weaken your resistance and make you afraid of being disgraced in the eyes of a sovereign capable of inflicting this unfortunate existence upon you. To spend a lifetime abroad voluntarily is one thing; if we are forced into it, though, we keep imagining that the people we love might be sick, and we would not be able to go to them, or perhaps ever see them again. Everything is compromised—the affections, social habits, financial interests. Sadder still, these links themselves grow weaker, and we end as strangers in our own homeland.

During the twelve years of exile to which Napoleon condemned me, I often thought that he would be unable to bear the misery of being deprived of France, having no memory of France in his heart. Nothing but the rocks of Corsica retraced his childhood days; Necker's daughter was more French than he. I will speak elsewhere about the circumstances of my exile and the trips I took to the edge of Asia as a result; but I have virtually forbidden myself to portray living people, so I would not have been able to make a personal history interesting in the way such things should be. I will recall here only what will be relevant to the general plan of this work.[18]

I guessed Napoleon's character and political schemes more quickly than most people, and I am proud of that. An infallible instinct enlightens all real friends of liberty about such things. But my position at the beginning of the Consulat was dreadful, because good society in France at the time thought Bonaparte the very man to save them from anarchy or Jacobinism.[19] As a result, my spirit of opposition earned me a lot of disapproval. Anyone who can see as far as tomorrow in politics arouses the wrath of people who can see no farther than today. I must say it took even more strength to bear the persecution of society than to expose myself to the persecution of power.

I have always kept the memory of one of those society tortures (if it is all right to speak that way) that French aristocrats are so good at inflicting whenever it suits them on people who do not share their opinions. A large part of the old nobility had rallied to Napoleon; some, as we have seen since then, trying to recapture their former habits as courtiers, others hoping that the first consul would bring back the old monarchy. Everyone knew I was strongly against the system of govern-

ment Napoleon was preparing, and the supporters of arbitrary government followed their usual custom of calling opinions that tended to elevate the dignity of nations "antisocial." If anyone were to remind the
émigrés who came back under Bonaparte how furiously they blamed the
friends of liberty who were still loyal to the same theory, they might learn
indulgence from remembering their mistakes.

I was the first woman exiled by Napoleon, though he
banished many women of opposing opinions soon afterward. One of the
most interesting was the Duchess of Chevreuse, who died of the heart
condition brought on by her exile. As she lay dying, she could not get
Napoleon's permission to come back to Paris one last time to consult her
doctor and see her friends again. Where could such luxuriating in evil
come from, if not from a hatred of all independent beings? Women annoyed Napoleon as rebels; they were of no use to his political designs, on
the one hand, and were less accessible than men to the hopes and fears
dispensed by power, on the other. As a result, he took pleasure in saying
hurtful and vulgar things to women. His pursuit of etiquette was
matched by his hatred of chivalry: a bad choice to make from the manners of former times. From his early habits of Revolutionary days he also
retained a certain Jacobin antipathy to brilliant Paris society, which was
greatly influenced by women; he was afraid of the art of teasing which we
must admit is characteristic of Frenchwomen. If Bonaparte had been
willing to keep to the proud role of great general and first magistrate of
the Republic, he would have floated with the height of genius above all
the little stinging barbs of salon wit. Once he decided to become a parvenu king, however, the bourgeois gentleman on the throne, he was exposing himself to the kind of society satire which can only be repressed
by the use of espionage and terror: and that is how, in fact, he
repressed it.

Bonaparte wanted me to praise him in my writings. It is not
that one more eulogy would have been noticed in the fumes of incense
surrounding him. But he was annoyed that I was the only well-known
French writer to publish during his reign without making the least mention of his stupendous existence, and he finally suppressed my book On
Germany with incredible fury.[20] Until that time my disgrace had merely
consisted in having to leave Paris. After that, however, I was forbidden to
travel anywhere, and threatened with life imprisonment. The worst
aggravation of this distress was the contagion of exile, an invention

worthy of the Roman emperors. Anyone who visited banished persons exposed himself to exile in turn; most of my French acquaintances fled as if I had the plague. When it was not too painful, this seemed like a comedy to me; when I happened to meet one of Bonaparte's courtiers in the streets of Geneva I was tempted to frighten him with my courtesy, the way quarantined travelers throw their handkerchiefs to passersby, out of malice, to make them share the trouble of the lazar house.

My great-hearted friend, M. Mathieu de Montmorency, once came to see me at Coppet; four days after his arrival he received a *lettre de cachet* exiling him for having given the consolation of his presence to someone who had been his friend for twenty-five years.[21] I would have done anything at that moment to prevent such a painful thing from happening. At the same time, I received a visit from Mme. Récamier, who had no relationship to politics at all except for her courageous interest in exiled people of various opinions; we had already had several reunions there at Coppet.[22] Can it be believed? The loveliest woman in France, who could have found champions anywhere in the world for that alone, was exiled because she had entered the château of an unhappy female friend one hundred fifty leagues from Paris. The conqueror of the world found this coalition of two women on the shores of Lake Geneva too threatening, and he made himself look ridiculous by persecuting them. But he had once said, "Power is never ridiculous," and he certainly put this maxim to the proof.

We have seen so many families divided by fear of contact with the exiled! At the onset of tyranny, there are always a few acts of courage, but little by little anxiety alters sentiments, and obstacles become wearisome. People come to believe that their friends' misfortunes are their own fault. The family pundits get together and announce that there is no point in too much communication with M. or Mme. so-and-so; their excellent feelings are not at issue, but they do have such lively imaginations! The truth is that everyone would be willing to proclaim these poor exiles great poets, on condition that their imprudence forbade one's seeing or writing to them. This is the way friendship and even love grow cold in every heart; intimate qualities and public virtues are lost forever; love between oneself and another is no longer possible once one has stopped loving one's country. All one learns is how to use a hypocritical language of sugary blame for those out of favor, adroit apology for the powerful, and the hidden doctrine of egoism.

Bonaparte knew better than anyone else the secret of creating a frozen isolation that presented men to him one by one, never united together. He did not want a single individual of his time to have an independent existence: no one was to get married, or have any kind of fortune, or choose a place to live, or exercise talent, or make any decision at all without his permission. Strange to say, he entered into the least detail of every individual's relationships, combining the empire of a conqueror with the inquisition of a gossip, so to speak, and holding the finest of threads and the strongest of chains in his hands.

In Napoleon's reign, the metaphysical question of man's free will had become completely pointless: no one could follow his own wishes in the most important situations, in the most trivial, in anything at all.

12.

Ten Years of Exile

WHY BONAPARTE HATED ME (1.1)

The reason why I have decided to tell the story of my ten years in exile is not to make the public pay attention to me. However bitterly I may have experienced my misfortunes, they count for so little amid the public disasters we have seen that I would feel it a disgrace to talk about myself if my personal life were not related to the major problem of humanity besieged. The Emperor Napoleon's character is completely visible in every detail of his life; he has persecuted me with painstaking care, ever-increasing intensity, and inflexible harshness, and my relationship to him helped me understand him long before Europe had found an answer to the riddle.

I am not going into all the events preceding Bonaparte's arrival on the European political scene. If I ever fulfill my plan of writing my father's life, I will tell what I saw of those first days of the Revolution that changed the fate of us all.[1] Right now, I will trace only my own part in that enormous tableau. Even so, with an occasional glance at the whole picture from this very limited point of view, I flatter myself I will often be able to make myself forgotten as I tell my own story.

The Emperor Napoleon's biggest grudge against me was my constant respect for true liberty. These feelings were handed down to me as a legacy, and I adopted them as soon as I was capable of reflecting on the noble ideas they come from and the beautiful actions they inspire. Since the cruel scenes that dishonored the French Revolution were nothing but a popular version of tyranny, it seemed to me that the cult of liberty remained untouched. At worst, the Reign of Terror might discourage one about the prospects for liberty in France—but even if this country were so unfortunate as to lose the greatest good of all, that would be no reason to outlaw liberty everywhere on earth. When the sun goes down on the northern horizon, the inhabitants of those countries do not blaspheme the rays still shining in lands that enjoy more of heaven's favors.

Shortly after the Eighteenth Brumaire, Bonaparte was given a report that I had spoken out in private society against the burgeoning oppression whose growth I could foretell as clearly as if I could see into the future. Joseph Bonaparte, whose wit and conversation I liked, came to me saying: "My brother is complaining about you. Only yesterday he asked me, 'Why isn't Mme. de Staël supporting my government? What does she want? Payment on her father's account? I will order it. To live in Paris? I will give my permission.'"[2] "Good Lord," I replied. "It's a question of what I think, not what I want." I do not know if that answer was ever reported to Bonaparte, but I am convinced at any rate that he made no sense of it if he did hear it, because he doesn't believe anybody can have sincere opinions about anything. Bonaparte considers every kind of morality a formula which has no more significance than the complimentary close of a letter. After you have assured your correspondent that you are his humble servant, he has no right to require anything of you. In the same way, Bonaparte believes that anyone who says he loves liberty, or believes in God, or prefers a clear conscience to self-interest, is just a man following the forms of etiquette to explain his ambitious pretentions or selfish calculations. The only kind of human being he does not understand is people who are sincerely attached to an opinion, whatever the consequences. Bonaparte considers such men either fools or shopkeepers trying to raise their own prices. As we shall see, the only mistakes he has ever made in this world have been about decent people, whether as individuals or, even more, as nations.

BONAPARTE'S SYSTEM OF
FUSION; PUBLICATION OF
MY BOOK *ON LITERATURE* (1.3)

Just as Christian kings used to take on two different confessors, the better to examine their consciences, Napoleon chose two ministers—one from the old regime, one from the new—so as to have the Machiavellian methods of two contradictory systems at his disposal.

Bonaparte followed this rule more or less closely in all his appointments, taking a little from the right, a little from the left, picking his agents from aristocrats and Jacobins in turn. He was least fond of the party in the middle, the friends of liberty, because it consisted of the few men left in France who had any opinions of their own. He preferred to do business with men linked to royalist interests or despised because of popular excesses. He went to the length of trying to nominate as Counsellor of State a Convention delegate stained by the vilest crimes of the Terror, but he was stopped by the shudders of those who would have had to sit on the bench with him. He would have loved to give this striking proof of his ability to regenerate as well as destroy.

Bonaparte's government is characterized by profound contempt for the richness of human nature. The eternal enemies of the Continent, to quote him, are virtue, moral dignity, religion, and enthusiasm. He would like to reduce man to force and deception, calling everything else stupidity or folly. The English particularly annoy him, because they have found a way to combine success and honesty, which Napoleon would prefer people to think impossible. This shining light of the world has offended his eyes from the first days of his reign; he has been unable to make a military attack on England, so he has aimed the whole artillery of his sophisms at her.

I do not think Bonaparte had already made his plan for universal monarchy when he first took charge of things. I believe his system was, as he told one of my friends shortly after the Eighteenth Brumaire, to do "something new every three months, so as to capture the imagination of the French nation. In France, anyone who does not move ahead is lost." He had promised himself to stamp out French liberty and European independence day by day; he did not lose sight of this goal, but he was able to adapt to circumstances. If the obstacle was too big, he would go around it; if the wind was blowing too strongly in the opposite direction, he stopped short. He is a most impatient man at heart, but he has a talent for standing still when necessary. He gets this from the Italians, who are capable of controlling themselves to reach their heart's desire exactly as if they had picked out this goal in cold blood. It was by alternating trickery and force that he conquered Europe. Europe is a big word, though. What was Europe? At the time, it consisted of a few ministers, none of whom had as much wit as one would find in a random sample of the men they governed.

Toward the spring of 1800, I published my book *On Literature*. Its success meant that I was back in society's favor. My salon was crowded with people once again, and I rediscovered the pleasure of talking—talking in Paris—which I must admit has always been the most stimulating pleasure I have ever known. My book said not one word about Bonaparte—but it did contain some very liberal sentiments, rather forcefully expressed. At that time the press was not bound in chains as it is today. The government was censoring newspapers, but not books. It would have been possible to defend this distinction, if only the censorship had been moderate: newspapers have a popular influence, while books, which are usually read by educated men, may be able to enlighten opinion without inflaming it. Later on a commission for the liberty of the press was established in the Senate—I believe as some sort of joke—and another for individual liberty. New members are still appointed to these commissions every three months. There must be more work to do in honorary bishoprics and English sinecures than there is on those committees.

Since that time, I have published *Delphine, Corinne*, and finally *On Germany*, which was suppressed just as it was ready to be published.[3] This last work earned me a good deal of harsh persecution. Nevertheless, a life of letters still seems to me a source of pleasure and respect, even for a woman. I attribute everything I have suffered in life to the circumstances associating me, at the time of my entrance into society, with the cause of liberty supported by my father and his friends. But the kind of talent that has made me talked about as a writer has always given me more pleasure than pain. Criticism directed at one's work can be borne quite easily if one has some elevation of soul, loving great ideas for themselves even more than for the success they may win. Besides, it seems to me that the public is almost always fair sooner or later. Pride has to let praise go on credit for a while; one gets one's just deserts sooner or later. And even if one has to suffer injustice for a long time, I can imagine no better protection against it than the meditation of philosophy and the emotion of eloquence. These faculties put a whole world of truths and feelings at our command: a world in which we can always breathe freely, at our ease.

SUPPRESSION OF *ON GERMANY*; EXILE FROM FRANCE (2.1)

As I could no longer stay in the château of Chaumont, whose owners had come back from America, I went to live on an estate called Fossé, lent to me by a generous friend, a Vendée military man who took no particular care of his house, but whose loyal kindness made everything easy and whose original mind made everything fun. Hardly had we arrived when an Italian musician whom I had engaged as a teacher for my daughter began to play the guitar; my daughter accompanied my lovely friend Mme. Récamier's singing on the harp; the peasants gathered around the windows, amazed to see this colony of troubadours who had come to enliven their master's solitude.[4] That is where I spent my last days in France, with a few friends whose memory lives in my heart. There can have been no harm in this intimate reunion, this solitary life, this pleasant occupation of the fine arts. We often sang a charming song composed by the Queen of Holland, with the refrain "Do what you have to, whatever may happen." After dinner, we had invented a game of sitting around a green baize-covered table and writing to each other instead of conversation. We enjoyed these varied, multiple tête-à-têtes so much that we would be impatient to get up from the dinner table, where we were all talking, so as to come to this green table and write to one another. If any strangers happened to visit, we could not bear to interrupt our habits, and our "petty post," as we called it, kept going.[5] The inhabitants of the nearby town were somewhat amazed by these novel procedures, and took them for pedantry, whereas this game was only a resource against the monotony of solitude. One day, a gentleman of the neighborhood who had never thought of anything but hunting all his life, came to take my sons hunting in his woods; he sat for some time at our active, silent table. Mme. Récamier wrote a little note to this big hunter, so that he should not feel too much of a stranger in this circle. He excused himself from taking it, saying he could not read her handwriting in that light. We all laughed a little at the upset to our lovely friend's kind coquetry, and remarked that a note from her hand would not always have found the same fate. This was how our life was spent, and as far as I am concerned it was a burden to no one.

The opera *Cinderella* was then creating quite a stir in Paris; I decided to go and see it played in a poor provincial theater in Blois.[6] As I walked on the street, the townspeople followed me curiously, more eager to see me as an exile than for any other reason. This triumph, granted me by misfortune more than talent, annoyed the minister of police, who wrote shortly afterward to the prefect of Loir-et-Cher that I was surrounded by a court. "At least they are not paying court to power," I replied.

I was still determined to go to America and thence to England, but I wanted to see through the printing of my book *On Germany* first. We were fairly far into the season, the fifteenth of September, and I could foresee that the difficulty of embarking with my daughter would keep me through the winter in some unknown town forty leagues from Paris. At that time I was hoping for Vendôme, a town where I knew some intelligent people, in easy communication with Paris. After having had one of the most brilliant houses in Paris, I was thinking of life in Vendôme with lively satisfaction; fate did not grant me this modest happiness.

On September 23, I was correcting the last proofs of *On Germany*: after six months of work, I took real delight in writing "The End" to my three volumes. I made a list of a hundred people to whom I wanted to send copies in various parts of France and Europe; I prized this book, which I thought could spread new ideas to France. It seemed to me inspired by feelings of elevation without hostility, expressed in a language people had stopped speaking.

Armed with a letter from my publisher, who had assured me that the censors had authorized my work, I thought I had nothing to fear,

and left with my friends for an estate belonging to M. Mathieu de Montmorency, five leagues outside Blois.[7] The house is in the middle of a
forest; I was walking in it with a man I respect more than any other man
in the world, now that I have lost my father. The beautiful weather and
magnificent forest, the historic memories of the place where the Battle of
Fretteval took place between Philippe-Auguste and Richard the Lion-
hearted, all put me in the sweetest, calmest mood.[8] In this conversation
as in all our conversations together, my worthy friend, whose whole occupation on this earth has been deserving heaven, took no notice of
current events, and sought only to do my soul good. We set off again the
next day, and got completely lost on the Vendômois plains, which look
the same everywhere, like the sea. It was midnight, and we did not know
which path to take: the country is the same on every side, its fertility as
monotonous as other places' sterility. Suddenly a young man on horseback, suspecting our embarrassment, came to invite us to spend the night
in his family's château. Accepting this invitation, which was a true service, we found ourselves suddenly surrounded by Asiatic luxury and
French elegance. The owners of the house had spend a good deal of time
in the Indies, and had decorated their château with everything they had
brought back from their travels. My curiosity was aroused by this visit,
and I was having a wonderful time.[9]

    In the morning, M. de Montmorency handed me a note
from my son, urging me to come home because my book was having
fresh difficulties with the censor. My friends who were at the château
with me begged me to leave; I did not guess what they were hiding from
me, and taking Auguste's words literally, I spent my time examining the
rarities of the Indies, with no notion of what was awaiting me. At least I
got into my carriage, and my kind, intelligent Vendeean soldier, who had
never been touched by his own dangers, shook my hand with tears in his
eyes. Suddenly I realized that everyone was keeping some new persecutions from me, and I interrogated M. de Montmorency, who told me
that the minister of police had sent his agents to destroy the ten thousand copies of my book that had already been printed, and that I had
been ordered to leave France within three days. My friends and children
had not wanted me to learn such news among strangers; but they had
taken all possible precautions to keep my manuscript from being seized,
and managed to save it a few hours before it was asked for.

    This fresh pain struck me with great force. I had flattered

myself that publishing my book would be an honorable success for me. If the censors had refused me authorization to print it, that would have been simple. But after all their observations, after all the changes they required of me, to learn that my book was being pulped, and that I had to leave the friends who were keeping up my courage—that made me cry. I tried to control myself one more time, though, to reflect on what should be done in a situation where my decision would influence my family's fate so greatly. As we approached the house, I gave my writing desk, containing a few more notes on my book, to my younger son; he jumped over a wall to enter the house through the garden. An Englishwoman, Miss Randall, a very good friend of mine, came to meet me to warn me of what was going on.[10] I could see the police wandering around in the distance, but apparently not looking for me; they must have been hunting for other unfortunate beings, prisoners, exiles, persons under surveillance: all the classes of oppressed people created by the present regime in France.

[. . .]

Notes

Introduction

1. Ellen Moers, *Literary Women* (New York: Anchor Press/Doubleday, 1977), p. 267.

2. Ghislain de Diesbach, *Madame de Staël* (Paris: Perrin, 1983), pp. 413, 393.

3. Moers, *Literary Women*, p. 299.

4. Lawrence Lipking, "Aristotle's Sister: A Poetics of Abandonment," *Critical Inquiry* (September 1983), 10(1):73.

5. Carol Gilligan, *In a Different Voice: Psychological Theory and Women's Development* (Cambridge: Harvard University Press, 1982), p. 48.

6. Paul de Man, "Madame de Staël et Jean-Jacques Rousseau," in *Madame de Staël et l'Europe: Colloque de Coppet* (Paris: Klincksieck, 1970), p. 37.

7. Georges Poulet, "La pensée critique de Madame de Staël," in *Madame de Staël et l'Europe: Colloque de Coppet* (Paris: Klincksieck, 1970), p. 27.

8. Madelyn Gutwirth, *Madame de Staël, Novelist: The Emergence of the Artist as Woman* (Urbana: University of Illinois Press, 1978), p. 71.

9. De Man, "Madame de Staël," p. 37.

10. Simone Balayé, *Madame de Staël, Lumières et Liberté* (Paris: Klincksieck, 1979), p. 130.

11. Gutwirth, *Madame de Staël*, p. 146.

12. Lipking, "Aristotle's Sister," p. 73.

13. Balayé, *Madame de Staël*, pp. 148f.

14. Gutwirth, *Madame de Staël*, pp. 155–56.

15. J. Christopher Herold, *Mistress to an Age: A Life of Madame de Staël* (Indianapolis: Bobbs-Merrill, 1958), p. 263.

16. Balayé, *Madame de Staël*, p. 136.

17. Jean Starobinski, "Suicide et mélancolie chez Madame de Staël," in *Madame de Staël et l'Europe: Colloque de Coppet* (Paris: Klincksieck, 1970), p. 46.

1. Letters on Rousseau

1. Despite this disclaimer, the young Mme. de Staël is thought to have been aware of the publication of her *Letters.*

2. For a comic version of this observation expanded, see *The Mannequin.*

3. His *Letter to d'Alembert on Spectacles* (1758).

4. The poet Sappho of Lesbos (first century B.C.) wrote lyrics and epigrams of which some 6,000 words survive; most of her intense love poetry is directed toward the girls at her school. She was also married and the mother of a child, and was reputed to have died for love of the youth Phaon (*The Influence of the Passions,* note 6). Mme. de Staël was to write a play on her in 1811.

5. This is the major line taken by Rousseau's contemporaries. The comparison was first made in an anonymous essay in the *Critical Review* (London, 1761), vol. 12, translated by the philosophe Jean-Baptiste Suard in the *Journal Etranger.* An example in Mme. de Staël's time is Robert Alves' "Shall we compare [Rousseau] to Richardson, whom he so much admired as a sentimental novelist? We shall find the latter more moral in action and design." *Sketches of a History of Literature* (Edinburgh, 1794), p. 103.

6. Pierre Abelard was the lover of his student Héloïse, niece of a Notre-Dame canon who had her put in a convent and him castrated. She later became the head of her order, and he found refuge in a series of monasteries. The "old story" is found in their famous correspondence, which includes the story of their affair, a plea from Héloïse that Abelard write to her, and his instructions as to how she should run her convent.

7. Not melodrama in our sense, but a form alternating music and speech, as Mme. de Staël goes on to indicate. Rousseau is often credited with the invention of this form in his *Pygmalion* (1762). His *Village Soothsayer* (1752) had been more popular, partly because of his lively libretto but also because of the music, which drew upon traditional French folk dances. It is generally considered one of the sources of French *opéra comique.*

8. See Ovid, *The Metamorphoses.*

9. Henchmen and patricides; from the character in Voltaire's play *Mahomet* (1743), in which Seide is made to kill his father.

10. The man from Geneva was Paul Moultou. Rousseau's common-law wife, Thérèse Le Vasseur, was a servant; all their children were sent to the Foundling Hospital.

11. The noble savage Oroonoko was the hero of Aphra Behn's novel *Oroonoko, or The Royal Slave* (1678). The idea of the nobility of primitive man became a Romantic topos, not least because of this kind of interpretation of Rousseau. Compare Mme. de Staël's own treatment of this theme in *Zulma.*

12. Jean-Jacques Rousseau, *The Confessions* (1781), J. M. Cohen, tr. (Harmondsworth: Penguin, 1953), p. 78. The gesture may have been an ambiguous one. The "insane dialogue" is *Rousseau Judge of Jean-Jacques* (1775–76).

13. Modern scholars do not doubt that Rousseau died a natural (though sudden) death, whatever Moultou may have told Mme. de Staël. Rousseau had requested an autopsy, which concluded that he died of cerebral congestion brought on by arteriosclerosis of the kidneys. This did not prevent rumors that he had been murdered by Thérèse, as well as that he had killed himself. Mme. de Staël's response to these rumors helped perpetuate the legend of his suicide.

2. Essay on Fictions

1. Later published as *The Origin, Forms, and Development of Religion* (1824–1831). Benjamin Constant de Rebecque (1767–1830), known today chiefly for his autobiographical love story *Adolphe,* was the longtime companion of Mme. de Staël, and the father of her daughter Albertine. They collaborated on writing and on plans for the political reform of France.

2. Dido, Queen of Carthage (*Aeneid,* book 4), falls in love with Aeneas and is abandoned by him. Mme. de Staël compares her heroine with Dido in the last chapter of *Corinne.*

3. Priam visits Achilles in *The Iliad,* book 24.

4. These "bloody crimes" are the Reign of Terror (1793–94), when 20,000 people suspected of opposing the French Revolution were executed, at one point without trial. Dante's *Inferno* was just begin-

ning to become popular outside Italy during these years. Mme. de Staël will refer to the *Inferno* to describe the Reign of Terror in her *Considerations*: see note 7 to that chapter.

5. The enchantress Armida's spells make Rinaldo fall in love with her in Torquato Tasso's epic poem *Jerusalem Delivered* (1576; book 26).

6. "Comparisons" include figurative language.

7. *Gil Blas* (1715–1735) is Alain-René LeSage's picaresque novel; *Tartuffe* (1664) and *The Misanthrope* (1666) are comedies by Jean-Baptiste Molière.

8. Fénelon's *Telemachus* (1699) was based on characters from Homer's *Odyssey*. The young hero sets out in search of his father and is rescued from various perils by his tutor Mentor.

9. Thélème is the lively heroine of the verse tale *Thélème and Macare* (1764); Macare is her tranquil lover. This is a minor work of the philosophe François-Marie Arouet de Voltaire (1694–1778).

10. Edmund Spenser's *The Faerie Queene* (1589–1596).

11. Jean de La Fontaine's very popular *Fables* were published in 1668–1694.

12. Samuel Butler's *Hudibras* (1663–1678) was criticized by some English critics of the eighteenth century, notably Samuel Johnson, for the same reasons.

13. Jean-Baptiste Massillon (1663–1742) was bishop of Clermont-Ferrand and a famous preacher.

14. Pierre Corneille's play (1640). The exchange is famous for its simplicity. The hero's father, asked, "What would you have wished that he do against three?" answers, "That he die . . . " (3.6).

15. Charles-Louis de Secondat de Montesquieu, *The Spirit of Laws* (1748), book 5, ch. 13: "When the savages of Louisiana are desirous of fruit, they cut the tree to the root, and gather the fruit. In this we behold an emblem of despotic government" (Dublin, 1750), 1:83.

16. Jonathan Swift published *A Tale of a Tub* in 1704, *Gulliver's Travels* in 1726; Voltaire published *Micromégas* in 1752.

17. This famous anecdote about Zeuxis (not Apelles) appears in Pliny's *Natural History*, book 35.

18. Voltaire published his epic poem *The Henriad* in 1723; Genghis Khan is the central figure of his tragedy *The Orphan of China* (1755); his tragedy *Tancred* appeared in 1760. *Mithridate* (1673) is a tragedy by Jean Racine.

19. By Marguerite de Lussan and the Abbé de Boismorand (1733, 1748).

20. Tales by Voltaire: *Zadig* was published in 1747, *Memnon* in 1749, *Candide* in 1759.

21. See Tacitus' *Annales*, 2.72; books 1 and 2.

22. William Godwin published *Caleb Williams* in 1794.

23. Jean-François Marmontel, *Moral Tales* (1761, 1789–1792); Laurence Sterne, *A Sentimental Journey* (1768); Joseph Addison and Richard Steele, *The Spectator* (1711–12).

24. Lovelace is the hero-villain of Richardson's *Clarissa* (1748).

25. Clementina is the Italian woman who renounces the eponymous hero of Richardson's *Sir Charles Grandison* (1754), enabling him to marry Harriet Byron. Prévost's translation retains Richardson's title, but Mme. de Staël sees Clementina as primary. For the influence of this character on Corinne, see Ellen Moers, *Literary Women* (Garden City, N. Y.: Doubleday, 1977), p. 306.

26. All these works are novels. *The Princess of Clèves* is by Mme. de La Fayette (1678); *The Count of Comminge* is by Mme. de Tencin (1735); *Paul and Virginia* is by Jacques-Henri Bernadin de Saint-Pierre (1787); *Cecilia* (1782) and *Camilla* (1796) are by Fanny Burney; Marie-Jeanne Riccoboni wrote a number of novels in the mid-eighteenth century. *Caroline* is probably *Caroline de Lichtfield*, by Isabelle de Montolieu (1785). Isabelle de Charrière, later Constant's intimate friend, wrote *Caliste* (1787).

27. Alexander Pope's poem "Eloisa to Abelard" (1717); Johann Wolfgang von Goethe's *The Sorrows of Young Werther* (1774); *The Portuguese Letters*, said to have been written by a Portuguese nun to her lover, but probably written by the translator, Gabriel-Joseph de Guilleragues (1669); Jean-Jacques Rousseau's *Julie, or The New Héloïse* (1761). All of these are epistolary fictions.

3. Novellas

Mirza

1. Gorea is an island in the Atlantic off the coast of Senegal, in western Africa, near Dakar. Plantation owners in Saint-Domingue,

now Haiti, were notorious for the cruel treatment of their slaves; the plantations were very large, and this was the richest colony of France in the eighteenth century. For Mme. de Staël's awareness of the problem, see *Considerations.*

2. The marble statue of Apollo in the Belvedere Courtyard of the Vatican, now generally thought to be a Roman copy of a Greek original, was considered the ideal of male beauty. Benjamin West exclaimed on seeing it in 1760, "My God, how like it is to a young Mohawk warrior." A number of others in the late eighteenth century thought it the depiction of a noble savage.

3. A coastal region of northern Senegal in western Africa.

4. The Hottentots are a South African people, believed to be related to the Bantus and Bushmen.

Adelaide and Theodore

5. Emile is the hero of Rousseau's famous educational treatise (*Emile* [1762], book 5). At this point Sophie is chaste; the use of the word "mistress" would not necessarily imply sexual activity. In her *Letters on Rousseau,* Mme. de Staël objects to the inferior education Rousseau gives Sophie, but is touched by the thought of Emile's making her win the race.

Pauline

6. For Saint-Domingue, now Haiti, see *Mirza*, note 1.

7. Cap-Haïtien, the capital of Saint-Domingue.

8. A busy port in western France, at the mouth of the Seine.

9. Attendance at the sickbed of a person one liked or respected was considered a courtesy, even for members of the opposite sex. Members of the nobility often rented out wings or floors of their large houses in town, so Mme. de Staël feels no need to explain Édouard's living quarters. Pauline's "apartment," however, would simply have been a suite of rooms.

Zulma

10. The Orinoco river flows through Venezuela to the Caribbean. Lima is the capital and principal city of Peru.

4. The Influence of the Passions

1. "He looked for the light from the sky, and groaned when he found it." Virgil, *Aeneid*, 4.692.

2. For example, the remains of the Revolutionary leaders Marat and Mirabeau were reverently placed in the Pantheon by the Convention and later rudely disinterred; in Marat's case the interval was only five months. For Marat and Mirabeau, see *Considerations*, notes 1 and 11.

3. Constant's *On the Strength of the Present Government of France, and the Necessity of Joining It* (1796).

4. Cato Uticensis (Cato the Younger) stabbed himself after losing a battle to Julius Caesar. He was known for his opposition to corruption and was an opponent of Catiline. Marcus Junius Brutus was the leader of the conspiracy that assassinated Caesar. He committed suicide after Philippi (42 B.C.). Algernon Sidney, son of an earl, was executed for treason in 1683 for his putative complicity in the Rye House plot and his authorship of *Discourses Concerning Government*, which vindicates regicide and supports commonwealth ideas.

5. Exod. 13:21.

6. The poet Sappho of Lesbos (first century B.C.) supposedly killed herself for love of the youth Phaon; this tale is found in Ovid, among others. (See *Letters on Rousseau*, note 4.) Queen Elizabeth I had Robert Devereux, Earl of Essex, executed for rebellion; the notion that she died for love of him is based on a story current in the eighteenth century that she had given him a ring to send her in time of need; this stratagem having failed, she died of grief.

7. Mezentius, ruler of the Etrurians, was expelled by them for his cruelty. He appears several times in the *Aeneid*, centrally in book 10.

5. On Literature

1. Jean-Baptiste Molière's *School for Wives* (1662), 1.1.

2. Voltaire's allegory in prose and verse, *The Temple of Taste* (1733); Jean-François Marmontel's *The Elements of Literature*, containing his articles for the philosophes' *Encyclopedia*, published 1787; Jean-François de La Harpe's *Lyceum, or Course in Ancient and Modern*

Literature, a collection of the lectures he gave for the Lycée founded in Paris by the philosophes, published 1799–1805.

3. Ossian is generally believed to be the creation of James Macpherson, who started publishing the Ossianic texts as *Fragments of Ancient Poesy* (1760). His poetry was very popular, and Mme. de Staël was in good literary company in being deceived. She is referring here to Paul-Henri Mallet's "Odes and Other Ancient Poems," in his *Monuments of Celtic Mythology* (1756).

4. See *Corinne*.

5. The *Elder Edda* is a collection of old Norse poems on cosmogony and mythology (c. 1200); the *Younger Edda* (c. 1230) contains a compendium of Odinic myths.

6. Macpherson published *Fingal* in 1762.

7. Ossian was often compared with Homer in England in the later eighteenth century—by Hugh Blair, for example, in *A Critical Dissertation on the Poems of Ossian* (1763).

8. Edward Young, *Night Thoughts on Death* (1742–45), James Thompson, *The Seasons* (1726–1730), Friedrich Klopstock, *The Messiah* (1748–1773), all of which had a European vogue.

9. Deism emphasized a belief in a Supreme Being without the trappings of religion.

10. In Euripedes' play the Eumenides are spirits that pursue the parricide Orestes; in Shakespeare's play Lady Macbeth's guilty conscience is what makes her sleepwalk.

11. Mme. de Staël has in mind Petrarch's sonnets to Laura, *The Canzoniere* (1327–1353), Goethe's *The Sorrows of Young Werther* (1776), Pope's "Eloisa to Abelard" (1717; see her comment in the *Essay on Fictions*, p. 77), Thompson's *The Seasons*, and Thomas Otway's *Venice Preserved* (1682).

12. Lacedaemonia was also known as Sparta. Lycurgus was a fourth-century B.C. Spartan legislator.

13. Montesquieu, *The Spirit of Laws* (1748); Rousseau, *Discourse on the Origin and Foundations of Inequality Among Men* (1754); Etienne de Condillac, *General History of Men and Empires* (1769–1773).

14. A novel published in 1790.

15. "Ma vie est un témoin qu'il faut entendre aussi." Mme. de Staël may be quoting an alexandrine from French classical drama.

16. In Tasso's *Jerusalem Delivered* (1581), the princess Erminia wears borrowed armor to seek her love Tancred in the Christian camp.

6. Delphine

1. Lack of sympathy with Rousseau is typical of characters who are themselves unsympathetic. See above, p. 58.

2. A spirited Polish folk dance, adopted by the nobility in Poland and Russia in the eighteenth century.

3. Mme. de Vernon is dying.

4. Montpellier is a city in southern France.

5. Léontine de Ternan, the Mother Superior of the convent where Delphine has found refuge, is the sister of Mme. de Mondoville and therefore Léonce's aunt. She bears a strong physical resemblance to her nephew and is also strongly attracted to Delphine, whom she is determined to keep in the convent as a nun.

6. Matt. 25:29.

7. Corinne

1. Petrarch, *The Canzoniere*, 146.

2. The worst period of the Reign of Terror in France ended in July 1794.

3. He is crossing the North Sea from northern England to Germany.

4. Territory belonging to the Roman Catholic Church at this time, not limited to the Vatican City.

5. The dome of St. Peter's was designed by Michelangelo in 1558; that of St. Louis des Invalides in Paris by Jules Mansart in 1675. The Count d'Erfeuil, a clever but shallow Frenchman, appreciates only the values and beauties of his own country.

6. Wilhelm von Humboldt (1767–1835), German diplomat, encouraged Mme. de Staël to study German literature. (For his brother, see *On Germany*, note 21.)

7. Petrarch was crowned poet laureate in 1341. Tasso was to be crowned, but the ceremony was postponed because of bad weather and the poet died (1595).

8. In 1794, at the time of Oswald's visit, Italy was a series of petty kingdoms under Austrian influence, repressing the spread of French Revolutionary ideas and soon to be occupied by the army of Napoleon in 1796.

9. Ludovico Ariosto was the author of the epic poem *Orlando Furioso* (1532).

10. *The Sibyl* (Galleria Borghese, Rome), by Domenichino (1581–1641), shows a turbaned girl with an open, eager face as the priestess of Apollo, listening attentively for the voice of inspiration and holding a scroll of music and a book. Mme. de Staël was called a "sibyl" as a girl, and she strongly identifies the Sibyl with her heroine, as opposed to Correggio's Madonna, who represents Corinne's half-sister and rival, Lucile. Corinne refers to the Cumaean Sibyl during her improvisation.

11. In 1805, Mme. de Staël herself had been made an honorary member of the Accademia dell'Arcadia in Rome at a public reception during which she had read her translation of an Italian sonnet into French, and the Italians had responded with applause, several sonnets in her honor, and a poem improvised by a nobleman about her book *On Literature*.

12. For the Greek poet Sappho, see *Letters on Rousseau*, note 4, and *The Influence of the Passions*, note 6.

13. Mme. de Staël heard several improvisators in Italy; poetic improvisation was still being practiced as an art. The most famous improvisator of her time, Corilla Olimpica (Maria Madelena Morelli, 1727–1800), was crowned with laurels at the Capitol. (Madelyn Gutwirth, *Madame de Staël*, p. 173.)

14. Petrarch, *The Canzoniere*, 213. Mme de Staël substitutes "parlar" (speech) for the accepted "cantar" (song). She may have known a variant text, but often quoted from memory.

15. The lyre, admired for its Greek simplicity, became popular in the later eighteenth century.

16. "Cantilena" is a term used for the plainchant of non-biblical poetic texts. Mme. de Staël was a friend of the neoclassical poet Vicenzo Monti (1754–1828), whom she met in Milan; Corinne quotes him (see note 41). The "episode" of Ugolino, the traitor who is starved to death with his sons and grandsons, is from Dante's *Inferno* (c. 1314), canto 33; Francesca, who dies for love of her brother-in-law Paolo, ap-

pears in canto 5. The Amazon Clorinda is unwittingly killed by Tarquin, who loves her, in Tasso's *Jerusalem Delivered.*

17. Propertius, *Elegies*, 2.10.21.

18. The Castel Sant'Angelo in the Vatican gardens was originally planned as a tomb for the Emperor Hadrian (A.D. 135), then enlarged and made into a fortress in the fifteenth century. The baroque statues on the Sant'Angelo bridge were by Giovanni Bernini (1598–1680), though parts of it date from Hadrian's time.

19. Virgil, *Georgics*, 4.563–64. Parthenope, now Naples, was founded by Greeks from Cumae.

20. Near Averno was the cave by which Aeneas descended to Hades; the Phlegeton was one of its rivers.

21. The northern tip of the Bay of Naples, supposedly the burial place of Aeneas' trumpeter Misenus, drowned by an envious Triton for boasting of his music.

22. Aeneas plucks the Golden Bough before descending to Hades to make Charon ferry him across the river Acheron. *Aeneid* 6.136.

23. *Aeneid* 6.173.

24. Pliny the Elder's *Natural History*, book 37.

25. The ancient town of Capua transferred its allegiance from Rome to Carthage during the Punic Wars, but when Hannibal made it his winter headquarters it destroyed the morale of his troops.

26. Cicero (106–43 B.C.), Roman orator and statesman, was murdered by Mark Antony's agents for his loyalty to the ideal of liberty.

27. Scipio the Younger (185–129 B.C.), consul and patron of the arts, died in suspicious circumstances after making a speech in the Senate.

28. Marius (157–86 B.C.), tribune of the plebeians, was captured in the marshes after a struggle for power, but escaped to Africa.

29. Tiberius (b. 42 B.C.), Roman emperor (A.D. 14–37), retreated to his Capri villa at the end of his life, embittered by intrigue.

30. Agrippina the Younger was the mother of Nero, who tried to scuttle her ship and had her killed after she fled (A.D. 59).

31. Cornelia, second wife of the Roman triumvir Pompey, returned to Italy after seeing him murdered in Egypt (48 B.C.). Agrippina

the Elder, Germanicus' wife and Caligula's mother, was exiled by Tiberius and starved herself to death (A.D. 29). Portia, who shared Brutus' republican ideals and, in the plot to assassinate Caesar, killed herself after her husband left Italy (see *The Influence of the Passions*, note 4).

32. After being honored for his poetry, Tasso was exiled from Ferrara because of a quarrel with the duke's courtiers. This story is told in Goethe's play *Torquato Tasso* (1790).

33. Goethe's poem "The Fisherman" (1778).

34. Florence, the birthplace of Dante, was an artistic and literary center during the medieval and Renaissance periods.

35. Northumberland, the northernmost county of England, is best known for mining and sheep farming.

36. Edinburgh, home of the Scottish Enlightenment, was a major European intellectual center during the eighteenth century.

37. In Dante's *Inferno*, canto 23, it is the hypocrites who are weighed down by cloaks of lead. Corinne (or Mme. de Staël) may have confused these figures with "the sad souls of those who have lived without infamy and without praise," canto 3, and who are condemned to race endlessly in pursuit of a whirling banner. It would be a characteristic mistake for Mme. de Staël to make: she does not associate motion with mediocrity. Corinne goes on to apply an appropriately Dantesque image to herself: in canto 26 Ulysses is swathed in a flame that appears to consume him, among the false counselors who have misused their great intellectual gifts.

38. In book 1 of Swift's *Gulliver's Travels* (1726), a crowd of tiny Lilliputians ties down Gulliver, a comparative giant.

39. Pietro Trapassi (1698–1782), known as Metastasio, wrote poetry and numerous opera libretti.

40. Genoa and Leghorn (Livorno) are port cities in Italy.

41. Monti, "After the Battle of Marengo" (1799). For Monti, see note 16.

42. Corinna was a Greek poet who lived between the fifth and fourth centuries B.C.; some 2,000 words of her lyric poems survive. Her friendship with the poet Pindar (518–438 B.C.) is probably apocryphal.

8. On Germany

1. Friedrich Gottlieb Klopstock was a German poet, author of patriotic odes; his best-known work is *The Messiah* (1748–1773), inspired by John Milton's *Paradise Lost.*

2. Denis Diderot (1713–1784) was one of the leading figures of the French Enlightenment and responsible, as director of the Encyclopedia, for disseminating many of its ideas. He himself wrote works of fiction, philosophy, art criticism, and drama.

3. In Greek mythology, the Erinyes, sometimes euphemistically called the Eumenides ("the kindly ones"), inflicted curses on criminals and pangs of conscience on the guilty. See *On Literature*, note 10.

4. For giving the fire of the gods to men, thus offering their abilities wider scope, Prometheus had his heart and liver torn out afresh by eagles every day. Mme. de Staël also uses this allusion elsewhere; it was a favorite myth of the Romantics. See *Reflections on Suicide*, pp. 300, 356.

5. Pedro Calderón de la Barca (1600–1681) was a Spanish playwright, popular author of *Life is a Dream* and 120 other plays. Luis de Camoëns (1524–1580) was the Portuguese author of *The Lusiad* (1572), an epic poem. Spanish and Portuguese poets were not widely read outside their own countries at this time; Mme. de Staël wrote an article on Camoëns for Joseph Michaud's biographical dictionary (1811–1828).

6. Gottfried August Bürger, German poet, was best known for ballads such as "The Wild Hunter" (1773) and "Lenore" (1774).

7. *The Critique of Pure Reason* was published in 1781, *The Critique of Practical Reason* in 1788, and *The Critique of Judgment* in 1790.

8. The teacher was Euclid, the Greek founder of geometry (third century B.C.).

9. John Locke published *An Essay Concerning Human Understanding* in 1690.

10. René Descartes, philosopher and mathematician, published his *Discourse on Method* in 1637. Gottfried Wilhelm Leibnitz gave his response to Locke in his *Monadology* (1714).

11. In the legend, when seers claimed that an abyss in Rome

would not close until the city's most valued possession was thrown into it, Marcus Curtius rode in on horseback.

12. David Hume, *An Inquiry Into Human Understanding* (1748).

13. The Abbé Roch-Ambroise Cucurron, called Sicard (1742–1822), founded the first school for deaf-mutes in Bordeaux.

14. St. Augustine, *Confessions* (written 397–98), 10.8. Mme. de Staël was apparently thinking of this passage, though Augustine actually speaks of a mind too narrow.

15. Nicolas Malebranche (1638–1715) was the author of *The Search for Truth*, a response to Descartes.

16. Exod. 13:21.

17. Mme. de Staël's use of the French word "romanesque" is impossible to translate: it implies the kind of sentimentality that comes from a misguided reading of novels. This translation settles for "romantic," to be distinguished from the critical concept "Romantic."

18. Goethe's *The Sorrows of Young Werther* (1774). Mme. de Staël sees that Goethe is more critical of his man of feeling than many readers recognized. She may also be thinking here of another text of Goethe's, *The Triumph of Sentiment* (1780), as Countess Jean de Pange and Simone Balayé suggest in their edition (Paris: Hachette, 1958), 3:358.

19. According to the biographical notice written by her cousin, Mme. Necker de Saussure, Mme. de Staël used to add, "I could say the same thing of myself, about the least little sorrow." Bernard de Fontenelle (1657–1757) was the author of *Conversations on the Plurality of Worlds* (1686).

20. *Twelfth Night*, 4.2.

21. Pange and Balayé suggest that this detail may have come from the descriptions of his Mexican explorations published in 1807–1808 by Mme. de Staël's friend, the statesman and naturalist Alexander von Humboldt (5:211); see *Corinne*, footnote to p. 249, where she calls him "the famous traveler."

9. The Mannequin

1. The Edict of Nantes (1598) granted French Protestants the right to worship and hold office; its revocation by Louis XIV in 1685 made many Protestants leave the country permanently.

2. Frederick II of Prussia (1712–1786), known as Frederick the Great, was a patron of the arts.

3. The Almanach de Gotha, founded 1763 in Germany, is a register of the royal and princely families of Europe.

4. In heraldry, a shield could be quartered to show alliances with other noble families. The ability to show sixteen quarters was considered proof of nobility; German shields were noted for more.

5. Jacob Gotthelf Schiele or Schiel of Leipzig, fl. 1755–1774.

6. Marie de Rabutin de Sévigné (1626–1696) left a portrait of private and court life in her famous *Letters*, first published 1725; Marie-Madeleine de La Fayette (1634–1693) is credited with writing the first psychological novel, *The Princess of Clèves*.

7. A marriage contract was a prenuptial legal settlement.

8. A closet was a small room off a larger one, typically used for reading or writing in private.

9. That is, he is ready to duel. The fact that the Count does not make fun of this offer is proof that Frederic is accepted as a gentleman.

10. Reflections on Suicide

1. See "On Philosophy."

2. This idea is expressed by the Roman Platonist Plotinus (205–270) and his followers.

3. The game of chance is Blaise Pascal's famous "bet" on eternity: one has nothing to lose. See his *Pensées* (published posthumously 1670), Louis Lafuma, ed. (Paris: Delmas 1952), no. 343.

4. Luke 15:18.

5. Luke 21:19.

6. For Prometheus, see *On Germany*, note 4.

7. Tantalus was punished by having food and drink forever just out of his reach.

8. The Styx was one of the rivers of Hades; any mortal dipped in it became invulnerable. The most famous example is Achilles, whose heel was unfortunately kept dry.

11. Considerations on the Main Events of the French Revolution

1. The Count Honoré-Gabriel de Mirabeau, Revolution-

ary statesman (1749–1791), was a believer in constitutional monarchy. His debt-ridden, venal, and sexually irregular personal life was well known; he was ungainly in appearance, but a great orator.

2. Montmorin had sided with Necker in agreeing that the Third Estate needed more representation; the ultimate result was a vote by head count, in which the Third Estate would be in the majority, rather than by order, where it would be outnumbered by the clergy and the aristocracy.

3. Niobe, who boasted of her fourteen children, was turned to stone after they were killed by Apollo and Diana, only children of the affronted goddess Latona; she continued to weep. See Ovid, *Metamorphoses*, book 6.

4. These distinctions are important: the carefully defined use of different chairs was a jealously guarded symbol of social status among the nobility. Under the old regime it was a sign of high rank to have the right to sit on even a footstool in the King's presence.

5. Jacques Necker, Mme. de Staël's father and Louis XVI's Minister of Finance, had just been dismissed and recalled by popular demand; it was believed that he could balance the budget. The public euphoria at his return to Paris created a scene that Mme. de Staël called the strongest impression of her life. See introduction, p. 4.

6. The Old Man of the Mountain, the Imam Hassan Ben-Sabbah el Homairi, was an eleventh-century Syrian prince of a Mohammedan sect called the Assassins.

7. The Girondins were moderate Republicans, advocating the overthrow of the monarchy and harsh measures against the clergy and émigrés but opposed to the fanaticism of the Reign of Terror. Dante's *Inferno* is a picture of hell; for other allusions, see *Essay on Fictions*, note 4; *Corinne*, notes 16 and 37.

8. See "Novellas," note 1.

9. In July 1793 the military situation had seemed desperate; angered by the French occupation of Belgium, the rest of Europe had mobilized to threaten invasion from the Alps, the Pyrenees, and the Rhone. By October this threat abroad had been put down as part of the same effort, led by Robespierre, that created the Reign of Terror at home.

10. After the fall of the Girondins, Hérault de Séchelles' constitution of 1793 provided for democratic elections, though it also encouraged legislation by decree instead of lawmaking.

11. Jean-Paul Marat (1743–1793), powerful Revolutionary journalist and deputy, believed himself the Apostle of Liberty; he was to be assassinated in his bath by Charlotte Corday. François Maximilien Joseph de Robespierre (1758–1794) was the leader of the party that displaced the Girondins, and the moving spirit of the Reign of Terror until he was executed by it.

12. Antoine-Nicolas de Condorcet (1743–1794), philosophe and friend of Voltaire, wrote his most famous work, the *Historical Tableau of the Progress of the Human Mind,* while proscribed as a Girondin; he took poison to avoid the guillotine.

13. Assignats, originally interest-bearing bonds, became issued as increasingly worthless paper currency.

14. Louis XVI, Queen Marie-Antoinette, and "Madame Elisabeth," the King's sister, were guillotined in 1793; Mme. de Staël published her *Reflections on the Trial of the Queen* that year. Chrétien-Guillaume de Malesherbes (1721–1794), minister of Louis XVI, softened censorship under the old regime and wrote a *Report on the Liberty of the Press* (1790); he was guillotined for defending Louis XVI before the Convention. Sylvain Bailly (1736–1793) was the author of a history of astronomy and onetime president of the National Assembly. Antoine Laurent Lavoisier (1743–1794) was one of the discoverers of oxygen and founders of modern chemistry. The St. Bartholomew's Day massacre of French Protestants was ordered by Charles IX in 1572, prompted by his mother Catherine de Médicis; the ensuing bloodbath lasted until the issuing of the Edict of Nantes (see *The Mannequin,* note 1).

15. Jean-Claude Gorjy, *The New Sentimental Journey* (1784); *The Dangerous Friendship, or, Célimaur and Amélie* (1786, published anonymously).

16. *Lettres de cachet,* so called because they bore the King's seal, ordered the imprisonment or exile without trial of the person named in them. Mirabeau, imprisoned for bad behavior by his family as a youth, had written a treatise against these letters (1782).

17. Themistocles (528–462 B.C.), Athenian statesman and fleet commander, was ostracized by antidemocratic forces and fled to Asia. Cicero (see *Corinne,* note 26) fled to Macedonia and was briefly declared an exile by Clodius in 58 B.C. The public writings of Henry St. John, Viscount Bolingbroke (1678–1751), protested that he did not mind his exile in France, but in his private letters he struck a very different note.

18. See *Ten Years of Exile*.

19. The Consulat was established by Napoleon's coup d'état, November 9, 1799 (18th Brumaire, year VIII of the Revolutionary calendar).

20. Napoleon ordered Mme. de Staël to stay forty leagues away from Paris.

21. Mathieu de Montmorency had once been Mme. de Staël's lover and was also the son of the mistress of another former lover, Louis de Narbonne.

22. The beautiful Juliette Récamier, Mme. de Staël's close friend, was adored by Benjamin Constant and many other admirers and was the hostess of her own salon.

12. Ten Years of Exile

1. She had already written "On the Character of M. Necker and His Private Life," to accompany an edition of his writings (1804).

2. Necker had advanced the French treasury 2,400,000 livres in 1778; the Revolutionary government had paid 400,000 of it back in 1790, and Mme. de Staël was claiming the rest from Napoleon.

3. *Delphine* was published in 1802, *Corinne* five years later; for Napoleon's suppression of *On Germany*, see p. 378.

4. Mme. de. Staël had been renting the château of Chaumont, in the Loire valley, to fulfill Napoleon's terms of her exile forty leagues from Paris. In a footnote to the 1821 edition, Auguste de Staël identifies her host as Charles Marie de Salaberry (1766–1847), a former captain in the counterrevolutionary army from the royalist Vendeé region and the author of travel books, fiction, and memoirs. For Mme. Récamier, see *Considerations*, note 22. Other guests at various points included several of Mme. Récamier's suitors and various men with whom Mme. de Staël had been involved: Mathieu de Montmorency, August Wilhelm Schlegel, Prosper de Barante, and Benjamin Constant, as well as Fanny Randall (see note 10).

5. Former Queen Hortense of Holland, the deserted wife of Louis Bonaparte (who had abdicated in 1810), agreed to try to get her brother-in-law Napoleon to consent to the publication of *On Germany*. "Petty post" was a round-robin game that involved folding pieces of

paper into pleats, writing half-playful sentimental questions or messages on the intricate folds, and explaining the results.

6. *Cinderella* was a comic opera (1810) by Nicolas Isouard; Blois is a small town in the Loire valley. M. de Corbigny, the prefect of this Loir-et-Cher region, identified and described by Auguste de Staël in a footnote as "a likeable, enlightened man," was very soon to be dismissed from his post for taking Mme. de Staël's word that the manuscript of *On Germany* she gave him to be confiscated was the only one in existence.

7. The censors had *not* endorsed the book, and had examined only the first two volumes at this point, which the publisher, Gabriel-Henri Nicolle, had begun printing without their permission. Napoleon issued a direct order to stop the printing on September 29, and did not change his mind on receiving a copy of the bound proofs from Queen Hortense.

8. Necker had died in 1804. Her companion was Mathieu de Montmorency; see *Considerations*, note 21. The battle of Fretteval was fought in 1194.

9. Auguste de Staël identifies this château as "the château of Conan, belonging to M. Chevalier, today the prefect of Var." He adds in another note, "Anxious at not seeing my mother arrive home, I rode out to meet her, trying the best I could to soften the news she would hear on her return; but losing my way like her in the unvarying Vendôme plains, I did not reach the château that had offered her hospitality until the middle of the night, and by a stroke of luck. After having M. de Montmorency awakened and letting him know that the Emperor's police had increased their persecution of my mother, I went back to finish putting her papers in order, leaving it to M. de Montmorency to prepare her for the new impending blow."

10. The writing desk would have been a portable one, for use on a table or in traveling. Fanny Randall was an Englishwoman taken on by Mme. de Staël as a companion for herself and her daughter Albertine, and devoted to them both.

Selected Bibliography

This list suggests some secondary reading available in English.

Andrews, Wayne. *Germaine: A Portrait of Madame de Staël.* New York: Atheneum, 1963.

Forsberg, Roberta J. and H. C. Nixon. *Madame de Staël and Freedom Today.* New York: Astra, 1963.

Gutwirth, Madelyn. *Madame de Staël, Novelist: The Emergence of the Artist as Woman.* Urbana: University of Illinois Press, 1978.

Herold, J. Christopher. *Mistress to an Age: A Life of Madame de Staël.* Indianapolis: Bobbs-Merrill, 1958.

Levaillant, Maurice. *The Passionate Exiles: Madame de Staël and Madame Récamier.* Translated by Malcolm Barnes. New York: Farrar, Straus, and Cudahy, 1958.

Lipking, Lawrence, "Aristotle's Sister: A Poetics of Abandonment." *Critical Inquiry* (September 1983), 10(1):61–81.

Moers, Ellen. *Literary Women.* New York: Anchor Press/Doubleday, 1977.

Posgate, Helen B. *Madame de Staël.* New York: Twayne, 1968.

Poulet, Georges. "The Role of Improvisation in *Corinne. ELH* (1971), 41:602–12.

Tenenbaum, Susan. "Montesquieu and Mme. de Staël: The Woman as a Factor in Political Analysis." *Political Theory* (February 1973), 1(1):92–103.

Winegarten, Renée. *Madame de Staël.* Leamington Spa: Berg, 1985.

Index

Abelard, Pierre, and Heloise, 384n6
Addison, Joseph, and Richard Steele, 387n23
Affiliation, *see* Connection
Africa, 79–80; *see also* Slavery
Americans: an enlightened people's language and literature, 185; religious fanaticism banished by Penn, 364
Ancien régime, 188–200, 202, 359–62, 365–66, 369; *see also* Revolution
Ariosto, Ludovico, 64, 251, 392n9
Artist: "Apelles" (Zeuxis), 68, 386n17; belongs to all ranks and nations, 327; difficulty of envisaging woman as, 14, 83; Goethe's views on, working in cold blood, 297; Klopstock not what anyone would call an, 296; Rousseau as, 53; *see also* Genius; Romantic; Sappho; Women, woman writer
Augustine, 312, 396n14

Balayé, Simone, 23, 26, 32, 396n18, 396n21
Barante, Prosper de, 400n4
Bernardin de Saint-Pierre, Jacques-Henri de, 76, 387n26
Bolingbroke, Henry St. John, 369, 399n17
Bonaparte, Joseph, 375
Bonaparte, Napoleon, *see* Napoleon
Brontë, Charlotte, 25
Bürger, Gottfried August, 301, 395n6
Burney, Fanny, 76, 387n26
Butler, Samuel, 67, 386n12

Calderón de la Barca, Pedro, 301, 395n5

Camoëns, Luis de, 301, 395n5
Catholicism, 4, 23, 48, 232, 270; *see also* Protestantism
Charrière, Isabella de (Belle de Zuylen), 76, 387n26
Christianity, 299–301; and origin of Romanticism, 300; and women's equality, 317
Cicero, 266, 369, 393n26, 399n17
Class hatred, 364–65
Classical, 29–30; ancient Greek and Romans identify with nature, 299–302; French poetry the most, modern, 301; not a result of reflection, 300
Climate, influence on literature, 176; *see also* Northern; Southern
Condillac, Étienne de, 192, 390n13
Condorcet, Antoine-Nicolas de, 20, 367, 368, 399n12
Connection: between artist and audience, 22, 26, 58, 157, 158; between author and text, 14, 25, 151; between classes must be multiplied, 364–65; and consciousness, 9; between ideas and feelings, 188; between ideas and interrelationship of objects, 144; between individuals destroyed by Napoleon, 373; and manners, 198; through memory, 245; between political parties needed now, 200, 364; and "Southern," 20–21, 176; women's happiness connected to feelings, 160
Constant, Benjamin, 8, 10, 22, 26, 33, 35, 61, 154, 385n1, 389n3, 400n22, 400n4